SAP Crystal Reports For Microsoft Visual Studio Made Easy

By Dr. Indera E. Murphy

Tolana Publishing
Teaneck, New Jersey

SAP Crystal Reports For Microsoft Visual Studio Made Easy

Published By:
Tolana Publishing
PO Box 719
Teaneck, NJ 07666 USA

Find us online at www.tolanapublishing.com
Inquiries may be sent to the publisher: tolanapub@yahoo.com

Our books are available online at www.barnesandnoble.com. They can also be ordered from Ingram.

Quantity discounts are available for corporations, non-profit organizations and educational institutions for educational purposes, fundraising or resale. www.tolana.com/wholesale.html

ISBN-13: 978-1-935208-19-8
ISBN-10: 1-935208-19-5

Library of Congress Control Number: 2013942583

Printed and bound in the United States Of America

Cover by Mary Kramer, owner of Milkweed Graphics, www.milkweedgraphics.com

v1.0

About The No Stress Tech Guide Series

SAP Crystal Reports For Microsoft Visual Studio Made Easy, is part of a series of computer software books that are designed to be used as a self-paced learning tool. Our books can also be used in a classroom setting or in an online class. The books in this series contain an abundance of step-by-step instructions and screen shots to help reduce the "stress" often associated with learning new software.

Titles In The Series

Title	ISBN
ACT! 2007	978-0-9773912-5-7
ACT! 2009	978-1-935208-07-5
ACT! 2010	978-1-935208-09-9
ACT! Pro 2011	978-1-935208-13-6
ACT! Pro 2012	978-1-935208-17-4
Sage ACT! Pro 2013	978-1-935208-22-8
Using Crystal Reports 2008 With ACT! 2010 Databases	978-1-935208-10-5
Getting Started With Alpha Five Desktop Applications	978-1-935208-23-5
Alpha Five Desktop Applications Beyond The Basics	978-1-935208-24-2
Creating Reports & Charts For Alpha Five Desktop Applications Made Easy	978-1-935208-26-6
Using SAP Crystal Reports With Alpha Five Databases Made Easy	978-1-935208-25-9
Crystal Reports XI For Beginners (2nd Edition)	978-1-935208-00-6
What's New In Crystal Reports 2008	978-1-935208-01-3
Crystal Reports 2008 For Beginners	978-0-9773912-9-5
Crystal Reports 2011 For Beginners (2nd Edition)	978-1-935208-15-0
Crystal Reports Beyond The Basics	978-1-935208-18-1
Crystal Reports For Visual Studio 2005	978-0-9773912-6-4
Crystal Reports Basic For Visual Studio 2008	978-0-9773912-8-8
Crystal Reports For Visual Studio 2010	978-1-935208-12-9
SAP Crystal Reports For Microsoft Visual Studio Made Easy	978-1-935208-19-8
Crystal Xcelsius 4.5	978-1-935208-02-0
Xcelsius 2008	978-1-935208-05-1
SAP Crystal Dashboard Design 2011 For Beginners	978-1-935208-11-2
Microsoft Office Starter 2010 (Word & Excel)	978-1-935208-14-3
Microsoft PowerPivot For Excel 2010	978-1-935208-16-7
Microsoft Works 7	978-0-9773912-2-6
Microsoft Works 8 & 8.5	978-0-9773912-1-9
Microsoft Works 9	978-0-9773912-7-1
Windows XP	978-0-9773912-0-2
OpenOffice.org 2 Writer	978-0-9773912-4-0
OpenOffice.org 3 Writer	978-1-935208-08-2

Why A Book Specifically For Crystal Reports For Visual Studio?

There are a few reasons that I decided to write a book for Crystal Reports for Visual Studio. They are listed below.

⇒ In general, there are not a lot of beginner level books with hands-on exercises for this complex software.
⇒ I felt that users, especially new report writers and designers would prefer to have more assistance in learning how to get the most out of the version of Crystal Reports specifically for Visual Studio.
⇒ I could not find a book specifically for this version of Crystal Reports.

Who This Book Is For

This book is primarily for beginners and end-users, as well as, report designers and developers that have never used the version of Crystal Reports that is specifically for Visual Studio. You do not have to know Visual Basic or Visual C++ to use this book because the functionality of these software packages is not covered in this book, except to create a project.

Over the years, I have come to realize that many people only use a small percent of the features that software has to offer. One of my goals in all of the books that I write is to point out as many features as possible. My theory is that if more people knew about more than 10% of the features that a software package has, at the very least, they would try a few of them.

I know that many books claim to have "step-by-step" instructions. If you have tried to follow books that make this claim and you got lost or could not complete a task as instructed, it may not have been your fault. When I decided to write computer books, I vowed to really have step-by-step instructions that actually included every step. This includes steps like which file to open, which option to select, when to save a file and more. In my opinion, it is this level of detail that makes a computer book easy to follow. I hope that you feel the same way.

About The Author

Dr. Indera E. Murphy is an author, educator and IT professional that has over 20 years of experience in the Information Technology field. She has held a variety of positions including technical writer, programmer, online adjunct professor, consultant, web designer, course developer and project leader. Indera has designed and developed software applications and websites, as well as, manage technology driven projects in several industries. In addition to being an Executive Director, she has taught courses in a variety of areas including project management, technical writing, Crystal Reports, information processing, Access, HTML, Windows, Excel, Dreamweaver and critical thinking.

Thank you for purchasing this book!

CONTENTS

GETTING STARTED WITH CRYSTAL REPORTS FOR VISUAL STUDIO

After reading this chapter and completing the exercises you will be able to:

- ☑ Have a better understanding of what Crystal Reports is and what you can use it for
- ☑ Understand the options on the Start Page tab
- ☑ Check for Crystal Reports updates
- ☑ Download the practice files

CHAPTER 1

Welcome To Crystal Reports!

Crystal Reports is a software package that is used to create reports. It is the leading report writing software on the market. Almost all businesses today that maintain data, have a need for reports to help them get their job done and to make business decisions. Often, businesses have data in a variety of data sources and need a way to pull data from several data sources to create a variety of reports including business intelligence analysis and proprietary business requirements.

Reports allow one to be able to read and make sense of large amounts of data that is most often stored in a database. Most databases have limited reporting capabilities and only allow reports to be created in that "type" of database. Database types include Sybase, Microsoft SQL Server and Oracle, to name a few. These are often called SQL databases and are usually stored on a database server. If you need to create a report that has data (information) in both Oracle and Sybase databases for example, you would have to use Crystal Reports because neither database allows you to create reports that have data in other types of databases.

Crystal Reports provides the ability to use data from a variety of database types and display the data in one report. Crystal Reports can use databases of any size. In addition to the SQL databases mentioned above, you can also use mainframe databases and what I call desktop or PC databases like Microsoft Access and Visual FoxPro. This type of database usually contains a lot less data than SQL databases and they do not have the capacity to support hundreds or thousands of end-users like SQL databases do. Crystal Reports also comes bundled with several leading software packages like PeopleSoft. In addition to creating paper reports, reports can be exported to Word, Excel and PDF formats from Crystal Reports. You can create almost any type of report that you can dream up.

Normally, Crystal Reports is a read-only program, meaning that when you create or modify reports, the data in the database is not changed. You can however, include SQL commands in the report, which will allow the report to edit, delete and add records to a database.

The primary goal of Crystal Reports is to allow a wide range of users to have the ability to work with the raw data in databases to be able to create reports that allow data to be interpreted and analyzed. Crystal Reports makes creating basic reports easier through the use of report wizards, which are similar to wizards that you may have used in other software packages. You can also create complex reports that include subreports, formulas, charts and much more.

A hands-on approach is usually the best way to learn most things in life. This book is a visual guide that shows you how to create or modify over 100 reports. There are over 500 illustrations that practically eliminate the guess work and let you know that you are doing the steps correctly.

Another goal of this book is to discuss report design issues and potential solutions on how to resolve them. The good thing is that you have taken a great first step towards learning Crystal Reports by purchasing this book. Now, all you have to do is use this book to learn how to overcome the hurdles. From time to time, I will point out functionality that may not work as expected. When I do this, I am not complaining, merely pointing out things that you should be aware of.

It is my sincere hope that whatever your current skill level is with Crystal Reports, that you will learn more about features that you are already familiar with as you go through this book and that you learn about features that you did not know existed. Learning new tips and shortcuts will let you work faster and smarter. The more you know about Crystal Reports, the easier your day to day report design experiences will be.

So sit back and lets get started!

How This Book Is Organized

Topics and exercises in one chapter build on ones covered in previous chapters. To get the most out of this book, it is not advised that you skip around. The first reason is because some of the reports used in later chapters are created in exercises earlier in the book. The other reason is that a topic or option may have been covered in more detail earlier in the book. If you decide to skip around and cannot complete an exercise because there is something that you do not understand, you will have to go back and find the section that covers the topic in question. Below is an overview of what is covered in each chapter.

Chapter 1, Getting Started With SAP Crystal Reports For Visual Studio covers background information about Crystal Reports, the Visual Studio Start Page and how to check for software updates.

Chapter 2, Toolbars, Menus And Customization Options covers the toolbars and menus in Crystal Reports, as well as how the workspace can be customized.

Chapter 3, Database Terminology And The Crystal Reports Workspace covers data types, the report design process, sections of a report, save data options, the Design and Preview tabs, the Preview Panel, Workbench and Group Tree.

Chapter 4, Create Your First Report covers creating a connection to a data source, linking tables and creating a basic report with a wizard.

Chapter 5, Creating Reports From Scratch covers the Database Expert, relational databases and creating a report without using a wizard.

Chapter 6, Aligning Objects On A Report covers how to line up objects on a report, resize objects, use the grid and guidelines.

Chapter 7, Editing And Formatting Reports covers adding images to a report, using the Format Editor and Format Painter.

Chapter 8, Selecting Records covers using the Select Expert to determine which records will appear on the report, using operators and creating report summary information.

Chapter 9, Grouping, Sorting And Summarizing Records covers the grouping and sorting techniques that are used to select how records will appear on the report.

Chapter 10, Creating Custom Groups covers using the Group Expert, setting up a user defined sort order and user defined groups.

Chapter 11, Using The Report Creation Wizards covers using the report and mailing label wizards to create reports.

Chapter 12, Exporting Reports covers report exporting options.

Chapter 13, Creating Formulas And Using Functions covers what formulas and functions are, selecting a syntax editor, using the Formula Workshop and creating formulas.

Chapter 14, Conditional Formatting covers using the Highlighting Expert and If Then Else statements to create conditional formatting. Suppressing fields and sections of the report are also covered.

Chapter 15, Using The Section Expert covers formatting entire sections of a report at one time and creating formulas for options on the Section Expert.

Chapter 16, Creating Charts covers creating the majority of chart types that Crystal Reports has.

Chapter 17, Parameter Field Basics covers using the Create Parameter Field dialog box to create parameter fields to customize reports, using parameter fields with the Select Expert and creating a static list of values for a parameter field.

Chapter 18, Creating Dynamic And Cascading Parameter Fields covers creating a dynamic list of values for parameter fields, create cascading parameter fields, creating parameter fields for Top N reports and using parameter fields to suppress data.

Objectives Of This Book

This book is written to accommodate classroom and online training, as well as, to be used as a self-paced training course. While there are no required prerequisites to successfully complete the exercises in this book, having a general knowledge of any of the following would be helpful.

- ☑ Prior version of Crystal Reports
- ☑ Database structures
- ☑ Basic programming
- ☑ Report design

Step-by-step instructions are included throughout this book. This book takes a hands-on, performance based approach to teaching you how to use Crystal Reports and provides the skills required to create reports efficiently. After completing the exercises in this book, you will be able to perform the following tasks and more:

- ☑ Create a connection to a database and link tables
- ☑ Utilize report design and planning techniques
- ☑ Understand database concepts
- ☑ Use the report wizards and create reports from scratch
- ☑ Modify existing reports
- ☑ Format and edit reports
- ☑ Create report selection criteria
- ☑ Sort and group data
- ☑ Create charts
- ☑ Create reports that have subtotals, counts, running totals and summary information
- ☑ Export data
- ☑ Add Special Fields to reports
- ☑ Create mailing labels using a wizard
- ☑ Use the Formula Editor and Formula Workshop to create formulas and add functions to a report
- ☑ Use the Highlighting and Section Experts to format data conditionally
- ☑ Create If...Then...Else Statements
- ☑ Create parameter fields

Conventions Used In This Book

I designed the following conventions to make it easier for you to follow the instructions in this book.

- ☑ The `Courier` font is used to indicate what you should type.
- ☑ **Drag** means to press and hold down the left mouse button while moving the mouse.
- ☑ **Click** means to press the left mouse button once, then release it immediately.
- ☑ **Double-click** means to quickly press the left mouse button twice, then release the mouse button.
- ☑ **Right-click** means to press the right mouse button once, which will open a shortcut menu.
- ☑ Click **OK** means to click the OK button on the dialog box.
- ☑ Press **Enter** means to press the Enter key on your keyboard.
- ☑ Press **Tab** means to press the Tab key on your keyboard.
- ☑ Click **Save** means to click the Save button in the software.
- ☑ Click **Finish** means to click the Finish button on the dialog box.
- ☑ **SMALL CAPS** are used to indicate an option to click on or to bring something to your attention.
- ☑ This icon indicates a shortcut or another way to complete the task that is being discussed. It can also indicate a tip or additional information about the topic that is being discussed. Some of this information comes from my personal experience using Crystal Reports.
- ☑ This icon indicates a warning, like a feature that has been removed or information that you need to be aware of. This icon can also represent what I call a quirk, meaning a feature that did not work as I expected it to.
- ☑ [See Chapter 3, Database Concepts] refers to a section in a different chapter then the one you are currently viewing that you can use as a reference for the topic that is being discussed.
- ☑ [See Chapter 2, Figure 2-8] refers to an illustration (screen shot) in a different chapter then the one you are currently viewing that you can use as a reference for the topic that is being discussed.
- ☑ When you see "**YOU SHOULD HAVE THE OPTIONS SHOWN IN FIGURE X-X**", or something similar in the exercises, check to make sure that your screen does look like the figure. If it does, continue with the next set of instructions. If your screen does not look like the figure, redo the steps that you just completed so that your screen does match the figure. Not doing so may cause you problems when trying to complete exercises later in the book.
- ☑ The section heading **EXERCISE X.Y:** (where X equals the chapter number and Y equals the exercise number) represents exercises that have step-by-step instructions that you should complete. You will also see sections that have step-by-step instructions that are not an exercise. Completing them as you go through the book is optional, but recommended.
- ☑ "Chapter 15 Report Name" refers to a report in the zip file for this book.
- ☑ "Save the My practice report as" means to open the My practice report and save it with the new file name specified in the instruction. The reason that I have you do this is if you want to view a report after completing this book, all of the reports will be intact.
- ☑ Many of the dialog boxes in Crystal Reports have OK, Cancel and Help buttons. Viewing these buttons on all of the figures adds no value, so they are not shown.

☑ "E2.1 Report Name" is the naming convention for reports that you will create. E2.1 stands for Chapter 2, Exercise 1. You may consider some of the report file names to be long. I did this on purpose, so that it is easier to know what topic the report covers. If you do not like to type or do not want to type the full report name, you can just type the first part as the report file name. That way when you have to find a report to complete another exercise, you will be able to find the correct report. For example, if the report name is E5.5 Orders shipped between 4-1-2010 and 6-30-2010, you can type E5.5 as the file name for the report.

☑ **FILE ⇒ NEW ⇒ PROJECT** means to open the **FILE** menu, select the option **NEW**, then select the option **PROJECT**, as shown in Figure 1-1.

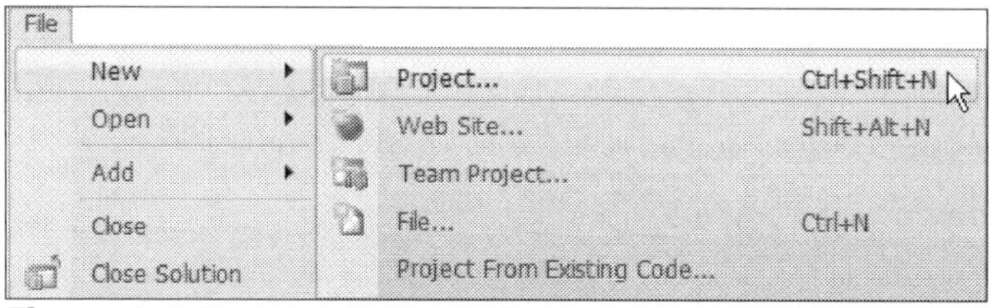

Figure 1-1 Menu navigation technique

Assumptions

Yes, I know one should never assume anything, but the following assumptions have been made. It is assumed that . . . .

☑ You have Visual Studio 2010 or higher and Crystal Reports developer for Visual Studio installed. The first link is for Crystal Reports, developer version. The second link is for the updates and support packs.
http://www.sap.com/software-free-trials/index.epx
http://scn.sap.com/docs/DOC-7824

☑ You know that the operating system used to write this book is Windows XP. If you are using a different version of Windows, any or all of the following can apply:

① Some of the screen shots may have a slightly different look.

② Some of the instructions for Windows tasks may be different.

③ The path to folders and files on your computer may be different then the paths listed in this book.

☑ You are familiar with the Windows environment including Windows Explorer and are comfortable using a mouse.

☑ You know that the version of Crystal Reports developer for Visual Studio is a scaled down version of Crystal Reports 2011.

☑ That you know to click OK or the appropriate button to close a dialog box and know to save the changes before going to the next section or exercise.

☑ You have access to the Internet to download the practice files needed to complete the exercises in this book and to download any updates to Crystal Reports that are available.

☑ Know that I am not perfect and sadly, you may find minor mistakes in this book. It is not intentional and I apologize for any inconvenience.

☑ When you see <smile>, that signifies my attempt of adding humor to the learning process.

☑ Understand that there will be options on dialog boxes that will not be referenced in the step-by-step instructions. When that is the case, accept the default value.

☑ Optional: That you have access to a printer, if you want to print any of the reports that you will create.

☑ Optional: That you have Microsoft Excel installed if you want to view the reports that will be exported to this format.

Crystal Reports For Visual Studio Forum

If you have a question about Crystal Reports for Visual Studio, you can post a message in the forum on the SAP.com website. Before you can post to the forum, you will have to create an account if you do not already have one. The account is free. The link below is for the forum that is specifically for the version of Crystal Reports for Visual Studio. After you click on the link, click on the Content tab.

http://scn.sap.com/community/crystal-reports-for-visual-studio

Exercise 1.1: Create A Folder For Your Reports

You will create and modify several reports in this book. It is a good idea to store all of them in the same folder on your computers hard drive so that you can find them easily. The instructions below create the folder at the root of the C drive. If you want to create the folder in another location or under an existing folder, navigate to that location prior to starting step 2 below.

> **Using The Practice Files And Sample Database**
> While you can create and use a different folder then the one listed below in step 3, the reports in the zip file may not display the correct data because the report will be looking for the database in a different location then the location saved in the report. If you are using a different folder, open each report in the zip file and select the location of where your copy of the crystalextreme database is located.

1. Open Windows Explorer, then click on the C drive.
2. File ⇒ New ⇒ Folder.
3. Type `CR For VS Book` as the folder name, then press Enter.

Visual Studio Settings

As shown in Figure 1-2, Visual Studio has settings that you can select from.

The **GENERAL DEVELOPMENT SETTINGS** option, is the one that I used for this book.

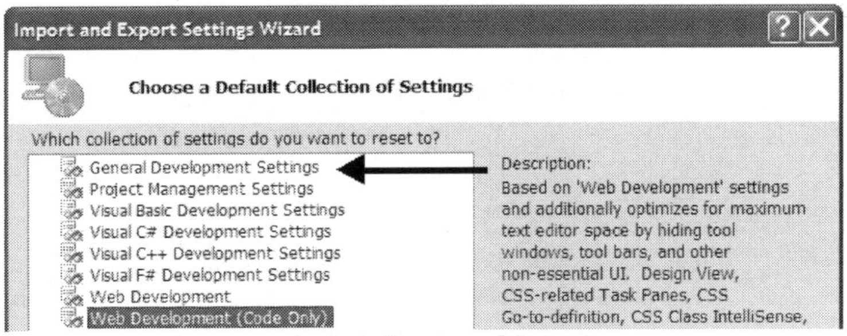

Figure 1-2 Choose Default Collection of Settings screen

Tools ⇒ Import and Export Settings, displays this dialog box if you have not selected any settings in Visual Studio. If you have selected settings, you will be prompted to save or reset your current settings, before you see this screen.

The reason that I am using this option is because I do not need any features of a specific development tool to use Crystal Reports in the Visual Studio environment.

Start Page Tab

Once Visual Studio is open you should see the **START PAGE** tab shown in Figure 1-3. The Start Page tab provides a lot of options that you may find helpful when using a development tool in the Visual Studio environment.

The **RECENT PROJECTS** section lists the last X number of projects that you have opened. X is determined by an option that you select on the Options dialog box. [See Chapter 2, Visual Studio Customization Options For Crystal Reports]

The **GETTING STARTED** tab has links to topics that would be of interest to people using Visual Studio for the first time.

The **GUIDANCE AND RESOURCES** and **LATEST NEWS** tabs contain information about Visual Studio. This is a good way to stay current.

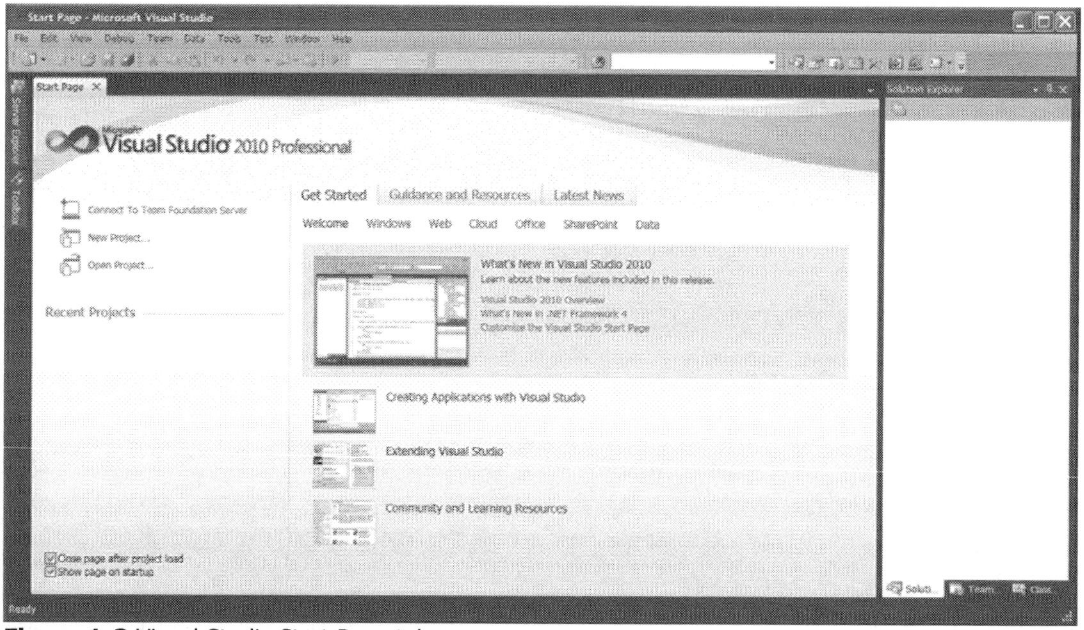

Figure 1-3 Visual Studio Start Page tab

Start Page Tab Shortcut Menu

The Start Page tab has the shortcut menu shown in Figure 1-4.

Selecting the **NEW HORIZONTAL TAB GROUP** option, creates a new tab as illustrated in Figure 1-5.

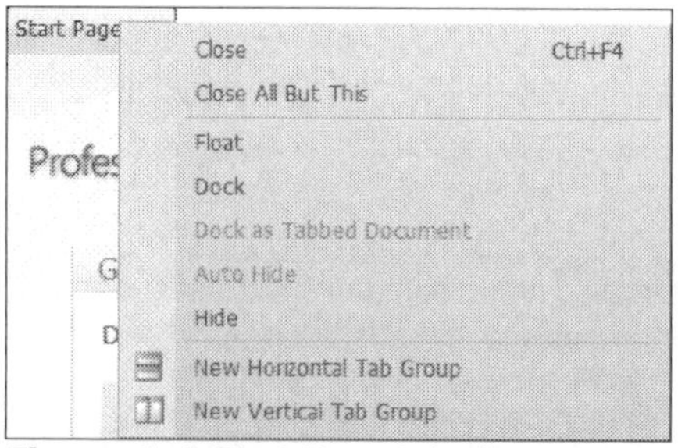

Figure 1-4 Start Page tab shortcut menu

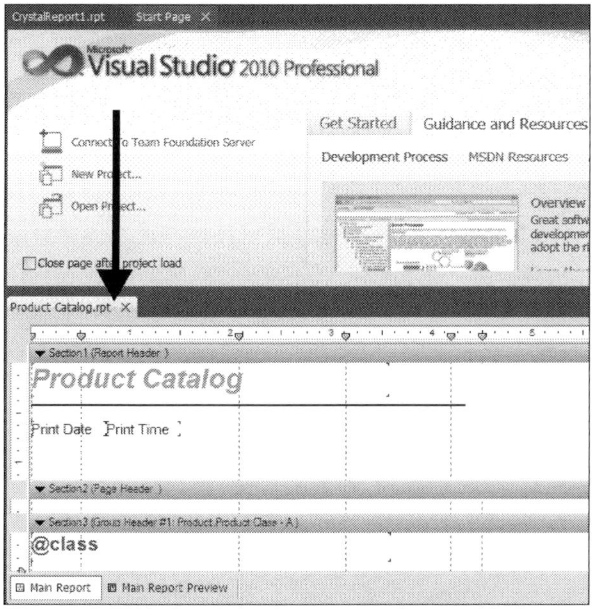

Figure 1-5 Horizontal tab group option enabled

> If you close the Start Page tab either on purpose or by accident, you can still get to all of the options on the Start Page tab through the menu, toolbar or shortcuts.
> View ⇒ Start Page, will display the Start Page tab.

Exercise 1.2: Creating A Project

If you have already created an application in Visual Studio, you already know how to create a project. The reports that you create must be stored in a project. The types of projects that you can create are based on the programming language (Visual Basic, Visual C#, Visual C++ or Visual F#) used for the application.

The functionality of Crystal Reports is the same for each type of project. How you connect to a database, the types of databases that you can use or how you deploy a report may be slightly different, but it doesn't effect how you create a report.

The project that you will create in this exercise will be used to save all of the reports that you create and modify in this book. I am aware of the fact that some readers think that authors should have you create a new project for each chapter in the book. I personally think that is unnecessary. You have better things to do then create 18 projects for this book. The report naming convention that I use for reports will let you easily know which chapter each report was created or modified in.

1. On the Start Page tab, click the **NEW PROJECT** link. You will see the dialog box shown in Figure 1-6.

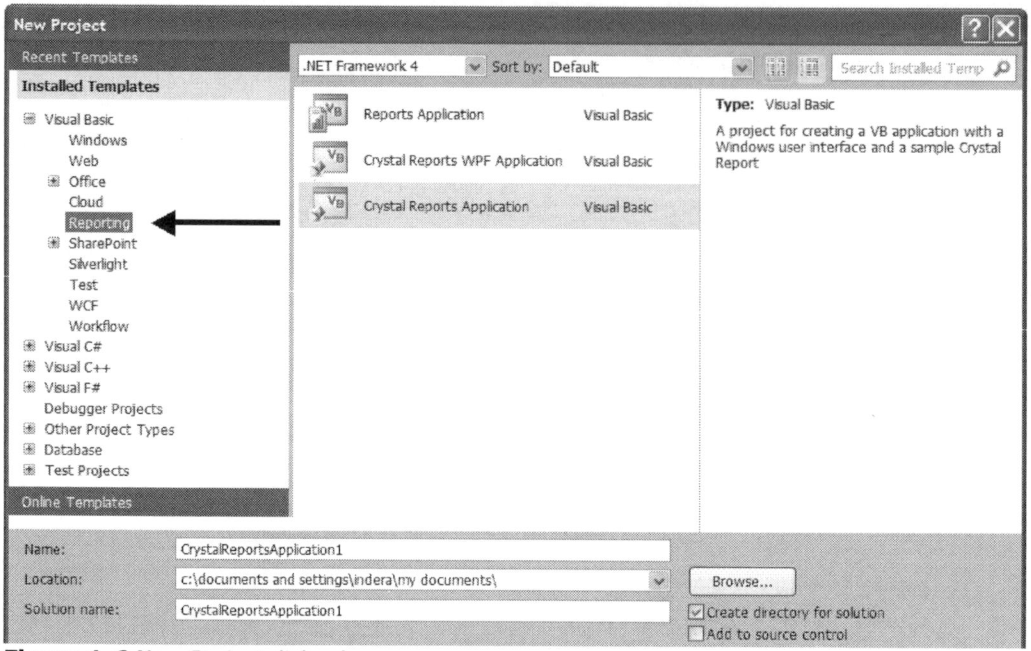

Figure 1-6 New Project dialog box

2. Click on the **REPORTING** option under Visual Basic on the left, as illustrated above in Figure 1-6, then click on the Crystal Reports Application option in the middle of the dialog box.

3. In the Name field, type `My_CrystalReports_Project`. This is the folder that you will save the reports in.

4. Click the Browse button at the end of the **LOCATION** field. Navigate to and click on the folder that you created earlier in this chapter, then click OK.

5. Type `CrystalReports_Book` in the **SOLUTION NAME** field.

6. Make sure that the **CREATE DIRECTORY FOR SOLUTION** option in the lower right corner is checked. You should have the options shown at the bottom of Figure 1-7. Click OK. It will take a few seconds for the project to be created.

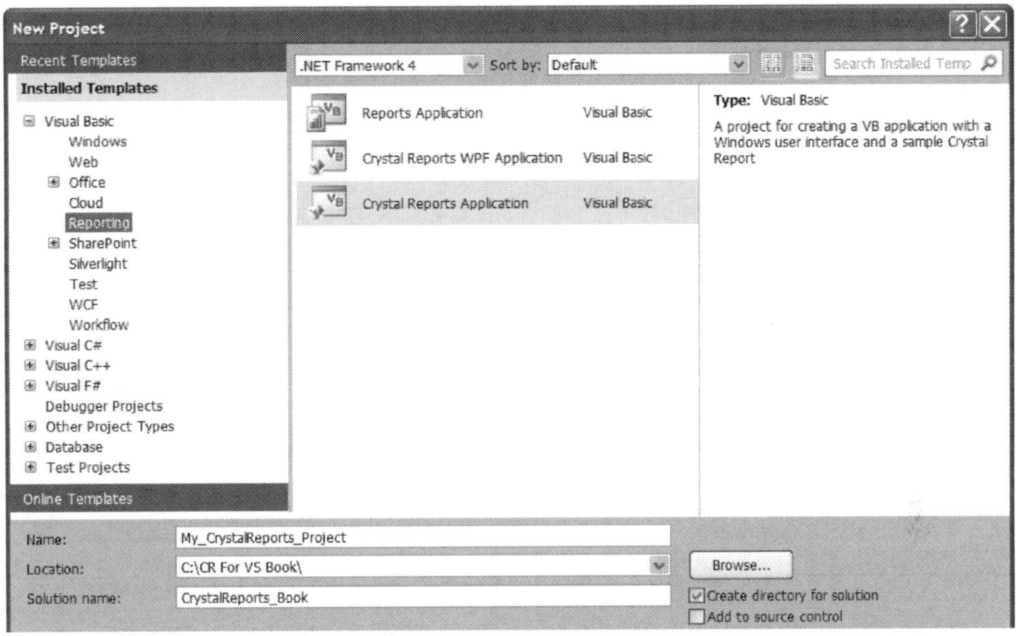

Figure 1-7 Options to create a project

7. After the project is created, you will see the dialog box shown in Figure 1-8.

   Click the X in the upper right corner of the dialog box.

   A new report window will open.

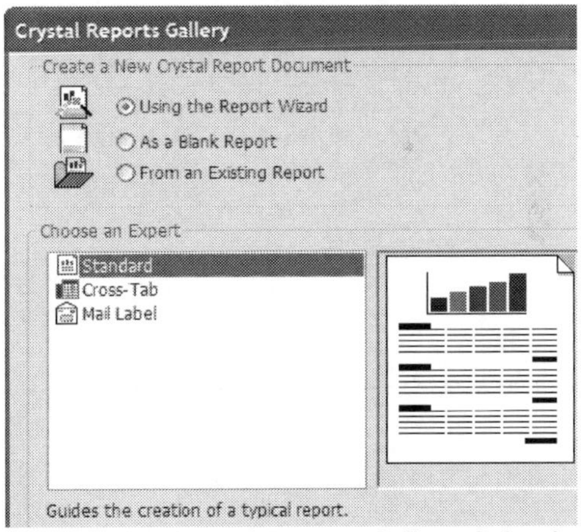

Figure 1-8 Crystal Reports Gallery dialog box

Exercise 1.3: Download The Practice Files

This book has practice files that you can download to use and follow along in the book. The steps below show you how to get the files.

1. The reports and files needed for this book are in a zip file named crvs.zip. To have the link for the zip file sent to you, send an email to crvs@tolanapublishing.com. If you do not receive an email in a few minutes with the subject line Crystal Reports Developer For Visual Studio Files, check the spam folder in your email software.

2. Download the zip file from the web site to the My_CrystalReports_VSProject folder.

3. Open Windows Explorer and click on the project folder that you just downloaded the zip file to.

   Right-click on the zip file and select **EXTRACT TO HERE**, as shown in Figure 1-9.

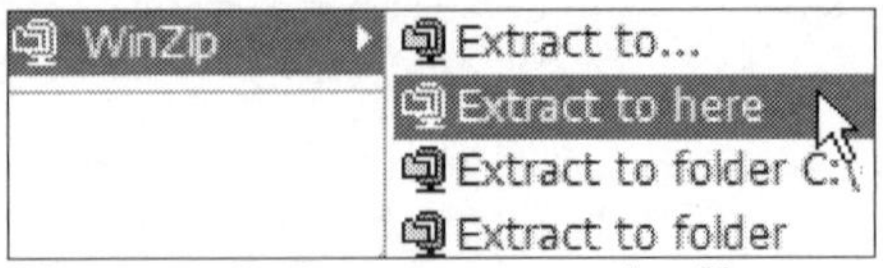

Figure 1-9 How to extract the files

TOOLBARS, MENUS AND CUSTOMIZATION OPTIONS

In this chapter you will learn about the options on the toolbars and menus. You will also learn about the report design customization options.

CHAPTER 2

Crystal Reports Toolbars

The Standard toolbar is part of Visual Studio, but is also used in Crystal Reports.

There are three toolbars that are specific to Crystal Reports in Visual Studio: Crystal Reports - Insert, Crystal Reports - Layout and Crystal Reports - Main, as illustrated on the shortcut menu in Figure 2-1.

These toolbars are not enabled by default. When selected, they are placed below the Standard toolbar. To add them to the workspace, View ⇒ Toolbars.

The other toolbars that you may want to add to the workspace when you are creating reports on your own are the **REPORT BORDERS** and **REPORT FORMATTING** toolbars near the bottom of the figure. These two toolbars are not needed to complete any exercise in this book.

The arrow at the top or bottom of the Toolbar shortcut menu means that there are more options on the menu that are not visible. Click on the arrow and you will see the additional options.

Like toolbars in other applications, you can rearrange the toolbars by clicking on the dots at the beginning of the toolbar with the left mouse button and dragging the toolbar to a new location in the workspace. You can add or delete buttons on the toolbars. You can also create your own toolbar.

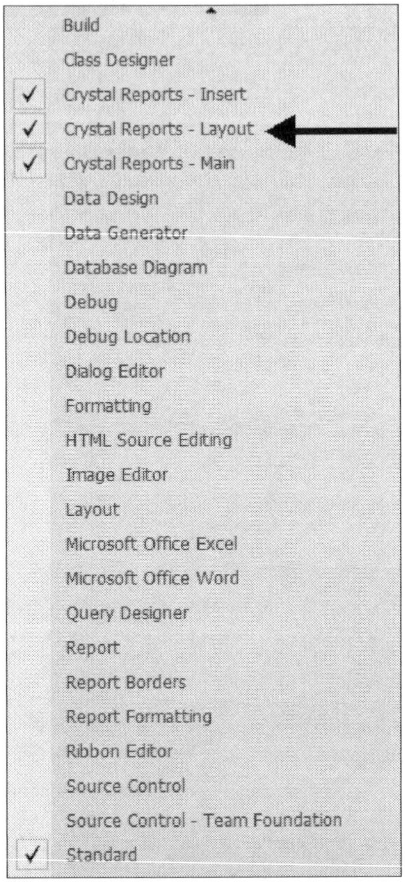

Figure 2-1 Toolbar shortcut menu

> Keep in mind that the buttons on the toolbars are available based on the task that you are performing and the object that is selected. There are some differences between the toolbar buttons and their menu counterparts. These differences will be pointed out.

Standard Toolbar

The buttons on the toolbar shown in Figure 2-2 provide access to options to open and save projects and reports, as well as, display or hide tools used to create reports. Table 2-1 explains the buttons on the toolbar.

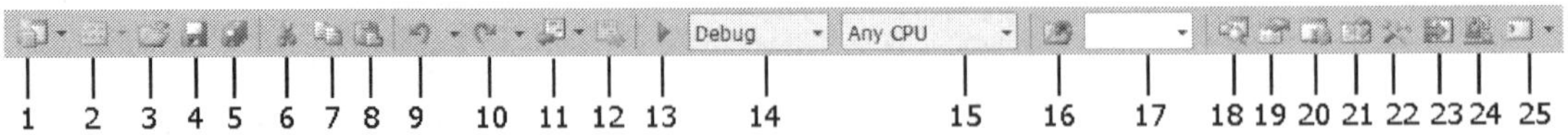

Figure 2-2 Standard toolbar

Button	Description
1	Create a new project.
2	Add a new or existing item to the project. If you click on the arrow at the end of the button, you will see all of the objects that can be added.
3	Opens a file.
4	Saves the report.
5	Saves all open reports and projects that have been changed.
6	Deletes the selected object(s).
7	Copies the selected object(s).
8	Pastes objects from the clipboard into the report.
9	Undoes an action.
10	Redoes the last action that was undone.
11	Navigate backward. (1)
12	Navigate forward. (1)
13	Starts the debugger. (1)
14	Selects the solution configuration. (1)
15	Selects the solution platform. (1)
16	Opens the Find and Replace dialog box, which is used to search for files in the project or search for words in files and replace them.
17	The Quick search option is used to search in the open report.
18	Displays or hides the Solution Explorer window.
19	Displays or hides the Properties window.
20	Displays the Team Explorer window.
21	Opens the Object Browser. (1)
22	Displays or hides the Toolbox.
23	Switches to the Start Page tab.
24	Opens the Extension Manager.
25	Opens the Command window. (1)

Table 2-1 Standard toolbar buttons explained

(1) This option is used for debugging an application.

Crystal Reports - Insert Toolbar

The buttons on the toolbar shown in Figure 2-3 are used to add objects to the report. Table 2-2 explains the buttons on the toolbar. These options are also on the design window shortcut menu.

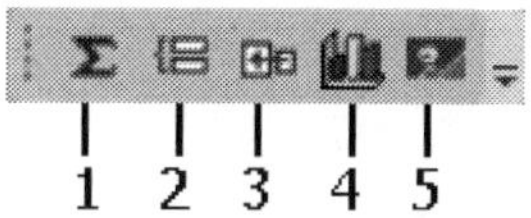

Figure 2-3 Crystal Reports - Insert toolbar

Button	Description
1	Opens the Insert Summary dialog box, which is used to create a calculated field.
2	Opens the Insert Group dialog box, which is used to create a group.
3	Opens the Insert Subreport dialog box, which is used to create a new report that will be used as a subreport or select an existing report to use as a subreport.
4	Opens the Chart Expert, which is used to create a new chart.
5	Is used to add an image or picture file to the report.

Table 2-2 Crystal Reports - Insert toolbar buttons explained

Crystal Reports - Layout Toolbar

The buttons on the toolbar shown in Figure 2-4 contain options that are used to align and resize objects on the report. Table 2-3 explains the buttons on the toolbar.

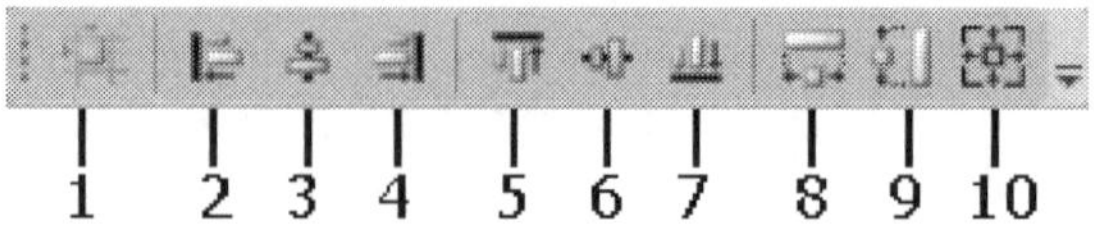

Figure 2-4 Crystal Reports - Layout toolbar

Button	Description
1	Aligns objects to the grid.
2	Aligns objects on the left.
3	Centers the object between the top and bottom of the frame.
4	Aligns objects on the right.
5	Aligns objects on the top.
6	Aligns objects in the middle of the frame.
7	Aligns objects on the bottom.
8	Makes objects the same width.
9	Makes objects the same height.
10	Makes objects the same size.

Table 2-3 Crystal Reports - Layout toolbar buttons explained

Crystal Reports - Main Toolbar

The buttons on the toolbar shown in Figure 2-5 provide access to formatting options and the Experts. Table 2-4 explains the buttons on the toolbar.

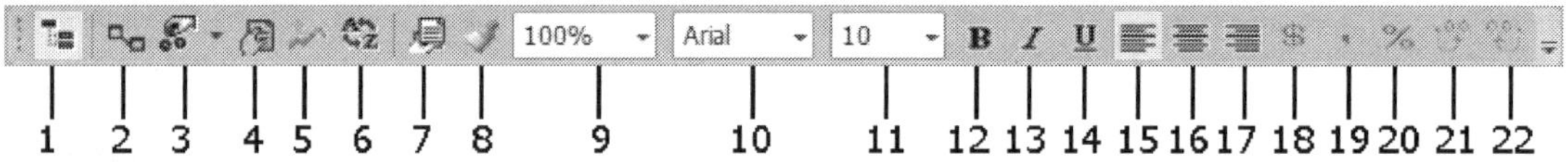

Figure 2-5 Crystal Reports - Main toolbar

Button	Description
1	The Toggle Field View button opens and closes the Field Explorer.
2	Opens the Database Expert, which is used to add or remove data sources for the report.
3	Opens the Select Expert, which is used to create criteria to select the records that will appear on the report.
4	Opens the Section Expert, which is used to manage the sections of the report.
5	Opens the Group Sort Expert, which is used to find the Top or Bottom N records or sort the data on summary fields.
6	Opens the Record Sort Expert, which is used to set the order that the detail records will be sorted in.
7	Opens the appropriate Format Editor, which is used to modify the formatting properties of the selected object.
8	Copies the formatting options from one object to another.
9	Is used to select a pre-set zoom level for viewing a report. Unlike other zoom fields that you may have used, this one does not allow you to type in the percent that you want.

Table 2-4 Crystal Reports - Main toolbar buttons explained

Button	Description
10	Select a font.
11	Change the size for the font that is currently selected. (2)
12	Makes the selected object bold.
13	Makes the selected object italic.
14	Underlines the selected object.
15	Aligns the selected object flush left.
16	Centers the data in the selected object.
17	Aligns the data in the selected object flush right.
18	Adds or removes the currency symbol in the selected numeric field.
19	Adds or removes the comma in the selected numeric field.
20	Adds or removes the percent sign in the selected numeric field.
21	Moves the decimal point in the selected numeric field one place to the right, each time this button is clicked. (3)
22	Moves the decimal point in the selected numeric field one place to the left, each time this button is clicked. (3)

Table 2-4 Crystal Reports - Main toolbar buttons explained (Continued)

(2) **Font Size Tip**
If the font size that you want is not in the drop-down list, highlight whatever font size is showing and type in the size that you want. You can also type in half sizes like 9.5.

(3) Rounding is set to the number of decimal places in the field.

Crystal Reports Menu

When Crystal Reports is installed, one menu for Crystal Reports is installed in the Visual Studio environment. Figure 2-6 shows the menu in the design view. Figure 2-7 shows the menu in the preview view. Table 2-5 explains the options on the menu shown in Figure 2-6.

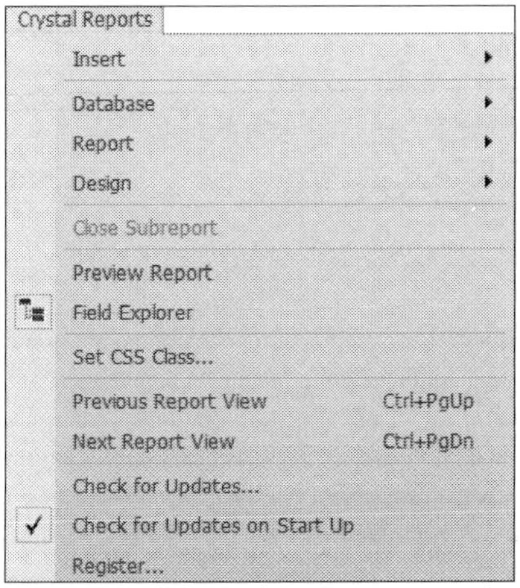

Figure 2-6 Crystal Reports menu in design view

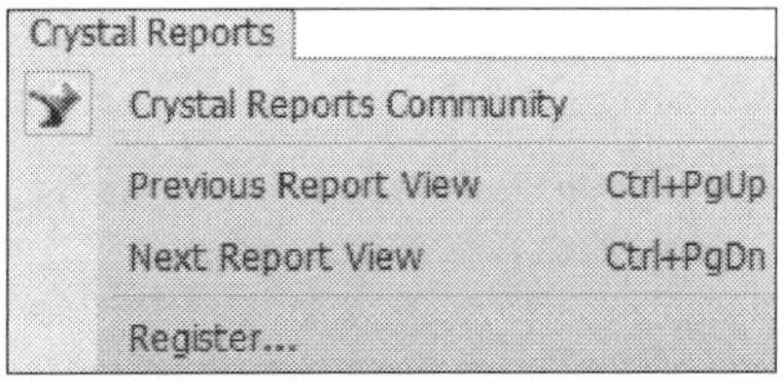

Figure 2-7 Crystal Reports menu in preview view

Option	Description
Insert	Displays the submenu shown in Figure 2-8. Table 2-6 explains the Insert submenu options.
Database	Displays the submenu shown in Figure 2-9. Table 2-7 explains the Database submenu options.
Report	Displays the submenu shown in Figure 2-10. Table 2-8 explains the Report submenu options.
Design	Displays the submenu shown in Figure 2-11. Table 2-9 explains the Design submenu options.
Close Subreport	This menu option is only available when viewing the subreport on its own tab. Select this option to close the subreport tab.
Preview Report	Is used to view what the report will look like when printed.
Field Explorer	Opens and closes the Field Explorer.
Set CSS Class	Is used to create HTML style sheets, which are used for reports that will be displayed on the web.
Previous Report View	Toggles between the design and preview workspaces.
Next Report View	Toggles between the design and preview workspaces.
Check for Updates	Is used to manually check for updates for Crystal Reports.
Check for Updates on Startup	If checked, this option will automatically check for software updates each time that you open Crystal Reports. I don't know about you, but this would get on my nerves. Clear this option if you do not want the software to check for updates every time that it is opened.
Register	Is used to register your copy of Crystal Reports.

Table 2-5 Crystal Reports menu options explained

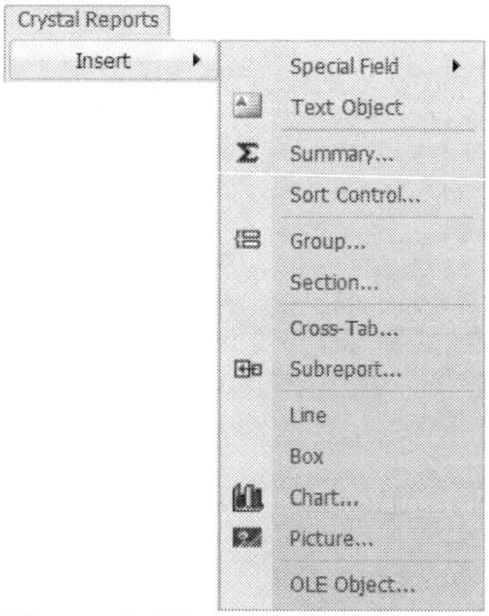

Figure 2-8 Insert submenu

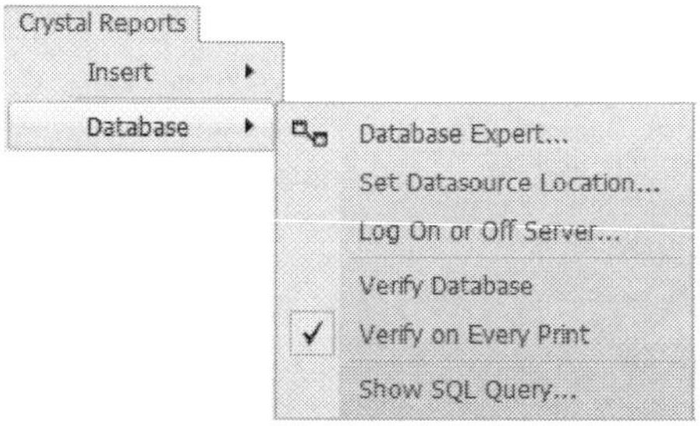

Figure 2-9 Database submenu

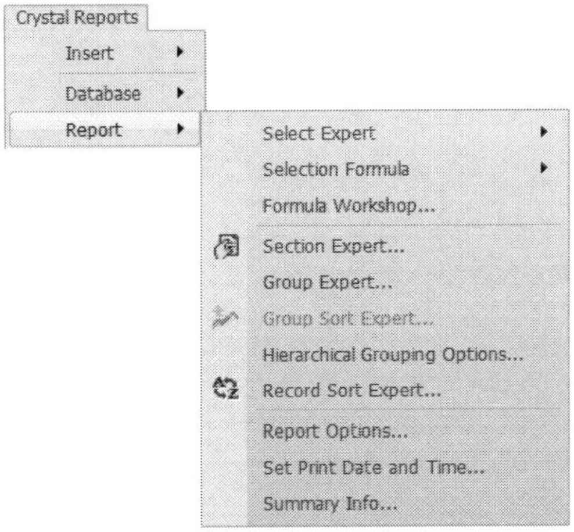

Figure 2-10 Report submenu

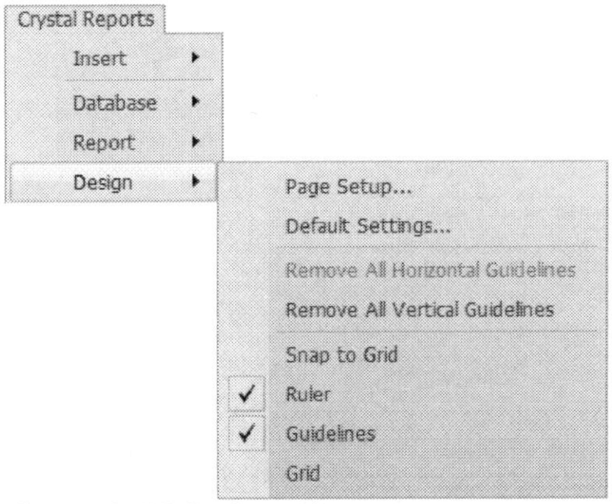

Figure 2-11 Design submenu

Insert Submenu Options

The options on this submenu are used to add objects to a report, as explained in Table 2-6. Many of these options are also available on the shortcut menu for the object.

Option	Description
Special Field	Add system fields to the report.
Text Object	Add a text object to the report.
Summary	Add a summary field to the report.
Sort Control	Add a control to a report that will let the person running the report sort the data in a different order or sort on a different field.
Group	Add a group to the report.
Section	Add a section to the report.
Cross-Tab	Opens the Cross-Tab Expert, which is used to create or edit a cross-tab object. There can be more than one cross-tab object on the report.
Subreport	Opens the Insert Subreport dialog box, which is used to create a subreport or select an existing report to use as a subreport.
Line	Draw lines on the report. You can draw horizontal or vertical lines. Lines can also be drawn across sections of the report.
Box	Draw a box on the report. Boxes can also be drawn across sections of the report.
Chart	Create a chart using the Chart Expert.
Picture	Add an image file to a report. The supported file types are Bitmap, JPEG, PNG, TIFF and WMF.
OLE Object	Add an OLE object, like a chart or sound file, to the report.

Table 2-6 Insert submenu options explained

Database Submenu Options

The options on this submenu are used to interact with databases that you use to create reports. The options are explained in Table 2-7.

Option	Description
Database Expert	Opens the Database Expert, which is used to add or delete data sources to or from the report.
Set Datasource Location	Is used to select a different database for the report or a different location for the database that the report is currently using. This option is useful when you are using a copy of the database to create and test the reports and are now ready to move the reports into production (go live). For example, this feature will let you change the database to point to the one on a production server.
Log On or Off Server	Is used to log on or off of an SQL or ODBC server, set database options and maintain the Favorites folder. Most of the tasks that you can complete on the Data Explorer can be done another way.
Verify Database	Is used to compare the structure of the data source that is used in the report to the structure of the actual database. This tool is helpful if you think that the database has changed.
Verify on Every Print	This option works almost the same as the Verify Database option. Either of these options can cause a processing delay and usually is not needed during development.
Show SQL Query	Is used to view SQL queries that a report may have. Parameter fields are included if they are used in the selection formula. Figure 2-12 shows the dialog box.

Table 2-7 Database submenu options explained

The query on this dialog box is automatically created when you create selection criteria for a report.

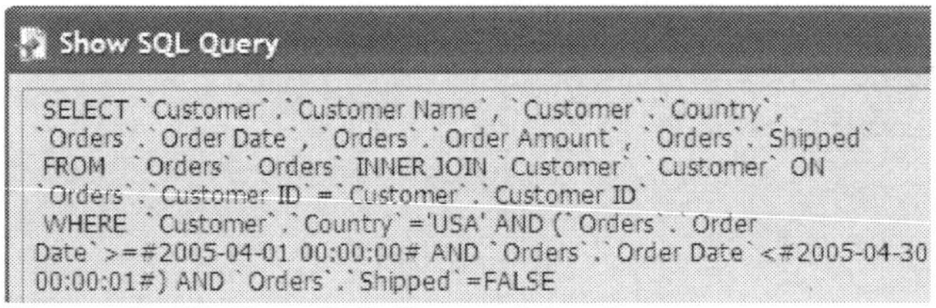

Figure 2-12 Show SQL Query dialog box

Report Submenu Options

Many of the options on this submenu will open an Expert. The options are explained in Table 2-8.

Option	Description
Select Expert	Opens the Select Expert, which is used to create selection criteria to filter records.
Selection Formula	Opens the Formula Workshop with the Formula Editor, based on the option that you selected on the submenu.
Formula Workshop	Opens the Formula Workshop, which is used to create, edit and view formulas and functions.
Section Expert	Opens the Section Expert, which is used to format the sections of the report.
Group Expert	Opens the Group Expert, which is used to create, modify and delete groups.

Table 2-8 Report submenu options explained

Option	Description
Group Sort Expert	Is used to sort the groups on the report by group summary fields.
Hierarchical Grouping Options	Is used to create a hierarchical report.
Record Sort Expert	Opens the Record Sort Expert, which is used to select the order that the detail records will be sorted in.
Report Options	Opens the Report Options dialog box, which is used to override or set how data is retrieved for the report.
Set Print Date and Time	Is used to override the values that would print if the Print Date or Print Time special fields are on the report.
Summary Info	Opens the Document Properties dialog box.

Table 2-8 Report submenu options explained (Continued)

Design Submenu Options

The options on this submenu are primarily used to select what is displayed in the design window. The options are explained in Table 2-9.

Option	Description
Page Setup	Opens the Page Setup dialog box so that you can change the report margins.
Default Settings	Opens the Options dialog box that you will learn about in the next section.
Remove All Horizontal Guidelines	Removes the horizontal guidelines from the design window.
Remove All Vertical Guidelines	Removes the vertical guidelines from the design window.
Snap to Grid	Is used to line up objects on a report.
Ruler	Displays or hides the rulers in the design window.
Guidelines	Displays the guidelines in the design window.
Grid	Displays or hides the grid in the design window. The grid is used to make it easier to line up objects.

Table 2-9 Design submenu options explained

Customizing The Crystal Reports Design Environment

If you need to customize the report design environment you can, by changing the options covered in the rest of this chapter. The options are used to set the default settings for the majority of features that you will use to create and modify reports. Once you have used Crystal Reports for a while and find yourself always having to change an option, you should come back to this section and review all of the options on the Options and Report Options dialog boxes and change the ones that you use, to better meet your needs.

Options Dialog Box

Modifying these options will save you time because they will automatically be applied as you are creating and editing reports. Some of the options that you may want to change would be the field formats and default fonts.

One option that you may want to change after completing the exercises in this book is the default date format if you think that you will use the same date format for the majority of reports that you will create. You do not have to change anything to complete the exercises in this book.

While looking at the options, pay particular attention to the options on the Layout, Database and Reporting tabs. They contain the options that you are likely to need to change first, because they are the options that most effect the functionality in the design window.

Options Dialog Box
The changes that you make on the Options dialog box effect all of the reports that you create or modify once the changes on this dialog box are saved. Any changes that are made will not be applied to reports that were saved prior to the changes made on the Options dialog box. If you want to apply changes that you make on the Options dialog box to existing reports, delete the object from the report that the change will effect and then add the object back to the report. It would be nice if there was an easier way to apply the change to existing reports.

1. Crystal Reports ⇒ Design ⇒ Default Settings. You will see the dialog box shown in Figure 2-13.

The **LAYOUT TAB** options determine how reports are displayed on the design window.

The options in the Grid Options section determine how the grid will or will not be displayed in the design window.

The options in the Field Options section determine how fields are displayed in the design window.

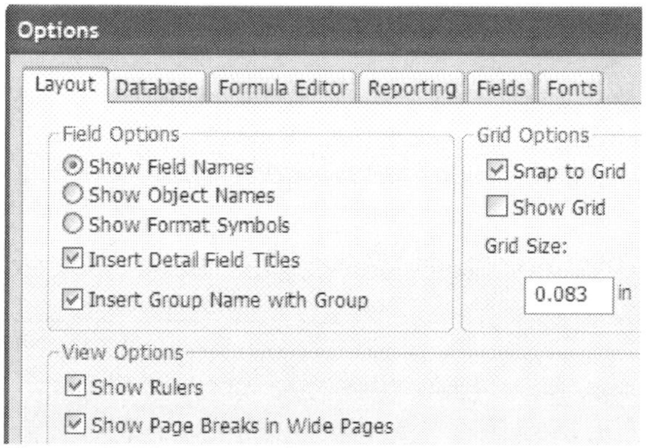

Figure 2-13 Layout tab options

The **INSERT DETAIL FIELD TITLES** option is what causes field headings to be added to a report when you add a field to the Details section. If the **SHOW FIELD NAMES** option is not checked, characters that indicate the field type will be displayed in fields in the design window instead of the field name.

If the **SHOW FORMAT SYMBOLS** option is checked, characters will be displayed in fields in the design window instead of the field name, as shown in Figure 2-14. This option will display X's in text fields and 5's in numeric fields.

Figure 2-14 Format symbols in the design window

2. Figures 2-15 to 2-18 and 2-20 show all of the other options that you can change. When you are finished viewing the options, close the dialog box.

The **DATABASE TAB** options are used to select how data appears and how queries are processed.

The options in the Tables and Fields section are used to configure how tables and fields are displayed.

The options in the Data Explorer section are used to select how database objects are displayed in the Field Explorer.

The options in the Advanced Options section are used to help resolve performance issues like determining how queries will run and when changes in the database structure will be checked. The first two options are only available for SQL tables, not queries that you create with the Select Expert.

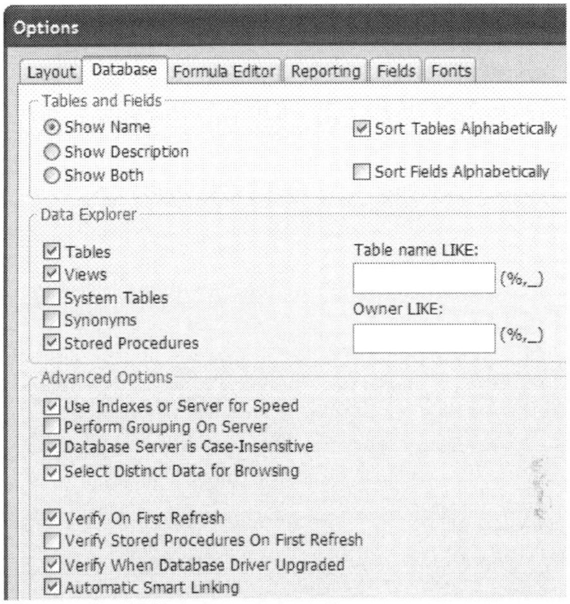

Figure 2-15 Database tab options

The **FORMULA EDITOR TAB** options are used to customize the fonts and colors used in the Formula Editor.

The **DEFAULT FORMULA LANGUAGE** option is used to select the default syntax language for the formulas that you create.

For the exercises in this book, this option should be set to Crystal Syntax.

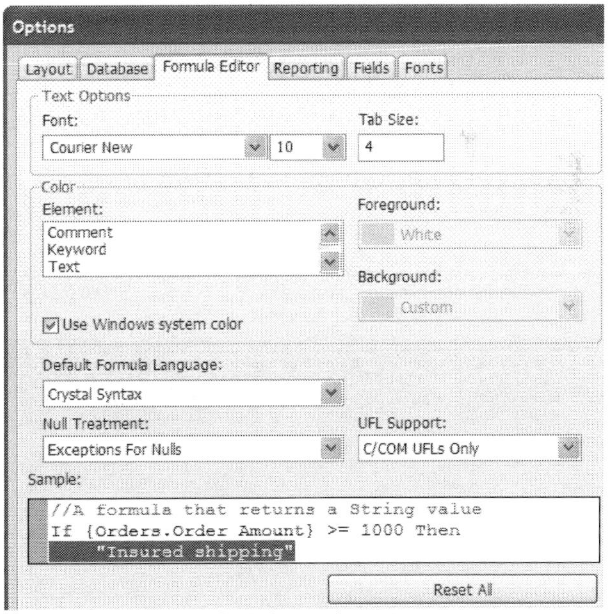

Figure 2-16 Formula Editor tab options

The **REPORTING TAB** options are used to select how the data is stored and retrieved for reports. These settings can be changed on a report by report basis, using the Report Options dialog box, which is covered later in this chapter.

The options in the **WHEN READING DATA** section are used to select how null values and sorting features will be handled.

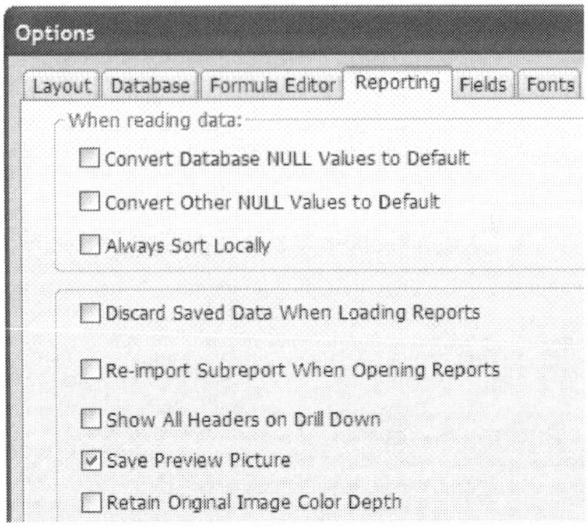

Figure 2-17 Reporting tab options

The **FIELDS TAB** options are used to select the default options for the field types that Crystal Reports supports.

You may want to click on these buttons now to become familiar with the default options.

For example, if you want all string fields to have the Can Grow option enabled by default, click the **STRING** button. You will see the dialog box shown in Figure 2-19. Select the option that you want applied to all reports, then click OK.

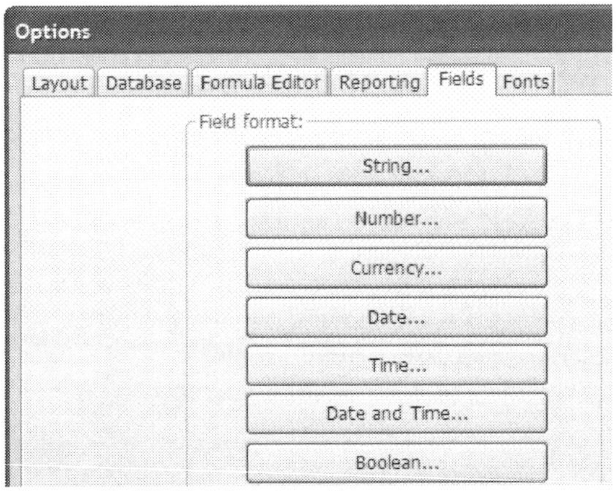

Figure 2-18 Fields tab options

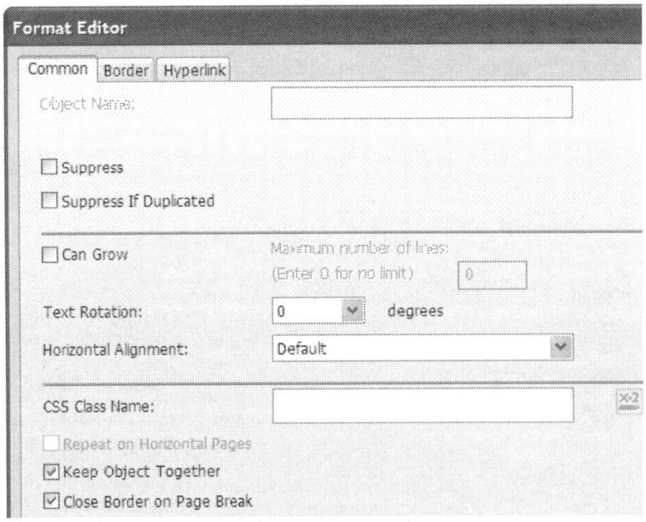

Figure 2-19 Format Editor string options

The **FONTS TAB** options are used to select the default font options for a variety of fields and objects that Crystal Reports supports.

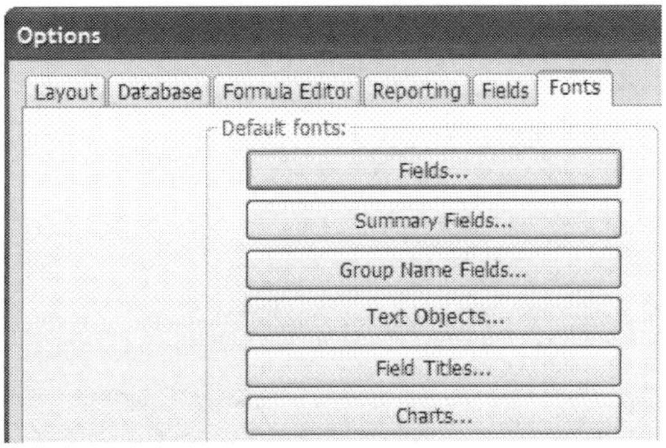

Figure 2-20 Fonts tab options

Report Options Dialog Box

The options that you see checked, like the **DATABASE SERVER IS CASE-INSENSITIVE** option, when you open the dialog box shown in Figure 2-21 are selected by the settings on the Options dialog box.

The pre-selected options are automatically applied to every report that you create.

The purpose of the Report Options dialog box is to select options for a specific report. Changes made on this dialog box are set on a report by report basis.

Crystal Reports ⇒ Report ⇒ Report Options, opens this dialog box.

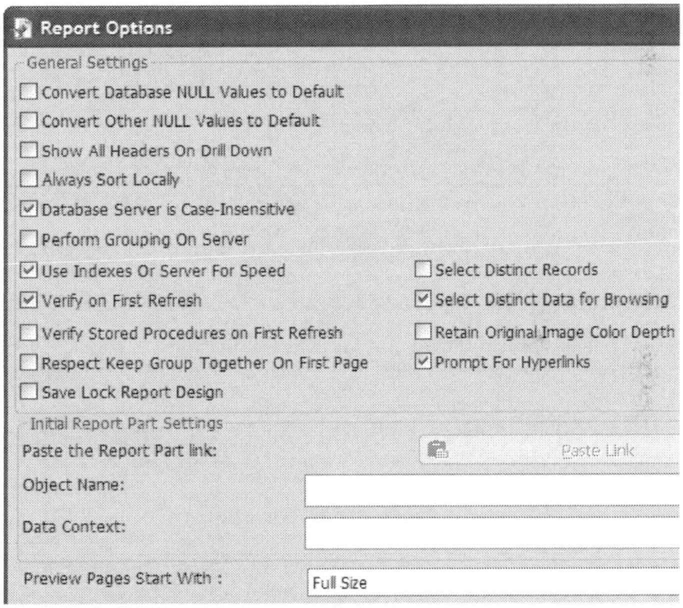

Figure 2-21 Report Options dialog box

The Role Of The Report Options Dialog Box
Changes made on the Reporting tab on the Options dialog box will change the default options on the Report Options dialog box. The options selected on the Report Options dialog box override the corresponding option on the Options dialog box (when applicable), for the active report. This means that the options on the Report Options dialog box will always be applied to the report, while the options on the Options dialog box will only be applied if there is no corresponding option on the Report Options dialog box.

Visual Studio Customization Options For Crystal Reports

You can change the number of files that are displayed on the File ⇒ Recent Files, submenu by following the steps below.

1. Tools ⇒ Options. Select the General option, if necessary. You will see the dialog box shown in Figure 2-22.

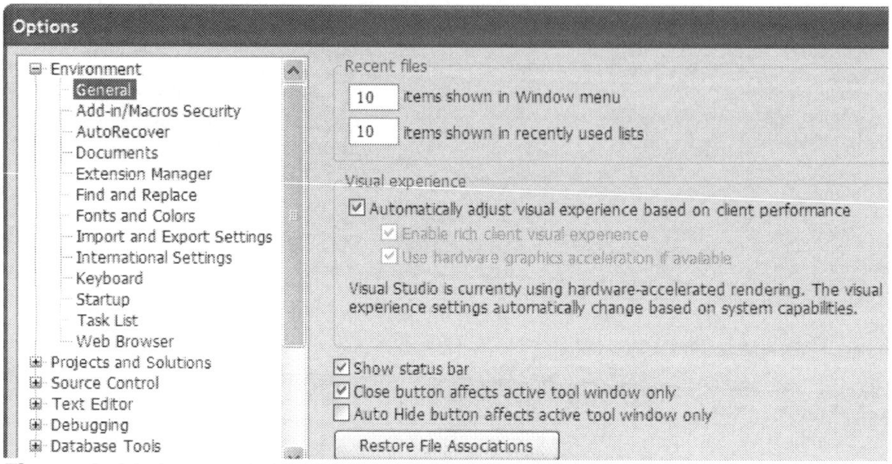

Figure 2-22 Options dialog box

2. Change the number in the **ITEMS SHOWN IN RECENTLY USED LISTS** option to the maximum number of files that you want to be able to select from. This option is also applied to the File ⇒ Recent Projects and Solutions submenu.

Customizing The Toolbars

In addition to being able to change the default values and options in Crystal Reports that you just read about, you can also customize the toolbars.

1. Tools ⇒ Customize ⇒ Commands tab.

   The options shown in Figure 2-23 are used to customize a menu or toolbar.

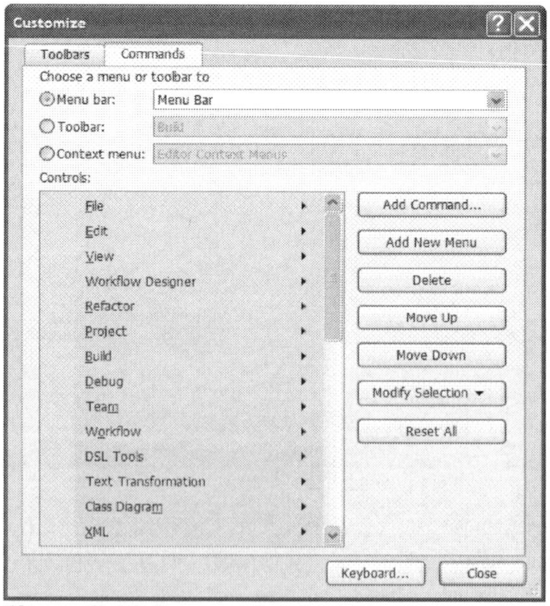

Figure 2-23 Commands tab

2. Make any changes that you want, then close the Customize dialog box.

How To Remove Toolbars

There are two ways to remove a toolbar, as discussed below.

① Tools ⇒ Customize. You will see the dialog box shown in Figure 2-24. Clear the check mark for the toolbar that you do not want displayed, then click Close.

② View ⇒ Toolbars, or right-click near the toolbars at the top of the Crystal Reports workspace.

You will see the **TOOLBAR SHORTCUT MENU** shown earlier in Figure 2-1.

Click on the toolbar that you want to remove. Notice the **CUSTOMIZE** option at the bottom of the shortcut menu.

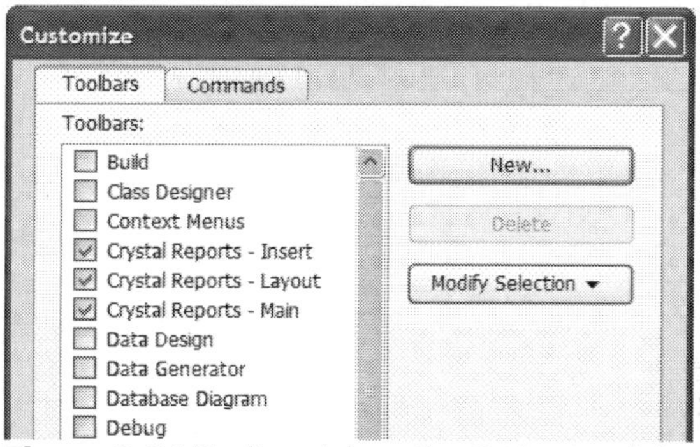

Figure 2-24 Toolbars tab on the Customize dialog box

Selecting this option will open the Toolbars tab on the Customize dialog box shown in Figure 2-24.

The **NEW** button is used to create your own toolbar.

DATABASE TERMINOLOGY AND THE CRYSTAL REPORTS WORKSPACE

After reading and competing the exercises in this chapter you will be able to:

- ☑ Have a foundation of database terminology
- ☑ Understand data types
- ☑ Have a foundation of Crystal Reports terminology
- ☑ Understand the report design process
- ☑ Understand the sections of a report
- ☑ Understand the report creation options
- ☑ Use the Design and Preview tabs in the workspace
- ☑ Use the Group Tree
- ☑ Use the Field Explorer
- ☑ Dock and undock the explorer windows

CHAPTER 3

Database Terminology

Below are key terms that you need to understand about databases in order to work with them effectively.

① **Field** A field contains one piece of information and is stored in a record. Examples of fields include customer name and customer address.
② **Record** A record has one or more fields. Each of the fields in a record are related. A record looks like a row of data in a spreadsheet.
③ **Table** A table is stored in a database and is a collection of records. Most databases have more than one table. Tables are linked on fields. Tables may remind you of a spreadsheet, because SQL databases have rows and columns, which Crystal Reports refers to as records and fields. Each table contains information about a specific topic. For example, a customer table would only contain information about customers. The customer table would not contain information about products.
④ **Database** A database is a collection of information that is stored in one or more tables.
⑤ **Relational Database** A relational database is a collection of **RELATED** information that is stored in one or more tables in the database. It is important to note that there are different types of physical database structures.

Database Concepts

There are several database concepts that you need to be aware of. Having an understanding of these concepts is necessary to create reports effectively.

Data Source A data source is where the data is stored. Examples of data sources are databases, **.CUB FILES**, tables, views and spreadsheets.

Data Dictionary A data dictionary contains detailed information about a data source and includes the following types of information: database and table names, field names, types, sizes, indexes and related files. A data dictionary can be handwritten or typed. It can also be generated by some database software packages.

Relationship A relationship is how two or more tables are joined (linked). Tables can be joined when they have at least one field that is the same in each table. For example, an invoice table can be joined to a products table because each invoice record will have at least one item from the products table. Crystal Reports has a **SMART LINKING** feature that will automatically join tables that have related information. Crystal Reports also has a built-in visual utility that will help you link tables.

Length Is used to select the maximum number of characters that the field can have. If the length of a field is set to 20, the contents in the field cannot have more than 20 characters.

Null Any of the field data types discussed in Table 3-1 can be null (empty). Null means that the field does not have a value. Depending on the data source, an empty string may or may not be set to null. An empty numeric field is not equal to zero.

Index The purpose of indexes is to make the retrieval of records from tables faster. Knowing which fields in the table are indexed is important when you need to optimize a report. Crystal Reports can indicate which fields are indexed in some types of databases and in other types of databases it can't. If Crystal Reports does not recognize the indexes in the tables that you are using, you can get the information from the data dictionary for the database.

PRIMARY KEY FIELDS should always be indexed. **FOREIGN KEY FIELDS** are usually indexed. Other fields in a table that are used frequently to retrieve (select) records should be indexed. Fields that fall into this category are fields that are used to sort, group or link data.

Databases that have too many indexes will retrieve records slower. Indexes are usually created by the DBA (Data Base Administrator). If you need to have an index created contact the DBA, unless you have the rights to create an index in the database.

Data Types

Each field must have a data type. The data type determines what type of information can be stored in the field. Table 3-1 explains the data types that are available in most databases. Crystal Reports recognizes these data types. If you use a database that has data types other then the ones listed in the table, they will be mapped to a data type that Crystal Reports recognizes.

Data Type	Description
String	String fields primarily contain text. They can also have numbers, spaces and other special characters. String fields are also known as **TEXT FIELDS**. Numeric data that is stored in a string field is treated like text because there is no need to use the data in any type of calculation. An example of numeric data that is treated like text is zip codes. Numeric data stored in a string field cannot be formatted with any number formatting options.
Number	This data type can only contain numbers and decimal points. This data type can be used in a calculation like addition, multiplication and formulas.
Currency	This data type can only contain monetary data. You can use currency fields in calculations, just like number fields. Currency is a special number data type. By default, Crystal Reports will automatically display and print a dollar sign with this data type.
Date	Date fields are used to store dates, which can be stored in several formats. Date fields contain the month, day and year.
Time	This data type is used to store time, which can be stored in several formats. Time fields contain hours, minutes and seconds. Crystal Reports does not recognize fractional seconds, even if the underlying data source has them.
Date and Time	Displays the date and time in one field, in this format - MM/DD/YYYY HH:MM:SS. You can hide the time portion of this data type on reports.
Boolean	Boolean fields are used to set a logical value of true/false, yes/no or 1/0.
Memo	The memo data type is a free form text field, meaning that it can store almost any type of information. This data type may not be available in all databases. Memo fields can contain large amounts of data and embedded formatting. Crystal Reports can recognize **RICH TEXT (RTF)** and **HTML FORMATTING** in memo fields. A common use for memo fields is to store comments about the data in the other fields in the record.
Picture	This data type stores an image file or a link to the location of the image file. (This is known as the **DYNAMIC IMAGE LOCATION**.) Crystal Reports recognizes the following image file types: bitmap, JPEG, TIFF, PNG and Windows Metafile. Some databases refer to this data type as a **BLOB** (Binary Large Object). This field type can only be displayed on a report. It cannot be used in a formula.

Table 3-1 Data types explained

Crystal Reports Terminology

Below are some key terms that you need to understand about Crystal Reports in order to work with databases effectively. The four field types discussed below are not stored in a table like the data types discussed above are.

① **FORMULA FIELDS** can include any of the 300 built-in functions that Crystal Reports has, or you can create a formula from scratch. The result of a calculated field is created on the fly, meaning that each time the report is run, the formula field will be recalculated.

② **SPECIAL FIELDS** contain information that is system generated. Examples of system generated fields include the date the report was printed and page number. There are 22 special fields that you can use.

③ **SUMMARY FIELDS** are calculated fields and like formula fields, they are also calculated on the fly, each time the report is run. You create summary fields.

④ **TEXT OBJECT FIELDS** are free form fields that are used to place information on the report that can't be added to the report by any of the field types discussed above. Text objects are often used to create a report title or a heading for fields that you create.

Report Design Process

I know that you are anxious to create your first report, but there are several items that need to be addressed and worked out before you create a report, whether this is your first report or your 100th report. This section is an overview of the report design process and planning. Report design could be an entire chapter or two all by itself, but I am giving you the abridged version. The report design process is part of what is known as the "Business Requirements" phase of a project. As you gain experience, you will see that if you do not get the business requirements right, the project will be delayed, potentially be over budget and not produce the results that the business owner (requestor) or client is looking for. Many call this a "bad career move".

When you learn the concepts presented in this chapter, it will be easier for you to create reports. You should write down the answers to the questions that will be presented in the report design process. The more planning that you do before you create the report, the less you will have to modify a report after it is created. There are four primary steps to the report design process. Each step can have multiple tasks.

You will see how these steps come together through the exercises in this book. When creating reports, especially ones that other people will use, it is imperative that you fully understand the requirements, which often includes asking a lot of questions. This is not a task that you can be bashful about. Not asking questions or worse, asking the wrong questions will more than likely cause you grief down the road.

Step 1: Define The Purpose Of The Report

Yes, I know what you are saying: "How hard can it be to figure out the purpose of a report?". The answer is it depends on how well the person or group of people are able to explain what they want the report to provide and how well you understand what they tell you.

The majority of reports that you create will be used by someone other than yourself, which means that you should meet with the person or group of people that will use the report. These meetings are part of the requirement gathering process. Keep in mind that you may have to have more than one meeting to get a good idea of what the report needs to include, because the users may not tell you or be able to clearly articulate their needs in one meeting. Reports are often used as a decision making tool, which means that poor decisions will be made or the decision making process will be ineffective due to missing or incorrect data that is presented on the report. The data must be presented in a logical manner in order to be an effective decision making tool.

> Keep in mind that one report can be used by people at different levels in the company. This means that at each level, people can have slightly different needs. If this is the case, you will have to plan and design the report accordingly, so that it meets the needs for all of the users.

Your role as the report designer is to gather the information needed, which will help the users of the report to be able to read it easily, as well as, understand the data on the report. If the information is not presented in a way that works for the users, trust me, they will let you know and you will be spending a lot of time modifying the reports.

In my opinion and experiences that I have had, the more that users have you modify a report, the quicker your credibility goes down hill. That is not something that you want to happen. What I have discovered, as well as, many other Information Technology professionals, is that if you create a prototype (which is discussed later in this chapter) of the report for the users, they can discuss what they like and do not like about the prototype report. Usually, you will gain valuable information that is often hard to get users to discuss in a regular meeting. The worst thing that you can do in many cases, is give the users the impression that you know more about their needs then they do. I am not saying that in some cases that you won't know more about their data, just don't give them that impression, if you know what I mean. To define the expected outcome of the report, write a descriptive sentence or two about the purpose of the report or what the report needs to accomplish. Below are some example purpose statements.

① The purpose of the report is to compare last years sales data to this years sales data by region.
② The purpose of the report is to show products that are low on inventory and need to be reordered.
③ The purpose of the report is to show the top 10 best selling products by sales team.

In addition to defining the expected outcome of the report you have to take into consideration who will be using the report. It is very possible that managers and their staff will request similar reports. In many cases it is better to create separate reports, even if there is only one field that is different, then to try and get multiple parties to try and come up with one report that works for both groups of users. As you gain report design experience, understand business requirements and know the requestors, you will be able to quickly determine which is the best solution.

Step 2: Determine The Layout Of The Report

Now that you have determined the purpose of the report, you need to determine where each piece of data should be placed on the report. If you are creative you will like this step. In addition to determining where the data should be placed, you need to determine some or all of the following:

① Create a list of fields that need to appear on the report. If you know what database or table each field is in, include that on the list. If the data does not currently exist, include it on the list also. You will use this list to complete tasks in future steps in the report design process.
② What should the report title be and where should it be placed on the report. Should it only be printed on the first page or on all pages of the report?
③ Does the report need page numbers or dates? If so, what format should they be in and where should they be placed on the report; in the Page Header or Footer section or someplace else?

④ Are any Special Fields other then the page number or date needed on the report?

⑤ Which fields or sections of the report need totals, summary, statistical information or some other type of calculated field? (**Hint**: Summary fields do not currently exist in a table).

⑥ An important question to answer during this step is what format the report needs to be in. This is known as the **DELIVERY METHOD** (for example, paper, PDF or web based). The way that a report needs to be distributed, can influence the layout of a report. You should find out if the report needs to be distributed in more than one format.

Step 3: Find The Data For The Report

This step is very important because without the data there is no report. As the person creating the report, life will be much easier for you if you are familiar with the data needed for the report and how it is organized. If you are not familiar with the data or are not technical, you may have to rely on Information Technology specialists, like database administrators, to help you with the tasks in this step. There are three tasks that you have to work on to complete this step successfully.

Task 1 The first task that you have to complete is to find out which databases and tables contain the data for the report. Use the list of fields that you created in step 2, to find the databases and tables. You may also have to find out what servers the databases are on. There are several types of databases that the data can be stored in. The data may also be stored in a Crystal dictionary, an OLAP Cube or something other than a database, like an Excel spreadsheet. This task is known as finding the **DATA SOURCE**.

Task 2 This task involves selecting the actual fields in the tables that are needed for the report. Use the list that you created in step 2. Once the fields are selected, determine the formatting for each field and how the fields should be displayed on the report. You also have to determine if the field names in the table are the best choice for the field headings on the report. One example of when a field name needs to be changed on a report is for fields that have the word ID as part of the field name.

Task 3 Now that you have found some of the data in the tables, there are probably fields left on the list that you created in step 2 that you have not found. Some may be special fields that you read about earlier in this chapter. More than likely, many of the fields that are left on the list are calculated fields. This task involves writing out the formulas for the calculated fields. Some calculated fields may use a built-in function and others require a field that will not be placed on the report.

In order to be able to create calculated fields, you have to become familiar with the database field types and the Crystal Reports fields discussed earlier in this chapter. Several Crystal Reports functions are designed to only work with specific types of data. Examples of calculated fields include:

① Sales price times quantity

② Number of days between the order date and the ship date

③ How long the person has been employed at the company

Step 4: Organize The Data

This step involves organizing all of the data. Many of the options that you decide on in task 1 below, will automatically dictate which section of the report certain fields will be placed in.

Task 1 To complete this task you have to organize all of the data, both from the tables and calculated fields, as well as, any other data source. Organizing the data means at a minimum, answering the following questions.

① Does the data need to be sorted? If so, which fields should the data be sorted on?
② Does the data need to be grouped? If so, which fields should the data be grouped on?
③ Does the report need summary data? Summary data is a calculated field, like grand totals, averages and counts.
④ Does the report need to have any data flagged? If so, how should the data be flagged? The primary reason data would be flagged is so that it can be easily identified on a report. Make a list of any data that needs to be flagged. Crystal Reports has several options including borders, symbols, changing the font size and other formatting techniques that can be used to indicate that the data is flagged.
⑤ Decide if the report needs any of the following: charts, cross-tabs or alerts, which notify the person running the report that a specific condition has been met.

Task 2 To complete this task you have to determine which section of the report each field should be placed in. Task 1 had you make decisions on how to organize the data at a high level. There are several sections of a report that the data and objects can be placed in. The sections of a report are discussed later in this chapter.

Task 3 One way that you organize the data is by selecting which records will actually appear on the report. This is important because most reports do not require that all records in a table appear on the report. For example, if the report needs to display sales (orders) for a specific sales rep, you would create selection criteria that would only allow orders for the particular sales rep to appear on the report. Another example would be to display all customers that purchased a specific product or group of products.

In addition to record selection, it may be necessary to create parameter fields which will make the report more flexible in terms of record selection. Parameter fields allow the person running the report to select the criteria that will be used to retrieve the records that will appear on the report. Parameter fields allow one report to be run with a variety of selection criteria. An example of this would be an order report. If the report had parameter fields for the order date, order amount and sales rep fields, all of the following reports and more, could be generated from the same report.

① A report to show all orders for a specific date.
② A report to show all orders for a specific sales rep.
③ A report to show all orders over or under a specific total order amount.
④ A report to show all orders in a date range.
⑤ A report to show all orders in a certain date range for a specific sales rep.

Task 4 Depending on the company, it may be necessary to have the person or group of people sign a document that states that all of the tasks discussed above will produce the report that they need.

Report Prototype

Even though you will go through the entire report design process, it is very possible that the users are still somewhat unclear or cannot visualize what the finished report should look like. If that is the case, creating a report prototype will be a life saver. A report prototype can be hand drawn on paper or you can create a sample report that displays the data based on the information that you gather during the report design process.

Some report designers create this prototype as each of the steps and tasks that were discussed above are completed. Other report designers will create the prototype right after the report design process is over. The reason prototypes are helpful is because the users will get a pretty good idea of what the finished report will look like, based on the information that they supplied.

The feedback that you receive from the users about the prototype is invaluable in my opinion, because users get to "see" what they asked for. I have found this process to be a very effective way for users to tell me what they like, don't like, need and don't need.

Sections Of A Report

There are seven sections of a report that you can place data and other objects in. Each section has its own properties that can be customized. If you place the same calculated field in different sections of the report, it can produce different results (numbers, totals or amounts). It is important that you understand how each section of the report works because they work independently of each other. Keep the following items in mind when deciding where to place fields and objects on the report.

① If a report does not need a section, it can be suppressed so that it does not display blank space on the report.
② If you create a report using a wizard, the majority of fields are automatically placed in an appropriate section of the report.
③ All of the report sections except the Group Header and Footer, will automatically appear in the report, whether you use them or not. Grouping is optional.
④ The order of the default report sections cannot be changed.
⑤ Sections can be resized vertically as needed.
⑥ Formulas, charts and cross-tabs will display different results, depending on which section of the report they are placed in. These differences are explained below, in each report section.

Section 1: Report Header

Data fields and other objects placed in this section will only print at the top of the first page of the report. It is quite possible that many of the reports that you create will not have anything in this section. Something that you may want to include in this section is the criteria and parameters of the report. If the report needs a cover page, the Report Header section can be used for the cover page. If this is what you need to do, add a page break after this section so that the actual report starts on a new page.

FORMULAS are calculated for the entire report.
CHARTS and **CROSS-TABS** will contain data for the entire report.

> If the Report Header section requires more than one page, the information in the Page Header and Footer sections of the report will not print until all of the information in the Report Header section has printed.

Section 2: Page Header

Data fields and other objects placed in this section will appear at the top of every page in the report except the Report Header page, if it prints on a page by itself. This is where most people put the report title. Other objects that are commonly placed in this section include the date, page number and headings for the fields in the Details section of the report. Report wizards will automatically place field headings and the system generated "print date" field in this section.

FORMULAS are calculated at the beginning of every page of the report.
CHARTS and **CROSS-TABS** cannot be placed in this section.

Section 3: Group Header

This section is only used if the data is grouped. Data fields and other objects placed in this section will print at the beginning of each group section on the report. Each time the data in the field the group is based on changes, another Group Header and Footer section is dynamically created. This section is always right above the Details section. If a report is grouped on two or more fields, a new Group Header and Footer section will automatically be created for each field that the report is grouped on.

FORMULAS are calculated one time at the beginning of the group, based on the data in the group, not on all of the data in the report.
CHARTS and **CROSS-TABS** will only contain data or information based on the data in the group.

Section 4: Details

Data fields and other objects placed in this section will print for each record that meets the selection criteria. The data fields and other objects in this section usually have field headings in the Page Header section. This section is automatically repeated once for each record that will be printed on the report.

FORMULAS are calculated for each record in this section, unless the record does not meet the selection criteria.
CHARTS and **CROSS-TABS** cannot be placed in this section.

Section 5: Group Footer

This section is only used if the data is grouped. Data fields and other objects placed in this section will print at the end of each group section on the report. The Group Footer section often includes subtotals and other summary data for the group. This section is always right below the Details section.

FORMULAS are calculated one time at the end of the group, based on the data in the group, not on all of the data in the report.
CHARTS and **CROSS-TABS** will only contain data or information based on the data in the group.

Section 6: Report Footer

Data fields and other objects placed in this section will print once at the end of the report. This is usually where grand totals and other types of report summary information is placed.

FORMULAS are calculated once at the end of the report.
CHARTS and **CROSS-TABS** will contain data for the entire report.

> If the Report Footer section requires more than one page to print the information, the Page Header and Footer sections will print on the additional pages that the Report Footer section needs. This is the opposite of what happens if the Report Header requires more than one page. If you think about it though, that makes sense because by the time the Report Footer section is printed, the "switch" if you will, for the Page Header and Footer sections is turned on.

Section 7: Page Footer

Data fields and other objects placed in this section will print at the bottom of each page of the report. The Page Footer section is similar to the Page Header section. Page numbers are often placed in this section. Report wizards will automatically place the page number in this section.

FORMULAS are calculated at the end of every page of the report. This would be useful if the report needs to have totals by page.
CHARTS and **CROSS-TABS** cannot be placed in this section.

Report Creation Options

There are three ways (wizards, from an existing report and from scratch) that you can create a report. Each option has pros and cons. Once you understand all of the options, you can select the one that best meets the needs for each report that you have to create.

Wizards

This is the easiest way to create a new report. The wizards walk you through the steps required to create a report. The wizards are helpful when learning the basics of Crystal Reports. Experienced report designers often only use the wizards to save time to create a basic report and then add advanced features manually. Keep in mind that the wizards do not provide all of the options that are needed to create the functionality that all reports need. The wizards are limited because they use default options which often do not meet the needs of the report that you are creating.

Based on your selections on the wizard screens, the fields are placed in the most appropriate section of the report. This does not mean that if you make a mistake when using the wizard, that the wizard will correct the mistake. It is possible to create a report that displays results that are very different then you intended, when using a wizard.

There are three report wizards that you can select from. What you will find, depending on the options that you select, is that additional fields are automatically added to the report, which you may not need. If this happens, you can delete the fields once you have the report open in the Design tab.

Create A Report Based Off Of An Existing Report

If a report exists that is similar to the report that you now need to create, select this report creation option. Save the existing report with a new file name and make the necessary changes to the new report. An example of when to create a report based off of an existing report would be when two groups of people need to see the majority of the same fields and one group needs additional information that the other group does not need, or when one group needs the same fields in a different layout.

Create A Report From Scratch

This option provides the most flexibility to create a report. You start with a blank canvas so to speak and add the fields, formulas and other objects without any assistance. For many, this can be intimidating especially in the beginning, but being the fearless person that you are, I'm sure that when you get to the exercises that have you create a report from scratch, you will do just fine.

Wizard Types

As mentioned earlier, there are three report wizards that you can select from to create reports. They are discussed below.

① **Standard** This is probably the most used wizard because it provides the majority of options needed to create a wide variety of reports. The report wizards discussed below create specific types of reports.

② **Cross-Tab** This wizard will create a report that presents data in a grid. Cross-Tab reports resemble spreadsheets because they have rows and columns. The grid often contains totals at the end of each row and column. An example of when a cross-tab should be used would be if you needed to know how many of specific products were sold by each sales rep. You should only use this wizard if the cross-tab will be the only object on the report.

③ **Mail Label** This wizard is used to create labels. While you can format a report created with the Standard wizard to print labels, the advantage of using the mail label wizard is that it has an option to select the label size that you need. This means that you will not have to manually format the report to match the dimensions of the label size that you need.

Xtreme Database

This is the database that is often used to test and learn Crystal Reports. You will use a modified version of it (which I named crystalxtreme.mdb) as the basis for the reports that you will create in this book. This database is a Microsoft Access database and contains the data for a fictitious company called Xtreme Mountain Bikes. As the company name suggests, they sell mountain bikes and accessories. The database has tables that store the following types of information: Customers, Employees, Orders, Suppliers, Products and more.

Figure 3-1 shows the data model for some of the tables in the database. The fields in bold are the Primary Key fields. Table 3-2 contains information for tables that are shown in Figure 3-1.

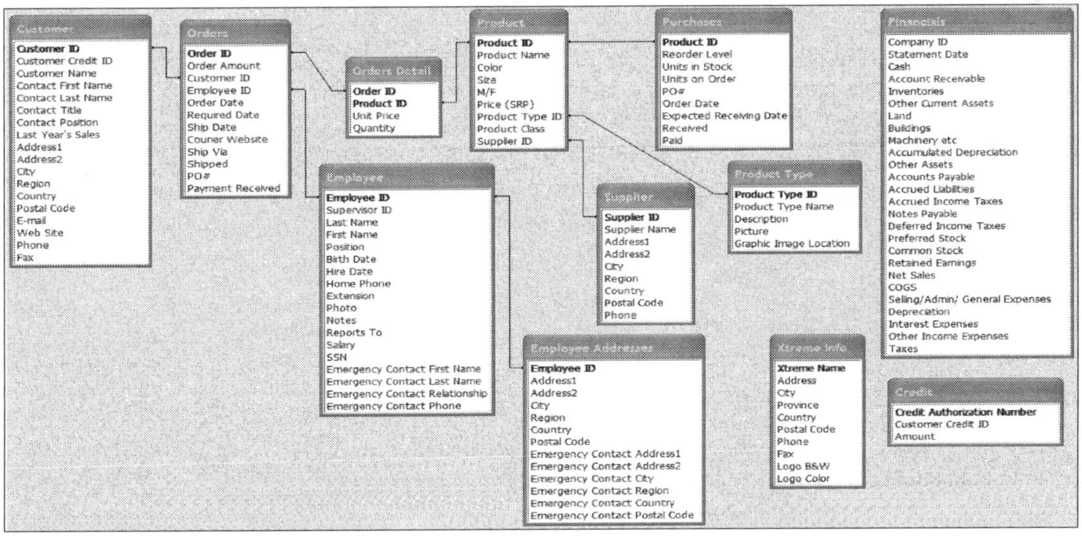

Figure 3-1 Database data model

Table	Primary Key	Indexed Fields	Records
Credit	Credit Authorization Number	Credit Authorization Number, Customer Credit ID	322
Customer	Customer ID	Customer ID, Postal Code	269
Employee	Employee ID	Employee ID, Supervisor ID, Reports To	15
Employee Address	Employee ID	Employee ID, Postal Code, Emergency Contact Postal Code	15
Financials	Company ID	Company ID	4
Orders	Order ID	Order ID, Customer ID, Employee ID	2,192
Orders Detail	Order ID, Product ID	Order ID, Product ID	3,684
Product	Product ID	Product ID, Product Type ID, Supplier ID	115
Product Type	Product Type ID	Product Type ID	8
Purchases	Product ID	Product ID	44
Supplier	Supplier ID	Supplier ID, Postal Code	7
Xtreme Info	Xtreme Name	Xtreme Name, Postal Code	1

Table 3-2 Database table information

Database Tables

In order to help you become more familiar with the data contained in each table, this section provides a description of the data in the tables that you will use. The table name is in bold.

Customer Contact and address information for all of the companies customers.

Employee Detail information for each employee. Some of the employees are sales reps for the company.

The Supervisor ID field in the Employee table contains the Employee ID of a different person in the Employee table. The Supervisor ID field contains who the employee reports to. This is known as a **RECURSIVE JOIN**, which you will learn about in Chapter 5.

Employee Addresses Home address and emergency contact information for each person in the Employee table.

Orders Information about each customer order. Fields that apply to the entire order, like the order date and order amount are in this table. This table is often referred to as the **ORDER HEADER** table. This table does not contain information about the items in the order.

Orders Detail Information about each item in each order.

Product Information for each item that Xtreme sells. Each product only has one product type and supplier. This does not mean that there cannot be two suppliers that have the same product. For example, Supplier A has blue hats. Supplier B has blue hats and brown hats. There would be a record in the Product table for each of these three hats.

Product Type General categories for the products like gloves, locks and helmets.

Supplier Information about companies that Xtreme purchases the products from that they sell. Contact and address information for each supplier is stored in this table.

Crystal Reports Workspace

The workspace is where you will create, edit and preview reports. Therefore, it is important to know what tools are available in the workspace. As you will see, the workspace has a lot of options. The toolbars, menus and customization options were covered in Chapter 2. The workspace has two tabs: The design tab (**MAIN REPORT TAB**) and the preview tab (**MAIN REPORT PREVIEW TAB**). When a report is opened, it is automatically displayed on the design tab.

Design And Preview Tabs

These two tabs are available for each report, as illustrated at the bottom of Figure 3-2.
The **MAIN REPORT** tab is where you create and modify reports. I will refer to this tab as the Design tab. The **MAIN REPORT PREVIEW** tab is where you view reports. I will refer to this tab as the Preview tab. The preview tab is used to view the report as it will look when it is printed. Reports can look different on this tab depending on the printer that is selected. Also notice that the report has its own navigation toolbar right above the report. You can use the options on this toolbar to move from one page to another in the report and to refresh the data in the report. This toolbar also lets you know what page of the report is currently displayed and how many pages in total the report has.

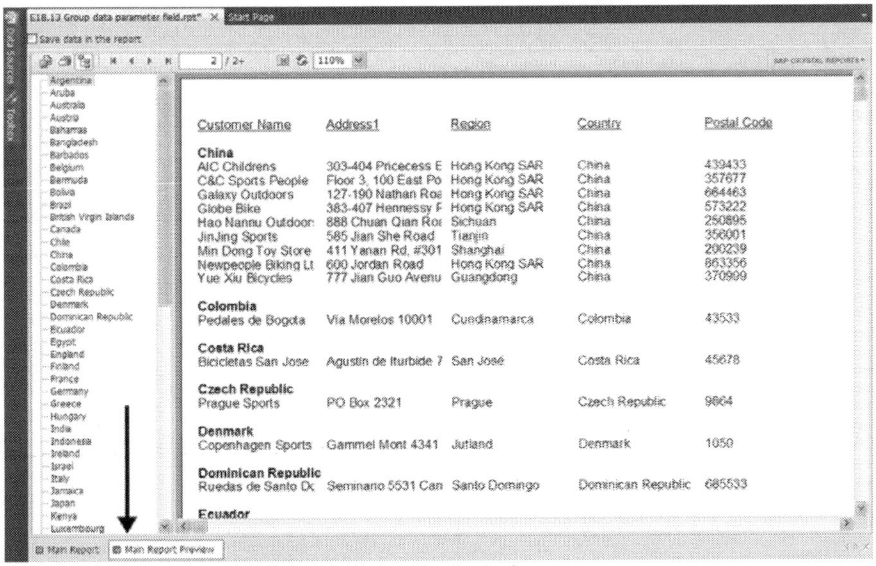

Figure 3-2 Design and Preview tabs illustrated

Design Tab (Main Report Tab)

The design tab is where you will create and modify reports, as well as, see the structure of the report.

Figure 3-3 illustrates the parts of the design tab.

Table 3-3 explains the parts of the design tab.

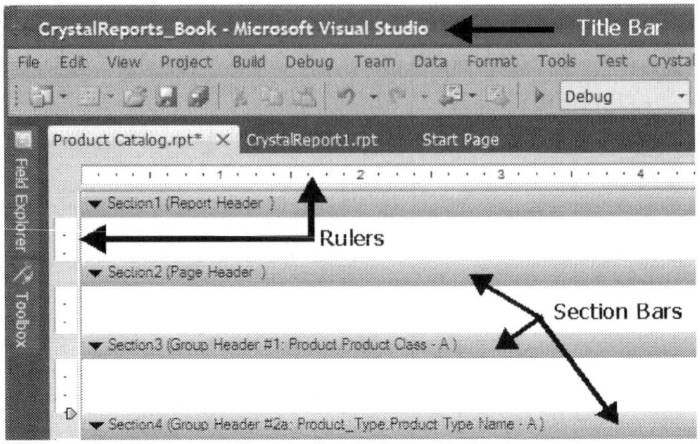

Figure 3-3 Parts of the design tab illustrated

Report tabs that have a * after the file name, as shown above in Figure 3-3, indicates that changes have been made to the report, but the changes have not been saved.

Option	Description
Title bar	Displays the solution name of the project.
Section bar	Like other parts of the design tab, each section of the report has a shortcut menu, which you access by right-clicking on the section bar that you want to work on.
Rulers	The rulers help you place fields in a specific location on the report.
Design area	This is white space under each section bar where you can add, change and format fields and other objects. The design area has a shortcut menu, that has different options then the section bars. You can place objects as close to the edge of this area as necessary because this area is inside of the page margins.

Table 3-3 Parts of the design tab explained

Everything on a report is an object. Each object has its own set of properties. Almost all of these properties can be modified. The properties can also be modified based on a condition that you set. You will learn about conditional formatting in Chapter 14.

Report Sections

As shown above in Figure 3-3, the design tab is divided into sections. The sections are divided by **SECTION BARS**. The sections can be resized by moving the section bar up or down. Figure 3-4 shows a smaller Page Header section and a larger Report Header section, then shown above in Figure 3-3.

If you do not need to display data in a section of the report, you can **SUPPRESS** (hide) the section and it will not appear on the preview tab or on the printed report. To resize a section of the report, place the mouse pointer over the section bar for the section that you need to resize, as illustrated in Figure 3-5. The mouse pointer will change to a double arrow, as illustrated. Drag the section bar up or down.

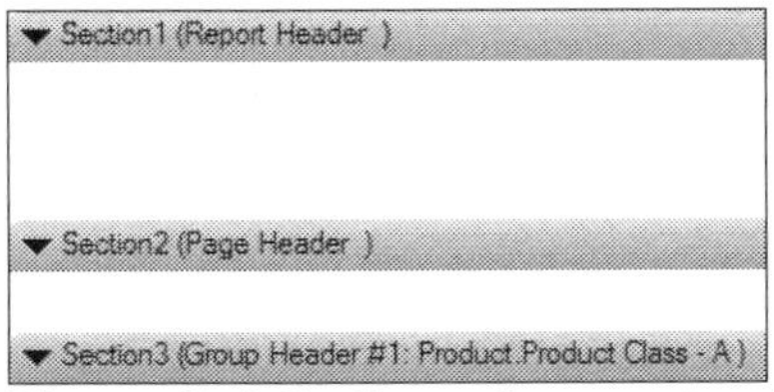

Figure 3-4 Sections of a report resized

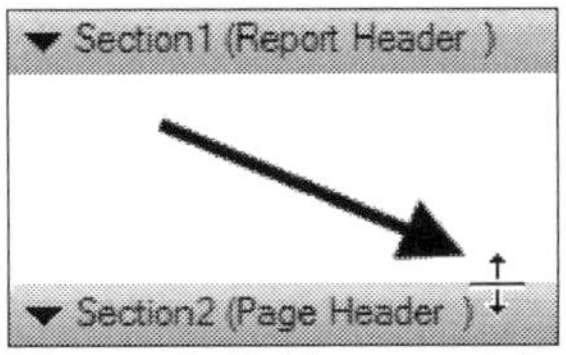

Figure 3-5 Mouse pointer in position to move the section bar

> You cannot make a section of the report smaller than the objects that are in the section.

Explorers

Crystal Reports comes with explorers that you can use to help create and manage reports. The one that you will probably use the most is the Field Explorer, shown in Figure 3-6.

The Solution Explorer is shown in Figure 3-7. The explorers are discussed below.

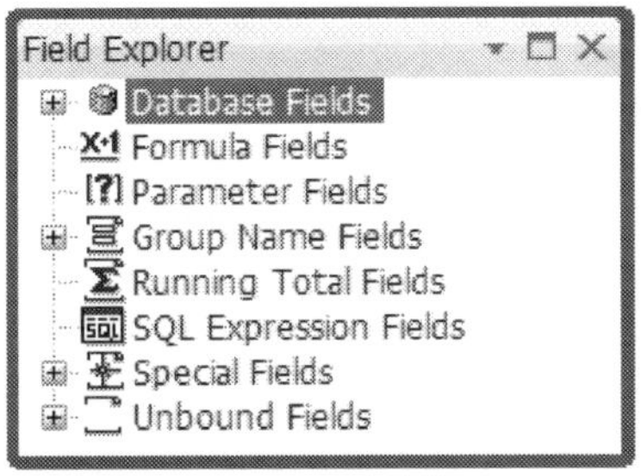

Figure 3-6 Field Explorer

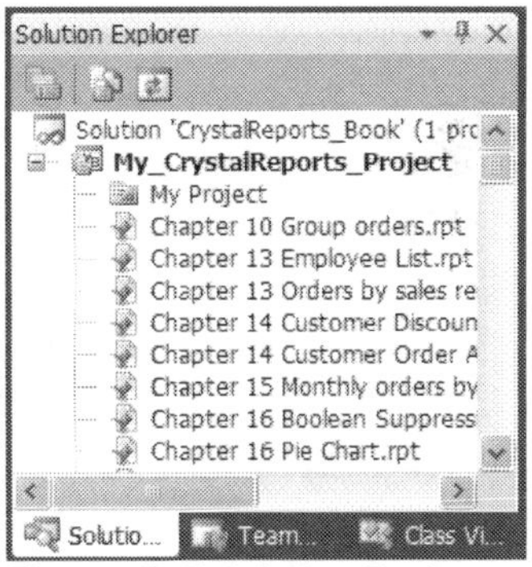

Figure 3-7 Solution Explorer

1. If the Field and Solution Explorers are not visible, display them now.

> By default, the Field Explorer docks on the left side of the design tab. Pay attention to the symbols (icons) that are next to each of the options in the Field Explorer. You will see them again when you learn how to create formulas.

Solution Explorer

The Solution Explorer is used to view and select the objects in the project, as well as, set properties for the project. Table 3-4 explains the buttons on the Solution Explorer window.

Button	Description
Properties	Displays the Properties window for the object that is selected.
Show All Files	Displays all of the files in the project. By default, only the report files are displayed.
Refresh	Refreshes and redisplays objects in the window.

Table 3-4 Solution Explorer buttons explained

> Reports that are created from an existing report do not appear in the Solution Explorer window without clicking the Show All Files button. If you want a report to always be displayed, right-click on it and select **INCLUDE IN PROJECT**, as shown in Figure 3-8.

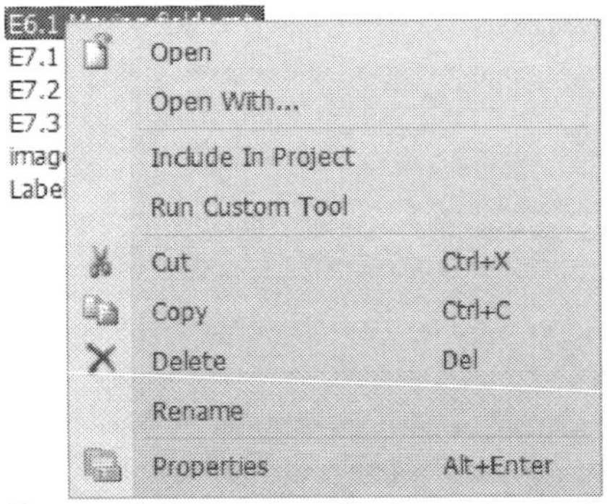

Figure 3-8 Solution Explorer shortcut menu

Rename A Report In The Solution Explorer

1. Right-click on the report name in the Solution Explorer window that you want to rename, then select Rename.

2. Type in the new report name, then press Enter. You should see the new report name in the Solution Explorer window.

Field Explorer

The Field Explorer is used to add the eight types of fields shown earlier in Figure 3-6 to a report. Table 3-5 explains each of the field types.

Field Type	Description
Database	The fields in this folder come from tables and are usually placed in the Details section of the report.
Formula	These are calculated fields that are created in the Formula Workshop. They are recalculated every time the report is run or previewed. (1) (2)
Parameter	Parameter fields prompt the person running the report to provide information. The information gathered from the parameter fields is used to query the tables to select records that meet the information in the parameter fields. (1) (2)
Group Name	This field type is automatically created for each group that the report has. When a group is created, by default the group name field is added to the Group Header section of the report and will display the value in the field. You can customize the group name to display something other than the value in the field. (1) (2)
Running Total	This is a formula field that sums (adds) the values in a numeric field (or column of data). Running Total fields can be placed in the Details section of the report and will provide a total up to the current record. Running Total fields can be reset to zero. They can be used to create totals by group or for the entire report. Summary fields can only be placed in the Group Header and Footer, Report Header and Footer sections of the report. (1) (2)
SQL Expression	This type of field is written in a language called SQL. This field type queries (searches) tables to select records that meet the criteria in the query. They are stored on and run from a server. (1) (2)

Table 3-5 Field types explained

Field Type	Description
Special	These are system generated fields. Some of the more popular special fields include page number, print date and Page N of M. Special Fields can be formatted like the other field types discussed in this table. (1)
Unbound	These fields were explained in Table 3-1. (1) (2)

Table 3-5 Field types explained (Continued)

(1) This field type is not stored in a database.
(2) You create this type of field.

Field Type Symbols And Naming Conventions

Crystal Reports will add a symbol to the beginning of the field name, as discussed below. This is done to help you know what type of field it is when you are viewing the field in the design window. Figure 3-9 shows what each field type looks like when displayed in the design window.

① **@ symbol** represents a formula or unbound field.

② **% sign** represents an SQL Expression field.

③ **? question mark** represents a parameter field.

④ **# sign** represents a running total or summary field.

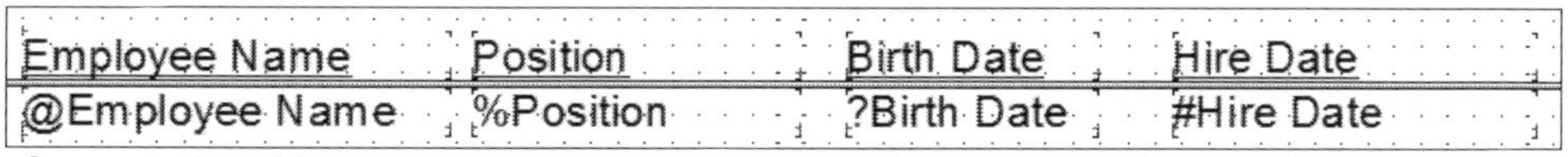

Figure 3-9 Field types and symbols

Do not use the field type symbols discussed above as part of a field name that you create.

Formula, SQL Expression, Parameter, Running Total and Unbound fields must have a unique name within each field type. Therefore, it is possible to use the same field name for a parameter, formula and running total field in the same report. This is why understanding what the field type symbols represent is important.

Docking The Explorers

There are three ways that you can dock explorer windows, as explained in Table 3-6.

Docking explorers is not a requirement to complete the exercises in this book, but doing so will make the explorer windows easier to find and use. I find it easier to dock the explorers in the same section on the right side of the window, as shown in Figure 3-10.

To rearrange your explorer windows to look like the ones in the figure, follow the steps below. Doing this is optional.

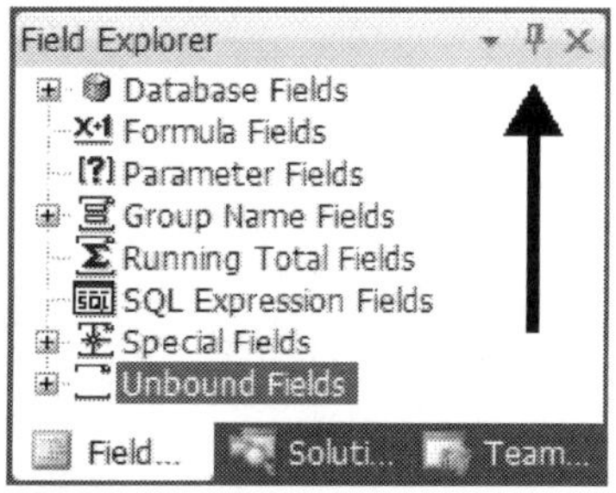

Figure 3-10 Docked explorer windows

Docking Type	Description
Float	Free form placement. You can move the window to any location in the workspace.
Dock	Two or more explorer windows share the same space, as shown above in Figure 3-10.
Tabbed Document	Will put the selected explorer window on a tab where the Start Page tab is.

Table 3-6 Docking type options explained

1. Open the Field Explorer window, if it is not already open. (Crystal Reports ⇒ Field Explorer)

2. Click on the down arrow in the upper right corner of the window and select **FLOAT**, as shown in Figure 3-11.

Figure 3-11 Explorer window position options

3. With the left mouse button, drag the Field Explorer window so that it is on top of the Solution Explorer window, then release the mouse button.

4. Right-click on the Title bar and select **DOCK**. You should see tabs for both explorers, as shown at the bottom of Figure 3-10 shown earlier.

Docking Tips

Below are several tips that you may find useful when using the explorers. It could be me, but when I mistakenly move an explorer window, I have difficulty getting it back to where it was. This truly drives me nuts. The reason that I am telling you this is so that if you have trouble getting the explorers exactly where you want them, you know that you aren't the only one that this bothers.

① To select the explorer that you want to use, click on the tab for it at the bottom of Figure 3-10 shown earlier.
② If you double-click on an explorer's title bar, it will toggle between being in docked and floating modes.
③ If you double-click on the title bar of a floating explorer window, it will go back to where it was the last time that you used Crystal Reports.
④ In floating mode, the explorer window can be moved to a new location in the workspace.
⑤ Other windows can also be docked with the explorers, as shown earlier in Figure 3-10. I like to keep the explorer windows in the same location because it frees up space in the workspace.
⑥ If you have several windows docked in the same location in the workspace, as shown earlier in Figure 3-10, you can rearrange the order of the tabs. Click on the tab that you want to rearrange and drag it to the location that you want.

The Push Pin

If you click on the push pin illustrated in the upper right corner of Figure 3-10 shown earlier, you will open the toolbar shown in Figure 3-12. This toolbar will give you more space to work on reports.

To access one of the explorers from this toolbar, hold the mouse pointer over the icon and the corresponding explorer window will open.

To close the toolbar and return to the docked explorer windows, open an explorer window from the toolbar and click on the push pin.

Figure 3-12 Explorer toolbar

Preview Tab (Main Report Preview Tab)

This tab is used to view reports.

Report Navigation Toolbar

Earlier I mentioned that the preview tab has its own toolbar. It is located above the report. The buttons on this toolbar are shown in Figure 3-13. Table 3-7 explains each button on the toolbar.

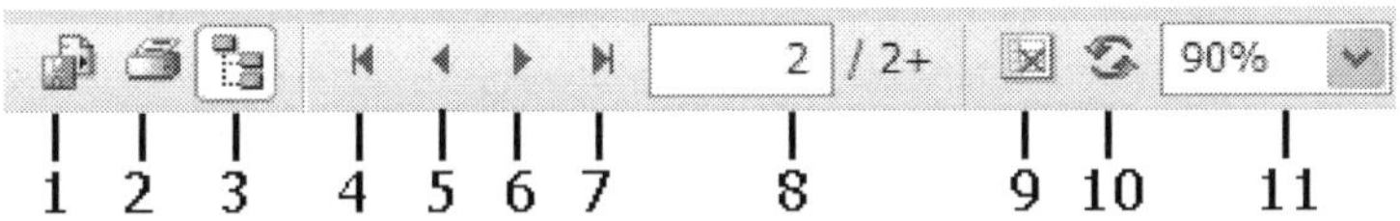

Figure 3-13 Report Navigation toolbar

Button	Description
1	Exports the report to another file format.
2	Prints the report.
3	Hides and displays the Group Tree.
4	Displays the first page of the report.
5	Displays the previous page of the report.
6	Displays the next page of the report.
7	Displays the last page of the report.
8	Displays the current page of the report and the total number of pages the report has. If you want to view a specific page, you can type the page number in this field, then press Enter. The plus sign in **2/2+**, shown above in Figure 3-13 lets you know that Crystal Reports has not formatted all of the pages in the report. This means that the total number of pages is currently unknown. If you want to know how many pages the report has, click the **GO TO LAST PAGE** button.

Table 3-7 Report Navigation toolbar buttons explained

Button	Description
9	Stops the processing of data and only displays the report with the data that has been processed, prior to clicking this button. This is helpful if the report has a lot of pages and you only need to see the first few pages of the report.
10	Refreshes the data in the report.
11	Sets the zoom level for viewing a report. If you need a zoom percent that is not in the list, you can type over the current percent that is displayed, then press Enter.

Table 3-7 Report Navigation toolbar buttons explained (Continued)

1. Click the Go to last page button on the Report Navigation toolbar. You should see the last page of the report.

2. Close a report by right-clicking on the tab for it. You will see the shortcut menu shown in Figure 3-14. Select the **CLOSE** option on the Report tab shortcut menu. You may see the dialog box shown in Figure 3-15.

Report Tab Shortcut Menu

Report tabs have the shortcut menu shown in Figure 3-14. These options are available from the design and preview windows. The options are explained in Table 3-8.

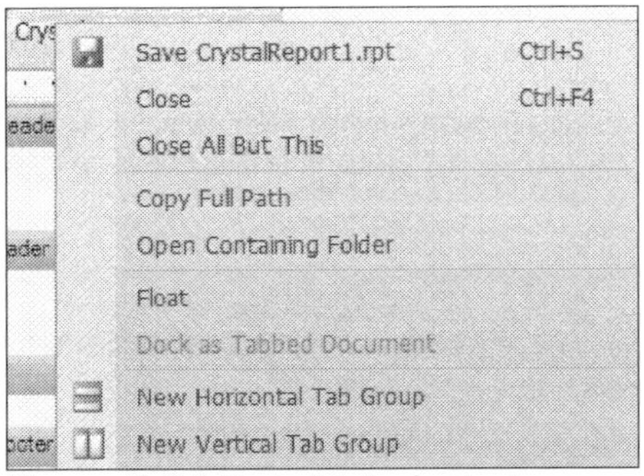

Figure 3-14 Report tab shortcut menu

Option	Description
Save (report name)	Saves the report.
Close	Closes the report.
Close All But This	Closes all reports that are open, except the one on the tab that you right-clicked on.
Copy Full Path	Is used to copy the path of the report and paste it in a document.
Open Containing Folder	Opens the folder that the report on the tab is in.
Float	Free form placement. You can move the window to any location in the workspace.
Dock as Tabbed Document	Will put the selected explorer window on a tab where the Start Page tab is.
New Horizontal Tab Group	Opens a tab group on the Start Page tab and moves the report to the new tab group. [See Chapter 1, Figure 1-5]
New Vertical Tab Group	Opens a tab group to the right of the current tab group and moves the report to the new tab group on the Start Page tab.

Table 3-8 Report tab shortcut menu options explained

Closing Visual Studio

When you close a report or Visual Studio you will see the dialog box shown in Figure 3-15 if you did not save all of the changes to the project.

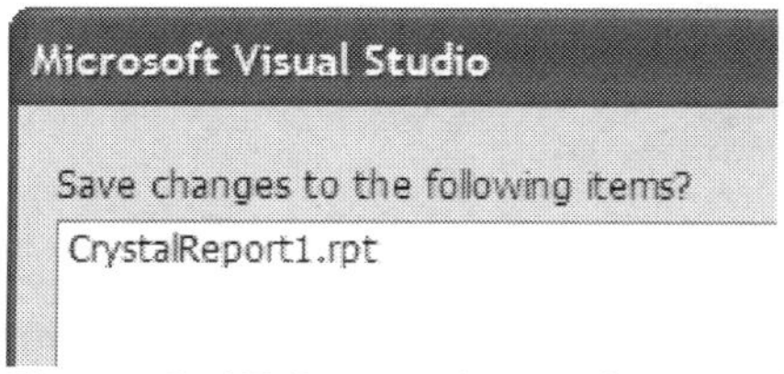

Figure 3-15 Save project and report changes dialog box

When you create or modify reports in a project, the project files (which are different then the report files) are updated.

If you click the **SAVE ALL** button on the Standard toolbar right before you close Visual Studio, the reports that you create or modify are saved, as well as, the project files.

Depending on what you have touched in the report, Crystal Reports will think that you have made changes. In this case, you did not make any changes and if you did, you would not want to save them in the sample report.

3. Click **NO** on the dialog box shown above in Figure 3-15. The report will close.

The Group Tree

The options shown down the left side of the preview window are the groups and subgroups that the report has. This section of the window is called the **GROUP TREE**. You can customize the group name, which you will learn how to do later in the book. The Group Tree is helpful when you need to navigate through a report that has a lot of groups. Clicking on an option in the Group Tree will display the corresponding section in the report.

If a group has a subgroup, you will see a plus sign (+) in front of the group name, as shown in Figure 3-16. Clicking on the plus sign will expand the group and show the subgroup(s) as shown in the figure.

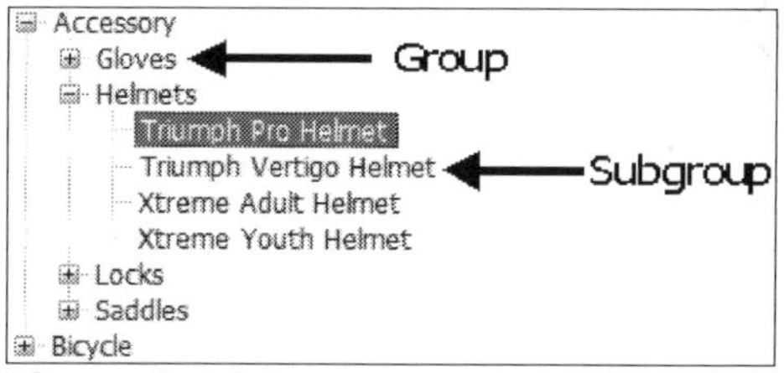

Figure 3-16 Group tree expanded

The plus sign is also known as the **EXPAND BUTTON**. The minus sign is also known as the **COLLAPSE BUTTON**.

To show or hide the Group Tree, click the **TOGGLE GROUP TREE** button on the Report Navigation toolbar or right-click in the Group tree section of the report and select **GROUP TREE**, as shown at the bottom of Figure 3-17. By default, the Group Tree is enabled even if the report does not have any groups.

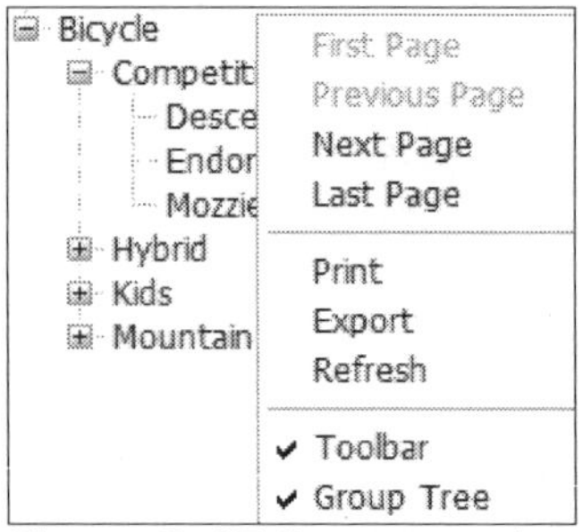

Figure 3-17 Group tree shortcut menu

Resizing The Group Tree Section

If you can't see the groups on the left side of the window, place the mouse pointer on the bar illustrated in Figure 3-18, then drag the bar over to the right, as much as needed.

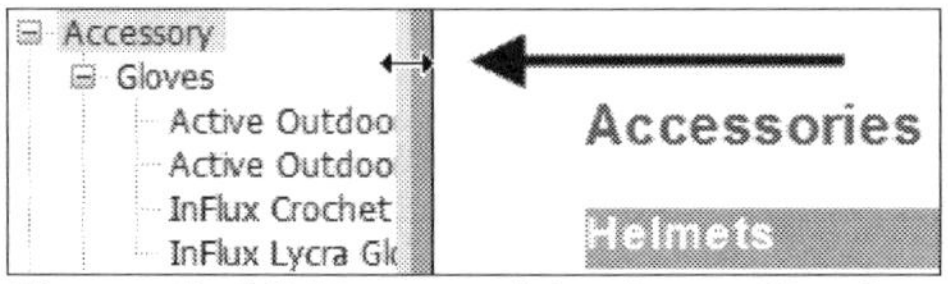

Figure 3-18 Mouse pointer in position to resize the Group Tree section

Drilling-Down In A Report

If you double-click on a detail row item in the report another window will open, as illustrated in Figure 3-19.

This new window displays the detail information for the item that you double-clicked on. This technique is known as **DRILLING-DOWN** in a report.

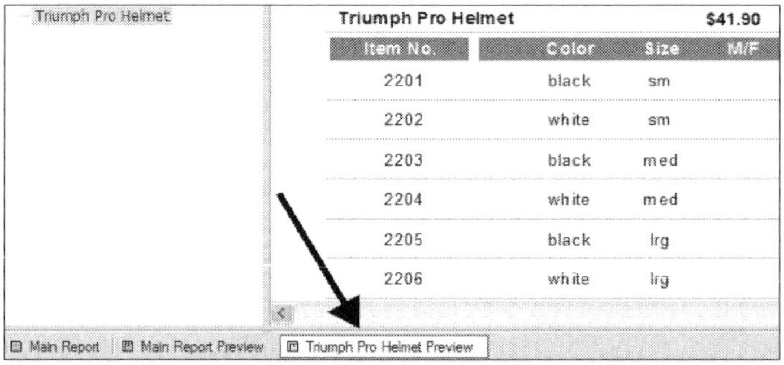

Figure 3-19 Detail information for a specific product

If you want more space for the report on your computer screen, close the Document Outline section on the left of the workspace by clicking on the X in that window.

Design And Preview Tab Differences

As much as these tabs have in common, there are some differences that you should be aware of, as discussed below.

① The preview tab has the Group Tree, page controls and refresh data options.

② The design tab has the "sections" of the report. Having the sections visible lets you know which section of the report each piece of data or object is in.

③ The design tab has a vertical and horizontal ruler.

CREATE YOUR FIRST REPORT

In addition to creating your first report, after completing the exercises in this chapter you will be able to:

- ☑ Create a connection to a database
- ☑ Understand the save data report options
- ☑ Link tables
- ☑ Have an understanding of the basics of the report processing model

CHAPTER 4

Learning To Create Reports

For some, learning to create reports can be intimidating. **LEARNING TO CREATE REPORTS REQUIRES TIME, PATIENCE, DEDICATION AND ATTENTION TO DETAIL.** Crystal Reports is a very robust package and has a lot of features and options. As you go through the exercises in this book, take your time and try to understand how the concepts that you are learning can be applied to reports that you will create on your own, once you have completed this book. It is possible to go through this entire book in a few days if you already have above average report design experience with another report design software package or if you have used a previous version of Crystal Reports and have a solid foundation of relational databases.

The reality is that you will make some mistakes along the way. If you have a fear of making mistakes, this is the time to let go of the fear because the fear will prevent you from learning. It is also normal to initially get confused on what to do next. Even though you may not understand why you are being instructed to do something, the steps in each exercise will allow you to achieve the expected result. This is how you will begin to build a foundation for creating reports and learning Crystal Reports.

The first time that a concept or technique is presented, a lot of information is provided. Each subsequent time that you have to perform the same task, less and less information (aka hand holding) will occur. As you will see, there are a lot of repetitious tasks involved in creating reports. These are the tasks that less and less information will be provided for as you go through the book. The purpose behind this learning technique is to allow you to rely more on your knowledge instead of flipping through this book months from now to find the answer.

Why Do I Have To Connect To A Data Source?

First, I should explain what a data source is. A data source contains the underlying data for the report that you will create or modify. The most common data source is a database. In addition to there being several types of data sources that you can connect to, there are multiple ways to connect to some data sources including the practice database used in this book. You can connect to this database via the Access/Excel (DAO) connection type or the ODBC connection type. There are two reasons that you would need to connect to a data source, as discussed below.

① If you viewed any of the reports that come with the Xtreme sample database you would see data. The reason that you are able to view data in the sample reports is because the data was saved with the report. If the data is not saved with the report, you would have to create a connection to the database that the report gets the data from to view data with the report.

② If you want to create a new report or modify an existing report that does not have the data saved with it.

Exercise 4.1: Create Your First Report

I suspect that this is the moment that you have been waiting for; to create your first report. The first report that you will create is a report that only uses data from one table. The report layout is basic, but you will use almost every screen on the Standard Report Creation Wizard dialog box so that you can become familiar with all of the options. In this exercise you will create a basic list report with a chart.

Step 1: Add A New Report To The Project

1. Click on the arrow on the **ADD NEW ITEM** button on the Standard toolbar, then select **ADD NEW ITEM**, as illustrated in Figure 4-1.

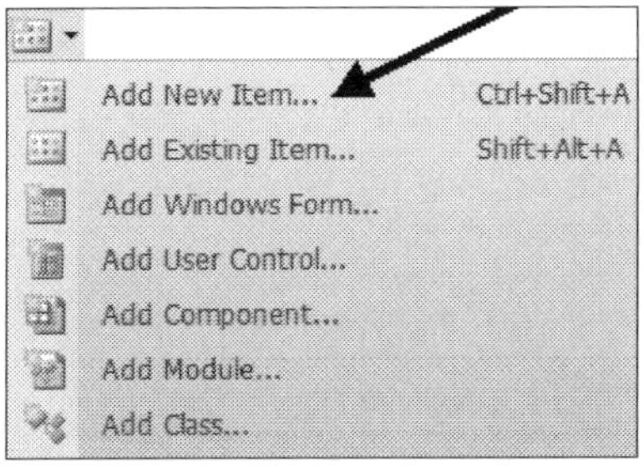

Figure 4-1 Add New Item button options

2. Click on the Reporting option on the left, then click on the Crystal Reports option in the middle. Notice that the default name (shown at the bottom of the window) for the report is **CRYSTAL REPORT**. You can use this name, but you should save the report with a file name that is more meaningful.

   Type `E4.1 My first report.rpt` in the Name field, as shown at the bottom of Figure 4-2, then click the Add button.

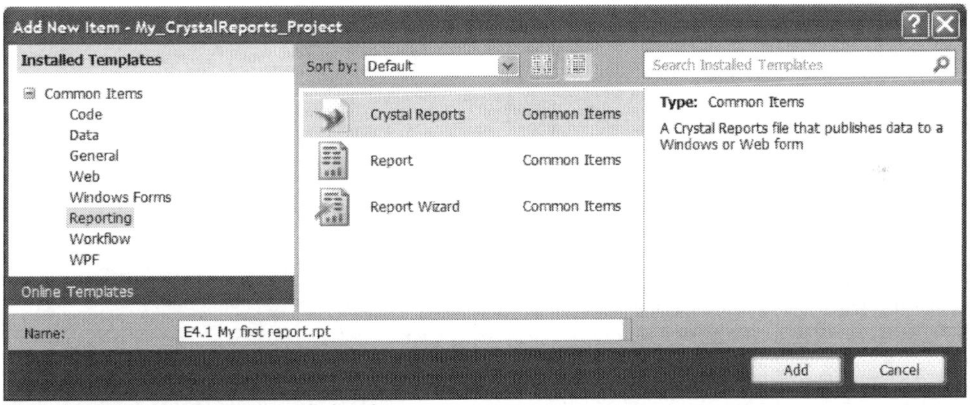

Figure 4-2 Add New Item dialog box

The default file extension for reports is **.RPT** in Crystal Reports. Report file names can have up to 255 characters and can include spaces and special characters. Reports can be stored in almost any folder on your computers hard drive or server. However, you should not store reports or any files for that matter, in operating system folders.

3. Accept the Report Wizard and Standard Expert options on the Crystal Reports Gallery dialog box, then click OK.

Step 2: Create A Connection To The Data Source

There are several types of data sources that you can use in Crystal Reports.

Figure 4-3 shows the categories of connection options that are available.

Table 4-1 explains some of the more popular connection options.

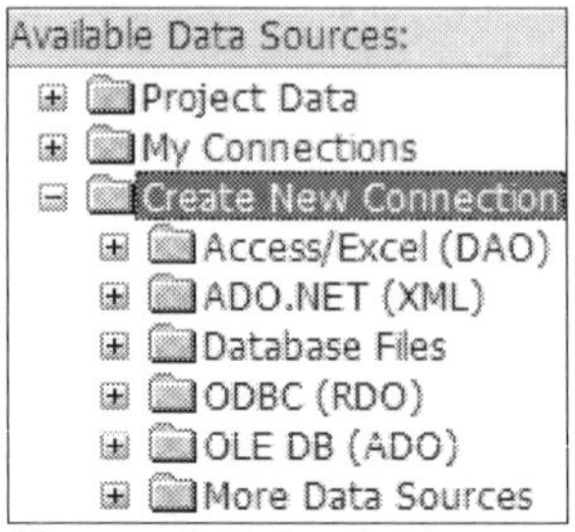

Figure 4-3 Available connection options illustrated

> You may see different data source options depending on the data components that were selected when you installed Visual Studio. You will also see data source options that you have added.

Connection Option	Is Used To Connect To . . .
Access/Excel (DAO)	Access databases and Excel files.
Database Files	Standard PC databases including FoxPro.
ODBC (RDO)	Any ODBC complaint database including Oracle, Sybase, Access and Visual FoxPro. This is probably the most common driver.
OLE DB (ADO)	Data link files that contain connection information (for a data source) that is saved in a file.
More Data Sources	Data sources that are available, but the driver was not installed during the Crystal Reports installation. These drivers will be installed on demand when you select the data source.

Table 4-1 Connection options explained

If you haven't created a connection, either for the Access/Excel (DAO) or the ODBC (RDO) connection type for the crystalextreme database, you will have to do that first. Follow the steps below to create an Access/Excel (DAO) connection. You can go to section, Step 3: Select The Tables, if you already have a connection to this database.

How To Create An Access/Excel (DAO) Connection

1. Click on the plus sign in front of the **CREATE NEW CONNECTION** folder, then click on the plus sign in front of the Access/Excel (DAO) folder.

   If this is the first Access/Excel (DAO) connection that you are creating, you will see the Access/Excel (DAO) connection dialog box shown in Figure 4-4.

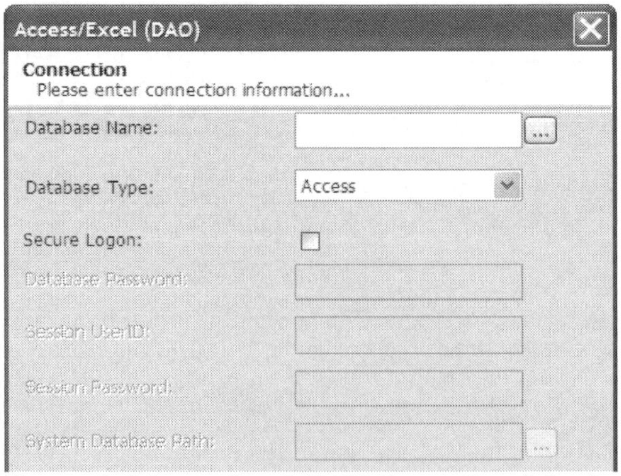

Figure 4-4 Access/Excel (DAO) Connection dialog box

2. Click the button at the end of the **DATABASE NAME** field on the Access/Excel (DAO) dialog box, then navigate to the following path:

   C:\CR For VS Book\CrystalReports_Book\My_CrystalReports_Project, as illustrated in Figure 4-5.

   If you did not put the crystalxtreme database in the folder that you created for this book, navigate to the folder that you put the database in.

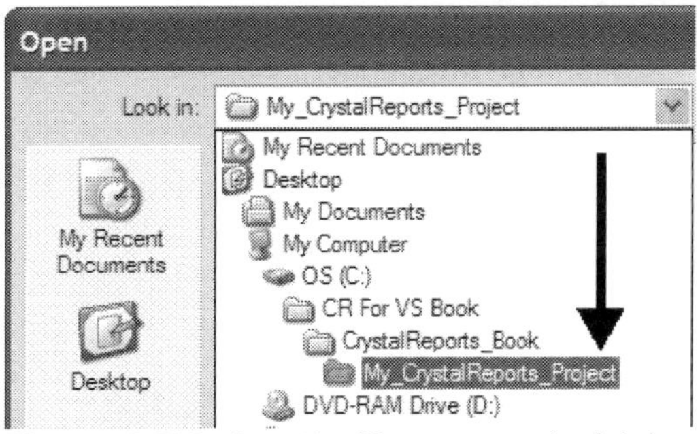

Figure 4-5 Path to the Xtreme sample database

3. Double-click on the **CRYSTALXTREME.MDB** database file. The database should have been added to the Database Name field on the dialog box, as shown in Figure 4-6. If you want to make sure that you added the correct database, click in the Database Name field, then press the **END** key.

   You will be able to see the database name at the end of the field, as shown in Figure 4-6.

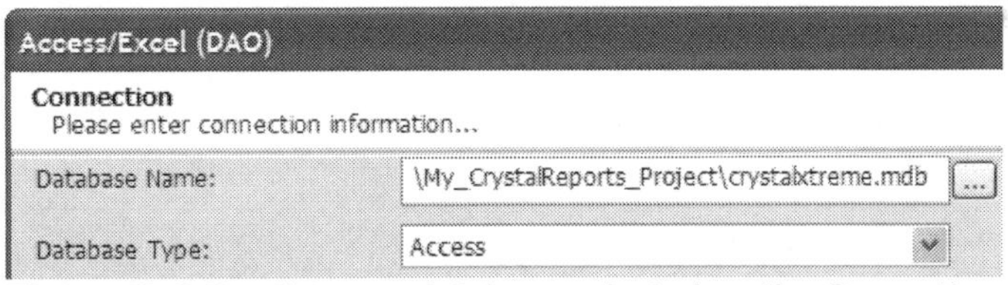

Figure 4-6 Crystlxtreme database selected on the Connection dialog box

> If the database required logon information, you would check the **SECURE LOGON** option shown earlier in Figure 4-4. The remaining fields on the dialog box would become available for you to enter the password information.

4. Click **FINISH**. You have completed creating your first connection to a database in Crystal Reports.

   That wasn't so bad, was it? You should see the connection to the database, as shown in Figure 4-7.

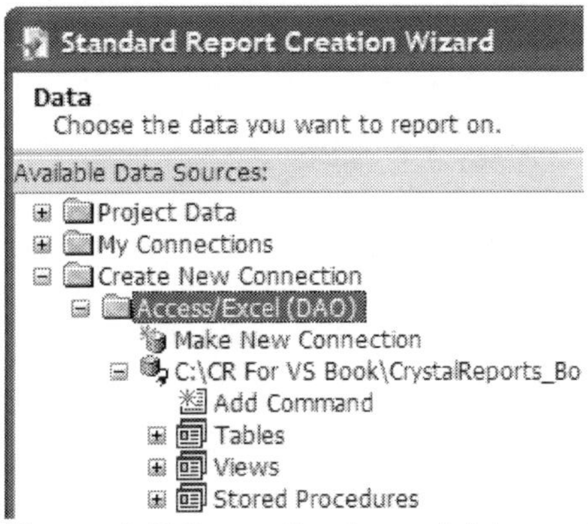

Figure 4-7 Connection to crystalxtreme database

Step 3: Select The Tables

Data is stored in tables in a database. In this step you will select the table for the report.

1. Click on the plus sign in front of the Tables folder, shown above in Figure 4-7. You should see the tables shown in Figure 4-8.

   These are the tables that are in the database. They are the tables that are used in the reports in the database.

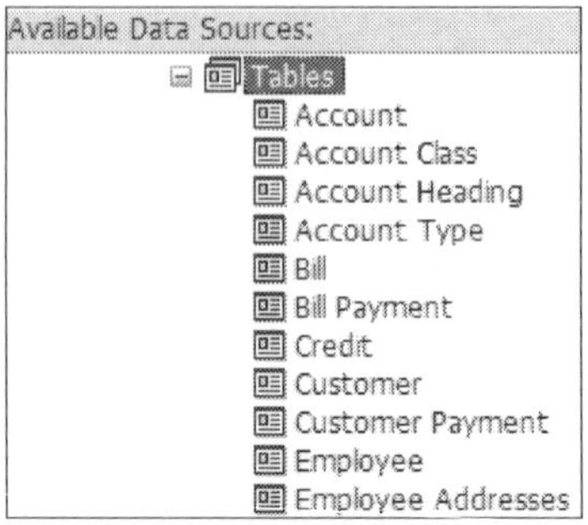

Figure 4-8 Tables in the database

> The only reason that I can think of to click the **CANCEL** button on a screen in the wizard is if you decide that you no longer want to create the report. You will lose all of the options that you have selected if you click the Cancel button. It is better to use the **BACK** button to go back and make changes because you cannot reopen the wizard to make changes or pick up where you left off.

2. Click on the **PRODUCT** table, then click the **>** button. The Product table should now be in the **SELECTED TABLES** list, as shown on the right side of Figure 4-9. Click Next.

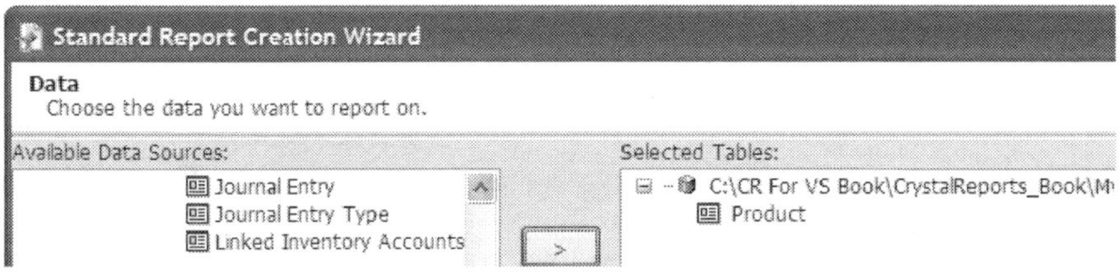

Figure 4-9 Product table selected

View The Data In A Field

The **BROWSE DATA** button on the Fields screen is used to view data. Being able to view the data in a field is helpful if you are not familiar with the data. This button is on several dialog boxes in Crystal Reports.

1. Click on the **PRODUCT NAME** field, then click the Browse Data button. You will see the dialog box shown in Figure 4-10. This is the data in the Product Name field.

   Notice that the field **TYPE** and **LENGTH** are displayed at the top of the dialog box shown in Figure 4-10. This information is helpful because you can learn more about the field and the data stored in it.

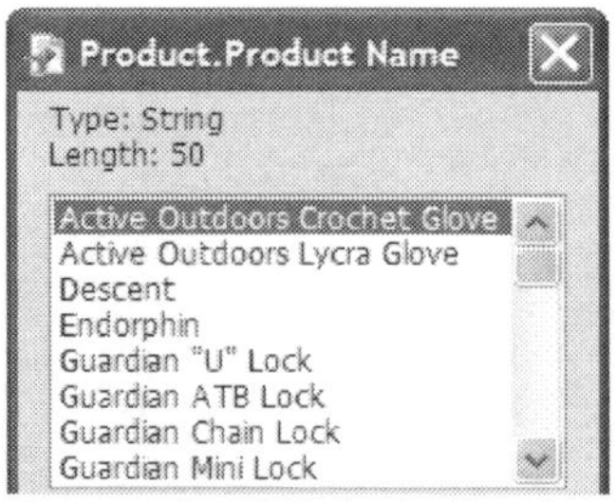

Figure 4-10 Data in the Product Name field

2. Click the Close button when you are finished viewing the data.

Selecting The Number Of Records To View
You can also view the data on the Design tab. By default, the first 500 distinct values in a field are displayed. The actual values that you see can be changed by clearing the **SELECT DISTINCT DATA FOR BROWSING** option on the Database tab on the Options dialog box or on the Report Options dialog box, if you only want the change applied the current report. OK, that's the way that it is suppose to work, but it doesn't. If this actually worked, it probably is not a good idea to turn this option off because you could see duplicate data in the Browse Data dialog box shown above in Figure 4-10. But since it doesn't work, turning it off has no effect. If you want to view a different number of records, you have to modify the following registry key. HKEY_CURRENT_USER\Software\SAP Business Objects\Suite XI 4.0\Crystal Reports\DatabaseServer. Change the **MAXNBROWSEVALUES** key to the maximum number of records that you want to see. Select the Decimal Base option.

How To Find A Field

The **FIND FIELD** button will open the dialog box shown in Figure 4-11. You can search for a field in the table. You will see this button on a few dialog boxes in Crystal Reports. I'm not sure that I understand the purpose of this button because all of the fields in a table are displayed on the wizard screen. It could be helpful if you didn't know which table a field is in and there were a lot of tables being used to create the report.

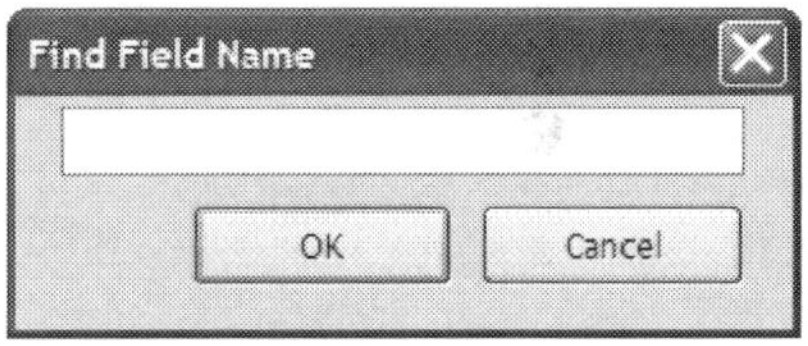

Figure 4-11 Find Field Name dialog box

The Find Field button will only find the first field that matches the text that you enter in the dialog box. You can also enter a partial field name. If the same field name is in more than one table, it does not continue searching. If you were creating a report on your own, in the report design process you would have already written down a list of fields and where they are located because you already learned how to do this in Chapter 3 <smile>.

Step 4: Select The Fields

In the previous step, you selected the table that has the fields for the report. In this step you will select the fields that will appear on the report.

1. Click on the Product Name field if it is not already selected, then click the **>** button. You should see the field in the **FIELDS TO DISPLAY** list.

2. Add the following fields to the Fields to Display list: Size, Price (SRP) and Product Class.

   Figure 4-12 shows the fields that should have been added. Click Next.

Figure 4-12 Fields selected

To add all of the fields in the table at the same time, click the **>>** button. You do not have to select any fields before clicking this button.

To remove a field that you do not need on the report click on the field in the Fields to Display list, then click the **<** button.

To remove all of the fields from the Fields to Display list click the **<<** button.

You can add several fields at the same time by clicking on the first field that you want to add, then hold down the **CTRL** key and click on the other fields that you want to add, one by one. When you have all of the fields selected that you want to add, click the **>** button.

The order that you add the fields to the Fields to Display list is the order that they will appear on the report in the Details section from left to right. If you discover that the fields are not in the order that you want them to appear in on the report, click on the field in the Fields to Display list, then click the **UP** or **DOWN** arrow buttons, illustrated above in Figure 4-12, to move the field to where it should be.

The order that the fields are in will change automatically if at least one field is selected to group on. Fields that are grouped on are moved to the beginning of the Details section. You can rearrange the fields after the wizard has created the report. This does not happen when you create a report from scratch that has groups.

Notice in Figure 4-12 above that fields in the Fields to Display list have the table name in front of the field name. This is done to let you know which table the field is in. This is helpful when you are using more than one table to create the report. Primary key fields in tables often have the same field name when the tables have related information. Without adding the table name you would not know which table a field is in.

Primary key fields are fields that are used to link one table to another table.

Step 5: Select The Grouping Options

Grouping allows you to organize and sort the data. Grouping data forces all records that are related by the field that is being grouped on to be displayed together. Grouping data makes reports that have a lot of data easier to read. Grouping the data in a report is optional. You can group on more than one field. You can group on fields that have already been added to the report or you can select fields to group on that will not appear on the report.

1. Add the Product Class field to the Group By list.

   The grouping option **IN ASCENDING ORDER** is correct. Figure 4-13 shows the grouping options that you should have selected.

   Click Next.

   There are two options that you can select from to group the records by, as discussed below. This is how you sort the values in the field that is being grouped on.

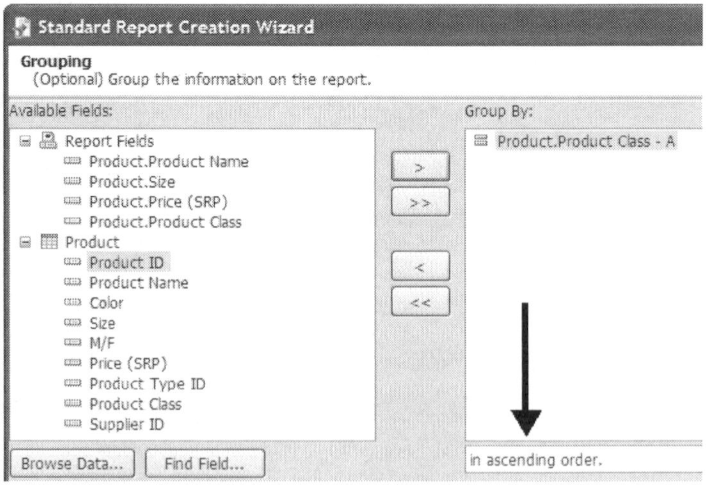

Figure 4-13 Field added to the Group By list

IN ASCENDING ORDER This is the default grouping option. The values in the field being grouped on will be sorted in A-Z order if the field is a string field. If the field being used to group on is numeric, the values will be sorted in 0-9 order.

IN DESCENDING ORDER The values in the field being grouped on will be sorted in Z-A order if the field is a string field. If the field being used to group on is numeric, the values will be sorted in 9-0 order.

Step 6: Select The Summary Options

Creating summary fields is optional. Summary options involve calculated fields. By default, the wizard will create a summary field for all numeric fields that were selected to appear on the report. You can remove the summary fields that are not needed.

There are built-in summary functions that you can use. Many of them are shown at the bottom of Figure 4-14.

The number of summary options that you see in the list depends on the data type of the field that you are summarizing on. Not all data types can use all of the summary function options. Many of the summary functions are only for numeric fields.

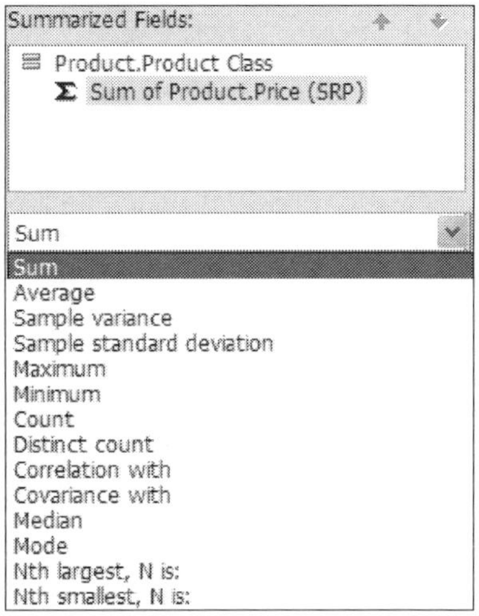

Figure 4-14 Summary options illustrated

1. Add the Product Class field to the **SUMMARIZED FIELDS** list.

2. Open the drop-down list shown above in Figure 4-14 and select **COUNT**.

   Notice that the Product Class field has different options in the drop-down list, then those shown above for the Product Price (SRP) field.

   Figure 4-15 shows the summary options that should be selected.

   Click Next.

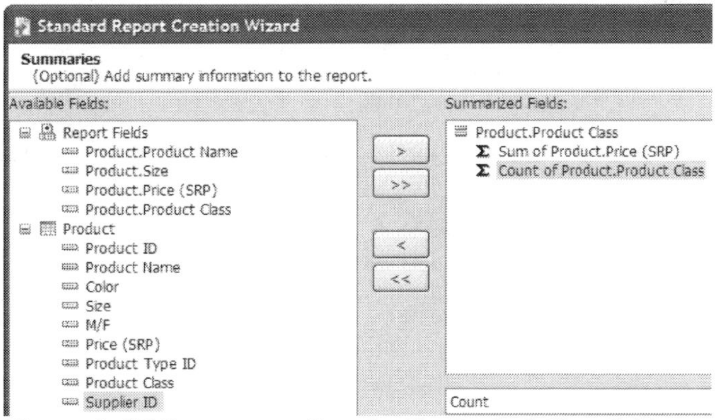

Figure 4-15 Summary options for the Product Class field

Step 7: Select The Group Sorting Options

The options on this screen are used to select options for the groups on the report.

1. Select the **TOP 5 GROUPS** option.

2. Select the Price field in the Summary values drop-down list.

   Figure 4-16 shows the options that should be selected.

   Click Next.

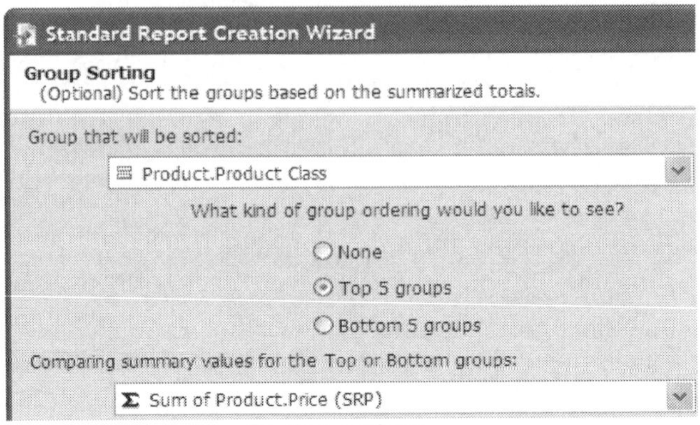

Figure 4-16 Group Sorting options

> The Top 5 Groups option will only display data for the five groups that have the highest value in the field selected in the **SUMMARY VALUES** field at the bottom of the Group Sorting screen. This is accomplished by sorting the groups based on the summary field in descending order for the Top N groups or sorting the groups in ascending order for the Bottom N groups. Selecting **NONE**, which is the default, will display all groups. It is possible that you will not get the five groups that you think should appear on the report. This is because of the way that Crystal Reports processes data. In Chapter 11, you will create a Top 5 group report that illustrates unexpected results because a wizard was used to create the report.

Step 8: Select The Chart Type

Adding a chart to a report is optional. Once you select a chart type the wizard will fill in information for the other fields on the screen. If you are not sure what options to select, accept the defaults, preview the report and then decide which chart options need to be modified.

1. Select the **PIE CHART** option.

2. Select the Price field in the Show summary drop-down list.

   Figure 4-17 shows the chart options that should be selected.

   Click Next.

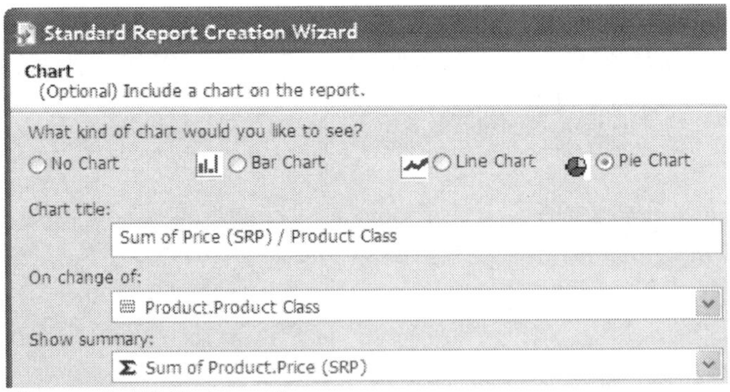

Figure 4-17 Chart options

Step 9: Select The Field(s) To Filter On

Creating filters is optional. Filters are another way that you can narrow down the number of records that will appear on the report. You can create as many filters as you need. In this step you will create a filter for the Product Size field to only select records that have a size that is in a specific range.

1. Add the Product Size field to the **FILTER FIELDS** list, then open the drop-down list and select **IS BETWEEN**.

2. Open the next drop-down list and select 16.

   Open the last drop-down list and select **XLRG**.

   Figure 4-18 shows the filter options that should be selected.

   Click Next.

   The filter that you just created will only display products that have a size that is between 16 and XLRG.

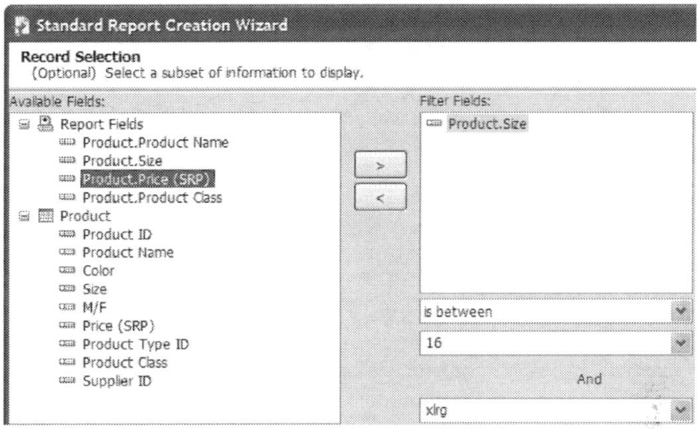

Figure 4-18 Record Selection options

> The data in the last two drop-down lists is actual data in the field that you are creating this filter for.

Step 10: Select A Report Style

Report styles apply formatting to the report. The styles are like templates, which allow you to quickly change the appearance of a report. You can preview what the other style options look like by clicking on them.

1. Select the **EXECUTIVE, TRAILING BREAK** style, as shown in Figure 4-19, then click Finish.

   On the Preview tab, the first page of the report should look like the one shown in Figure 4-20.

   The top of the second page of the report should look like the one shown in Figure 4-21.

   As you scroll through the report you may see things that you would like to rearrange on the report.

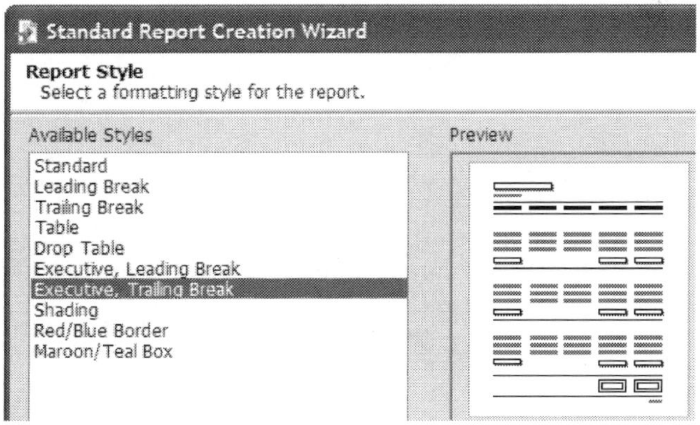

Figure 4-19 Report Style options

   Because grouping options were selected in Step 5, the **GROUP TREE** is displayed with data. Clicking on the options in the Group Tree will display that section of the report.

If for some reason the Group Tree is not visible or you do not want to see it, you can click the **TOGGLE GROUP TREE** button on the Report Navigation toolbar to turn it on or off.

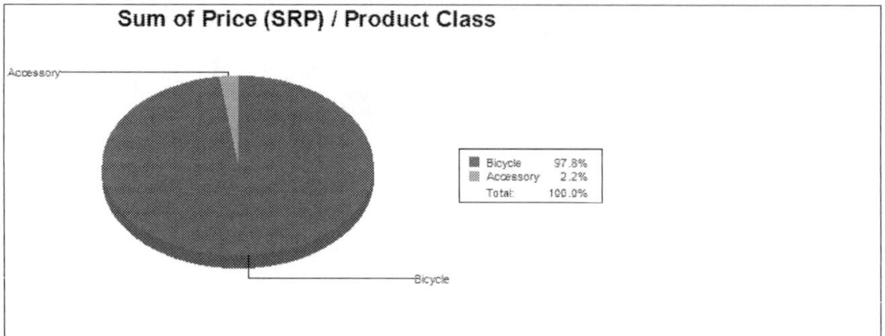

5/17/2013

Product Class	Product Name	Size	Price (SRP)
Bicycle	Descent	22	$2,939.85
Bicycle	Descent	17	$2,939.85

Figure 4-20 Page 1 of the E4.1 report

5/17/2013

Product Class	Product Name	Size	Price (SRP)
Bicycle	Wheeler	16	$539.85
Bicycle	Wheeler	18	$539.85
Bicycle	Wheeler	20	$539.85
Bicycle	Wheeler	22	$539.85
Bicycle	SlickRock	16	$764.85
Bicycle	SlickRock	18	$764.85
Bicycle	Endorphin	22	$899.85
Bicycle	**48**	**$50,215.80**	
Accessory	InFlux Lycra Glove	lrg	$15.50
Accessory	Triumph Vertigo Helmet	lrg	$53.90

Figure 4-21 Page 2 of the E4.1 report

Step 11: Save The Report

In addition to giving the report a meaningful name, you have to decide whether or not you want to save the data with the report.

Save The Report With Data

Unless you changed the default options after Crystal Reports was installed, the data is saved with the report by default. There are pros and cons to saving data with a report, as discussed below. As stated earlier, saving the data with the report is the default option. You can preview and print reports faster with this option selected because the data does not have to be retrieved. This option is also useful if you need to send the report to someone that does not have access to the data.

One downside to saving the data with the report is that the report requires more hard drive or server space. A second downside is that anyone that runs the report with saved data will not be using the most current data. A third downside occurs if the database has security. Unless the report has been published to Crystal Reports Server, the security is bypassed and anyone that opens the report will have access to the data, whether they should or not.

> If you are not sure if the report is being saved with the data, look at the **SAVE DATA IN THE REPORT** option above the Report Navigation toolbar on the preview tab. If the option is checked, the data will be saved with the report.

Save The Report Without Data

Selecting this option requires less disk space. With this option, the report uses live data each time it is run. The downside is when you need to preview or print the report, it will take a little longer to process, because the data has to be retrieved. Most of the time, you will not notice the delay. To save reports without data by default, check the **DISCARD SAVED DATA WHEN LOADING REPORTS** option on the Reporting tab on the Options dialog box.

> From a report developers perspective if you have the space, it will save time, a considerable amount of time if there are thousands of records, if you save the data with the report while you are creating and modifying it. The danger that some developers have <not us of course> is that they forget to change the save data option before putting the report into production. Another danger is not testing the report with live data. Remember that most data is volatile, meaning that it changes frequently. Not testing with live data before putting the report into production could be a bad career move, if you know what I mean. Testing with live data before putting the report into production, also means that the report will not go into production with the saved data.

Refreshing Report Data

As you just read, you have to decide whether to save the data with the report or not. If you decide to normally save data with a report to save processing time while designing the report, that's fine. Anytime that you want to work with the current data, click the **REFRESH** button on the Report Navigation toolbar.

If the changes that you make to a report fall in the formatting category, like changing fonts, moving fields around on the report or adding titles to summary fields that were already saved with the report, you do not have to refresh the data.

Automatic Data Refreshing

If any of the items below occur after a report have been saved, the data will automatically be refreshed, regardless of the save data option that is associated with the report.

① A new field is added to the report.
② If a formula is added to the report that uses a field that was not already being used on the report.
③ If an existing formula is modified that uses a field that was not already being used on the report.
④ If any report criteria or parameter fields are added or changed that include a field that was not already being used on the report.
⑤ If the grouping is not done on a server, the detail record data will be refreshed.

> If you drill-down on hidden data, the data is not a full refresh. If the grouping is taking place on a server, drilling down in the Details section will only retrieve the new data required by the drill-down for the Details section.

Yes, I can sense that you are shaking your head about the save data with report options. Keep in mind that only the fields on the report and fields needed for formulas or functions that the report uses are saved with the report. Other fields in the table are not saved with the report. As you become more familiar with modifying reports, you will know which save data option is best suited for each report that you are modifying or creating.

Real World Data

Many companies have what is known as a "development server" that has a copy of "live data" and applications (live data is also known as production data). This is done so that anyone that is creating new applications, modifying existing applications or testing software, can do so without putting the companies data in danger. If this is the type of environment that you are working in, keep in mind while going through this book, the differences between "live" and "refreshed" data, when these terms are referenced.

When creating reports on a development server and you click the **REFRESH** button in Crystal Reports, you are not getting a copy of the data from a production server. You are getting another copy of the data from the development server. The same is true if you have placed a copy of the production data on your hard drive. Usually, data on a development server is refreshed from a production server at pre-defined intervals (daily, weekly monthly). If you want to know when the data on a development server is refreshed, ask the DBA or the person that manages the databases that you are using.

Save The Report

> **Report File Extension**
> The default file extension for reports is **.RPT**. Report file names can have up to 255 characters and can include spaces and special characters. Reports can be stored in almost any folder on a computers hard drive or server. You should not store reports in operating system folders.

1. Right-click on the E4.1 tab, then select Save E4.1 My first report.

> You can also click the **SAVE** button on the Standard toolbar.

Selecting A Data Source

In the previous exercise you used the options in the Create New Connection folder to create a connection to the database. That connection stays live until you close Crystal Reports.

When you reopen Crystal Reports, any previous connections are automatically moved to the **MY CONNECTIONS** folder shown in Figure 4-22. If you right-click on the connection, you will see the shortcut menu shown in the figure.

The **PROPERTIES** option is used to view information about the data source of the connection.

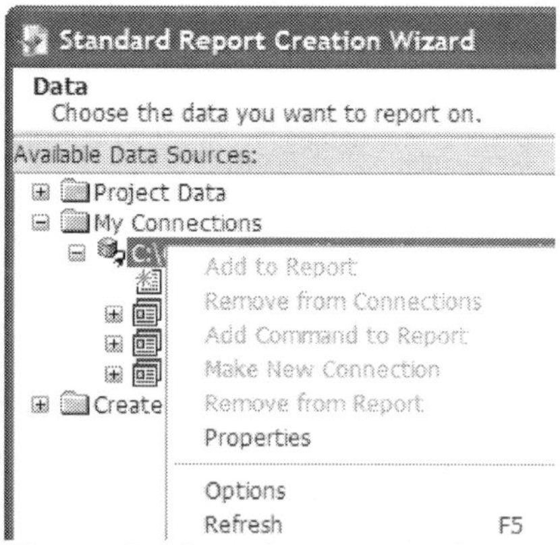

Figure 4-22 My Connections data source folder

The **OPTIONS** option opens the Database tab on the Options dialog box.

Exercise 4.2: Create A Product List Report

In this exercise you will create a product list report that will print the Product ID, Product Name and Price fields.

1. Create a new report and save it as `E4.2 Product list`.
2. Add the Product table to the Selected Tables list on the Data screen, then click Next.
3. Add the Product ID, Product Name and Price (SRP) fields to the Fields to Display list, then click Finish because the report does not require any of the options on the other wizard screens. Save the report. It should look like the one shown in Figure 4-23.

5/17/2013

Product ID	Product Name	Price (SRP)
1,101	Active Outdoors Crochet Glove	$14.50
1,102	Active Outdoors Crochet Glove	$14.50
1,103	Active Outdoors Crochet Glove	$14.50
1,104	Active Outdoors Crochet Glove	$14.50
1,105	Active Outdoors Crochet Glove	$14.50
1,106	Active Outdoors Lycra Glove	$16.50
1,107	Active Outdoors Lycra Glove	$16.50

Figure 4-23 E4.2 Product list report

Exercise 4.3: Create An Employee Contact List Report

The fields that are needed to create this report are stored in two tables. This report will be grouped by the Supervisor ID field so that each supervisor can have a list of their employees.

1. Create a new report and save it as `E4.3 Employee contact list.`
2. Add the Employee and Employee Addresses tables, then click Next.

Linking Tables

You will see the screen shown in Figure 4-24. You will only see this screen if two or more tables have been added to the report.

The options on this screen are used to select the appropriate links for the tables that you have selected.

Most of the time, the link that is automatically created is the one that you need. Fields are automatically linked if they have the same name and compatible data type.

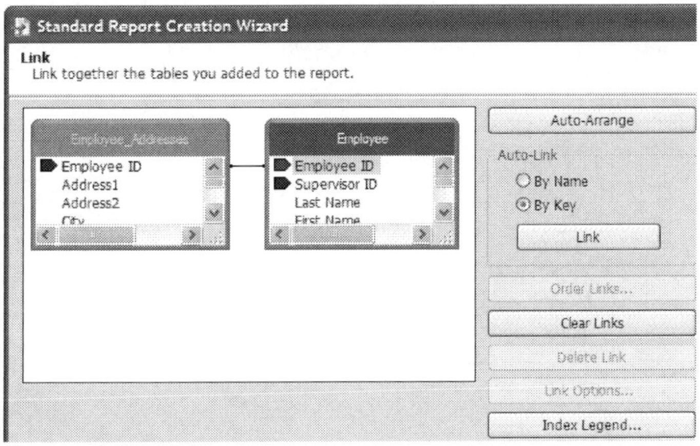

Figure 4-24 Link screen

In this exercise, the tables should be linked on the Employee ID field.

Link Screen Tips

① You may need to make the dialog box wider to see both tables. To make the dialog box wider, place the mouse pointer on the right side of the dialog box and drag the border of the dialog box to the right. You can also make the table boxes longer if you want to see all of the fields.

② If you right-click on a field in a table and select **BROWSE FIELD**, as shown in Figure 4-25, you will be able to see the first 500 unique values for the field. If you see more than one occurrence of the same value, it means that you have turned off the Select Distinct Data For Browsing option on the Database tab on the Options dialog box or on the Report Options dialog box.

③ By default, Crystal Reports only uses a link if the record selection query requires it. If you want to enforce a link, right-click on the link that you want to enforce and select **LINK OPTIONS**, as shown in Figure 4-26.

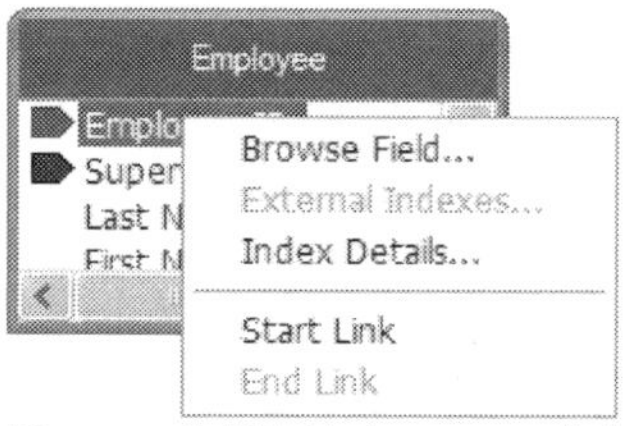

Figure 4-25 Link screen field shortcut menu

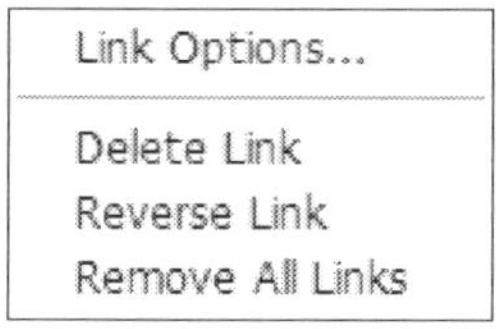

Figure 4-26 Link shortcut menu

Index Legend

As shown earlier in Figure 4-24, there are arrows next to some fields. If you click on the **INDEX LEGEND** button you will see the index that each color represents, as shown in Figure 4-27.

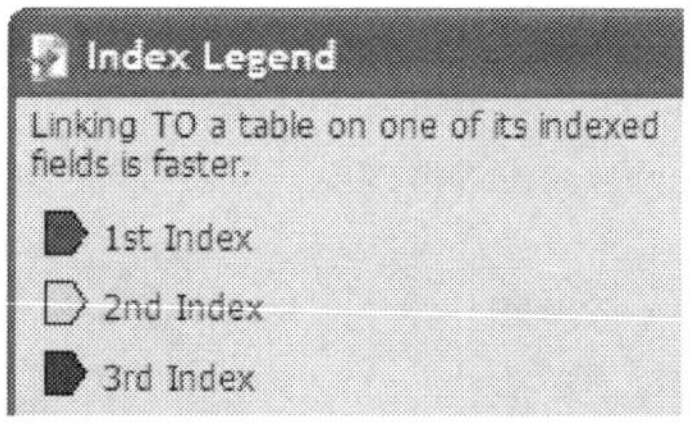

Figure 4-27 Index Legend dialog box

Fields in tables are indexed to reduce the time it takes to retrieve the records needed to create the report. Fields that are used in the record selection criteria are often used as an index.

Add The Fields To The Report

1. Click Next on the Link screen, then add the fields in Table 4-2 to the Fields to Display list.

   Figure 4-28 shows the order that the fields should be in.

   Click Next.

Employee	Employee Addresses
Supervisor ID	Region
First Name	
Last Name	
Home Phone	

Table 4-2 Fields to add to the report

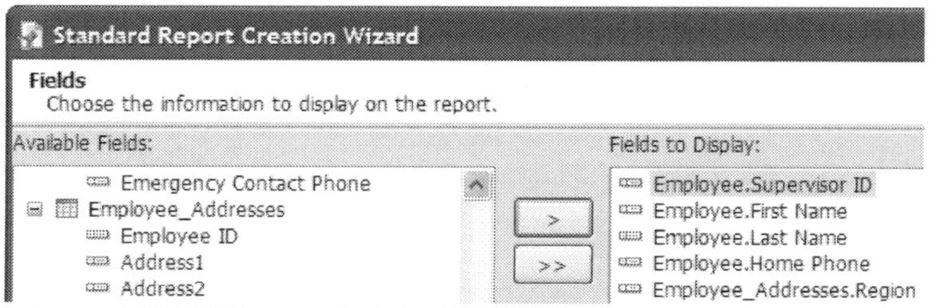

Figure 4-28 Fields selected for the report

Select The Grouping Options

This report would look better if it was grouped on the Supervisor ID field and within each Supervisor ID group, the employee names were sorted by last and first name. It would also be helpful if there was a count of employees per supervisor.

1. Add the Supervisor ID field to the **GROUP BY** list, then click Next.

2. Add the Employee ID field to the **SUMMARIZED FIELDS** list. This field is in the Employee table. Open the drop-down list and select **COUNT**. Figure 4-29 shows the summary options that should be selected.

   This option will count the number of employee ID's under each Supervisor ID. When you want a count of records, you should select a field that has unique values. Each employee is assigned a unique ID.

   Think of ID fields as being the equivalent of social security numbers, where each security number is unique.

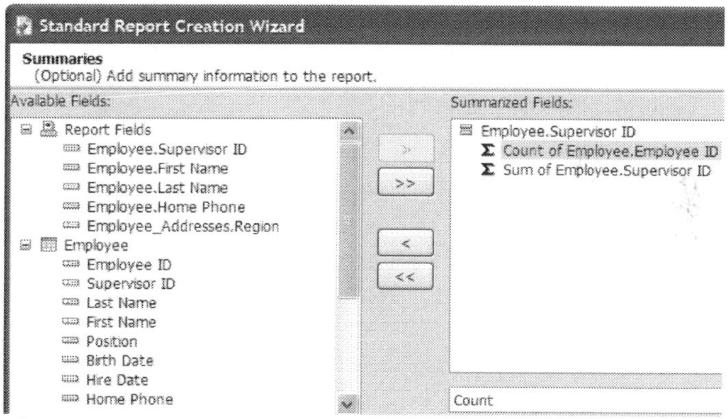

Figure 4-29 Summary options

3. Click Next. Click Next again on the Group Sorting dialog box because you do not need to change any of the options.

Select The Chart Options

1. Select the **BAR CHART** option.

2. In the **CHART TITLE** field, type `Count of employees per supervisor.`
   Figure 4-30 shows the chart options that should be selected. Click Next.

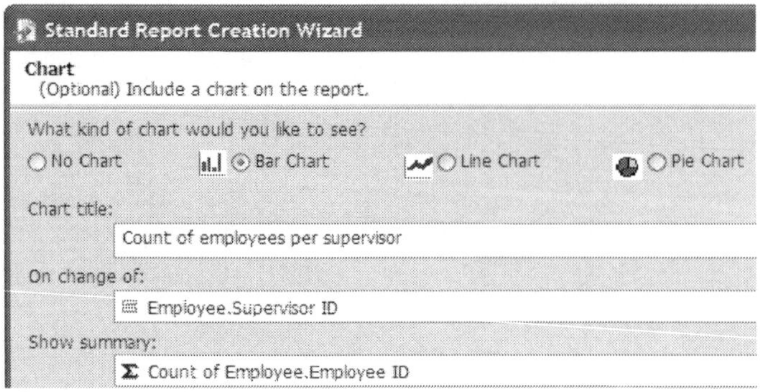

Figure 4-30 Chart options

Finish The Report

1. Click Next on the Record Selection screen because the report does not require any filters.

2. Select the Standard report style if it is not already selected, then click Finish.

   Your report should look like the one shown in Figure 4-31. It looks ok, but it needs to be modified.

   Save and close the report.

Figure 4-31 E4.3 Employee contact list report

Report Processing Model

Reports are processed in three main passes. The first pass reads all of the records, calculates the formulas and summary fields, suppresses fields and creates a temporary data file. This temporary file only contains the records needed for the report, opposed to all of the records in the database. The second pass sorts records, calculates totals for groups, calculates running totals, generates charts, maps, cross-tabs, OLAP grids and subreports, as needed. The second pass also formats the pages. The third pass calculates the total page count and Page N of M special fields if necessary.

Formulas can be placed in all sections of a report. Formulas are not processed in report section order. The report processing model uses the following criteria to help determine the order to process formulas in.

① Formulas that use database fields are processed while the records are being read in the first pass.
② There is no order to how formulas are processed in the same section of the report.
③ Formulas that only use variables are processed before records are read.

④ Formulas that use summary and group fields are processed after the records are read.
⑤ Cross-Tab summary fields are calculated in the first pass.

The link below provides more information on the processing model that Crystal Reports uses.
http://msdn2.microsoft.com/en-us/library/ms225477.aspx

If this report processing model seems complicated, remember the following:

① The first pass reads the records in the database, retrieves the records that match any selection criteria and calculates formulas when all of the fields in the calculation are fields in a table.
② The second pass selects data for groups and evaluates summary functions, calculates running total fields, in-place subreports and charts based on cross-tabs or OLAP data are generated.
③ The third pass is mainly used to calculate the total page count (Page N of M special field) if needed.

Report Creation Tips

When creating a new report for exercises in this book, select the Report Wizard and Standard Expert options on the Crystal Reports Gallery dialog box, unless instructed otherwise.

Create A Report From An Existing Report

There are three ways to create a report from an existing report, as discussed below.

① Open the report that you will base the new report from. File ⇒ Save (Report Name) As. Type in the new report file name.
② Create a new report, then open the Crystal Reports Gallery and select the **FROM AN EXISTING REPORT** option. Click OK, then double-click on the existing report that you want to use. This produces the same results as option 1.
③ On the Standard toolbar, Project ⇒ Add Existing Item. This option is similar to option 2. The difference is that this option does not use the Crystal Reports Gallery dialog box.

Saving An Existing Report With A New File Name

This is a task that you will do a lot in this book. The steps below will show you how.

1. Open the report that you want to save with a new file name.

2. File ⇒ Save (report name) As, as illustrated in Figure 4-32.

   For the exercises in this book, save the reports in the folder that you created. On your own, you can save the reports in any folder that you want.

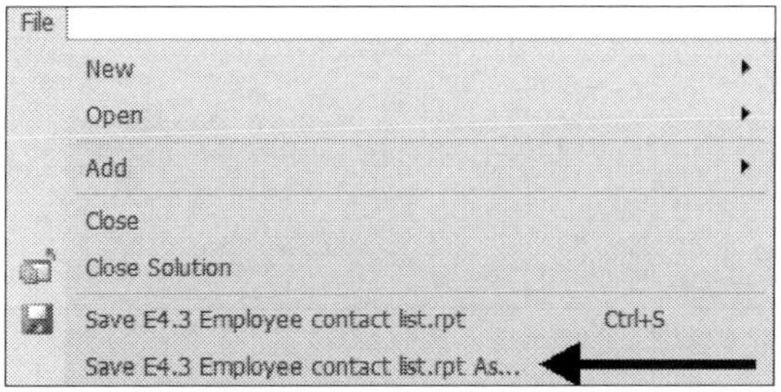

Figure 4-32 Save As option illustrated

CREATING REPORTS FROM SCRATCH

After completing the exercises in this chapter you will be able to:

- ☑ Use the Database Expert
- ☑ Create basic reports from scratch
- ☑ Use the Field Explorer
- ☑ Add and remove tables in the Field Explorer
- ☑ Understand relational databases
- ☑ Understand the different types of relationships
- ☑ Understand Linking, Join Types and Smart Linking techniques

Overview

While you may be frowning at the title of this chapter because you know that there are wizards that will help you create reports, you should keep in mind that the wizards may not be able to create a report that you need. If you only use the wizards to create reports, you will not learn how to use the majority of features that Crystal Reports has. If you create a report and do not get the output that you need, you could have a hard time trying to figure out how to modify it to get what you need, if you only know the options on the wizards. You will experience not getting the correct output when using a wizard in Chapter 11, Exercise 11.4. This makes learning to create reports from scratch essential for being able to create new reports and modify existing reports.

The Database Expert

The Database Expert shown in Figure 5-1 is used to select the data source for the report.

Crystal Reports ⇒ Database ⇒ Database Expert will open this dialog box.

Right-clicking on the Database Fields option on the Field Explorer and selecting Database Expert, also opens this dialog box.

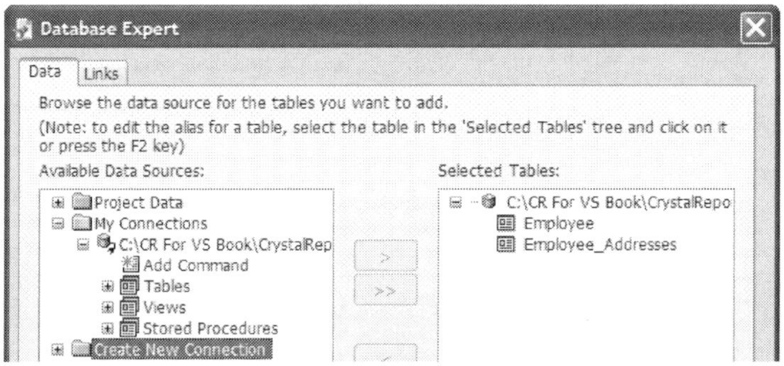

Figure 5-1 Database Expert dialog box

As you can see, this dialog box is very similar to the Data screen in the wizard that you used in the previous chapter. Like the Data screen, the Database Expert has a Links screen.

Data Source Options

Each of the four data source options (Commands, Tables, Views and Stored Procedures) provide a different way to access data for the reports that you create. As the report designer, for the most part, you will not be required to create or maintain the data sources. You do however, need a good understanding of them so that you can select the best option, based on the requirements for the report. These data source options are not supported by all database types.

Tables are probably the most used of the four data sources because accessing the tables does not require any code or programming skills, like the other three data source options require.

Views Business Views is the real name of this option. Business Views are a set of components, (Data Connections, Dynamic Data Connections, Data Foundations and Business Elements) that report designers and end-users can use to access the data that is needed to create the report. Business Views are created in the Business View Manager by a System Administrator, report designer or someone that has administrator rights to the databases. Business Views allow one to gather data from a variety of databases and combine the data into a "view". This makes it easier to access the data.

Many databases have the ability to present different views of the data. A view is a **RECORDSET** (the result) of a query. Views usually display a subset of the data in a data source. Views are stored in the database and are like tables, but they do not have the physical characteristics of a table. For example, records cannot be added or deleted from a view. Fields cannot be added to a view or the length of a field cannot be changed in a view.

Views are less complex queries then the ones in the Command section. These queries are similar to what you can create in Crystal Reports when you use the sorting, grouping and data selection options to create a report. Views are created when the same recordset, calculation or query needs to be used in several reports. If you know that you will create several reports that use the same sorting, grouping or data selection options, you could create and save a view, if you have the appropriate administrator rights to do so. Doing this means that you would not have to select the same options over and over again for each report. Instead of selecting all of the tables, fields and options, select the view that already has all of this information.

Views are one way to optimize reports that use tables that have a lot of data. For example, a customer table will hold all customers world wide. If there is a need to create several reports that are specific to a certain country, create a view (a query) that retrieves all of the customer records for the country. When the reports are created for that country, select the "country view" if you will, as the data source, instead of the customer table. The report will run faster because it does not have to read the entire customer table to find the records for the specific country. Instead, the "view" is read. The sample Xtreme database comes with business views that you can look at. The first one is explained below.

Top Customers This view contains customers that have purchased $50,000 or more worth of products last year.

Commands are queries (code that retrieves data from tables) that are created with a **STRUCTURED QUERY LANGUAGE (SQL)** and have been brought into Crystal Reports. These queries are often complex. They are usually created (by a DBA or programmer) in another software package.

Using a command as a data source allows the report to process faster, because the selection of records for the report is already done before the report that you create is run. Commands are very useful when you (the report designer) need data from several databases to create one report.

SQL This is the language that is most used to interact with databases. It is used to create and populate tables with data, modify data and retrieve data from a database. The **SQL SELECT** command is what is used to retrieve data. This is also known as a **QUERY**. Before you start to frown, the answer is no, you do not have to learn how to write SQL code to retrieve the data that you need for the reports that you will create in this book. Crystal Reports provides tools, like the Select Expert and Group Expert, that allow you to retrieve the data from the tables. At some point you may have requests for functionality that these tools can't provide, which means that you will have to write code. (1)

Stored Procedures These are mini programs that are stored (saved). They are created when it is difficult to retrieve the data from a table or when a view cannot handle the processing that is needed. Stored procedures are saved on a database server. From a report designers perspective, they function and have the same characteristics as a view. Don't worry, most report designers do not create stored procedures. If you have to create a complex report and have trouble getting the data the way that you need it, talk to the DBA to get their recommendation for the best way to get the data that you need or to create the stored procedure for you.

Stored procedures, like Commands and Views, do not contain data. They contain queries that are more complex then views, but less complex than commands. The majority of the time, stored procedures are created by a DBA or programmer. The Xtreme database comes with two stored procedures that you can use. The first one is explained below. (1)

Credit_Limits This view contains customer credit limits. It also has a parameter field that will let you specify the range limit that you need for the report that you are creating. The reason this view is in the stored procedure section is because views cannot have parameter fields in most databases. When Crystal Reports recognizes that a view has a parameter field, the view will be placed in the stored procedure section, because stored procedures can store a parameter field.

(1)

> **Command And Stored Procedure Advantage**
> The advantage that commands and stored procedures have over views is that they can use parameter fields. This means that the stored procedure can return a different recordset each time that it is run, based on the values in the parameter fields.

> Think of these tools (Commands, Views and Stored Procedures) as query generators. They let you "visually" select criteria that will be used to retrieve the records based on the criteria that you create.

Exercise 5.1: Create Your First Report From Scratch

1. Create a new report and save it as `E5.1 Customer information`.

2. Select the **BLANK REPORT** option on the Crystal Reports Gallery, then click OK.

3. Crystal Reports ⇒ Database ⇒ Database Expert.

4. Add the Customer table to the **SELECTED TABLES** list, then click OK. You will see an empty design window.

How To Add Fields To A Report

There are several ways to add fields in the Field Explorer to a report as discussed below. If you are not familiar with the techniques discussed, take some time to try them and see which one you like the best.

① Drag the field to the report.

② Select the field. Press Enter, then click in the report section where you want to place the field.

③ Right-click on the field that you want to add to the report section and select **INSERT TO REPORT** on the shortcut menu, then click in the report section where you want to place the field.

Add The Fields To The Report

1. Click on the plus sign in front of the **DATABASE FIELDS** option on the Field Explorer window. You will see all of the tables that you have added to the report. Clicking on the plus sign in front of a table name will display all of the fields in that table. Click on the plus sign in front of the Customer table.

2. Click on the Customer Name field with the left mouse button and drag the field to the far left of the **DETAILS** section. Notice that a field heading is automatically added to the Page Header section.

> If you add a field to a section other then the Details section, a field heading will not automatically be added to the Page Header section. Field headings are only added automatically when the field is added to the Details section.

3. Add the following fields to the **DETAILS** section: Address1, Region, Country and Postal Code. When you are finished, the report layout should look like the one shown in Figure 5-2.

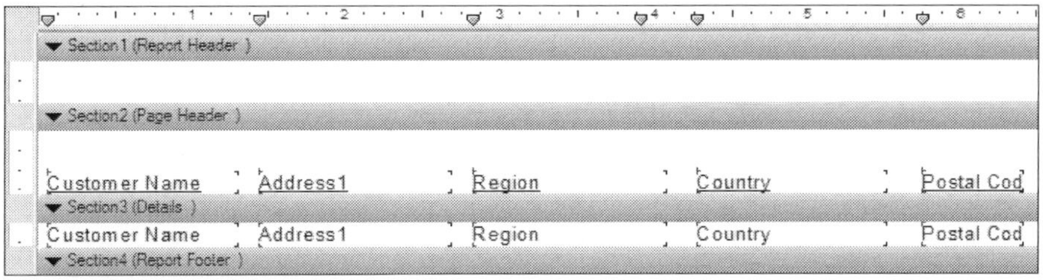

Figure 5-2 Report layout

The green check marks illustrated in the Field Explorer in Figure 5-3 indicate that the field has been added to the report or is being used in a formula field that has been added to the report.

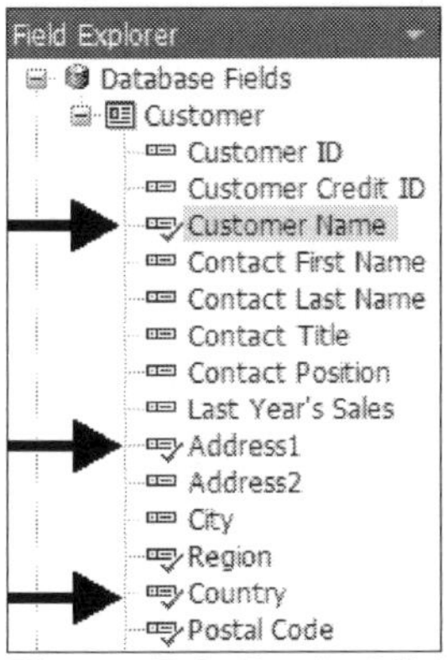

Figure 5-3 Checked fields illustrated

4. Save the report. It should look like the one shown in Figure 5-4. Not bad for your first time creating a report from scratch. Notice that the Address 1 header has a break in the underline. The underline does print correctly.

Customer Name	Address1	Region	Country	Postal Cod
City Cyclists	7464 South Kingswa	MI	USA	48358
Pathfinders	410 Eighth Avenue	IL	USA	60148
Bike-A-Holics Anony	7429 Arbutus Boulev	OH	USA	43005
Psycho-Cycle	8287 Scott Road	AL	USA	35818
Sporting Wheels Inc	480 Grant Way	CA	USA	92150

Figure 5-4 E5.1 Customer information report

Find In Field Explorer Option
This option will highlight the field in the Field Explorer window. I am not sure of the benefit of this feature because if you have the tool tips option turned on, you can see which table the field is in by holding the mouse pointer over the field on the Design tab. This option is on the shortcut menu when you right-click on a field.

Exercise 5.2: Create A Report Using Multiple Tables

In the previous exercise the report that you created was based on one table. Many of the reports that you will need to create will use two or more tables. The report that you will create in this exercise uses more than one table.

Select The Tables

1. Create a new report using the report wizard and save it as `E5.2 Employee list.`

2. Add the Employee, Employee Addresses and Orders tables, to the report.

> **Adding More Than One Table To The Report At The Same Time**
> You can add more than one table at the same time by clicking on the first table that you want to add, then press and hold down the Shift key and select the other tables. You can also double-click on the table in the **AVAILABLE DATA SOURCES** list to add it to the Selected Tables list.

3. Click Next. Make the Link screen larger. This will make it easier to see how the tables are linked. Notice that all of the tables have an Employee ID field.

> The Database Expert references the screen that you link tables on, the **LINKS** screen. The wizards reference the same screen the **LINK** screen. They both do the exact same thing, so I don't know why they have slightly different names.

The **ORDER LINKS** button opens the dialog box shown in Figure 5-5. It is used to verify the order of how the tables are connected. Most of the time, the order that is selected is what you need.

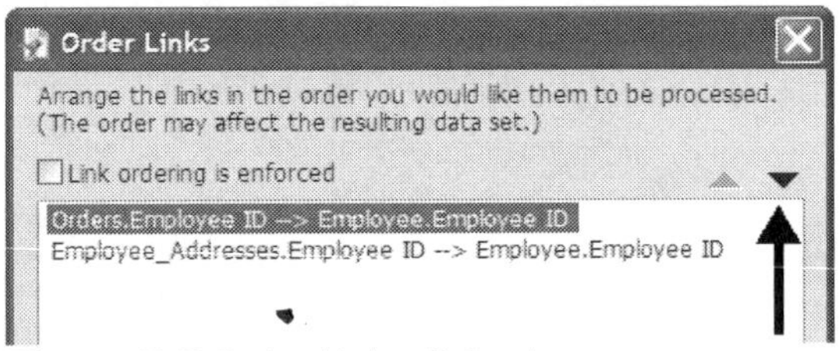

Figure 5-5 Order Links dialog box

When you are using several tables, it is a good idea to check the link order to make sure that the links are correct. Incorrect linking will produce an outcome different then what you expect.

If you need to rearrange the order of the links, click on the link that you need to move, then click the **UP** or **DOWN** arrow to move the link, as illustrated above in Figure 5-5.

If you are using a command or query as the basis of the report you do not have to create or have links, because the links are created and stored in the command or query. Linking data in tables is an important concept to understand and will be covered in detail after you finish creating this report.

4. Close the Order Links dialog box, then click Finish to close the Standard Report Creation Wizard dialog box.

Add The Fields To The Report

1. Delete the Print Date field in the Page Header section.

2. Add the following fields in the Employee table to the Details section: Photo, First Name and Last Name.

3. Add the following fields in the Employee Addresses table to the Details section: Address1 and Region.

   Figure 5-6 shows the report layout. Leave the report open to complete the next part of the exercise.

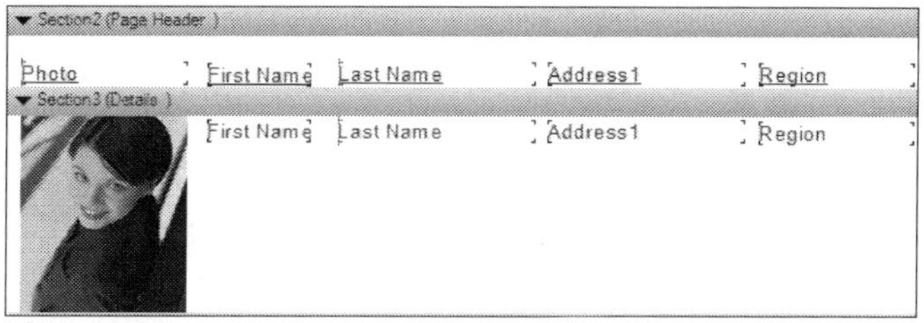

Figure 5-6 Fields from the Employee and Employee Addresses tables added to the report

How To Add And Remove Databases And Tables

It is possible that during the report design process you may need to add or delete a database or table. You just realized that you do not need any fields from the Orders table and want to remove the table from the report. You can make changes like this in the Field Explorer window by following the steps below.

1. Right-click on the **DATABASE FIELDS** option in the Field Explorer.

   You will see the shortcut menu shown in Figure 5-7.

   Select the **DATABASE EXPERT** option on the shortcut menu.

Figure 5-7 Field Explorer shortcut menu for databases

Other Ways To Open The Database Expert
① Right-click on a table in the Field Explorer and select Database Expert.
② Right-click on a field in the Field Explorer and select Database Expert.
③ Crystal Reports ⇒ Database ⇒ Database Expert.

2. Click on the Orders table in the **SELECTED TABLES** list, then click the **<** button.

   Your report should look like the one shown in Figure 5-8.

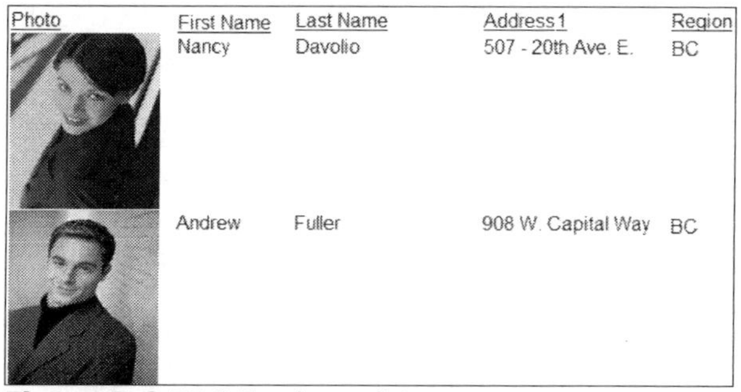

Figure 5-8 E5.2 Employee list report

> If you need to add a table select it from the **AVAILABLE DATA SOURCES** list, then add it to the Selected Tables list on the Database Expert dialog box.

Relational Databases

Earlier in this chapter you read a little about linking tables. The reason tables can be linked is because there is a relationship (at least one field in common) between them, thus the term "Relational Databases". Yes, this is a complicated topic and there are a lot of books on the concepts associated with relational databases and how to create them, so I won't bore you with the details, but please hear me out and don't skip this section.

If the databases that you will use out in the real world are created properly, you will not have to learn a lot about linking or relational databases, because Crystal Reports will create the links that you need. However, this doesn't mean that you do not have to learn anything about these topics.

While databases are not the primary focus of this book, it is important that you understand a little more than the fundamentals and basic database terminology that was covered in Chapter 3. The reason that you need to understand databases is because they are the foundation for the reports that you will create and modify. If you have never created a database, or have very little experience creating them, the next few sections in this chapter will be your crash course in databases, relationships and linking. You will learn how all of the components fit together. Figures 5-9 and 5-10 illustrate the layout of two tables.

Orders			
Order ID	Order Date	Order Amount	Cust ID
1000	1/2/2005	$263.99	48
1001	1/2/2005	$322.45	57
1002	1/3/2005	$196.00	3
1003	1/4/2005	$124.99	48

Table Name
Field Names
Records

Figure 5-9 Orders table layout

Orders Detail		
Order ID	Product ID	Quantity
1000	43	4
1000	76	2
1001	76	3
1001	10	2
1003	10	1
1004	25	3

Table Name
Field Names
Records

Figure 5-10 Orders Detail table layout

Primary Key Fields

In Chapter 3 you saw a table that listed the primary keys for tables in the database used in this book. The fields in the Primary Key column are the ID fields. You will see these two terms used interchangeably. I prefer to use the term ID field because primary key fields usually have "ID", as part of the field name.

> ID is short for identification. It is jargon that the programming community uses to reference a field that can be used to link the data in one table to the data in another table.

All of the tables that you will use in this book have at least one ID field. Hopefully, you will find that this is also true out in the real world. The reason ID fields are used is because by design, they provide a way for each record in the table to have a unique way to be identified.

I have taught several database classes and almost without fail, this topic causes a lot of confusion. For some reason, people want to create links on string (text fields). Please don't do that. It can cause you problems.

If you needed to create a report that showed all of the orders and what items were on each order, you would need a way to link the Orders and Orders Detail tables. Think of "linking" as having the ability to combine two or more tables "virtually" and being able to display the result of this "virtual linking" on a computer screen or on a printed report.

In Figures 5-9 and 5-10 above, the common ID field is the Order ID field. If you look at the data in the Orders Detail table, you will see that some records have the same Order ID number. That's ok. This means that some customers placed orders with more than one item. Each record in the Orders Detail table represents one item that a customer ordered. If you were to "virtually" join the data in the tables shown in Figures 5-9 and 5-10 above, it would look like the table shown in Figure 5-11.

Orders				Orders Detail		
Order ID	Order Date	Order Amount	Cust ID	Order ID	Product ID	Quantity
1000	1/2/2005	$263.99	48	1000	43	4
1000	1/2/2005	$263.99	48	1000	76	2
1001	1/2/2005	$322.45	57	1001	76	3
1001	1/2/2005	$322.45	57	1001	10	2
1002	1/3/2005	$196.00	3			
1003	1/4/2005	$124.99	48	1003	10	1
				1004	25	3

Figure 5-11 Virtually joined tables

This "virtual" join is what happens when tables are **LINKED**. If all of this data was stored in one table instead of two, at the very minimum, the Order Date and Order Amount fields would be repeated for every record that is in the Orders Detail table. Repetition of data is why this information is stored in two tables instead of one. It is considered poor table design to have the same information (other than fields that are used to join tables) stored in more than one table.

More then likely if you see a record in the Orders Detail table, like Order ID 1004 shown above in Figure 5-11, or any child table that is in a parent-child relationship, there is a problem with the data in at least one of the tables because all of the records in the child table should have at least one matching record in the parent table. Parent tables are used to get data from a child table.

Types Of Relationships

The Employee report that you just created required two tables. These tables are linked by a common field, the Employee ID field. This field is what connects (joins) data from both tables and allows you to use data from both tables.

The Employee ID field in the Employee table is how you find the matching record (known as a **ONE-TO-ONE RELATIONSHIP**) or records (known as a **ONE-TO-MANY RELATIONSHIP**, which is the most popular type of relationship) in the Employee Addresses table. These are two of the most common types of relationships. The **MANY-TO-MANY RELATIONSHIP** is a third type of relationship. It is not used as much as the other two.

How Linking Works

More than likely, most reports that you create will require data from more than one table. Reports like the Product list report that you created only used one table, so there is no linking involved. For reports that require two or more tables, the tables need to be linked. The tables are usually linked in the database. When you create a report and need to view or modify the links, you can do so by opening the Database Expert and clicking on the Link tab.

The best way to understand the basic concept of linking tables is to look at the records or a portion of the records in the tables that need to be linked. When you create a report that you are not familiar with the data that is needed, you should take the time to look at the data in the tables. Figures 5-12 and 5-13 show the records in the Employee and Employee Addresses tables. The field that these tables have in common is the Employee ID field, as shown below.

Employee : Table

Employee ID	Supervisor ID	Last Name	First Name	Position	Birth Date	Hire Date
1	5	Davolio	Nancy	Sales Representati	12/8/1972	3/29/1991
2		Fuller	Andrew	Vice President, Sal	2/19/1969	7/12/1991
3	5	Leverling	Janet	Sales Representati	8/30/1971	2/27/1991
4	5	Peacock	Margaret	Sales Representati	9/19/1973	3/30/1992
5	2	Buchanan	Steven	Sales Manager	3/4/1975	9/13/1992
6	5	Suyama	Michael	Sales Representati	7/2/1963	9/13/1992
7	5	King	Robert	Sales Representati	5/29/1972	11/29/1992
8	5	Callahan	Laura	Inside Sales Coordi	1/9/1974	1/30/1993
9	5	Dodsworth	Anne	Sales Representati	1/27/1976	10/12/1993
10	2	Hellstern	Albert	Business Manager	3/13/1968	3/1/1993
11	10	Smith	Tim	Mail Clerk	6/6/1973	1/15/1993
12	10	Patterson	Caroline	Receptionist	9/11/1979	5/15/1993
13	2	Brid	Justin	Marketing Director	10/8/1977	1/1/1994
14	13	Martin	Xavier	Marketing Associate	1/30/1975	1/15/1994
15	13	Pereira	Laurent	Advertising Speciali	12/9/1970	2/1/1994

Record: 1 of 15

Figure 5-12 Data in the Employee table

Employee Addresses : Table

Employee ID	Address1	Address2	City	Region	Country	Postal Code
1	507 - 20th Ave. E.		Port Moody	BC	Canada	V3D 4F6
2	908 W. Capital Way	Suite 100	Coquitlam	BC	Canada	V3H4J7
3	722 Moss Bay Blvd.		Vancouver	BC	Canada	V6M 8S9
4	4110 Old Redmond Rd.		Richmond	BC	Canada	V5S 6H7
5	14 Garrett Hill		London		UK	SW1 8JR
6	Coventry House		London		UK	EC2 7JR
7	Edgeham Hollow	Apt #243	London		UK	RG1 9SP
8	4726 - 11th Ave. N.E.		New Westmins	BC	Canada	V7J 5G5
9	7 Houndstooth Rd.		Nottingham		UK	WG2 7LT
10	13920 S.E. 40th Street		Burnaby	BC	Canada	V2C 8H3
11	30301 - 166th Ave. N.E.	Apt #3D	North Vancouve	BC	Canada	V3K 2G9
12	16 Maple Lane		West Vancouve	BC	Canada	V3L 5S3
13	2 impasse du Soleil		Haguenau	Bas-Rhin	France	67500
14	9 place de la Liberté		Schiltigheim	Bas-Rhin	France	67300
15	7 rue Nationale		Strasbourg	Bas-Rhin	France	67000

Record: 15 of 15

Figure 5-13 Data in the Employee Addresses table

> Fields that are used to link tables must be the same data type. You could not create a link between a date field and a string field.

Depending on the table structure, tables can have more than one field that they can be linked by. An example of this would be the Orders Detail table. This table has an ID field that would let you link it to the Orders table. There is a Product ID field in the Orders Detail table that would let you retrieve the Product Name from the Product table to print on the report, instead of printing the Product ID number. Displaying the product name on the report is more meaningful to the people that read the report then the Product ID field, which contains a number. If you are asking why the Product Name is not stored in the Orders Detail table, there are two reasons.

① The ID field takes up less space, thereby keeping the size of the Orders Detail table smaller.

② If a Product Name has to be changed for any reason, it only has to be changed in the Product table. Every place that the Product Name field is used on any report would automatically be updated with the revised product name. If the product name was stored in the Orders Detail table, every record in the Orders Detail table that had that product name would have to be changed, as well as, any other table that stored the product name. That would be a lot of extra work for you.

Join Types

Hopefully you are still with me. Don't worry, the relational database "lecturette" is almost over. There are several types of links that can be created. Figure 5-14 shows the link options. These different types of links are called **JOIN TYPES**. Crystal Reports has several join types that you can select from. Each join type will display different results from the same tables, which you will see in Figures 5-16 to 5-19. **INNER** joins are the most common.

If you use any of the three **OUTER** join types discussed below, the order that the tables are added to the report is important. The join types that are explained in Table 5-1 are the ones that are automatically created and are the most common. The other join types have to be created manually. They are covered later in this chapter.

To open this dialog box, right-click on the line between the tables, as illustrated in Figure 5-15, then select **LINK OPTIONS** on the shortcut menu.

You can also open the Link Options dialog box by clicking on the link between the tables, then click the Link Options button shown in Figure 5-15.

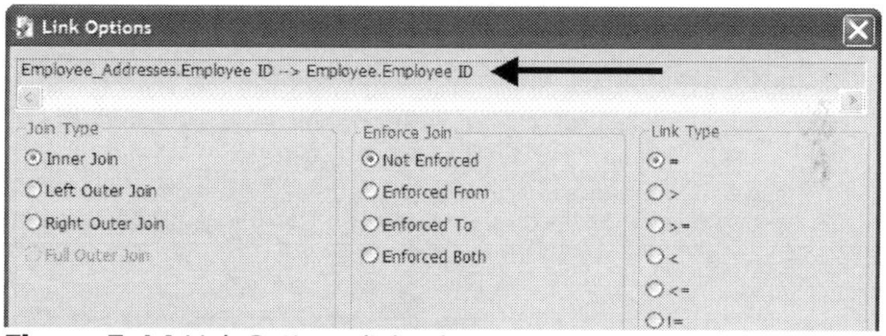

Figure 5-14 Link Options dialog box

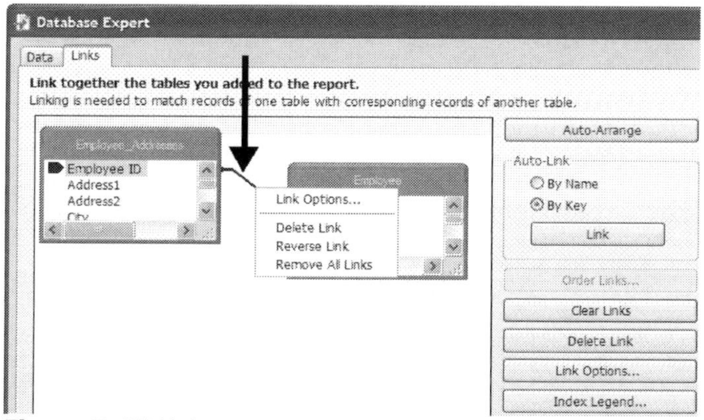

Figure 5-15 Link screen

The "matching" discussed in Table 5-1 is usually done on ID fields.

Join Type	Description
Inner	Records that have matching records in both tables, as illustrated in Figure 5-16.
Left-Outer	Selects all records from one table (usually the left most table on the Links tab) and only matching records in the table on the right, as illustrated in Figure 5-17.
Right-Outer	Selects all records from the right table and only matching records from the table on the left, as illustrated in Figure 5-18. This join type works the opposite of the Left-Outer join type.

Table 5-1 Join types explained

Join Type	Description
Full-Outer	Selects all records from both tables whether or not there are matching records in the other table, as illustrated in Figure 5-19. Full-Outer joins are also known as a **UNION** join type.

Table 5-1 Join types explained (Continued)

In the Orders and Orders Detail tables, the Orders table is known as the **LEFT** table and should be added to the list of tables for the report first. The Orders Detail table is known as the **RIGHT** table and should be added to the list of tables after the Orders table. The reason the tables need to be added in this order for outer joins is because for each record in the Orders table, there can be multiple records in the Orders Detail table that have the same ID. If the tables were added in the wrong order you can use the options on the Order Links dialog box to change the order.

Join Type Examples

When walking through these examples compare the data in Figures 5-16 to 5-19 to the data shown earlier in Figure 5-11. The data shown in these examples only represent the data that would be retrieved from the tables in Figure 5-11. The examples in this section illustrate how the same data would be retrieved differently depending on the join type that is selected. This is why it is important to understand linking and join types.

In Figure 5-16, the record for Order ID 1002 in the Orders table would not be retrieved in an Inner join because there is no related record in the Orders Detail table. The arrows between the tables represent the flow of the data.

In Figure 5-17, the record for Order ID 1004 would not be retrieved from the Orders Detail table in a Left-Outer join because there is no related record in the Orders table.

In Figure 5-18, the record for Order ID 1002 in the Orders table would not be retrieved in a Right-Outer join because there is no related record in the Orders Detail table.

In Figure 5-19, all records would be retrieved in a Full-Outer join whether there is a related record in the other table or not.

Orders			
Order ID	Order Date	Order Amount	Cust ID
1000	1/2/2005	$263.99	48
1001	1/2/2005	$322.45	57
1003	1/4/2005	$124.99	48

Orders Detail		
Order ID	Product ID	Quantity
1000	43	4
1000	76	2
1001	76	3
1001	10	2
1003	10	1

Figure 5-16 Inner join recordset

Orders			
Order ID	Order Date	Order Amount	Cust ID
1000	1/2/2005	$263.99	48
1001	1/2/2005	$322.45	57
1002	1/3/2005	$196.00	3
1003	1/4/2005	$124.99	48

Orders Detail		
Order ID	Product ID	Quantity
1000	43	4
1000	76	2
1001	76	3
1001	10	2
1003	10	1

Figure 5-17 Left-Outer join recordset

Orders			
Order ID	Order Date	Order Amount	Cust ID
1000	1/2/2005	$263.99	48
1001	1/2/2005	$322.45	57
1003	1/4/2005	$124.99	48

Orders Detail		
Order ID	Product ID	Quantity
1000	43	4
1000	76	2
1001	76	3
1001	10	2
1003	10	1
1004	25	3

Figure 5-18 Right-Outer join recordset

Orders			
Order ID	Order Date	Order Amount	Cust ID
1000	1/2/2005	$263.99	48
1001	1/2/2005	$322.45	57
1002	1/3/2005	$196.00	3
1003	1/4/2005	$124.99	48

Orders Detail		
Order ID	Product ID	Quantity
1000	43	4
1000	76	2
1001	76	3
1001	10	2
1003	10	1
1004	25	3

Figure 5-19 Full-Outer join recordset

Tables Without A Link

If you added the Orders and Orders Detail tables to a report but did not link them, Crystal Reports would not know which record in the Orders table went with which record in the Orders Detail table.

The result would be that each order record would be displayed (matched) with each of the records in the Orders Detail table, as shown in Figure 5-20.

In total, 24 records would print on the report. When a report uses more than one table, this is usually not what you want.

Orders			
Order ID	Order Date	Order Amount	Cust ID
1000	1/2/2005	$263.99	48
1000	1/2/2005	$263.99	48
1000	1/2/2005	$263.99	48
1000	1/2/2005	$263.99	48
1000	1/2/2005	$263.99	48
1000	1/2/2005	$263.99	48
1001	1/2/2005	$322.45	57
1001	1/2/2005	$322.45	57
1001	1/2/2005	$322.45	57
1001	1/2/2005	$322.45	57
1001	1/2/2005	$322.45	57
1001	1/2/2005	$322.45	57
		. . .	
1003	1/4/2005	$124.99	48

Orders Detail		
Order ID	Product ID	Quantity
1000	43	4
1000	76	2
1001	76	3
1001	10	2
1003	10	1
1004	25	3
1000	43	4
1000	76	2
1001	76	3
1001	10	2
1003	10	1
1004	25	3
	. . .	
1004	25	3

Figure 5-20 Tables not joined recordset

The reports shown in Figures 5-21 and 5-22 have the same three fields: Customer Name, Product ID and Order ID. The report shown in Figure 5-21 has the **LEFT-OUTER** join between the Customer and Orders tables. The report shown in Figure 5-22 has the **RIGHT-OUTER** join between the Orders and Orders Detail tables. As you can see, the output is completely different for these reports. Hopefully, these reports demonstrate why understanding table structures, types of relationships, linking and join types is important.

Customer Name	Product ID	Order ID
City Cyclists	2,201	1
Deals on Wheels	5,205	1,002
Deals on Wheels	102,181	1,002
Warsaw Sports, Inc.	2,213	1,003
Warsaw Sports, Inc.	5,402	1,003
Bikes and Trikes	402,002	1,004
SAB Mountain	1,101	1,005

Figure 5-21 Left-Outer join report

Customer Name	Product ID	Order ID
City Cyclists	2,209	1,387
City Cyclists	3,305	1,387
City Cyclists	302,201	1,387
City Cyclists	1,108	2,277
City Cyclists	2,207	2,277
City Cyclists	1,101	1,033

Figure 5-22 Right-Outer join report

Recursive Join

In addition to the join types discussed above, there is another join type called **RECURSIVE JOIN**. This type of join is not always obvious when looking at the table structures. A recursive join occurs when the same data is stored in two different ID fields in the same table. This is not the same as a parent/child (also known as a master/detail) relationship because this type of relationship does not require two tables like the Orders and Orders Detail tables that you read about earlier.

An example of a recursive join is in the Employee table. The Supervisor ID field in the Employee table contains the Employee ID of another record in the Employee table. This is because supervisors are also employees. Refer back to Figure 5-12. Seven employees have the number 5 in the Supervisor ID field (the second field from the left). This is because they all have the same supervisor, Steven Buchanan, whose Employee ID is number 5. Recursive joins are often used to create hierarchical reports.

Smart Linking

Smart linking is enabled by default. Crystal Reports uses this feature to create links based on an index or common fields in tables. You can change the default smart linking option on the Database tab of the Options dialog box. Some people turn this option off and always create the links manually to make sure that the correct join type is selected. The reason people turn this feature off is because tables are joined on fields that have the same name and data type, which may not be what you want.

View The Current Links

1. Open a blank report and name it what you want, then add the Customer, Orders and Orders Detail tables.

2. On the Links tab, click the **CLEAR LINKS** button. Click Yes, when prompted if you are sure.

How To Manually Create Links

When you have the need to manually create links, follow the steps below.

1. Select a field in one table and drag it to the field in the other table. In this example, select the Quantity field in the Orders Detail table and drag it to the Customer Name field in the Customer table, then release the mouse button.

> Both fields must have the same data type. If there is something wrong with the link that you are trying to create, you will see a warning message similar to the one shown in Figure 5-23. This message lets you know that the link that you are trying to create is not valid.

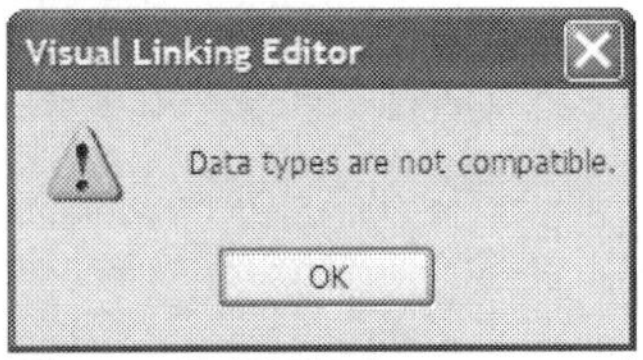

Figure 5-23 Link error warning message

2. Click OK to close the Visual Linking Editor message window shown above in Figure 5-23.

Manual Join Types

As discussed earlier, there are other join and link types that can be used to link tables. Table 5-2 explains the enforce join type options. Table 5-3 explains the link types.

Enforce Join Type	Description
Not Enforced	Selecting this option doesn't mean that the link will be included in the SQL statement. At least one field must be used to join tables in order for the linking criteria to be included in the SQL statement.
Enforced From	Selecting this option forces the link to the right table. When a field from the right table is used, but not one from the left table, the SQL statement requires that both tables be referenced.
Enforced To	This option forces the link from the left table, whether or not a field is used from the right table. This means that the SQL statement will include both tables.
Enforced Both	This option forces the link between the tables, regardless of where the fields that are used in the report are stored.

Table 5-2 Enforce join types explained

Link Type	Creates A Recordset Where The Link Field . . .
Equal Link =	Has related records in the left and right tables.
Greater Than Link >	From the left table is greater than the linked field in the right table.
Greater Than or Equal To Link >=	From the left table is greater than or equal to the linked field in the right table.
Less Than Link <	From the left table is less than the linked field in the right table.
Less Than or Equal To Link <=	From the left table is less than or equal to the linked field in the right table.
Not Equal Link !=	From the left table does not match the linked field in the right table.

Table 5-3 Link Types explained

Exercise 5.3: Create A Customer Orders Report

In this exercise you will create a report that displays customers and their orders.

1. Create a new report and save it as `E5.3 Customer orders`.
2. Select the Blank Report option. Open the Database Expert and add the Customer and Orders tables.
3. Add the Customer Name field in the Customer table to the Details section.
4. Add the Order Date and Ship Date fields in the Orders table to the Details section.

Add Another Table And More Fields To The Report

You have decided that the report would look better if it also had fields from the Orders Detail table. To add a table to the report, follow the steps below.

1. Right-click on the **DATABASE FIELDS** option in the Field Explorer, then select Database Expert. Add the Orders Detail table, then click OK. When you see the **LINKS** tab, Click OK. You will see the Orders Detail table in the Field Explorer window.

2. Add the Order ID, Unit Price and Quantity fields in the Orders Detail table to the Details section. Your report layout should look like the one shown in Figure 5-24. The report should look like the one shown in Figure 5-25.

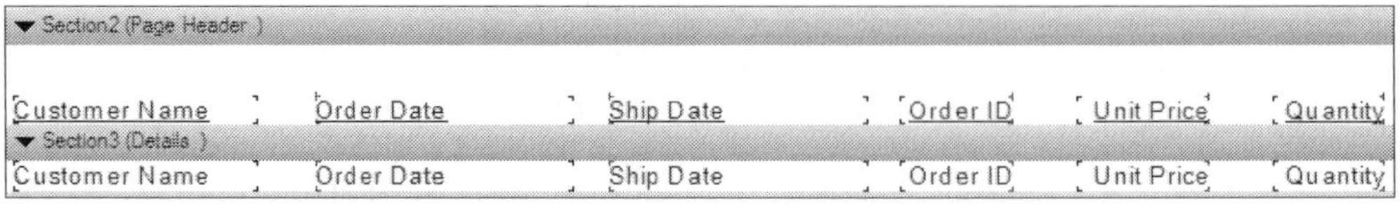

Figure 5-24 Customer orders report layout

Customer Name	Order Date	Ship Date	Order ID	Unit Price	Quantity
City Cyclists	12/2/2010 12:00:00AI	12/10/2010 5:32:23P	1	$41.90	1
Deals on Wheels	12/2/2010 12:00:00AI	12/2/2010 6:45:32AN	1,002	$33.90	3
Deals on Wheels	12/2/2010 12:00:00AI	12/2/2010 6:45:32AN	1,002	$1,652.86	3
Warsaw Sports, Inc.	12/2/2010 12:00:00AI	12/5/2010 12:10:12AI	1,003	$48.51	3
Warsaw Sports, Inc.	12/2/2010 12:00:00AI	12/5/2010 12:10:12AI	1,003	$13.78	3

Figure 5-25 Customer orders report

The reason that the information in the Customer Name, Order Date, Ship Date and Order ID fields is repeated, is because on some orders the customer ordered more than one item. (See Order ID 1002 and 1003). As you can see, all of the reports that you have created so far in this book need to be edited and formatted, so that they are more presentable. You will learn how to edit reports in the next chapter.

Using A Table Alias

There may be times when a table needs to be added to a report twice to be able to retrieve different data. The second time that a table is added to a report, you will see the message shown in Figure 5-26.

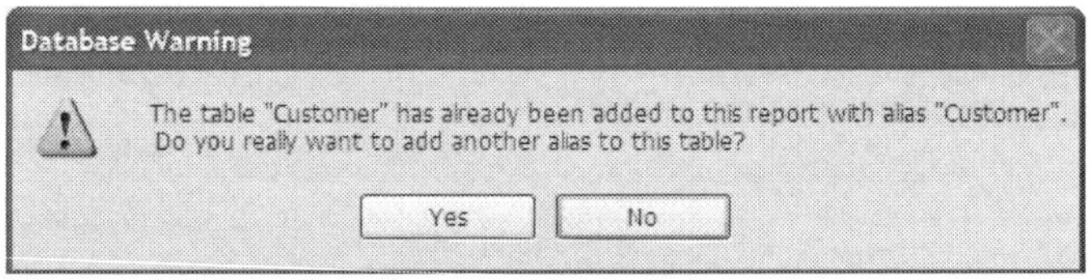

Figure 5-26 Adding the same table twice message

The second occurrence of the table is automatically renamed to include an underscore and incremental number, as illustrated in Figure 5-27. The second occurrence table is known as the alias table. You can rename the alias table.

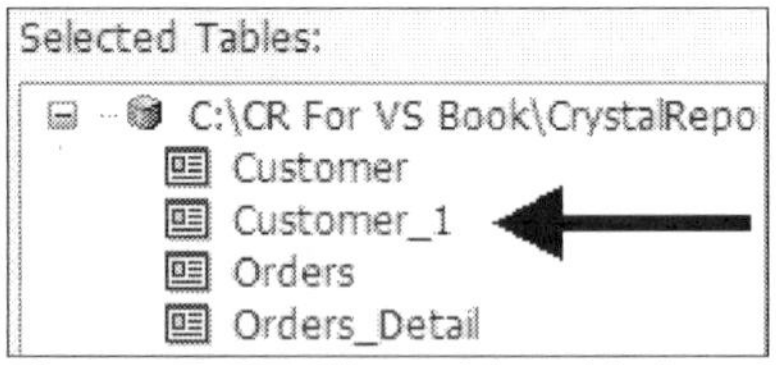

Figure 5-27 Alias table added to the report

ALIGNING OBJECTS ON A REPORT

As the title of this chapter indicates, you will learn alignment techniques that you can use to make the reports that you create look better. After completing the exercises in this chapter you will be able to:

- ☑ Understand the options on the field shortcut menu
- ☑ Select objects
- ☑ Align objects
- ☑ Use guidelines
- ☑ Understand the purpose of the grid
- ☑ Resize objects
- ☑ Nudge objects

CHAPTER 6

Shortcut Menus

Crystal Reports has several shortcut menus that you can use instead of selecting menu options or clicking on toolbar buttons. As you will see, you will spend a lot of time formatting and editing reports. A great time saver in completing these tasks is using the options on the shortcut menus.

The options on the shortcut menu will change depending on the object that is selected.

In addition to the object shortcut menu, there is a general shortcut menu available when you right-click on an empty space in the design window, as shown in Figure 6-1. These are the same options that are on the Crystal Reports menu.

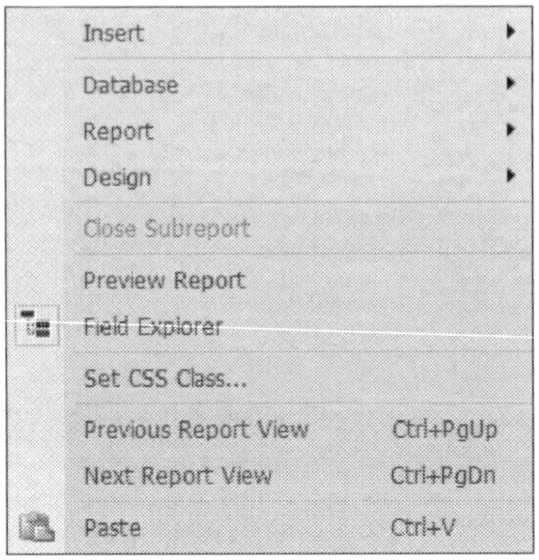

Figure 6-1 General shortcut menu

Selecting Fields And Objects

A lot of the report editing that you will do requires fields and other objects to be selected. Often, you will have the need to apply the same changes to several fields or objects.

To select a single field or object, click on it with the left mouse button.

When an object is selected you will see a frame around it, as illustrated in Figure 6-2. You will also see squares. These squares are called **RESIZE HANDLES**.

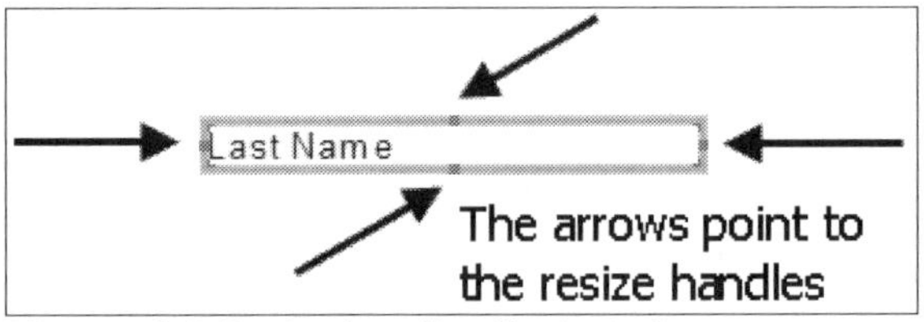

Figure 6-2 Resize handles illustrated

> In the Crystal Reports environment everything on a report is considered an object, including fields, text boxes, lines and images. When I use the word "field", I am referring to a field in the Details section of the report, or a field from a table or a calculated field that you create. "Objects" refer to items like the field heading, a text field or an image.

Selecting Multiple Fields And Objects

There are two ways to select the fields in the report that you need, as discussed below.

① Click on one field or object. Press and hold down the **CTRL** or **SHIFT** key, then click on the other fields or objects that you need to select.

② Draw what is called a **MARQUEE** or **LASSO** around the fields or objects with the mouse. To do this successfully, the objects need to be near each other, either side by side or up and down from each other. Click outside of the first field or object. Hold the left mouse button down, then draw around the objects that you need to select. You will see a frame being drawn. When you are finished selecting the objects and release the mouse button, you will see that several objects have been selected. To use this technique no objects on the report can already be selected.

Exercise 6.1: Moving Objects

One of the tasks that you will do from time to time is rearrange fields and other objects on a report. This exercise will show you how to move fields and objects on a report.

1. Save the E4.2 report as `E6.1 Moving fields`.

2. Click on the Product ID field in the Details section and move it to the left, as close to the edge as possible. Notice that the field heading moved with the field.

3. Move the Product Name and Price fields to the left.

Aligning Objects Vertically

In addition to moving objects, you will have the need to have multiple objects line up. The **ALIGN** option is used to line up several objects at the same time. Follow the steps below to learn how to align objects. Because everything on the report is currently aligned, you need to move an object to get it out of alignment to complete this exercise.

1. Click on the Price field heading and drag it to the right, as shown in Figure 6-3.

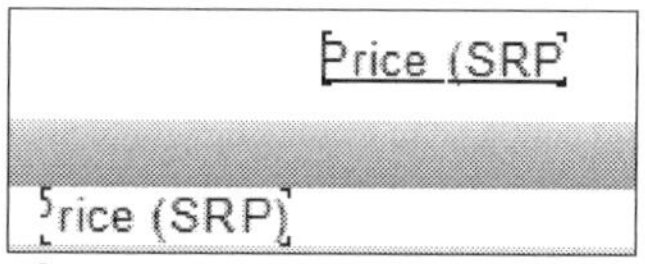

Figure 6-3 Field heading moved to the right

2. Select the Price field and heading, then right-click on the Price field.

> In the step 2, you have to right-click on the object that has the alignment that you want duplicate. In this exercise you want to align the field heading with the field. If you right-clicked on the field heading in the step above and selected Align ⇒ Rights, the field would have been aligned on the right with the field heading.

3. Align ⇒ Lefts, as shown in Figure 6-4. The field and heading should be where they were before you started this exercise. Table 6-1 explains the align options.

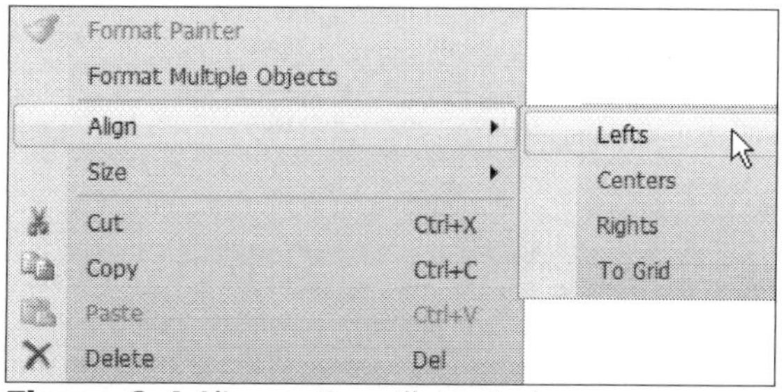

Figure 6-4 Align options illustrated

> At the top of the shortcut menu if you see the words **FORMAT MULTIPLE OBJECTS**, it means that you have more than one object selected. When selecting multiple fields or objects, whatever change you make will be applied to all of the selected fields or objects as long as the change can be applied to the data type. Not all data types can have the same changes applied.

Align Option	How It Aligns . . .
Lefts	On the left side of the object.
Centers	On the center of the object.
Rights	On the right side of the object.
To Grid	To the closest grid point of the object that you right-click on. The **GRID** option needs to be enabled to see how this works.

Table 6-1 Vertical align options explained

You can right-click on any object and select the **ALIGN** option. Just remember which object that you right-click on before selecting an align option, because you may get results different then what you expected. The alignment of the object that you right-click on will be applied to the other objects that are selected.

4. Save the changes and leave the report open to complete the next part of the exercise.

Aligning Objects Horizontally

This type of alignment is very similar to the align options that you just read about. The horizontal align option is useful when you manually add fields or objects to a report. If you rush and add fields to a report like I do, meaning that you just drop them on the report without paying attention to whether or not they are lined up properly, you will really appreciate this exercise. In order to demonstrate how this feature works, you need to rearrange objects on the report first.

1. Drag the Product ID and Price field headings up in the Page Header section, as shown in Figure 6-5.

Figure 6-5 Field headings moved

2. Select the Product ID, Product Name and Price field headings, then right-click on the Product Name heading.

3. Align ⇒ Bottoms, as shown in Figure 6-6. The field headings should be back where they were before you started this exercise.

   Table 6-2 explains the align options on the shortcut menu.

   The align options shown in Figure 6-6 are only available when all of the selected objects are in the same section of the report.

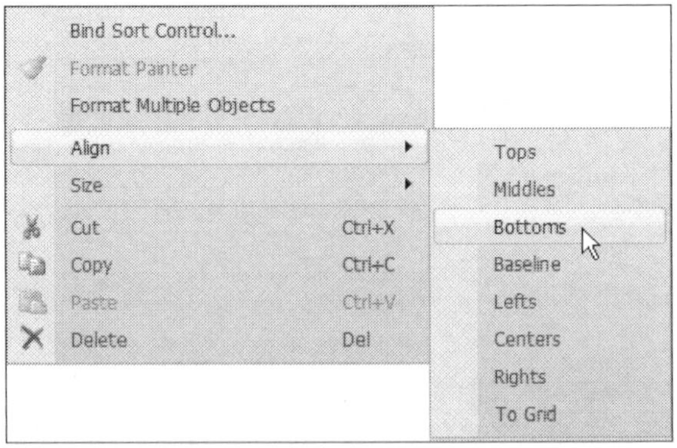

Figure 6-6 Horizontal align options

4. Move the Price field to the right, then save the changes and leave the report open.

Align Option	How It Aligns . . .
Tops	On the top of the object.
Middles	On the middle of the object.
Bottoms	On the bottom of the object.
Baseline	On the bottom of the text, not the bottom of the frame like all of the other alignment options discussed in this table. The baseline align option is useful when you are aligning objects that have a different font, font size or frame size.
Lefts	On the left side of the object.
Centers	On the center of the object.
Rights	On the right side of the object.
To Grid	To the closest grid point of the object that you right-click on. The **GRID** option needs to be enabled to see how this works.

Table 6-2 Horizontal align options explained

Guidelines

As you add fields to the report you will see triangles called **GUIDELINES**, automatically being added to the beginning or end of the field. Text and date fields will have the guideline marker at the beginning of the field. Numeric fields will have the guideline marker at the end of the field.
In Figure 6-7, the Customer Name (a text field) and Order Date (a date field) fields have the guideline markers at the beginning of the field. The Order ID and Unit Price fields are numeric and have the guideline marker at the end of the field. These markers let you know visually where a field starts or ends. Each field also has brackets around it to let you know how long the field is.

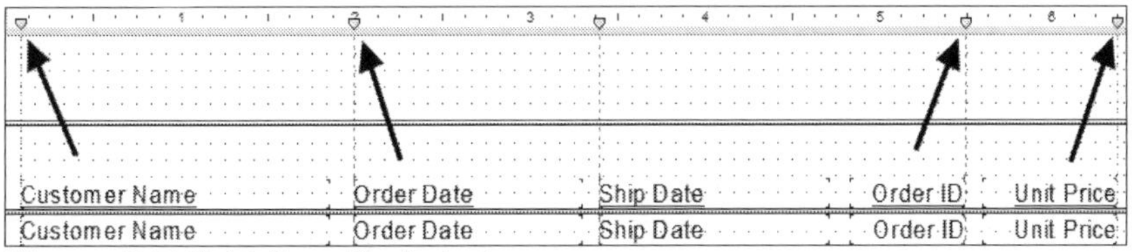

Figure 6-7 Guidelines illustrated

As a general rule, the brackets for one field should not be inside of the brackets for another field unless you are combining objects and fields. Overlapping fields, as illustrated in Figure 6-8 will cause the fields to print on top of each other, as shown in Figure 6-9.

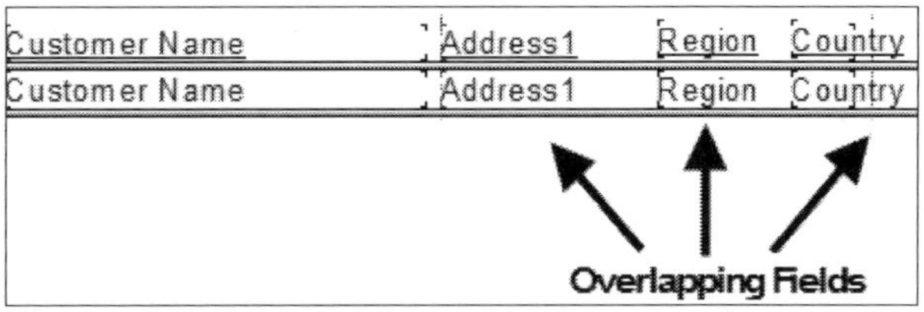

Figure 6-8 Fields overlapped in the report layout

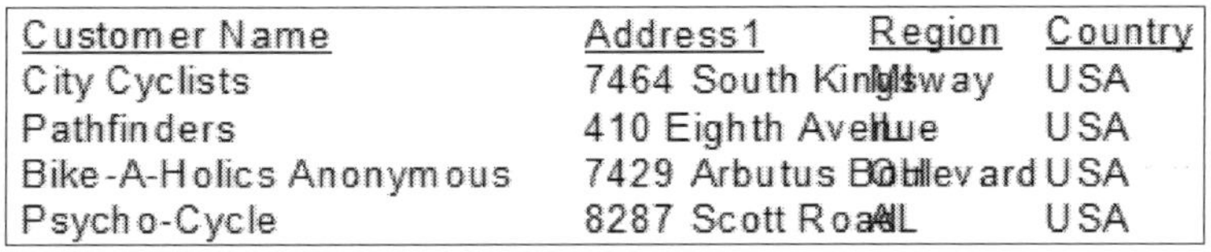

Figure 6-9 Overlapping fields illustrated in print preview

It may not always be easy to move or align objects. Guidelines are used to move all objects that are anchored to the guideline at the same time. This means that you can move the field in the Details section, the field heading in the Page Header section and all calculated or summary fields in other sections that are anchored to the same guideline at the same time, without selecting them individually.

Guidelines are the **TRIANGLE BUTTONS** on the ruler at the top of the report, as illustrated in Figure 6-10. The dotted lines that you see coming down from the guidelines in the Page Header and Group Header sections are **MARKERS** on the ruler.

The reason that you do not see the markers in the Report Header section in the figure is because the section has a chart. The dotted lines for the markers are behind the chart. The dotted lines do not print on the report.

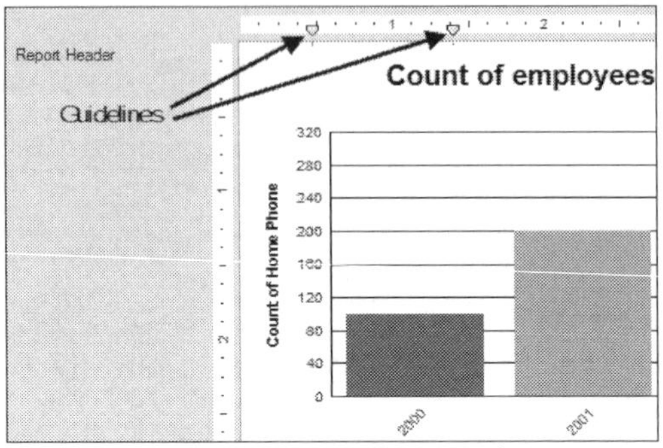

Figure 6-10 Guidelines illustrated

If you moved the guideline that is anchored to the Last Name field, all of the following objects would move at the same time: The field heading, the Sum of Employee.Supervisor ID field in the first Group Footer section and the Count of Employee.Home Phone field in the Report Footer section.

You will see red marks on the side of objects that the guideline is on, if the object is anchored to a guideline. If you do not see the red marks, drag the object towards the guideline or drag the guideline towards the object.

Guidelines are automatically added to a report if any of the follow actions occur:

① A field is added to the Details section.
② You right-click in a **REPORT SECTION** on the design tab, then select **ARRANGE LINES**.
③ A summary field is added to the report.

The horizontal guidelines for all fields are at the top or bottom of the field or the baseline of the text in the field. You will see red marks on the side of objects that the guideline is on, if the object is anchored to a guideline. If you do not see the red marks, drag the object towards the guideline or drag the guideline towards the object.

How To Manually Add Guidelines

If the need arises to manually add guidelines, you can use one of the options below.

① Click on the horizontal ruler where you want to add a guideline.
② Click on the vertical ruler where you want to add a guideline.

> To remove a guideline, drag the triangle marker off of the ruler. Removing guidelines does not delete the objects attached to it.

Turning The Guidelines On

If you do not see the guidelines, Crystal Reports ⇒ Design ⇒ Guidelines, will enable the guidelines.

Using Guidelines To Move Objects

You can move all of the objects that are attached to the same guideline at the same time, by following the steps below.

1. Click on the guideline marker for the Product ID field on the E6.1 report and drag the marker to the right, to the 4 inch mark on the ruler, as illustrated in Figure 6-11.

   The field and field heading should have moved.

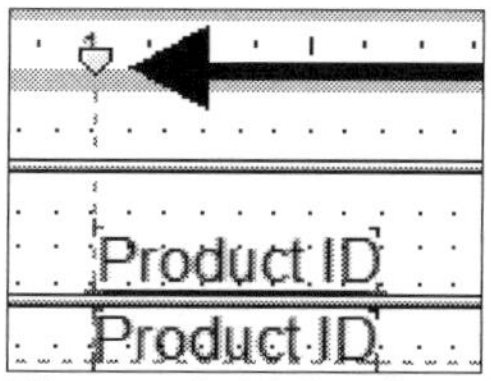

Figure 6-11 Product ID field marker moved

If there were other objects anchored to this marker, like a total or summary field, they would have moved also.

Guideline Issues

Depending on how much you use guidelines, you may notice that a few strange things happen with the guidelines. The ones that I have noticed are discussed in Table 6-3.

Issue	Solution
You delete objects from the report, but the guidelines stay.	Delete the guidelines that are no longer needed.
You moved an object, but the guideline did not move with it.	Move the object towards the guideline until the object snaps to the guideline.
You resized or moved an object and the object now appears to be attached to two guidelines.	Move the object away from the guideline that you do not want the object attached to and then resize the object and attach it to the guideline that you want.

Table 6-3 Guideline issues explained

Using The Grid

When you need to have greater precision over lining up objects on a report, you can turn on the **GRID** option. This option is not enabled by default. In addition to the grid option, turning on the **SNAP TO GRID** option provides additional precision.

The grid is the dot pattern in the background. When new fields or objects are added to the report manually, they are automatically placed on the closest grid position to where you release the mouse button. If you need to change any of the grid settings, they are located on the Layout tab on the Options dialog box.

Crystal Reports ⇒ Design ⇒ Grid, will turn on the grid on the design window, as shown in Figure 6-12.

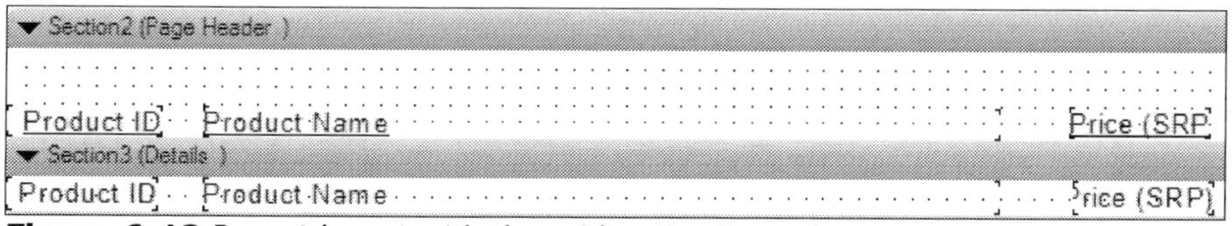

Figure 6-12 Report layout with the grid option turned on

It could be me, but I have noticed that if the **SNAP TO GRID** option is enabled and I create a report with a wizard, the objects are not always placed on a gridline. If you need to line these objects up with a gridline to make the spacing better or because you have manually added more fields, often it cannot be done. Instead, I use the Align options if I used a wizard to create a report.

Resizing Objects

When fields are added to a report, the size is the larger of the field or the field heading. It appears that Crystal Reports estimates the horizontal space needed for string fields. Sometimes this works and sometimes the data in a string field in the Details section of the report gets cut off using this method.

Product ID	Product Name		Price (SRP
1,101	Active Outdoors Crochet Glo		$14.50
1,102	Active Outdoors Crochet Glo		$14.50
1,103	Active Outdoors Crochet Glo	Truncated Data	$14.50
1,104	Active Outdoors Crochet Glo		$14.50
1,105	Active Outdoors Crochet Glo		$14.50
1,106	Active Outdoors Lycra Glove		$16.50
1,107	Active Outdoors Lycra Glove		$16.50

Figure 6-13 Truncated data illustrated

I suspect this happens because there is not enough space in the row to display all of the fields, so text fields are often truncated. This is what happened with the Product Name field on the report illustrated above in Figure 6-13. To fix this, the field needs to be resized. Depending on how close you placed the fields on the report, you may have to move fields to the right, before starting this exercise. When you need to resize a field, follow the steps below.

1. Click on the field that you need to resize. In this exercise, click on the Product Name field.

2. Place the mouse pointer on the right side of the field, as illustrated in Figure 6-14. The mouse pointer will change to a double headed arrow, as shown.

   Drag the **RESIZE HANDLE** that you saw earlier in Figure 6-2 to the right. Notice that the field heading was also resized.

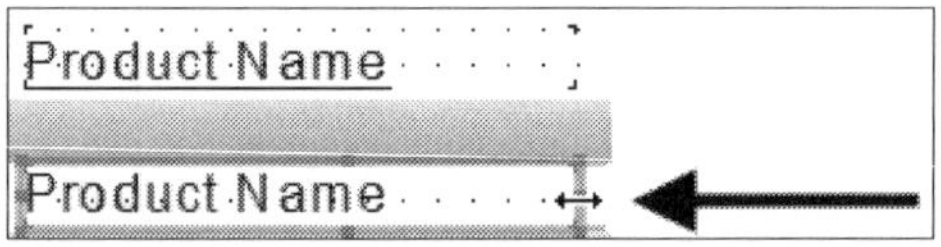

Figure 6-14 Mouse pointer in position to resize the field

3. Preview the report to see if you can now see all of the data in the Product Name field, as shown in Figure 6-15.

Product ID	Product Name	Price (SRP
1,101	Active Outdoors Crochet Glove	$14.50
1,102	Active Outdoors Crochet Glove	$14.50
1,103	Active Outdoors Crochet Glove	$14.50
1,104	Active Outdoors Crochet Glove	$14.50
1,105	Active Outdoors Crochet Glove	$14.50
1,106	Active Outdoors Lycra Glove	$16.50

Figure 6-15 Product Name field resized

It is a good idea to scan through several pages of the report while previewing it, to make sure that you do not see any data cut off (truncated) in the field that you are resizing. It is possible that the resized field may still not be wide enough.

Nudging Objects

So far in this chapter you have learned how to move and resize objects using the mouse. You can also move and resize objects using the keyboard. This is helpful if you use a laptop and do not use a mouse. Using the keyboard to move or resize objects is known as **NUDGING** an object.

> If the **SNAP TO GRID** option is enabled, the arrow key will move the selected object one grid point each time you press an arrow key.

How To Move An Object By Nudging It

1. Select the object that you want to move.

2. Use one of the four arrow keys on the keyboard to move the object in the direction that you need to reposition it.

How To Resize An Object Using The Nudge Feature

1. Click on the object that you need to resize, then press and hold down the **SHIFT** key.

2. Use the arrow key that points in the direction that you want to resize the object. Close the E6.1 report but do not save the changes.

EDITING AND FORMATTING REPORTS

You will learn editing and formatting techniques that you can use to make the reports that you create look better. Chapters 13 and 14 will teach you other ways to format reports. After completing the exercises in this chapter you will be able to:

- ☑ Edit text objects
- ☑ Add graphics to a report
- ☑ Use the Format Editor
- ☑ Use the Format Painter

CHAPTER 7

Overview

It can take an hour or more to create a report. You may struggle to write the formulas, make sure that the sorting and grouping options meet the report requirements and come up with an appropriate title for the report. You are pleased that you were able to accomplish all of these tasks and give a copy of the report to the person that requested it. You see them frown, but can't figure out why, especially because you checked the formulas by hand and know that the data is correct. You ask why they are frowning and they say, "Some of the fields are not lined up and there are too many fonts." As they say, "Perception is everything". Take from this what you will.

Crystal Reports has a variety of options that you can use to make the reports that you design look better. You can draw boxes, apply templates, add color (probably best suited for reports that will be viewed as a web page or printed on a color printer) and more. You can also apply formatting conditionally to fields or sections of the report, depending on whether the value in a field meets specific criteria. This type of formatting can be applied to any field on the report, including summary and group name fields.

Earlier in this book you read that everything on a report is an object, including charts, data fields, headings and formulas. I realize that this may take some getting use to. The good news is that each type of object has it's own set of properties that you can modify. The options on the Standard, Crystal Reports - Main, Crystal Reports - Layout and Crystal Reports - Insert menus, contain many of the options that are covered in this chapter.

Adding And Editing Text Objects

Text objects are used to add additional information to a report. Text objects include field headings, report titles or any text that you want to add to a report that is not based on a field in a table.

> Crystal Reports does not have a spell checker.

Exercise 7.1: How To Edit Text Objects

In this exercise you will learn how to edit text objects.

1. Save the E6.1 report as `E7.1 Text objects`. Delete the Print Date field.

The majority of the field headings on the report are clear and easy to understand. The one field heading that would be easier to understand is the Product ID field. Most end-users (people that will read the report) would not understand the term "ID", so it would be better to change this field heading.

2. Right-click on the Product ID field heading and select **EDIT TEXT OBJECT**.

> You can also double-click on the Product ID field heading to change the text.

3. Select (highlight) the text shown in Figure 7-1, then type `Product #` and click on a blank space on the report.

Figure 7-1 Text selected to change

You can also select a portion of the text in a field and change that. For example, you could select "ID" in Figure 7-1 above and just change that.

Pressing the **ENTER** key does not end the editing session like it does in other software packages. Pressing Enter in Crystal Reports starts a new line in the text object. When you finish adding or editing text, click outside of the text object to end the edit session.

Make The Page Header Section Longer

The report that you have open does not have a report title. As you can see, there is not a lot of space in the Page Header section above the field headings to add a report title. The Page Header section needs to be longer. Follow the steps below to learn how to make a section of the report longer.

1. Click on the Details section bar. The mouse pointer is in the right position when you see the double headed arrow. Drag the section bar down to the top of the Report Footer section.

2. Move all of the field headings down, then click on a blank space on the report.

The easiest way to move all of the field headings at one time is to select all of them first and then move them at the same time.

If you need to make a section in the report shorter, drag the section bar up.

How To Add A Text Object

1. Right-click in the report. Insert ⇒ Text Object. The mouse pointer will have an object attached to it, as shown in Figure 7-2.

Figure 7-2 Text object ready to be placed on a field

2. Click in the Page Header section above the field headings and type `Product List Report` in the text object.

When selecting fonts to use on a report, it is best to use the default fonts that come with Windows, otherwise the report will look different on computers that do not have the font that you selected. If you have to use a font that does not come with Windows, you should export the report to Adobe PDF format. Doing that will allow the report to be seen with the font that you selected.

How To Format A Text Object

As you can see, the text object is too small for the text that you entered. Follow the steps below to learn how to format a text object.

1. Click on the object that you want to apply formatting to. In this exercise, click on the report title that you just created.

2. Click the **BOLD** button and change the font size to 14, then make the object longer and wider so that you can see all of the text.

3. Move the report title so that it is centered (left to right) across the Page Header section.

   The top of the report should look like the one shown in Figure 7-3.

Figure 7-3 Modified Page Header section

> **Centering Text Across A Page**
> I use to find it difficult to center a report title across the page. I finally came up with the steps below to center a report title across the page.

① Make the report title object the width of the report, as shown in Figure 7-4.

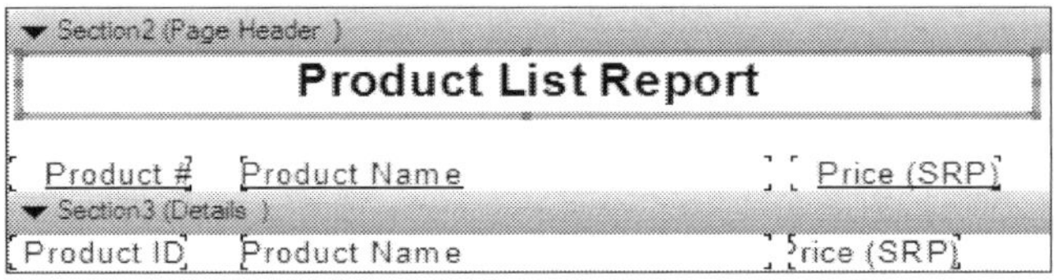

Figure 7-4 Text object resized to the width of the report

② With the text object still selected, click the **CENTER** button.

How To Import A Text File Into A Text Object

If there is text in a file that you want to add to a text object in the report, you can, by following the steps below.

1. Add a text object to the report. Make the object larger, then double-click in the text object to start the edit mode.

2. Right-click on the text object and select **INSERT FROM FILE**, as shown in Figure 7-5.

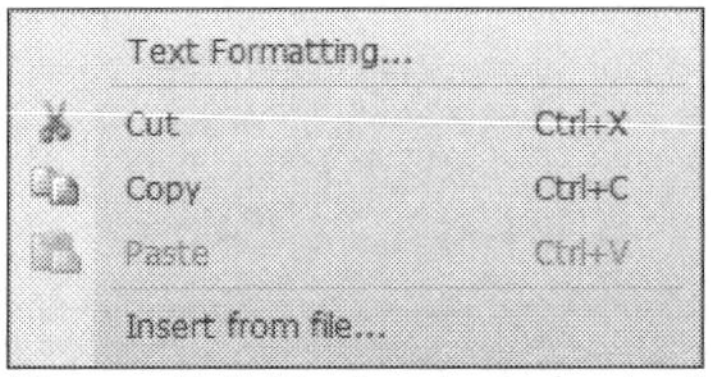

Figure 7-5 Text object shortcut menu

3. Find the file on your hard drive or in another location, then double-click on it. The content of the text file will be added to the text object. Save the changes.

Combining Text Objects And Database Fields

Text objects are more powerful then they may appear. If you have spent any time trying to get a text object and a field to line up side by side with spacing that looks right, but have had trouble doing so, you are in luck. Text objects can have data fields embedded in them. The steps below explain how to embed a database field in a text object.

1. Add a text object to the report, then add the text to the object.

2. Drag a database field from the Field Explorer into the text object, as shown in Figure 7-6, then release the mouse button.

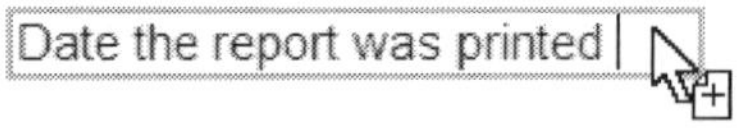

Figure 7-6 Database field being added to a text object

Combining Text Objects Tips
① You can edit the combined field or add more text or another database field to the text object.
② You can format part of a text object. If this is what you need to do, only select (highlight) the part that you want to format.
③ If you discover that you have added the wrong field to the text object, click on the text object and move it away from the database field. Click on the database field, then press the **DEL** key.
④ I find it easier to drag the fields that I want to add to the report and format them there and then drag them into the text object, instead of trying to format the fields inside of the text object.

Exercise 7.2: Adding Image Files To A Report

This exercise will show you how to add a logo or any image file to a report. There are two ways to add an image file to a report, as explained below.

① Click the **PICTURE** button on the Crystal Reports - Insert toolbar.
② Crystal Reports ⇒ Insert ⇒ Picture.

1. Save the E6.1 report as `E7.2 Insert picture`. Delete the Print Date field if its on the report.

2. Make the Page Header section longer by dragging the Details section bar down almost to the end of the Details section. Move the field headings down.

3. Select one of the options above to add an image file to the report. On the Open dialog box, navigate to the folder that you created for this book. Click on the image6.jpg file, then click the Open button.

4. The mouse pointer should change to a shadow box (which is the actual size of the graphic), as shown in Figure 7-7.

   Click in the upper left corner of the Page Header section.

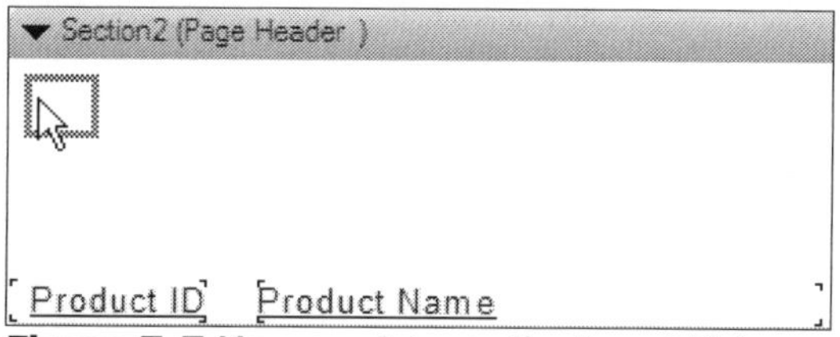

Figure 7-7 Mouse pointer in the Insert Picture mode

You should see the image. Leave the report open to complete the next part of the exercise.

How To Resize An Image

This image would look better if it were larger. Follow the steps below to resize the image.

1. Select the image if it is not already selected. Drag the mouse pointer down and to the right to make the image larger.

2. The report should look like the one shown in Figure 7-8. If you look at other pages in the report, you will see the image at the top of the page because it was placed in the Page Header section, which prints on every page. Save the changes.

Product ID	Product Name	Price (SRP)
1,101	Active Outdoors Crochet Glove	$14.50
1,102	Active Outdoors Crochet Glove	$14.50

Figure 7-8 E7.2 Insert picture report with an image

Exercise 7.3: Adding Graphics From Fonts

In addition to being able to add graphic images to a report, you can also add graphics that are stored in fonts like the Wingdings font. Fonts that have graphics can be accessed from the Character Map application in Windows. These graphics have to be placed in a text object. In this exercise you will add a graphic from a font to a report.

1. Save the E6.1 report as `E7.3 Graphics from fonts`.

2. Click the Start button (on the Windows taskbar) ⇒ All Programs (or Programs) ⇒ Accessories ⇒ System Tools ⇒ Character Map.

3. Open the Font drop-down list on the Character Map dialog box and select **WINGDINGS**, if it is not already selected.

   You should see the dialog box shown in Figure 7-9.

   Double-click on the document picture (the third picture from the right in the first row), then click the Copy button and close the dialog box.

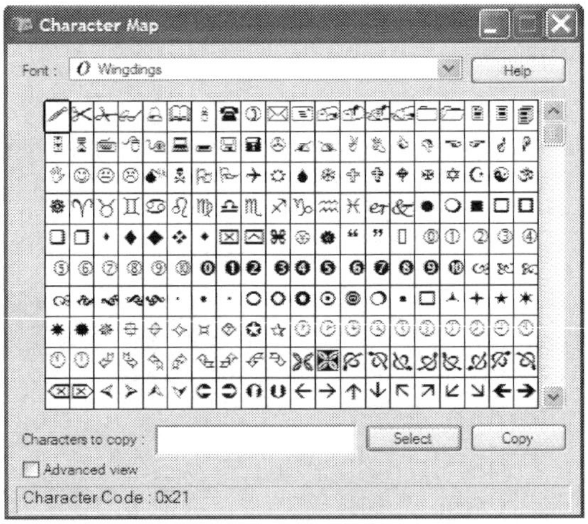

Figure 7-9 Character Map dialog box

4. Add a text object to the Details section after the Price field, then press the CTRL+V keys to paste the picture in the text object. The report should look like the one shown in Figure 7-10.

Product ID	Product Name	Price (SRP)	
1,101	Active Outdoors Crochet Glove	$14.50	🖹
1,102	Active Outdoors Crochet Glove	$14.50	🖹
1,103	Active Outdoors Crochet Glove	$14.50	🖹

Figure 7-10 E7.3 Graphics from fonts report

One reason to add an image next to each detail record is to create a hyperlink to another section of the report or to open a document or another report that has information that relates to the detail record.

The Format Editor

So far, all of the formatting that you have read about is considered basic formatting. For many reports that is all of the formatting that is required.

When you need to create additional formatting, you can use the Format Editor dialog box shown in Figure 7-11. Right-clicking on an object and selecting Format Object, opens this dialog box.

There are a lot of options for changing how objects look on a report. If the standard options on the Format Editor do not handle your needs you can create conditional formulas.

Many options on the Format Editor have a Formula button. Clicking on this button will let you create conditional formatting for a field or object.

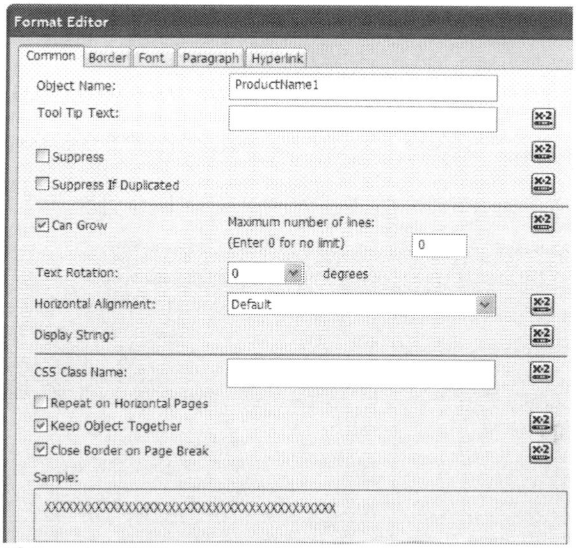

Figure 7-11 Common tab options

If you need to make the same change to several objects, select all of the objects that need the same change, prior to opening the Format Editor.

The options that are on the Format Editor dialog box will vary, depending on the type of object that is selected. When you open the Format Editor you will only see tabs that can be used for the field type that is selected. Table 7-1 explains all of the tabs on the Format Editor.

Tab	Data Type	Description
Common	All	The options shown above in Figure 7-11 can be used by most objects on a report. Table 7-2 explains the options on the Common tab.
Border	All	Add lines and drop shadows to fields.
Font	All except OLE & graphic objects	Select font, font size, font color, underlining, strike out and character spacing. Most of the options on this tab are also on the Crystal Reports - Insert toolbar.
Paragraph	String & Memo fields	Formats paragraphs that are stored in string or memo fields.
Hyperlink	All	Uses the selected object as a link to a web site, file, email address or a field on a web page.
Number	Number & Currency	Applies formatting options that are only for number fields. (1)
Date & Time	Date & Time fields	Applies formatting options that are only for date, time and date/time fields. (1)
Picture	Graphic	Crop, scale, reset and resize graphic images.
Boolean	Boolean	Select how Boolean values are displayed.

Table 7-1 Format Editor tab options explained

(1) Options on this tab support custom formatting.

Option	Description
Object Name	This field is filled in by default. You can accept the default name unless you have a need to use it in a formula and want to use a shorter or more descriptive name. It is not necessary to change the object name.
Tool Tip Text	Enter text in this field that you want displayed when the mouse pointer hovers over the field in Preview mode.
Suppress	Hides the object. When an object is suppressed it is grayed out. When a section is suppressed, it has diagonal lines through the section.
Suppress If Duplicated	Hides the object if it has the same value as the one in the prior record. In Figure 7-12, this option is enabled for the Product Name field.
Can Grow	Allows the field to expand vertically to accommodate more data. When selected, the **MAXIMUM NUMBER OF LINES** option is enabled, which is used to select the number of lines the field will display on the report.
Text Rotation	Is used to change the angle of the field.
Horizontal Alignment	Is used to select the horizontal alignment options for the selected objects.
Display String	Is used to create a formula to display a date, currency, number or Boolean field as a string field.
CSS Class Name	If the field will be formatted with a style sheet, enter the CSS Class Name that should be applied to the object.
Repeat on Horizontal Pages	This option is mostly used with a cross-tab or OLAP grid that will print horizontally across more than one page.
Keep Object Together	Keeps the object that will fit on one page from printing on more than one page. The object will be printed on the next page if it does not fit on the current page.
Close Border on Page Break	This option is used for fields that will print on more than one page and have a border. This option will print the bottom of the border of the object on the first page and print another border around the remaining data in the field that prints on the next page.
	The Formula button opens the Formula Workshop, which is used to create a formula to use with the option. You can also attach an existing formula to the option. You would use a formula when you need to control when the option is turned on or off, based on a condition. For example, if you wanted to highlight the order amount field of records that were in a certain dollar amount range.

Table 7-2 Common tab options explained

Product ID	Product Name	Product Type Name	Supplier Name
1,101	Active Outdoors Crochet	Gloves	Active Outdoors
1,102		Gloves	Active Outdoors
1,103		Gloves	Active Outdoors
1,104		Gloves	Active Outdoors
1,105		Gloves	Active Outdoors
1,106	Active Outdoors Lycra G	Gloves	Active Outdoors
1,107		Gloves	Active Outdoors

Figure 7-12 Suppress If Duplicated option illustrated

Sections that are manually suppressed have diagonal lines as shown in Figure 7-13. If you later add data to a suppressed section, as shown, it will not be displayed on the report. To remove the suppression, right-click on the section bar and select **DON'T SUPPRESS**, as illustrated.

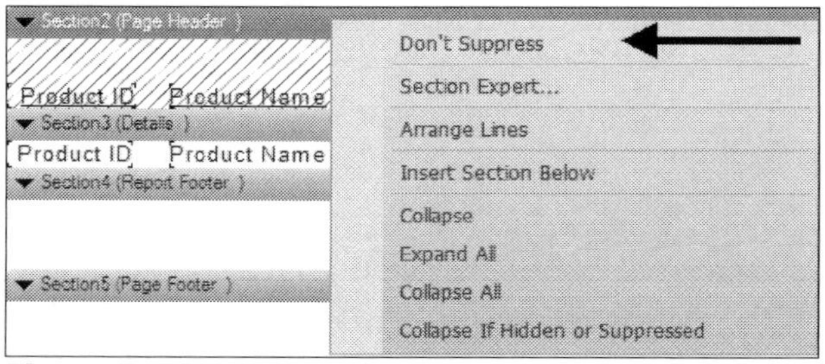

Figure 7-13 Suppressed section

The Toolbox

The Toolbox shown in Figure 7-14 contains options that you can use to enhance reports. By default when Crystal Reports is installed, the Toolbox is pinned to the left side of the workspace.

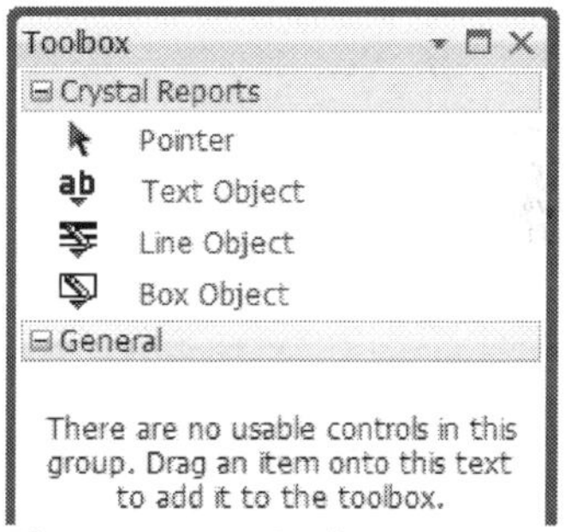

Figure 7-14 Toolbox

The **TEXT OBJECT** option is the same one that you have already read about.

The **LINE OBJECT** is used to draw a line on the report.

The **BOX OBJECT** is used to draw a box around an object on the report. This option is also available on the shortcut menu when you right-click in the report.

All of these options are also on the Crystal Reports ⇒ Insert menu. You can also access these options by right-clicking on a blank space in the report and selecting the Insert submenu. There are three ways to open the Toolbox as listed below.

① View ⇒ Toolbox.

② Click the Toolbox button on the Standard toolbar.

③ Click the Toolbox button on the Explorer toolbar.

Format A Text Object

1. Open the E7.1 report and right-click on the report title, then select **FORMAT OBJECT**.

2. On the **BORDER** tab you will see the options shown in Figure 7-15. Table 7-3 explains the options on this tab. Change the **LINE STYLE** to single for the Left, Right and Top options.

   Notice at the bottom of the dialog box in the **SAMPLE** section that you can see the options that you have applied to the object.

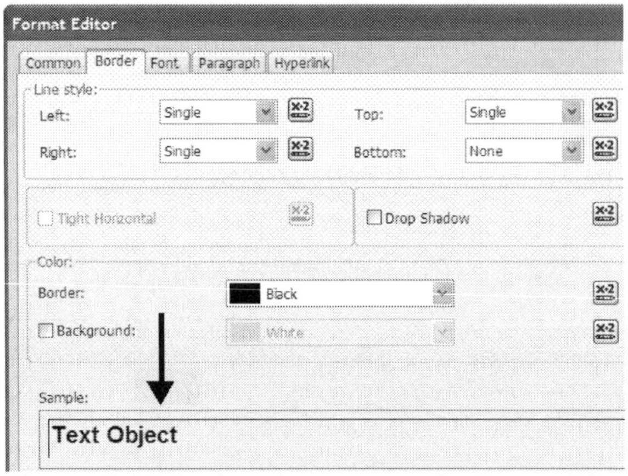

Figure 7-15 Border tab options on the Format Editor dialog box

Option	Description
Line Style	These four options are used to select the line style for each side of the object. Notice that these options can be set conditionally. You can use the Bottom option to apply a double line below a field. This is often used in financial reports.
Tight Horizontal	Removes space from around the border. This option can resize fields because the border is around the length of the value in the field, not the physical size of the field.
Drop Shadow	Adds the shadow effect to the lower right corner of the object.
Border Color	Select a color for the border and drop shadow.
Background Color	Select the color for the background of the object.

Table 7-3 Border tab options explained

3. Check the **DROP SHADOW** and **BACKGROUND** options.

   Open the Background drop-down list and select **YELLOW**, as shown in Figure 7-16.

   The report should look like the one shown in Figure 7-17.

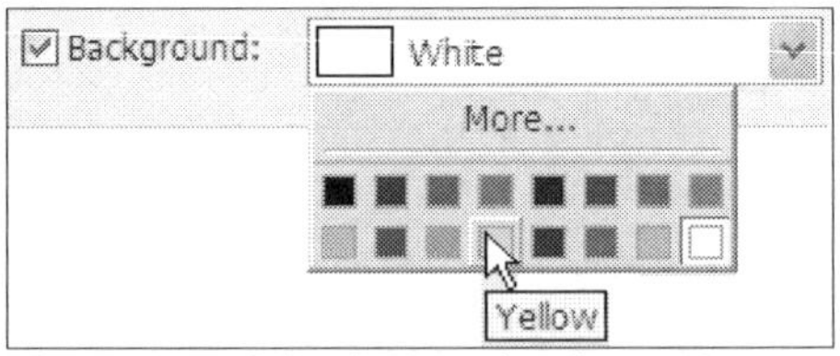

Figure 7-16 Background color options

> If selected, the **MORE** option shown above in Figure 7-16 will open the Color dialog box, which has additional colors that can be selected or create a custom color.

Figure 7-17 E7.1 report with formatting applied to a text object

4. Open the E5.3 report and add a title to the Report Header section that says `Customer Orders Report`. Format it like the one shown above in Figure 7-17.

The Can Grow Option

Earlier I mentioned that one reason data gets truncated is because there may not be enough room in the section of the report to accommodate all of the data. In the part of the exercise that you just completed, there was enough room to make the field longer. If you have tried everything possible to get all of the data to fit, but it won't, the **CAN GROW** option should fix the problem. This option will cause the data in the field to wrap to a new line, only when needed. Fields that have this option enabled, will only grow longer, not wider. Follow the steps below to learn how to use this option.

> The Can Grow option can only be used with string fields (also known as character fields), text objects and memo fields.

1. Open the E7.2 report. Right-click on the object(s) that you want to apply the Can Grow option to and select **FORMAT OBJECT**. For this exercise, right-click on the Product Name field.

> You can also click on the field and then click the **OBJECT PROPERTIES** button on the Crystal Reports - Main toolbar to open the Format Editor.

2. On the Common tab, check the **CAN GROW** option, then click OK.

If you want to limit the maximum number of lines that a field can print on the report, enter it in the **MAXIMUM NUMBER OF LINES** field to the right of the Can Grow option. For example, if you are applying the Can Grow option to a memo field that could have 500 characters or more of text, you may not want to have all of the text in the field print on the report. If this is the case, you would enter a number in the Maximum number of lines field so that only the first two or three lines of information in the field will actually print on the report. The Can Grow option, even when enabled will only be activated when needed. It does not force every record to expand to the number entered in the field.

If you use the Can Grow option on a field and there is another field below it, it is possible that the field below will be overwritten. To prevent this, the following options are available.

① Put the field with the Can Grow option at the bottom of the section.

② Not as effective as the first option, but you can check the spacing to make sure that the field with the Can Grow option is not close to other fields.

3. Resize the Product Name field so that it ends at the 2.5 inch mark.

   The report should look similar to the one shown in Figure 7-18.

Product ID	Product Name	Price (SRP)
1,101	Active Outdoors Crochet Glove	$14.50
1,102	Active Outdoors Crochet Glove	$14.50
1,103	Active Outdoors Crochet Glove	$14.50

Figure 7-18 Can Grow option applied to the Product Name field

Text Rotation

There may be times when some of the text on a report will look better if it is rotated. Figure 7-19 shows the degrees that text can be rotated. Select the text that you want to rotate, then select the degree rotation on the Common tab. Figure 7-20 shows the Product ID heading rotated 90 degrees.

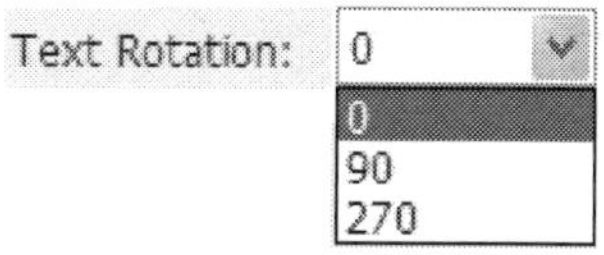

Figure 7-19 Text rotation options illustrated

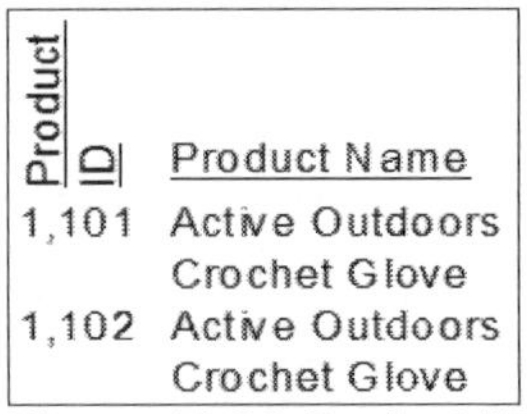

Figure 7-20 Product ID heading rotated 90 degrees

Paragraph Tab

When you are applying formatting to a text object, string or memo field, you will see the Paragraph tab shown in Figure 7-21.

The options on this tab are used to select how text fields that have multiple lines of data or text will be formatted.

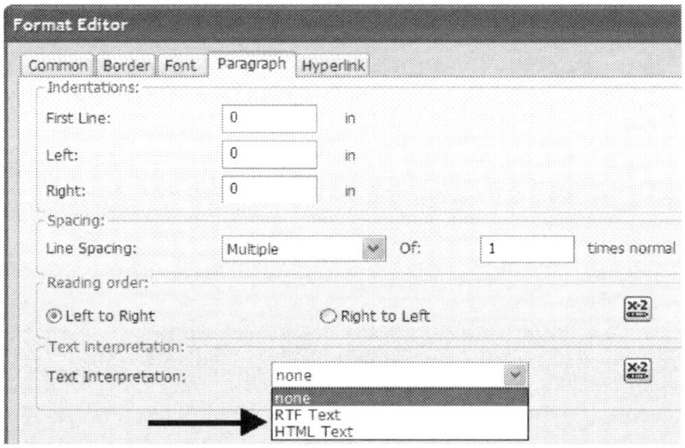

Figure 7-21 Paragraph tab on the Format Editor

> The **TEXT INTERPRETATION** option illustrated above in Figure 7-21 is not available for text objects. These options are helpful if the field has **HTML** (Hypertext Markup Language) formatting, which is used for web pages or **RTF** (Rich Text Format) formatting for text that may have special formatting from word processing or publishing software.

Hyperlink Tab

The options shown in Figure 7-22 are used to create a hyperlink to a website, email address, file, current website field value or current email field value.

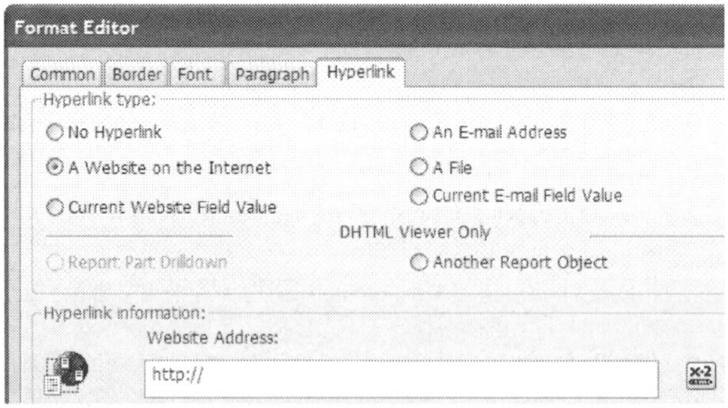

Figure 7-22 Hyperlink tab options

Exercise 7.4: Format Numeric Fields

Usually, order numbers do not have any formatting. As you saw earlier in Figure 7-20, the Product ID field has a comma. This field would look better if it did not have any formatting. Follow the steps below to change the formatting of the Product ID field.

1. Save the E7.2 report as `E7.4 Format a numeric field`.

2. Right-click on the Product ID field, then select **FORMAT OBJECT**.

   You will see the dialog box shown in Figure 7-23.

   Click on the option **-1123**.

   The minus sign will only print if the number is negative.

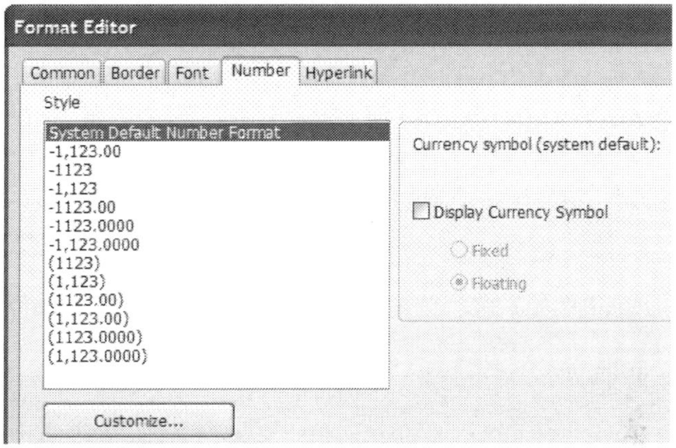

Figure 7-23 Number tab options

3. Preview the report. The Product ID field should not have a comma in it. Save the changes and leave the report open to complete the next part of the exercise.

If none of the options shown above in Figure 7-23 meet your needs to format currency or number fields, click the **CUSTOMIZE** button.

You will see the options shown in Figure 7-24 if the field that you are formatting is a currency field.

You will see the options shown in Figure 7-25 if the field that you are formatting is a number field.

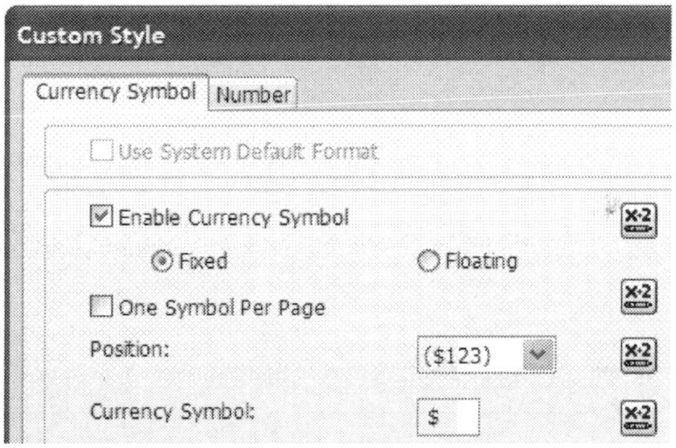

Figure 7-24 Currency symbol options

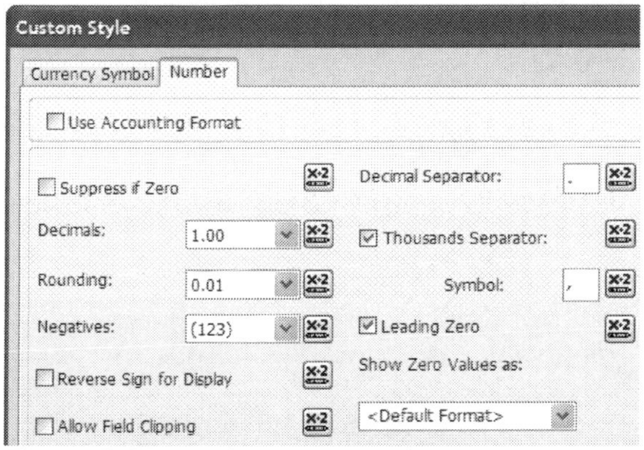

Figure 7-25 Number custom style options

Usually, the **DECIMALS** and **ROUNDING** options shown above in Figure 7-25 are set to the same number of decimal places.

Exercise 7.5: Format A Date/Time Field

Displaying the time as part of a date field is usually not needed on reports. To keep the time portion of a Date/Time field from printing on the report, the field needs to be formatted. Follow the steps below to change the formatting of a Date/Time field.

1. Save the E5.3 report as `E7.5 Format dates.`

2. Right-click on the Order Date field and select Format Object. You will see the dialog box shown in Figure 7-26.

   If you click the **CUSTOMIZE** button you will see the dialog box shown in Figure 7-27, which is used to change the formatting for a date.

   The options shown on Figure 7-28 are used to change the formatting for the time field or portion of a date/time field.

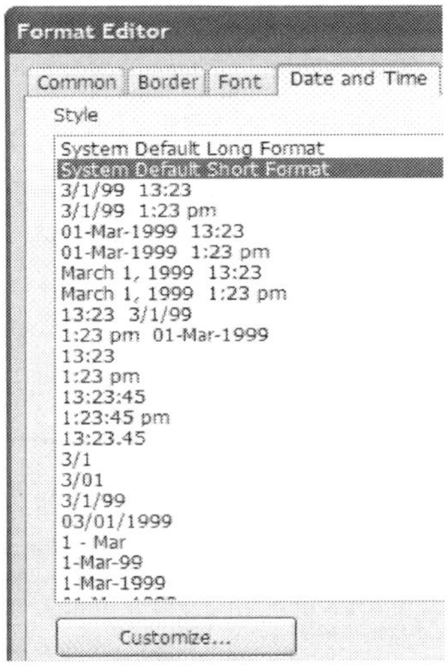

Figure 7-26 Date and Time tab options

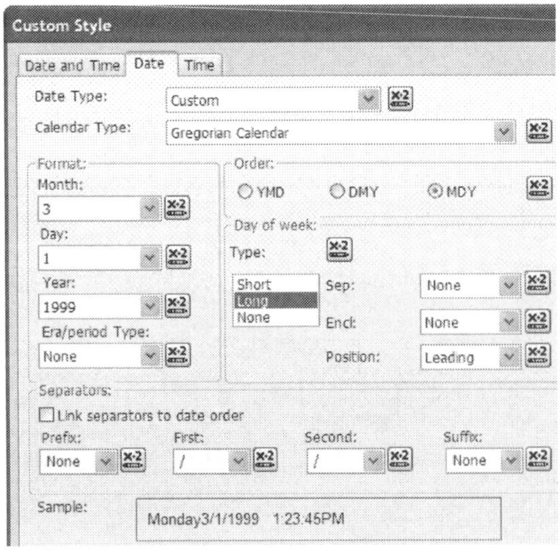

Figure 7-27 Date custom style options

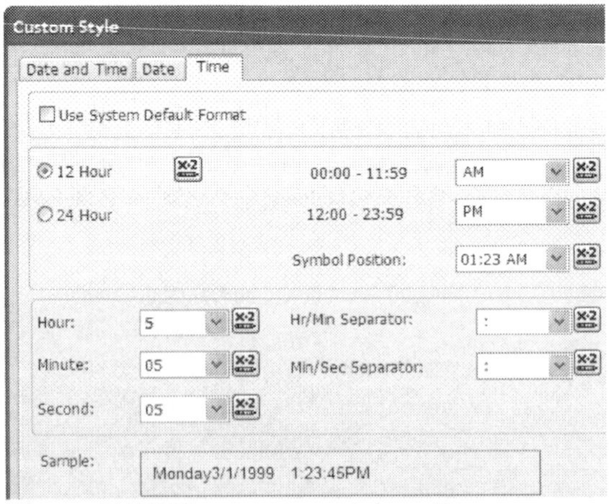

Figure 7-28 Time custom style options

3. Click on the option **3/1/99** on the Date and Time tab on the Format Editor dialog box.

4. Format the Order ID field so that it does not have a comma. The report should look like the one shown in Figure 7-29. You should not see the time on the Order Date field.

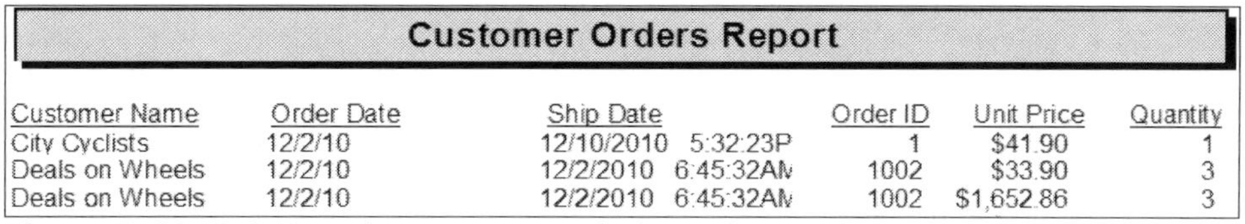
Customer Orders Report

Customer Name	Order Date	Ship Date	Order ID	Unit Price	Quantity
City Cyclists	12/2/10	12/10/2010 5:32:23P	1	$41.90	1
Deals on Wheels	12/2/10	12/2/2010 6:45:32AM	1002	$33.90	3
Deals on Wheels	12/2/10	12/2/2010 6:45:32AM	1002	$1,652.86	3

Figure 7-29 E5.3 Text objects report with the Order Number and Order Date fields modified

Picture Tab

Earlier in this chapter you added an image file to the E7.2 Insert picture report. The image would look better if it had a border and was resized. The options on the Picture tab are used to scale an image, as well as, crop and resize the image. The Picture object supports the following image formats: JPG, usually used for photos, TIFF, PNG and BMP, which is not used much these days.

Exercise 7.6: Resize The Image File

1. Save the E7.2 report as `E7.6 Resize the image file.`

2. Right-click on the image and select Format Object.

   Click on the **PICTURE** tab. You will see the dialog box shown in Figure 7-30.

   Table 7-4 explains the options on the Picture tab.

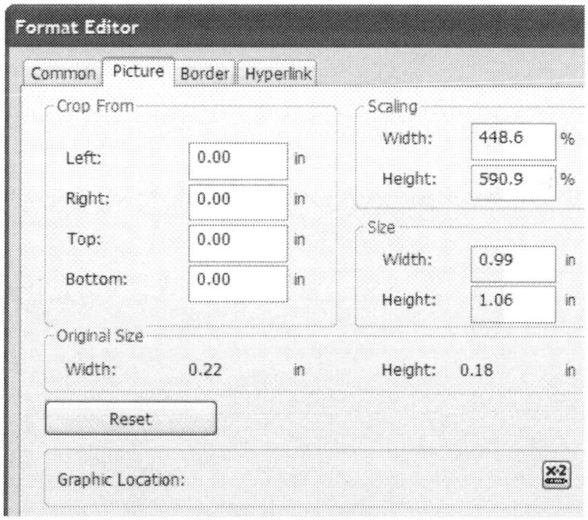

Figure 7-30 Picture tab options

Option	Description
Crop From	Removes the part of the image that is on the outside of the crop lines that are created when you enter the dimensions in any or all of the four crop options (left, right, top or bottom). Positive numbers cut into the image. Negative numbers add a white space between the edge of the image and the frame around the image. Cropping starts at the edge of the image.
Scaling	Enlarge or reduce the image by a percent.
Size	Change the width and height of the image.

Table 7-4 Picture tab options explained

Option	Description
Reset button	Removes all of the formatting that was applied to the image on the Picture tab. When you crop, scale or size an image, the original image file is not changed. It is only displayed differently on the report, based on the options that are selected.
Graphic Location	Is used to dynamically change images by listing a default image to use if the image in the report is not found.

Table 7-4 Picture tab options explained (Continued)

3. Change the scaling **WIDTH** option to `200`, then change the scaling **HEIGHT** option to `200`. Figure 7-31 shows the image before it was scaled. Figure 7-32 shows the image after scaling. Leave the report open to complete the next part of the exercise.

Figure 7-31 Image before scaling

Figure 7-32 Image after scaling

Add A Border To The Image

1. Click on the image, then open the Format Editor and click on the Border tab.

2. Change all four **LINE STYLE** options to Dotted. The image should look like the one shown in Figure 7-33.

Figure 7-33 Image border modified

Exercise 7.7: Format A Boolean Field

In this exercise you will change how the data in a Boolean field is displayed on a report.

1. Create a new report and save it as `E7.7 Boolean formatting`.

2. Add the following fields from the Orders table: Order ID, Order Date, Shipped and Payment Received. The report should look like the one shown in Figure 7-34.

The Shipped and Payment Received fields are Boolean fields. As you can see, they both are displaying true or false. You will format these fields so that they display Yes and No instead. Doing this does not change the data in the table.

Order ID	Order Date	Shipped	Payment Received
1	12/2/2010 12:00:00AI	True	True
1,002	12/2/2010 12:00:00AI	True	True
1,003	12/2/2010 12:00:00AI	True	True
1,004	12/2/2010 12:00:00AI	True	True
1,005	12/3/2010 12:00:00AI	True	True
1,006	12/3/2010 12:00:00AI	True	True

Figure 7-34 E7.4 Boolean formatting report

3. Select both Boolean fields, then right-click and select Format Multiple Objects.

4. On the Boolean tab, open the **BOOLEAN TEXT** drop-down list and select Yes or No, as shown in Figure 7-35. The value in the Shipped and Payment Received fields is now displayed as Yes or No instead of True and False. If you go to page 28 of the report and look for Order ID # 2800, you will see that not all of the data in these fields is Yes, as shown in Figure 7-36.

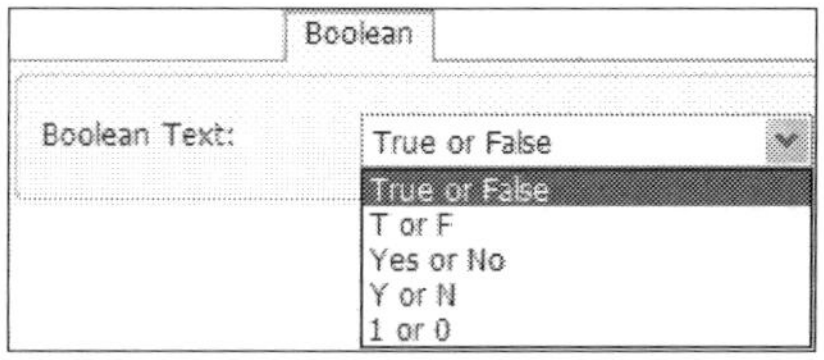

Figure 7-35 Boolean tab options

Order ID	Order Date	Shipped	Payment Received
2,797	3/7/2012 12:00:00AM	Yes	Yes
2,798	3/8/2012 12:00:00AM	Yes	Yes
2,799	3/8/2012 12:00:00AM	Yes	Yes
2,800	3/8/2012 12:00:00AM	Yes	No
2,801	3/8/2012 12:00:00AM	Yes	No

Figure 7-36 Boolean fields displayed differently on the report

Exercise 7.8: Using The Format Painter

This is a pretty cool feature. It is used to copy the formatting from one object to several other objects with a mouse click. Formatting properties like the font, font size, font color and borders can be taken from a text object and applied to a numeric object. This is because this type of formatting is not specific to a data type. Usually, number specific formatting cannot be applied to other data types. There are three ways to start the Format Painter as discussed below, **AFTER** you have clicked on the object that has the formatting that you want to apply (copy) to other objects.

① Right-click on the object and select Format Painter.

② Click the **FORMAT PAINTER** button on the Standard toolbar.

③ Format ⇒ Format Painter.

There are some things that the Format Painter cannot do, as discussed below.

① The Format Painter cannot copy a format that is created with the Highlighting Expert.

② Formatting cannot be copied from text objects or templates to fields in a table.

③ Formatted objects in the repository can be copied to reports. Formatting from reports cannot be copied to objects in the repository.

④ The Format Painter does not copy hyperlink properties.

⑤ The Format Painter will copy all formatting to other objects of the same data type. If formatting is copied from one data type to a different data type, only the formatting options that the objects have in common will be copied.

Change The Formatting Of An Object

To learn how to use this feature you need to change the formatting of an object.

1. Save the E7.2 report as `E7.8 Format Painter`.

2. Change the font of the Product Name heading to Times New Roman, Size 10 and Bold.

Apply The Formatting To Other Objects

1. With the Product Name heading selected, turn on the Format Painter.

2. When you hold the mouse pointer over the Product ID heading, it will change to a **PAINT BRUSH**, as illustrated in Figure 7-37.

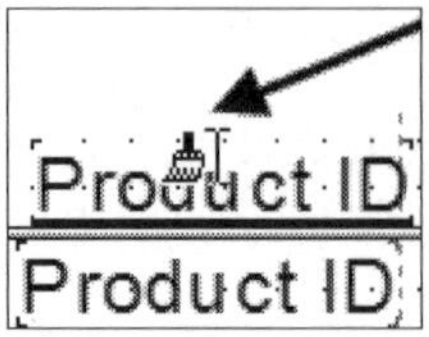

Figure 7-37 Mouse pointer in position to apply formatting

3. Click on the Product ID heading. The formatting from the Product Name heading should have been applied to the Product ID heading.

Using The Format Painter On Multiple Objects

If you need to apply the same formatting to more than one object, follow the steps below.

1. Select the object that has the formatting that you want to apply to other objects. For this exercise, click on the Product ID heading.

2. Turn on the Format Painter, then press and hold down the **ALT** key.

3. Click on the first object that you want to change. In this exercise, click on the Product Name heading, then click on the Price heading. The headings should all have the same formatting. Save the changes and close the report.

If you tried to apply this formatting to the image, the mouse pointer would change to the symbol illustrated in Figure 7-38.

This symbol is used to let you know that the formatting cannot be applied to the object that you are holding the mouse pointer over.

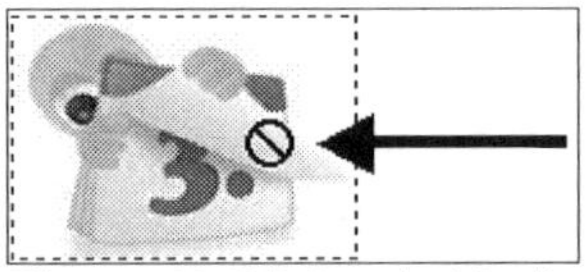
Figure 7-38 Symbol indicating that the formatting cannot be applied to the object

Exercise 7.9: Center Data Under A Heading

The Customer information report that you created in Exercise 5.1 would look better if the following changes were made.

① Center the Region field under the heading.

② Put a line under each detail record to make the report easier to read.

1. Save the E5.1 report as `E7.9 Modified customer information`.

2. Select the Region field and heading, then click the **CENTER** button on the Crystal Reports - Main toolbar.

3. Make the Region field and heading smaller. The data should now be centered under the heading. Move the Country and Postal Code fields left.

How To Add Horizontal Lines To A Report

One way to make the data in the Details section of a report easier to read is to place a line under the fields in this section. Like other objects, you can format lines that you add to a report. There are three ways to open the **LINE** tool, as discussed below.

① Right-click in the report ⇒ Insert ⇒ Line.
② Crystal Reports ⇒ Insert ⇒ Line.
③ Select the option on the Toolbox.

Follow the steps below to add a line to the Details section of the E7.9 report.

1. Move the Details section bar down a little.

2. Open the **LINE** tool. The mouse pointer will change to a pencil. Draw a line under the fields in the Details section.

Format The Line

Follow the steps below to learn how to format a line.

1. Right-click on the line and select **FORMAT OBJECT**. You will see the dialog box shown in Figure 7-39.

   Open the **STYLE** drop-down list and select Single, if it is not already selected.

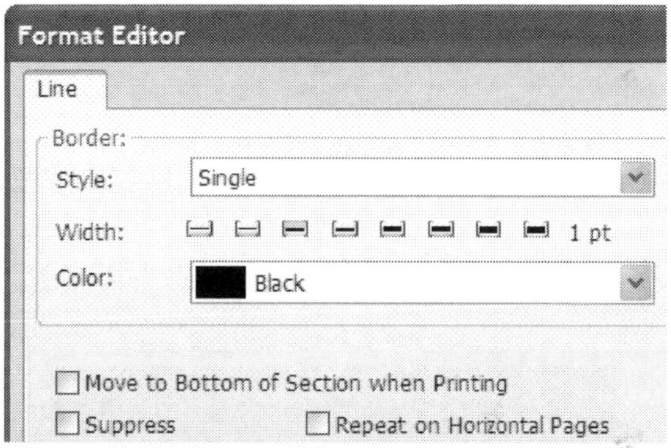

Figure 7-39 Format Editor horizontal line options

> The **MOVE TO BOTTOM OF SECTION WHEN PRINTING** option is often used for lines in a section of the report that has a field with the Can Grow option enabled, like a Notes field. Checking this option will force the line to print at the bottom of the section, which is what you usually want. You can test how this option works by checking the option and making the section of the report longer that has the line and preview the report.

2. Click on the first button in the **WIDTH** section. You should see the word **HAIRLINE** at the end of the Width options. The report should look like the one shown in Figure 7-40. Notice that the Region field data is centered under the heading.

Customer Name	Address1	Region	Country	Postal Code
City Cyclists	7464 South Kingswa	MI	USA	48358
Pathfinders	410 Eighth Avenue	IL	USA	60148
Bike-A-Holics Anony	7429 Arbutus Boule\	OH	USA	43005

Figure 7-40 E7.9 Modified customer information report with the Details section modified

Exercise 7.10: Add Vertical Lines To A Report

In the previous exercise you learned how to add horizontal lines to a report. In this exercise you will learn how to add vertical lines to a report.

1. Save the E5.1 report as `E7.10 Vertical lines`.

2. Make the Region and Country fields smaller, then move the Country and Postal Code fields over to the left.

3. Open the Line tool. Draw a vertical line in the Details section, after the Customer Name field.

4. Right-click on the vertical line that you just created and select Copy, then right-click anyplace in the report and select Paste. The mouse pointer will have a picture of the line next to it. Repeat this step to place a vertical line after every field in the Details section except the Postal Code field. The report should look like the one shown in Figure 7-41.

Customer Name	Address 1	Region	Country	Postal Code
City Cyclists	7464 South Kingsway	MI	USA	48358
Pathfinders	410 Eighth Avenue	IL	USA	60148
Bike-A-Holics Anonymous	7429 Arbutus Boulevard	OH	USA	43005
Psycho-Cycle	8287 Scott Road	AL	USA	35818
Sporting Wheels Inc.	480 Grant Way	CA	USA	92150

Figure 7-41 E7.10 Vertical lines report

You can also draw vertical lines through sections of the report. In the report that you just added vertical lines to, you can make the vertical lines longer by clicking on the line and dragging the top blue square on the line up, so that it is above the field heading in the Page Header section. The report would look like the one shown in Figure 7-42.

Customer Name	Address1	Region	Country	Postal Code
City Cyclists	7464 South Kingsway	MI	USA	48358
Pathfinders	410 Eighth Avenue	IL	USA	60148
Bike-A-Holics Anonymous	7429 Arbutus Boulevard	OH	USA	43005
Psycho-Cycle	8287 Scott Road	AL	USA	35818
Sporting Wheels Inc.	480 Grant Way	CA	USA	92150

Figure 7-42 Report with lines extended into the Page Header section

If an object has the Can Grow option enabled, the object will grow but the vertical line will not grow by default, as shown in Figure 7-43. You will see breaks in the vertical line. To fix this, check the **EXTEND TO BOTTOM OF SECTION WHEN PRINTING** option shown in Figure 7-44.

Customer Name	Address1	Region	Country	Postal Code
City Cyclists	7464 South Kingsway	MI	USA	48358
Pathfinders	410 Eighth Avenue	IL	USA	60148
Bike-A-Holics Anonymous	7429 Arbutus Boulevard	OH	USA	43005
Psycho-Cycle	8287 Scott Road	AL	USA	35818
Sporting Wheels Inc.	480 Grant Way	CA	USA	92150

Figure 7-43 Can Grow option and vertical lines

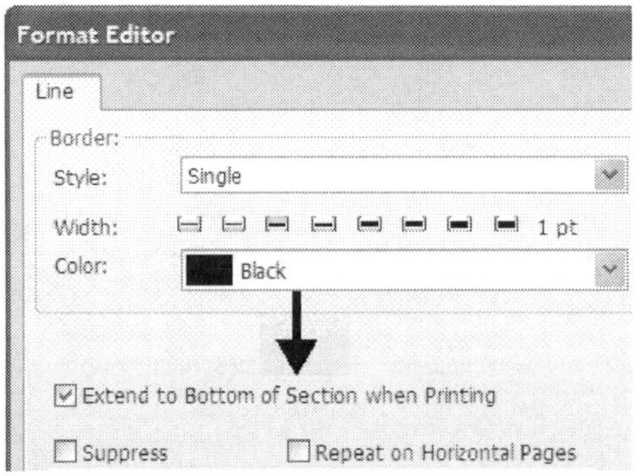

Figure 7-44 Format Editor options for a vertical line

SELECTING RECORDS

After completing the exercises in this chapter you will be able to use the following techniques to control which records will appear on a report:

- ☑ The Select Expert
- ☑ Filter and query records
- ☑ Create report summary information

CHAPTER 8

Selecting Records Overview

So far you have learned to create a variety of basic reports. All of the reports that you created without a wizard retrieved all of the records in the tables. As you saw, many of the reports contained 500 or more detail records. Most of the time reports provide specific information, which means that all of the records in the tables selected should not be on every report that is created. For reports that use tables similar to the size of the ones used in this book, this may not be a problem. But if the report is using tables or other data sources with thousands or millions of records (think credit card statements), the report will take a long time to run. Not only will you notice this on your computer, which may run out of memory, the network will also take a performance hit.

One way that Crystal Reports lets you narrow down the records that will appear on the report is through a selection process. This selection process uses the **SELECT EXPERT**. This tool is used to specify which records will appear on the report by entering **CRITERIA** that a record must meet. Records that do not meet the criteria will not appear on the report. This process is also known as **FILTERING RECORDS** or **QUERYING THE DATABASE**. Other ways to select records include writing formulas and using functions.

When you used a wizard to create a report, you created a filter on the Record Selection screen. The Record Selection screen has similar functionality to the Select Expert that you will learn how to use in this chapter.

Examples of the types of information that can be retrieved when selecting, filtering records or querying the database, include the following:

① Orders that were placed during a specific date range, like the month of June, last year.
② Customers that purchased a specific product.
③ Orders that are over a certain dollar amount.
④ Products that need to be reordered.

Selecting, filtering or querying the database lets you ask a question about the data and then retrieve the records that meet the criteria that you specify. The records that are retrieved are known as a **RECORDSET**. The examples above are only asking one question. More than one question can be asked in the same query. The following types of multi-part questions can be asked.

① Orders that were placed during a specific date range and are more than $500.
② Customers that purchased a specific product and live in a specific state.
③ Orders that are over a certain dollar amount that are for a specific salesperson.
④ Customers that have a credit limit of $1,000 or more and have placed at least one order over $2,500, that shipped during a specific date range.
⑤ Orders that were placed or shipped during a specific date range.

Like SQL, the selection process produces the same results. Think of the Select Expert as an SQL code generator, without actually having to write code. The Select Expert creates the SQL code for you, which makes the Select Expert easy to use. The SQL code though, is what Crystal Reports uses to select records for the report.

In addition to selecting individual records, the Select Expert can also select groups. A group selection example would be to only display records in states that have an order total amount between $100,000 and $400,000.

The Select Expert provides two ways to select records as discussed below:

① Use the built-in **OPERATORS**. Table 8-1 explains the operators. Not all of the operators listed in the table are available for all field types.

② **FORMULAS** are used to write the SQL code. This is not a contradiction to what I said earlier about not having to write code to use the Select Expert, because writing code in the Select Expert is not mandatory.

Operator	This Operator Selects Records That . . .
Is Equal To	Are equal to the value that you specify.
Is Not Equal To	Are not equal to the value that you specify. (1)
Is One Of	Match at least one of the values that you specify. If the criteria is NY, NJ or PA for the state field, any record that has one of these values in the State field would appear on the report.
Is Not One Of	Are not one of the values that you specify. (1)
Is Less Than	Are less than the value that you specify. If you want to see products that have a reorder level of less than 10 items in stock, enter 10 in the criteria field and the report will display products with a reorder level of nine or less. (2)
Is Less Than Or Equal To	Are less than or equal to the value that you specify. It works similar to the Is Less Than operator. The difference is that this operator will also select records that have the value that you specify. In the less than example above, the report would not display records with a reorder level of 10 items. The less than or equal to operator will. (2)
Is Greater Than	Have a value greater than the value that you specify. If you want to see all orders with an order amount over $500, enter $500 in the criteria field and the report will display records with an order amount of $500.01 or more.
Is Greater Than Or Equal To	Are greater than or equal to the value that you specify. It works similar to the Is Greater Than operator. The difference is that this operator will also select records that have the value that you specify. In the greater than example above, the report would not display records with an order amount of exactly $500. The greater than or equal to operator will.
Is Between	Fall between two values. If you want to see order amounts between $1,000 and $5,000 or orders between 6/1/10 and 6/15/10, this is the operator that you would use. This operator also selects records equal to the two values that you enter for the range.
Is Not Between	Are not in the range of values that you enter. It will retrieve records outside of the range that you select. (1)
Starts With	Begin with a specific character or set of characters. If you want to retrieve records of employees whose last name starts with the letter "M", use this operator. (3)
Does Not Start With	Do not start with the character or set of characters that you specify. (1) (3)
Is Like	Meet the wildcard criteria that you specify. The wildcard characters that you can use are a ? (question mark) and an * (asterisk). (3)
Is Not Like	Do not meet the criteria that you specify with the wildcards. (1) (3)
Is In The Period	Meet the criteria of one of the functions explained in Table 8-2. These functions will save you a lot of time because you do not have to figure out how to write the formula. (4)

Table 8-1 Select Expert operators explained

Operator	This Operator Selects Records That . . .
Is Not In The Period	Are not in the period that you select. (1) (4)
Is True	Have a value of true in the Boolean field. (5)
Is False	Have a value of false in the Boolean field. (5)
Formula	Meet the criteria of one of the functions explained in Table 8-2. These functions will save you a lot of time because you do not have to figure out how to write the formula. (4)

Table 8-1 Select Expert operators explained (Continued)

(1) This operator works the opposite of the operator above it in the table.
(2) This operator can also be used with a string field.
(3) This operator can only be used with a string field.
(4) This operator can only be used with date and date/time fields.
(5) This operator can only be used with a Boolean field.

In addition to the operators listed above in Table 8-1, there is another operator, **IS ANY VALUE**, which is the default operator that you see when the Select Expert is first opened. This operator does not apply any condition to the field that it is associated to. In reports that do not have criteria, this is the operator that is used when the report is run.

Is In The Period Functions

The functions in Table 8-2 provide a date range. You can create the same criteria using the Is Between operator, but using these built-in functions is easier and does not require dates to be hard coded.

Function	When It Starts And Ends . . .
Week To Date From Sun	From last Sunday to today
Month To Date	From the beginning of the current month to today
Year To Date	From the first day of the current year to today
Last 7 Days	From 7 days ago to today
Last 4 Weeks To Sun	From 4 weeks prior to last Sunday to last Sunday
Last Full Week	From Sunday of last week to Saturday of last week
Last Full Month	From the first day of last month to the last day of last month
All Dates To Today	From the earliest date in the table up to and including today
All Dates To Yesterday	From the earliest date in the table up to and including yesterday
All Dates From Today	From today forward
All Dates From Tomorrow	From yesterday forward
Aged 0 To 30 Days	From 30 days ago to today
Aged 31 To 60 Days	From 31 days ago from today to 60 days ago
Aged 61 To 90 Days	From 61 days ago from today to 90 days ago
Over 90 Days	More than 90 days ago
Next 30 days	From today to 30 days in the future
Next 31 To 60 Days	From 31 days from today to 60 days in the future
Next 61 To 90 Days	From 61 days from today to 90 days in the future
Next 91 To 365 Days	From 91 days from today to 365 days in the future
Calendar 1st Qtr	From January 1 of the current year to March 31 of the current year

Table 8-2 Is in the period criteria functions explained

Function	When It Starts And Ends . . .
Calendar 2nd Qtr	From April 1 of the current year to June 30 of the current year
Calendar 3rd Qtr	From July 1 of the current year to September 30 of the current year
Calendar 4th Qtr	From October 1 of the current year to December 31 of the current year
Calendar 1st Half	From January 1 of the current year to June 30 of the current year
Calendar 2nd Half	From July 1 of the current year to December 31 of the current year
Last Year MTD	From the first day of the current month last year to the same month and day last year
Last Year YTD	From January 1 of last year to today's month and day last year

Table 8-2 Is in the period criteria functions explained (Continued)

Using The Select Expert

As shown in Figure 8-1, the Select Expert is used to create criteria by record, group or saved data.

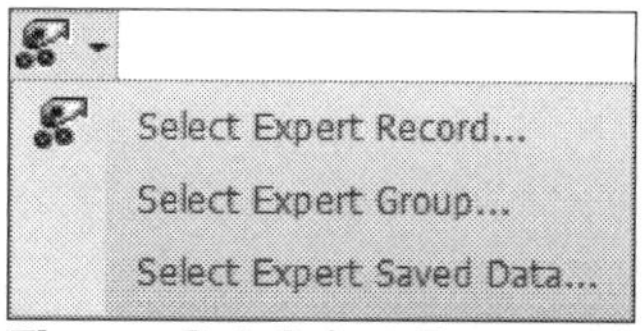

Figure 8-1 Select Expert submenu options

The **SELECT EXPERT RECORD** option creates criteria for a field. This option filters records from being retrieved from tables.

Use the **SELECT EXPERT GROUP** option when the criteria has to be based on a group name or summary field. This option displays the groups based on the group selection criteria after the record selection has retrieved records. Group selection hides groups that do not meet the criteria.

Use the **SELECT EXPERT SAVED DATA** option when you want to filter data that has been saved with the report. This option does not cause data to be refreshed like the record and group options do. Chapter 4 covered indexes and how they cause records to be retrieved faster because tables that are indexed are optimized.

For the most part, using the Select Expert is point and click. The only time that you have to type is if the value that you want to use is not in the drop-down list. This sometimes happens because the drop-down list only displays the first 500 unique values in a field. Any field that has multiple values that are identical will only display the value once in the drop-down list. An example of this would be a date field because it is possible that multiple records have the same date in the same field.

If you want to create a customer order report and only want to display records for the Wheels Company, this company name may not appear in the drop-down list because there could be more than 500 companies in the table and this company name is near the end of the alphabet. This is an example of when you would have to type something in the Select Expert.

The other time that you would need to type something in the Select Expert is if you are using a value that you know is not one of the values for the field. For example, if you want to select records that have an order amount greater than $600. You may have to type 600 in the field if the Order Amount field does not have that value in any of the first 500 values that are in the drop-down list.

Unless stated otherwise, when opening the Select Expert to complete exercises in this book, select the Record option or just click the Select Expert button. There are three ways to open the Select Expert, as explained below:

① Right-click on the field that you want to create criteria for and select, Select Expert.

② Click the **SELECT EXPERT** button on the Crystal Reports - Main toolbar.

③ Crystal Reports ⇒ Report ⇒ Select Expert.

If you click on the field that you want to create the criteria for before you select option two or three above, the Select Expert will open with the field selected and you can start to create the selection criteria.

The exercises in this chapter will show you how to create a variety of queries using the operators that you read about earlier in Table 8-1. Hopefully after completing these exercises, you will feel comfortable using the Select Expert.

Exercise 8.1: Using The Is Equal To Operator

In this exercise you will use the Select Expert to find customers that are in the CA region. The region field contains the same data as a state field.

1. Save the E7.9 report as `E8.1 Region = CA`.

2. Add the Record Number special field to the Report Footer section. Preview the report. Go to the last page of the report. Notice that there are 269 records in the report.

3. Use one of the last two options discussed earlier to open the Select Expert.

   You will see the dialog box shown in Figure 8-2. You will learn how to use the first option in the next exercise.

   The reason that you see the Choose Field dialog box is because a field was not selected in the report prior to opening the Select Expert.

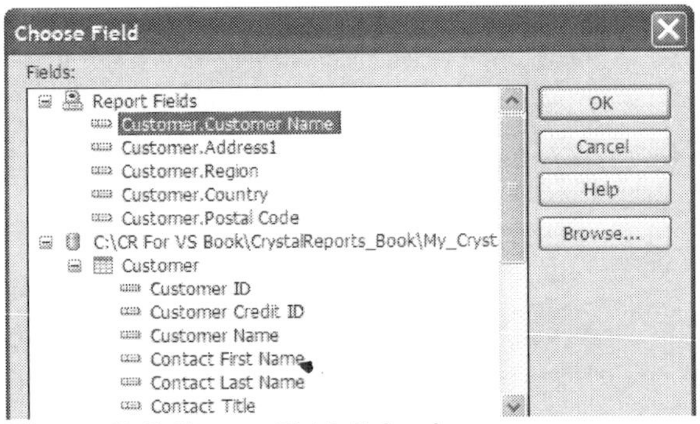

Figure 8-2 Choose Field dialog box

The **REPORT FIELDS** section at the top of the dialog box lists the fields that are currently on the report. Below that section you will see all of the data sources that are connected to the report. You can use any field in the Choose Field dialog box as a field for the selection criteria, whether or not it is being displayed on the report.

> **Selecting Records Limitation**
> You cannot use summary fields or formula fields that use summary fields as selection criteria. This is because of the three pass data collection model that Crystal Reports uses. Summary fields are not calculated until the second pass. Selecting records for the report is done in the first pass, which means that the summary field calculations have not been processed when the records are being selected. The work around is to create group selection summary fields which you will learn about.

4. Click on the **CUSTOMER.REGION** field in the Report Fields section, then click OK. You will see the dialog box shown in Figure 8-3. Notice that the field that you selected is the name on the first tab. Multiple tabs means that there is more than one set of selection criteria for the report.

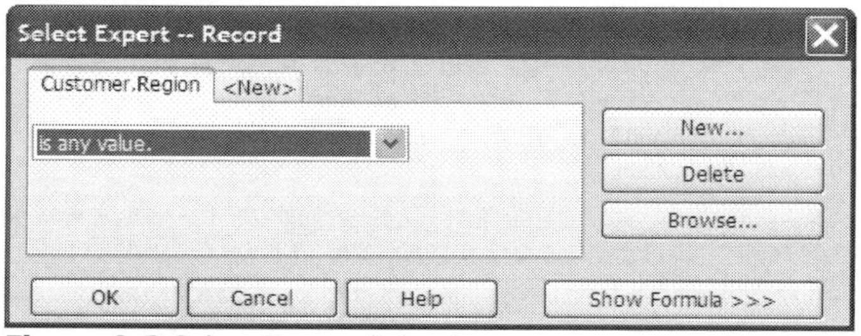

Figure 8-3 Select Expert dialog box

The **NEW** button opens the Choose Field dialog box.
The **DELETE** button deletes the tab that is selected.
The **BROWSE** button is used to view data in the field that is selected.
The **SHOW FORMULA** button displays the formula that was created by the selection criteria.

5. Open the drop-down list and select **IS EQUAL TO**. You will now see another drop-down list. This drop-down list is connected to the field that is selected.

   The values in the second drop-down list are from the Region field in the table, as shown in Figure 8-4.

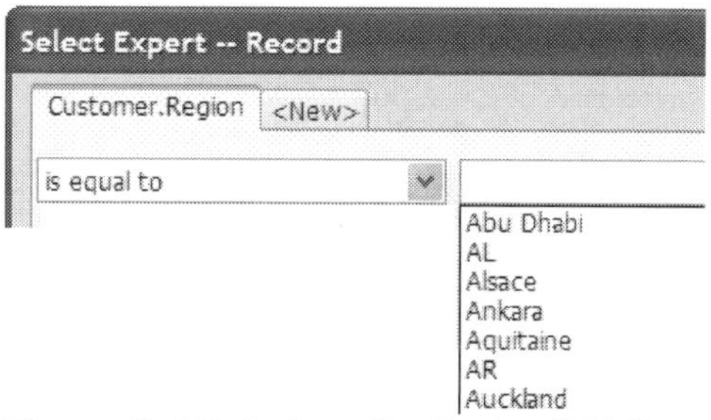

Figure 8-4 Data from the Region field illustrated

6. Select **CA** from the drop-down list shown above in Figure 8-4. Figure 8-5 shows the criteria that should be selected. When the report is run, it will use this criteria to find records that have CA (the state) in the Region field.

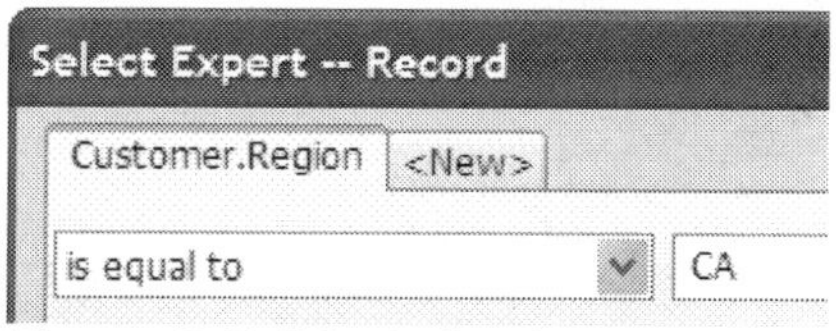

Figure 8-5 Criteria for the report

If you were creating this report and using live data, you would probably click the Refresh button the first time that you run the report after creating the selection criteria. Keep in mind that refreshing data can take a little longer than using saved data if there are thousands of records in the table. Under certain conditions you may have to refresh the data, regardless of how long it takes. Don't worry, even with thousands of records, it only takes a few seconds. If the record selection criteria changes, Crystal Reports does not know if the database has to be re-queried.

If you changed the selection criteria to include more records then the original selection criteria, you should refresh the data unless you know for sure that the Discard saved data when loading reports option is checked. It is possible that no records will be displayed on the report depending on the revised selection criteria, if the data is not refreshed.

7. Click OK. Preview the report.

   You may see the message shown in Figure 8-6.

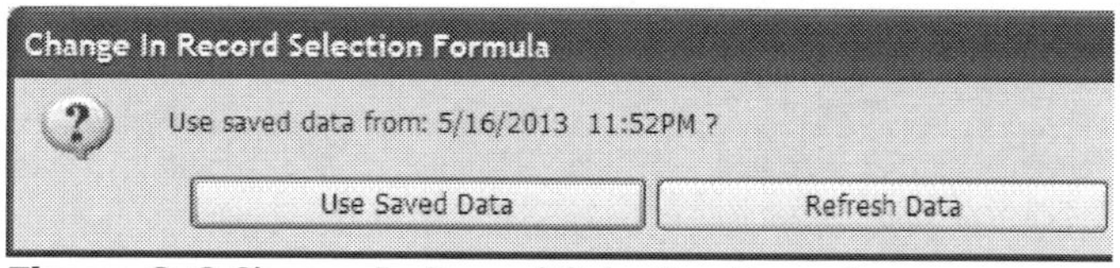

Figure 8-6 Change In Record Selection Formula message

The message in Figure 8-6 is asking if you want to use the data that is currently saved with the report or if you want to refresh the data. It also displays the date and time the data was last refreshed. If you know that the data in the report is current or you want to use the data that is saved with the report, click the **USE SAVED DATA** button. If you are not sure, click the **REFRESH DATA** button. When in doubt, refresh the data.

8. Click the **REFRESH DATA** button. The report should look like the one shown in Figure 8-7. Notice that there are six records displayed on the report. This means that there are only six records in the Customers table in the CA region. Save the changes and close the report.

Customer Name	Address 1	Region	Country	Postal Code
Sporting Wheels Inc.	480 Grant Way	CA	USA	92150
Rowdy Rims Company	4861 Second Road	CA	USA	91341
Changing Gears	1600 Hyde Crescent	CA	USA	92750
Off the Mountain Biking	192 St. Luke Boulevarc	CA	USA	92725
Tyred Out	3687 Kerrisdale Street	CA	USA	92721
Bike Shop from Mars	7071 Dundas Crescent	CA	USA	91338
6				

Figure 8-7 E8.1 Region = CA report

Exercise 8.2: Using The Is One Of Operator

In the previous exercise you used the Is Equal To operator to find customers in one region. In this exercise you will use the Is One Of operator to find customers that are in the OH or FL region.

1. Save the E7.9 report as `E8.2 Region = OH or FL`.

2. Right-click on the **REGION** field and select, Select Expert ⇒ Record.

3. Open the drop-down list and select **IS ONE OF**, then open the next drop-down list and select OH.

> If you type in the first letter of the value that you are looking for in the drop-down list after you open the list, the first value that starts with that letter that you type in will be displayed. You can also type in the exact value that you want.

4. Open the same drop-down list that you just used and select FL.

   Figure 8-8 shows the criteria that should be selected.

   The report should look like the one shown in Figure 8-9.

Figure 8-8 Criteria for the report

Customer Name	Address 1	Region	Country	Postal Code
Bike-A-Holics Anonymous	7429 Arbutus Boulevarc	OH	USA	43005
Wheels and Stuff	2530 Bute Avenue	FL	USA	34666
Uni-Cycle	1008 Kerr Street	OH	USA	43042
Extreme Cycling	1925 Glenaire Avenue	FL	USA	34638
Karma Bikes	1516 Ohio Avenue	OH	USA	43092

Figure 8-9 E8.2 Region = OH or FL report

Exercise 8.3: Modify Selection Criteria

The report that you will modify in this exercise has criteria to find orders that have an order date greater than or equal to a specific date. You will add to this criteria to find orders that have an order amount greater than $2,500.00.

Adding additional criteria via the Select Expert will reduce or increase the number of records that will appear on the report. As you have probably noticed, the report that you just added selection criteria to does not have the Order Amount field. If you need to have additional fields on the report you can add them at anytime. If you need to create a filter on a field, but do not need to see the field on the report, you can create a filter without adding the field to the report.

> Creating the criteria **IS GREATER THAN** 2499.99 will produce the same results as creating the criteria, **IS GREATER THAN OR EQUAL TO** 2500.00.

1. Save the Chapter 8 Order Date report as
   `E8.3 Order date GTE 6-24-10 and Order Amt GT 2499.99.`

2. Add the Record Number special field to the Report Footer section.

3. Delete the Quantity field from the report. Add the Order Amount field from the Orders table and place it after the Ship Date field, as shown in Figure 8-10.

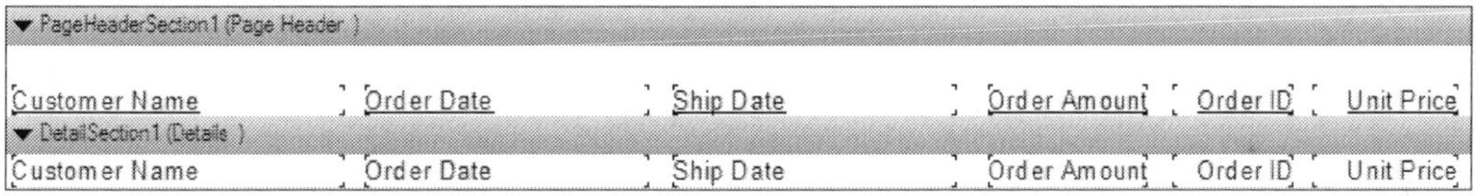

Figure 8-10 Order Amount field added to the report

4. Open the Select Expert to use with the Order Amount field. Notice that you see existing criteria on the Select Expert dialog box. I created the criteria when I created the report.

   Open the drop-down list and select **IS GREATER THAN**, then type `2499.99` in the next drop-down list.

   Figure 8-11 shows the criteria that should be selected.

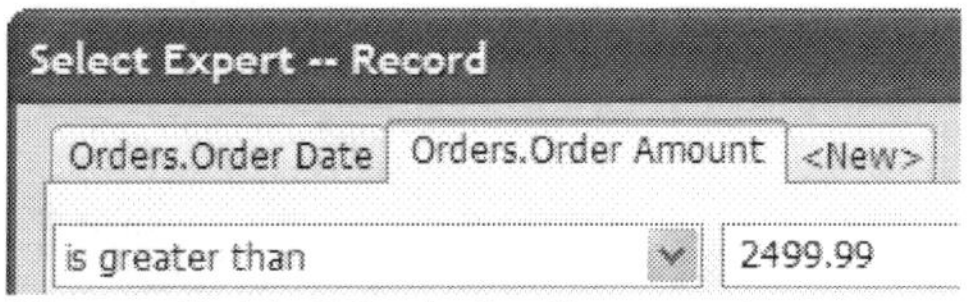

Figure 8-11 Criteria for the report

5. Refresh the data. Your report should look like the one shown in Figure 8-12. The report should have 1,142 records.

Customer Name	Order Date	Ship Date	Order Amount	Order ID	Unit Price
Deals on Wheels	12/2/2010 12:00:00AM	12/2/2010 6:45:32AM	$5,060.28	1,002	$33.90
Deals on Wheels	12/2/2010 12:00:00AM	12/2/2010 6:45:32AM	$5,060.28	1,002	$1,652.86
Cyclopath	12/3/2010 12:00:00AM	12/3/2010 11:11:11PM	$14,872.30	1,010	$2,939.85
Cyclopath	12/3/2010 12:00:00AM	12/3/2010 11:11:11PM	$14,872.30	1,010	$2,645.87

Figure 8-12 Order date GTE 6-24-10 and Order Amt GT 2499.99 report

Exercise 8.4: Using The Is Between Operator

In this exercise you will use the Is Between operator to find all of the orders that were shipped between 4/1/2011 and 6/30/2011.

1. Save the E5.3 report as `E8.4 Orders shipped between 4-1-2011 and 6-30-2011.`

2. Add the Record Number special field to the Report Footer section.

3. Open the Select Expert to use with the Ship Date field. Select the Is between operator, then open the top drop-down list on the right and select 4/1/2011.

4. Open the bottom drop-down list and select 6/30/2011. The report should have 780 records.

Exercise 8.5: Using Multiple Selection Criteria

In this exercise you will create a new report that selects records that meet the following criteria: Country = USA, the Order Date is between 4/1/2012 and 4/30/2012 and the order was not shipped.

> Once you open the Select Expert and create the first set of criteria, you do not have to close it to add additional criteria. Click on the **NEW** tab to add more criteria.

- ☑ Save the report as `E8.5 US orders not shipped in April 2012.`
- ☑ Table 8-3 contains the tables and fields for the report. The table names are in bold.
- ☑ Figure 8-13 shows the report layout.
- ☑ Figure 8-14 shows the report, which should have 44 records.

Customer	**Orders**
Customer Name	Order Date (Change the format of this field to MM/DD/YYYY)
Country	Order Amount
	Shipped

Table 8-3 Tables and fields to add to the report

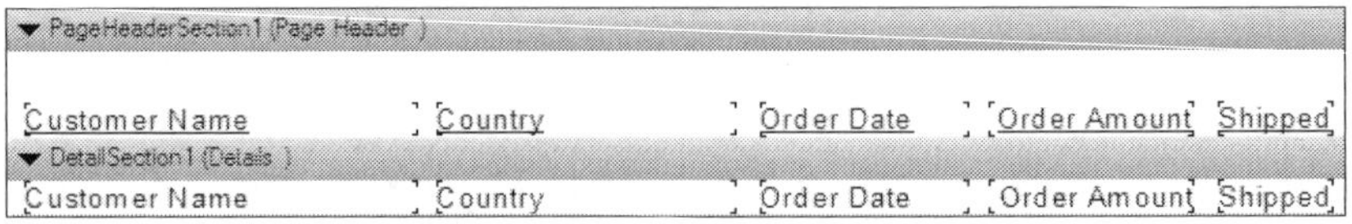

Figure 8-13 E8.5 report layout

Customer Name	Country	Order Date	Order Amount	Shipped
City Cyclists	USA	04/29/2012	$63.90	False
Pathfinders	USA	04/26/2012	$3,185.42	False
Rockshocks for Jocks	USA	04/25/2012	$8,933.25	False
Rockshocks for Jocks	USA	04/30/2012	$31.00	False
Poser Cycles	USA	04/14/2012	$83.80	False

Figure 8-14 E8.5 US orders not shipped in April 2012 report

Viewing Formulas

In Exercise 8.4 you created criteria that selected orders shipped between 4/1/2011 and 6/30/2011. In Exercise 8.3 you added criteria to retrieve records that had an order amount greater than $2,499.99 to the Select statement. To view the formula, click the **SHOW FORMULA** button on the Select Expert.

In Exercise 8.5 if the syntax in your formula looks different then what is shown in Figure 8-15 and your report looks exactly like the one shown earlier in Figure 8-14, you are probably using the **BASIC SYNTAX** formula language instead of **CRYSTAL SYNTAX**. [See Chapter 13, Syntax Language And Editors]

Depending on the tab that is selected prior to clicking the Show Formula button, the formula will be in a different order then what is shown in Figure 8-15. The Country tab was selected for this figure.

```
not {Orders.Shipped} and
{Customer.Country} = "USA" and
{Orders.Order Date} in DateTime (2012, 04, 01, 00, 00, 00) to DateTime (2012, 04, 30, 00, 00, 00)
```

Figure 8-15 E8.5 Selection criteria formula

The zeros at the end of the date/time fields in the formula shown above in Figure 8-15 represent the time in HH MM SS format (hours, minutes, seconds).

And vs Or Operators In Selection Criteria

The bottom of Figure 8-16 shows the formula that was created for the E8.3 report shown earlier in Figure 8-12. It also shows all of the criteria that must be met. At the end of the first line of the formula, you see the word **AND**.

If you changed the "and" to **OR**, the report would look like the one shown in Figure 8-17. If you made this change and ran the report, you would see that there are 3,622 records in this report, compared to the 1,142 records in the E8.3 report shown earlier in Figure 8-12.

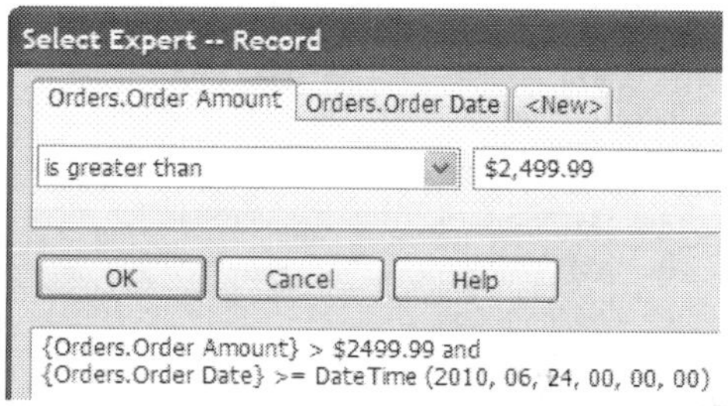

Figure 8-16 Formula for the selection criteria for the E8.3 report shown earlier in Figure 8-12

The **RECORD** and **GROUP SELECTION** options were removed from the Select Expert dialog box in Crystal Reports 2008.

Customer Name	Order Date	Ship Date	Order Amount	Order ID	Unit Price
City Cyclists	12/2/2010 12:00:00AM	12/10/2010 5:32:23PM	$41.90	1	$41.90
Deals on Wheels	12/2/2010 12:00:00AM	12/2/2010 6:45:32AM	$5,060.28	1,002	$33.90
Deals on Wheels	12/2/2010 12:00:00AM	12/2/2010 6:45:32AM	$5,060.28	1,002	$1,652.86
Warsaw Sports, Inc.	12/2/2010 12:00:00AM	12/5/2010 12:10:12AM	$186.87	1,003	$48.51
Warsaw Sports, Inc.	12/2/2010 12:00:00AM	12/5/2010 12:10:12AM	$186.87	1,003	$13.78

Figure 8-17 Order date GTE 6-24-2010 OR Order Amt GT 2499.99 report

Reports can have more than one selection criteria. When this is the case, in order for records to appear on the report, they have to meet all of the selection criteria. That is because by default, Crystal Reports uses the logical **AND** operator on the Select Expert. If you need to create selection criteria where only one of the selection criteria options must be true in order for a record to appear on the report, you have to use the logical **OR** operator. To change the operator, you have to manually edit the selection formula that is created by the Select Expert.

How To Delete Selection Criteria

After you have created selection criteria you may decide that one or more of the criteria that you created is not needed. You do not have to delete everything and start over. The steps below show you how to delete specific criteria on the Select Expert dialog box.

1. Open the report that has the selection criteria that you want to delete.

2. Open the Select Expert. Click on the tab that has the selection criteria that you want to delete, then click the **DELETE** button shown earlier in Figure 8-3. Click OK to close the Select Expert.

Understanding How Date/Time Fields Work In Selection Criteria

In Exercise 8.3, a date/time field was used as part of the selection criteria. You entered a date and the records that have an order date greater than or equal to 6/24/2010 were retrieved, even though you did not enter a time for the date that you selected. That is because Crystal Reports will use midnight as the time when a date is entered without a time. This is fine for selection criteria that only uses a date/time field once. If the selection criteria uses the **IS BETWEEN** operator for example (or any operator that requires that two dates be entered for the selection criteria), the records that are retrieved may not be exactly what you are expecting.

The first date in the selection criteria will be compared to midnight as the time, meaning that all records that have a time of midnight or later will be included. So far, so good. The problem is with the second date in the selection criteria. If a time is not entered for the second date, only records that have midnight as the time will be retrieved. This means that a record that has the same date as the second date field in the selection criteria, but the time is something other then midnight will not appear on the report. To include all records on the date in the second date field, you should enter 23:59:59 (or 11:59:59 PM) as the time. If you enter 17:00:00 (or 05:00:00 PM) as the time, for the second date, records that have a time that is greater than 5 PM will not be included on the report.

If you were going to modify the E8.5 report to show all of the orders that were shipped between 1/1/2011 and 1/15/2011, Figure 8-18 shows what many people would enter as the selection criteria. When the report is run with this selection criteria, 49 records will be retrieved. This is incorrect because it does not account for records that have a time other than midnight on the Ship Date field. If the selection criteria shown in Figure 8-19 was entered, the report would retrieve 58 records. As you can see in Figure 8-20, the times on the Ship Date field are different. Notice that there are nine records that have a ship date of 1/15/2011.

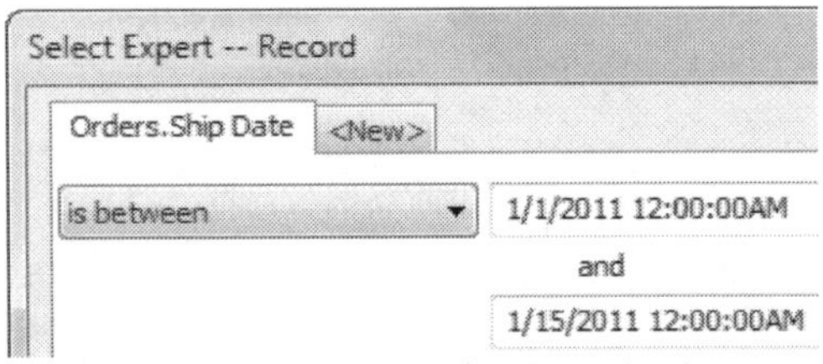

Figure 8-18 Incorrect selection criteria

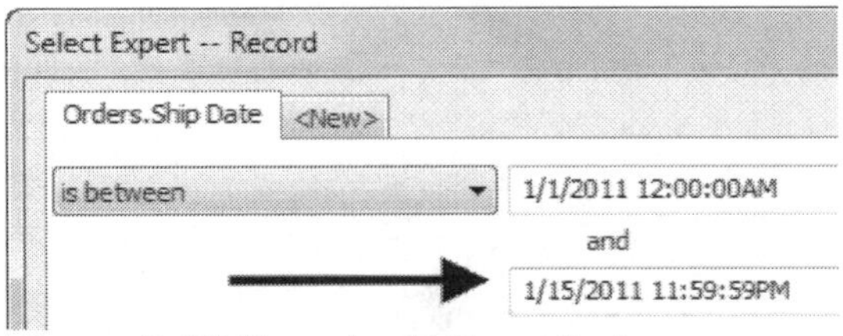

Figure 8-19 Correct selection criteria

If the second Ship Date field has the time entered as 03:00:00 PM, as shown in Figure 8-21, the last three records on the 15th, shown in Figure 8-20 would not be displayed on the report because the time for these three records is after 3 PM.

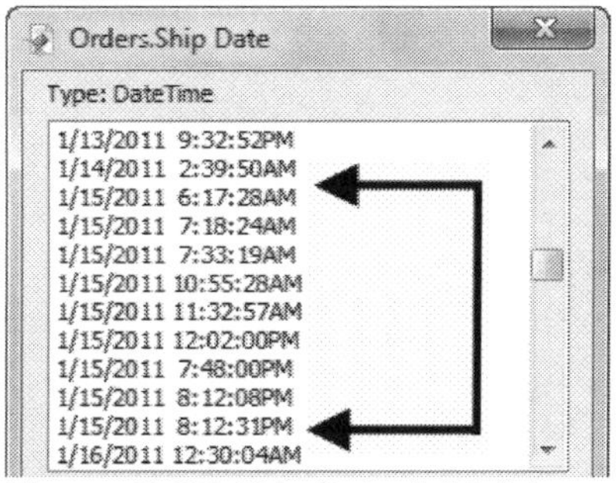

Figure 8-20 Ship Date field data

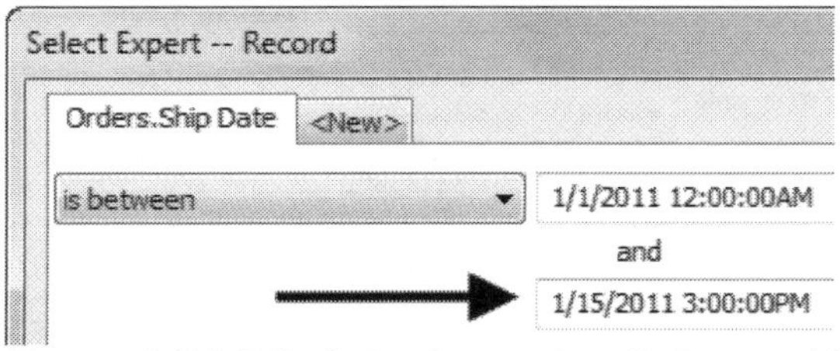

Figure 8-21 Criteria to show orders that were shipped between 1/1/2011 and 1/15/2011 by 3 PM

If you want to try this yourself, save the E8.5 report as `E8.5A Time Problem (Incorrect Criteria)` and delete all of the current selection criteria, then create the criteria shown earlier in Figure 8-18. Add the Ship Date field to the report and sort this field in ascending order. Refresh the data and run the report. If you scroll to the end of the report you will see that the last record on the report has a ship date of 1/14/2011. There are no records with a ship date of 1/15/2011 on the report.

Save the E8.5A report as `E8.5B Time Problem (Correct Criteria)`. Use the criteria shown earlier in Figure 8-19. If you scroll to the end of the report you will see that there are nine records with the date 1/15/2011. These are the records that you were expecting to appear on the report when you created the criteria.

Save the E8.5A report as `E8.5C Time criteria with a specific time`. Use the criteria shown above in Figure 8-21. You will see that there are 55 records. This is what you were expecting because the time on the Ship Date criteria was 3 PM.

I don't know about you, but when I first figured this out it was somewhat scary. You do have options. You can always type in the time that you need on the second date field in the selection criteria or you can type in the day after the last day that you want to include records for on the report. Instead of typing 1/15/2011 for the second date, you could type 1/16/2011 and let the time default to 00:00:00 AM. Doing this will produce the same result. Keep this in mind when you are creating reports on your own. In an effort to save time, when you create reports in this book that have similar selection criteria, you do not have to enter a time on the Select Expert dialog box.

Being able to enter a time is helpful for reports that are time sensitive. If you needed to create a report that displayed a list of medications that were given to patients between 8 AM and 2 PM, you would enter the times as part of the selection criteria.

Date/Time Field Update
As if all of the above time issues are not complicated enough, Crystal Reports now uses the current time as the default time instead of using 00:00:00 as the default time, regardless of the data that you are using. The best advice that I can give you if you do not want to use a formula to fix this, is to always type in the time that you need on all date/time fields.

If you do not mind modifying the selection criteria formula, you can add the Date function to the Date/Time field in the selection criteria. Doing this will force Crystal Reports to ignore the time portion of the field. Figure 8-22 shows the selection formula created for Figure 8-18 shown earlier. Figure 8-23 shows the same formula modified that uses the Date function. Another option is to change the default Date/Time option. [See Chapter 7, Figure 7-26]

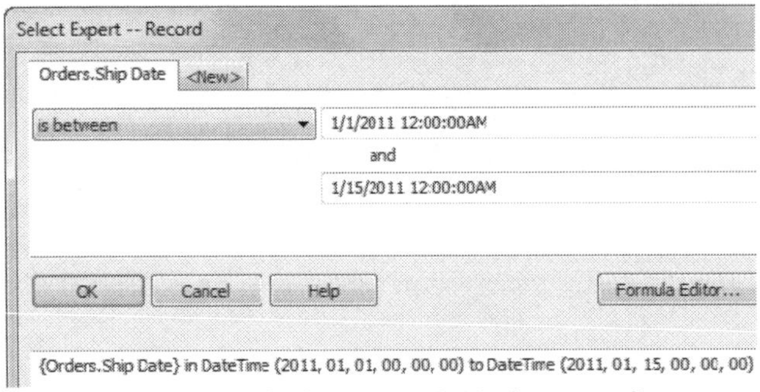

Figure 8-22 Formula for Figure 8-18 shown earlier

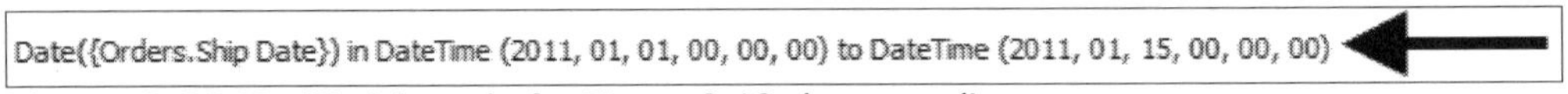

Figure 8-23 Modified formula for Figure 8-18 shown earlier

By now I think that you have figured out how important it is to understand how to create selection criteria to meet the requirements of the report. If the wrong criteria is created for the report, the output will not be what the user is expecting. This means that they could make decisions based on incorrect data and not know that the data is incorrect. If you aren't familiar with the data, it is a good idea to open the tables and look at the raw data.

Edit An Existing Formula

In Exercise 8.2, the criteria for the Region field is that it has to contain one of two values. If you needed to add another value, you could use the Select Expert to add the value from the drop-down list or you could edit the formula that is at the bottom of the Select Expert dialog box.

If you type in the **FORMULA** field, Crystal Reports will disable the top portion of the Select Expert dialog box, as shown in Figure 8-24. Compare this to the Select Expert dialog box shown earlier in Figure 8-18.

In Figure 8-24 you do not see anything in the top portion of the dialog box.

That is because I typed "PA" in the formula field at the bottom of the dialog box.

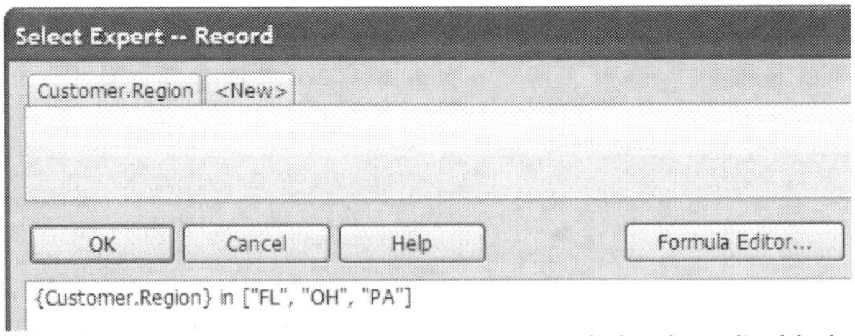

Figure 8-24 Top half of the Select Expert dialog box disabled

The reason Crystal Reports disables the top half of the Select Expert when you create or edit a formula at the bottom of the dialog box is because the formula can't be duplicated by the options that the Select Expert has at the top of the dialog box.

Opening The Formula Editor From The Select Expert

If you can create or edit the formula at the bottom of the Select Expert shown above in Figure 8-24, you do not have to use the Formula Editor. If you cannot remember the function or need help creating the formula, there are two ways that you can open the Formula Editor from the Select Expert as discussed below. You will learn more about the Formula Editor in Chapter 13.

① Click the **FORMULA EDITOR** button shown above in Figure 8-24.

② Open the operator drop-down list, scroll to the bottom of the list and select the **FORMULA** option illustrated in Figure 8-25. The Select Expert will change, as illustrated in Figure 8-26 to let you create a formula.

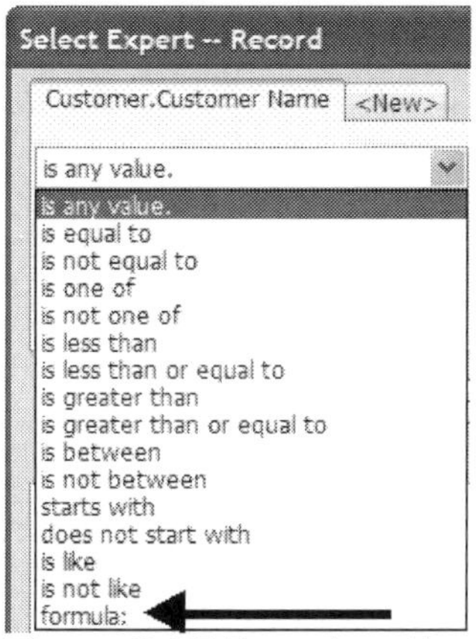

Figure 8-25 Formula option illustrated

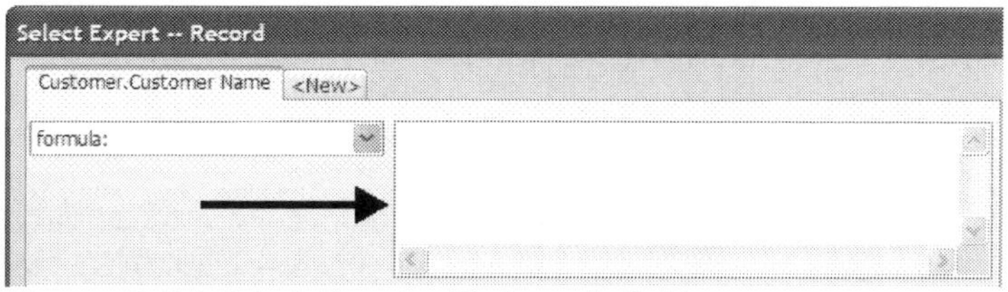

Figure 8-26 Select Expert with formula field

Record Selection Performance Considerations

The type of database that the report is using determines the record selection process that Crystal Reports uses. Databases that are stored on a database server or desktop databases that use an ODBC connection have more performance issues than desktop databases that are local or are on a network drive, as discussed below.

① If the database is on a server, Crystal Reports creates a **WHERE CLAUSE** and adds the clause to the query and sends the query to the database server. The query is run on the server and returns the records to Crystal Reports to use, to generate the report. If the database is on a server, performance improves if this record selection process is used.

② If the database is local or is a desktop database that is stored on a network drive (which is different then a database server), Crystal Reports runs the query that is created from the record selection criteria itself. Depending on the number of records, the report selection process can take some time.

Making changes to a formula created with the Select Expert via the **SHOW FORMULA** button can really slow down the record selection process if the database is on a database server, especially if the underlying tables have a lot of records.

The **USE INDEXES OR SERVER FOR SPEED** option if selected, will improve performance. If you want to use this option for the current report, it is on the Report Options dialog box. If you want this option to be the default for all reports that you will create going forward, select the option on the Database tab of the Options dialog box.

Using indexed fields will improve performance during the record selection process, especially when using tables that have a lot of records. When possible, you should use indexed fields for the record selection process because the fields index stores all of the values that are in the field, in sorted order, which makes retrieving records faster.

Case Sensitive Considerations

When Crystal Reports is installed, case insensitivity is set as the default. This means that entering "new orleans" or "New Orleans" will retrieve the same records. When creating selection criteria on text fields, keep the following in mind.

① PC and SQL databases that are connected to via an ODBC connection usually ignores case sensitivity.
② Some databases and ODBC drivers may not support case insensitivity when used with Crystal Reports, even though the **DATABASE SERVER IS CASE-INSENSITIVE** option is enabled.
③ If the server that the database is stored on is set to be case sensitive, you cannot override it by enabling the Database server is case-insensitive option. If you select the same option on the Report Options dialog box, you can enable the option, only for the report that you are currently working with. If this is the case, you would have to convert the text field that you need to create the selection criteria for to all upper case and enter the criteria to support all upper case.
④ If the database is not stored on a server that is set to case sensitive and the database is set for case insensitivity, you can use the Database server is case-insensitive option to control what the selection criteria returns.

If you want the **DATABASE SERVER IS CASE-INSENSITIVE** option applied to reports that have already been created, you have to open each of the reports and select the option on the Report Options dialog box.

Using Wildcard Characters As Selection Criteria

Earlier in the chapter you learned that you could use the ? and * wildcard characters as selection criteria using the Is Like and Is Not Like operators.

Wildcard characters provide another way to retrieve records. Wildcard characters are used to substitute all or part of the data in a field.

You can also use wildcards to search for data that has a pattern. You can use these wildcard characters, as shown in Figure 8-27, at the beginning or end of the search criteria that you enter.

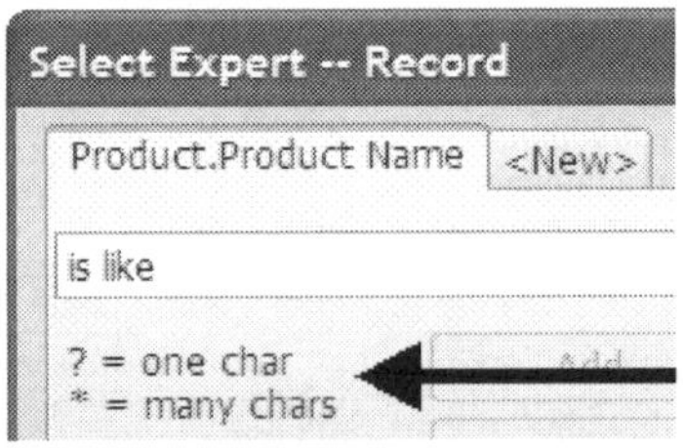

Figure 8-27 Wildcard characters illustrated

① The question mark is used to replace one character in the data. If you entered t?n in the criteria field, the selection criteria would return records that have ten, tan, tune and ton, but not toon.
② The asterisk is used to replace more than one character in the data. If you entered s*r in the criteria field, the selection criteria would return records that have star, start and sour, or any records that had the letter "s" come before the letter "r" in the field that the selection criteria is for. This wildcard character selection criteria is more flexible, but often returns a lot of results that are not needed.

Document Properties

Some of the special fields come from the Summary tab on the Document Properties dialog box shown in Figure 8-28. Crystal Reports ⇒ Report ⇒ Summary Info, opens this dialog box.

Summary Tab Options

The information that is entered on this tab is used for identification purposes. These are properties of Windows files and are not specific to Crystal Reports. Other software packages have similar dialog boxes. For example, Microsoft Word has the Properties dialog box.

The **TITLE** field does not appear on the tab in place of the report file name like it does in the full version of Crystal Reports.

The **TEMPLATE** field does not provide any use. It does not let you apply a template to the report or save the active report as a template. If the report is based off of a template, you could enter the template name in this field so that you will know which template the report is using.

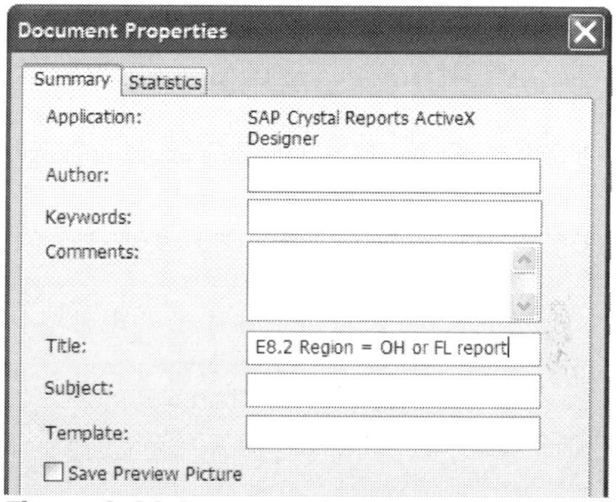

Figure 8-28 Summary tab options

If checked, the **SAVE PREVIEW PICTURE** option, is used to view a thumbnail size picture of the first page of the report in the Open dialog box in Crystal Reports.

Statistics Tab Options

The options shown in Figure 8-29 are **READ-ONLY,** which means that you cannot modify them.

The **REVISION NUMBER** field is incremented each time the report is saved. If you are modifying a report that you did not create, the information on this tab may be helpful.

The **TOTAL EDITING TIME** field displays how long the report has been open and whether it has been edited.

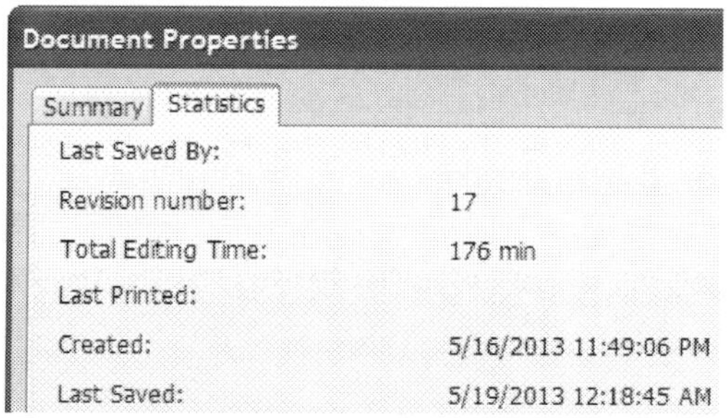

Figure 8-29 Statistics tab options

Adding Summary Information To A Report

The special fields on the Document Properties dialog box can be added to a report. The report shown in Figure 8-30 has the **FILE AUTHOR** and **REPORT TITLE** special fields in the Report Header section. I had to refresh the data for these fields to appear on the report.

Indera Murphy	E8.2 Region = OH or FL report			
Customer Name	Address1	Region	Country	Postal Code
Bike-A-Holics Anony	7429 Arbutus Boulev	OH	USA	43005
Wheels and Stuff	2530 Bute Avenue	FL	USA	34666
Uni-Cycle	1008 Kerr Street	OH	USA	43042

Figure 8-30 Report with summary information added

GROUPING, SORTING AND SUMMARIZING RECORDS

After completing the exercises in this chapter you will be able to use the techniques listed below to control which records appear on a report and how they are organized.

- ☑ Grouping records
- ☑ Sorting records
- ☑ Create summary subtotals and group totals

CHAPTER 9

Grouping And Sorting Overview

Sorting rearranges the order that records will appear on the report without changing the layout or structure of the report. Grouping takes sorting one step further by displaying records that have the same value in a field or a value that is in a range of values together. Grouping changes the structure of the report by automatically creating another Group Header and Group Footer section for each group. If either of these group sections are not needed, you can suppress them. You can also create formulas that determine if or when the section is displayed or hidden. After all of the records in a group print, there are often totals or some type of summary information about the records in the group. You can sort records whether or not there are groups on the report.

Grouping Records

Grouping displays records together that meet specific criteria. Consider the following two examples:

① In the E8.2 Region = OH or FL report, at a glance, it is hard to tell how many records are in the OH region versus how many are in the FL region. If the report was modified to print all of the records in the same region together, it would be easier to see how many records are in each region. This is known as grouping records.
② In the E8.5 US orders not shipped in April 2012 report, you cannot tell how many orders were not shipped on any particular day. If the records were grouped by ship date, you would be able to create a count summary field to show how many orders were not shipped by day. You could also have a total by day of the total dollar amount, based on the Order Amount field, of orders that were not shipped.

There are three main tasks that need to be completed when records in a report need to be grouped. The three tasks are listed below and are discussed in this chapter.

① Select the fields to group on.
② Decide if the detail records in each group need to be sorted.
③ Decide if any fields in the Details section of the report need summary information.

The name of the group is usually placed in the Group Header section. The summary information, which is not a requirement, is usually placed in the Group Footer section.

Being able to add this type of functionality to reports will make them much more useful in many cases, then the reports that were created in Chapter 8. Reports that have groups can also use the drill-down feature. In addition to creating the groups, Crystal Reports also provides summary functions including statistical, averaging and totals that you can add to a report.

Records are placed together because they have the same value in a field (or fields). This is how the Group Header and Footer sections are automatically re-created each time the value in the field being grouped on, changes. You will not see this in the Design window. The process of creating another group each time the value changes is dynamic processing that happens behind the scenes, as they say. This is how you can create totals for a group. If you are shaking your head, after you complete the first exercise in this chapter, this should make more sense.

Selecting The Field To Group On
As you will see, you can create a group on just about any field in a table. It is best to select a field that has unique values like an ID field. Using a text field like a customer name or city field would work, but would probably produce unexpected results because there could be two or more customers that have the same name.

Selecting The Field To Group On (Continued)
In this scenario, the unexpected result would be that all customers with the same name would be grouped together. This means that the totals for the group would be incorrect because they included amounts for more than one customer. Grouping on the Customer ID field instead, would prevent this from happening.

Grouping Tips
Below are some tips that I follow to help determine if a report needs a group and if so, which field(s) to group on.

① Reports that retrieve hundreds or thousands of records, probably would be easier to read if there were one or two groups.
② If you need to provide a count or subtotal for a field.
③ If the report needs statistical information.

Insert Group Dialog Box

The options on the **COMMON** tab of this dialog box are used to create the groups. At a minimum, the field to group on (the first drop-down list shown in Figure 9-1) and the sorting order of the group (the second drop-down list) have to be selected. Date and Boolean fields have an additional option that can be set. The **OPTIONS** tab will be discussed later. There are three ways to open the **INSERT GROUP** dialog box, as discussed below.

① Click the **INSERT GROUP** button on the Crystal Reports - Insert toolbar.
② Right-click on a blank space on the report and select Insert ⇒ Group.
③ Crystal Reports ⇒ Insert ⇒ Group.

The **GROUP BY** field is the first drop-down list on the Common tab. It contains all of the fields that the report can be grouped on.

This list contains the fields that are on the report and the fields in tables that are connected to the report. You can also use formula fields as the field to group on.

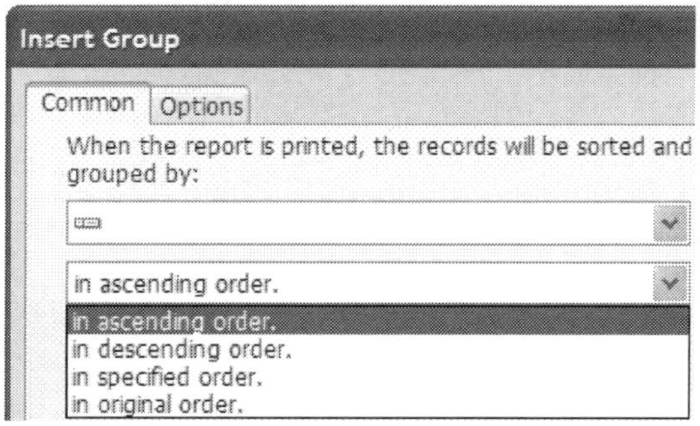

Figure 9-1 Insert Group dialog box

The **GROUP SORT ORDER** field is the second drop-down list on the Common tab. The sort order determines the order that the groups will appear on the report. Table 9-1 explains the group sorting options.

Memo fields will not appear in the group by drop-down list because they cannot be used as a field to group on.

Option	Description
In Ascending Order	Text fields will be sorted in A-Z order. Numeric fields will be sorted in low to high order. Date group fields will be sorted in oldest to most recent date order.
In Descending Order	Text fields will be sorted in Z-A order. Numeric fields will be sorted in high to low order. Date group fields will be sorted in most recent to oldest date order.
In Specified Order	This option is used to select the order of the groups. This is known as **CUSTOM GROUPING** and is discussed below. An example of a custom group would be to rank customers by the amount of sales they placed last year. The option causes two tabs (Specific Order and Other) to appear on the dialog box.
In Original Order	This option will leave the data in the order that it is retrieved from in the database. It may be me, but I don't find this option very useful.

Table 9-1 Group sorting options explained

Once a field is selected to be grouped on, it will appear under the text, **THE SECTION WILL BE PRINTED ON ANY CHANGE OF** at the bottom of the Insert Group dialog box.

The **DATE/TIME** option is only available when a date, time or date/time field is selected in the Group By drop-down list. Figure 9-2 shows the options for date/time fields.

The **BOOLEAN** group sort order option is only available when a Boolean field (ex. true/false or yes/no field) is selected in the group by drop-down list. Figure 9-3 shows the Boolean field options. Table 9-2 explains the Boolean field options. The Boolean sort process does not work like the other sort options. Boolean fields sort false before true, when the ascending sort order option is selected. The groups are created when there are changes from yes to no, or from true to false in the report data. The exception to this is the **ON ANY CHANGE** option.

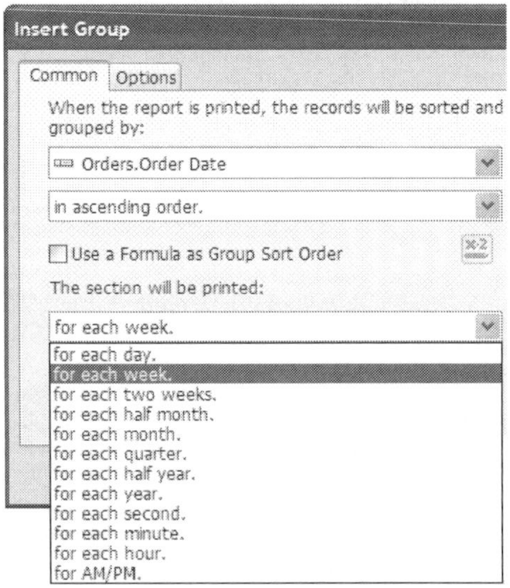

Figure 9-2 Date/Time field group sorting options

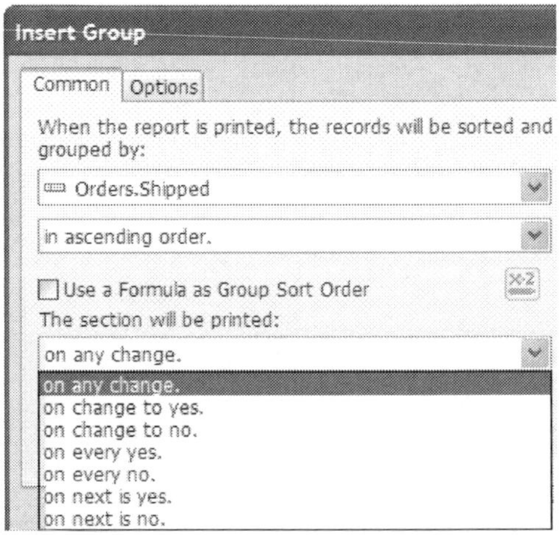

Figure 9-3 Boolean field group sorting options

In addition to using the Insert Group dialog box to create and edit groups, you can also use the Group Expert to create and edit groups.

Option	Description
On any change	This is the default option and will sort the values and place them next to each other.
On change to yes	Creates a new group each time a True value comes after a False value. (1)
On change to no	Creates a new group each time a False value comes after a True value. (1)
On every yes	Creates a group that always ends with a True value and includes any records in the middle that have a False value, back to the previous True value. (1)
On every no	Creates a group that always ends with a False value and includes any records in the middle that have a True value, back to the previous False value. (1)
On next is yes	Creates groups that always start with a True value and includes all records in the middle that have a False value until the next record with a True value is found. (1)
On next is no	Creates groups that always start with a False value and includes all records in the middle that have a True value until the next record with a False value is found. (1)

Table 9-2 Boolean field group options explained

(1) The records are not sorted if this option is selected.

Custom Grouping

If the ascending and descending sort options are not sufficient, you can create custom groups by selecting the **IN SPECIFIED ORDER** option in the second drop-down list shown earlier in Figure 9-1. There are two custom group options available on the Insert Group dialog box: User defined sort order and User defined groups.

User Defined Sort Order

When you select this option, a tab named **SPECIFIED ORDER** will appear on the Insert Group dialog box, as shown in Figure 9-4. The options on this tab are used to create the list of how the values in the groups will be sorted.

The **NAMED GROUP** drop-down list contains all of the values for the group field. Select the values that you want the groups to appear in on the report, as shown at the bottom of Figure 9-5.

You can change the order of the values by clicking on the value that you want to move, then click the Up or Down arrow to the right of the list.

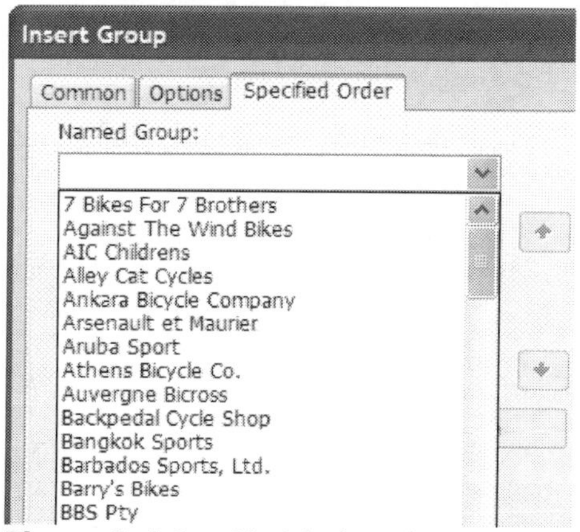

Figure 9-4 Specified Order tab

In addition to being able to select individual values in a field that will be used as a group, you can also create your own groups. To do this, click the New button on the Specified Order tab to create a named group. Named groups let you specify a range that a value has to be in to be added to the group. For example, if you want to group order records by the week that they were shipped, you would create named groups in seven day intervals. The operators that are available to create the selection criteria for the group range are a subset of the select operators in Chapter 8, Table 8-1.

Once you add one value to the Named Group list, the **OTHERS** tab shown in Figure 9-6 will open. The options on this tab are used to select what you want to happen to the group values that are not added to the Named Group list on the Specified Order tab. Table 9-3 explains the options on the Others tab.

> You do not have to order all of the group values. You can select just the ones that you need.

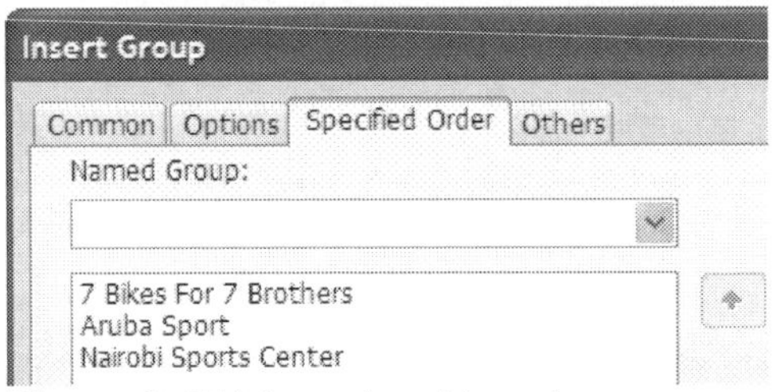

Figure 9-5 Values placed in order

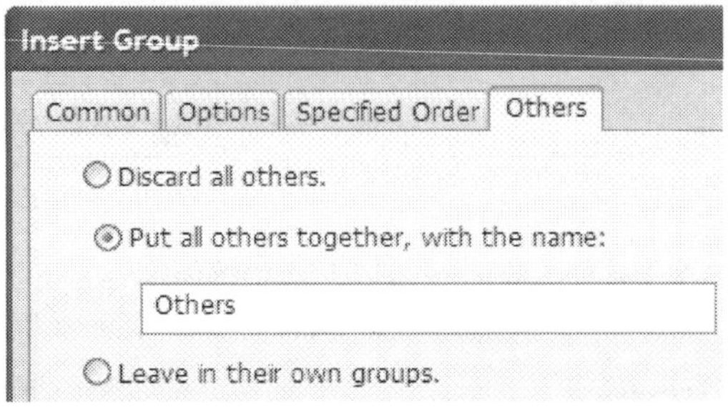

Figure 9-6 Others tab options

Option	Description
Discard all others	Causes the group values (and their detail records) that are not selected on the Specified Order tab to not be displayed on the report.
Put all others together, with the name	Is used to put all of the group values that are not selected on the Specified Order tab together under one group name that you type in the text box.
Leave in their own groups	Prints all of the group values that you selected on the Specified Order tab first on the report. The remaining group values will be printed after, in ascending order.

Table 9-3 Others tab options explained

Sorting Records

Sorting records is the second task that has to be completed. Like grouping, sorting is used to rearrange the order that records appear on the report. Data can be sorted by any database field, formula or SQL Expression. Data cannot be sorted by a memo field. The data can be sorted on more than one field including fields that are not on the report. There are two types of sorting, as discussed below.

① You can sort the report as it is. The E8.1 report could be sorted by customer name. Another way to sort this report would be by postal code.

② You can sort the records within a group. After the groups for a report have been determined, you may decide that the report would be more meaningful if the detail records in the group were sorted. If you do not specify a sort order, the records in each group will print in the order that they are retrieved from the table.

The **RECORD SORT EXPERT** dialog box shown in Figure 9-7 is used to select the options to sort the records in the Details section. The Record Sort Expert will show group fields in the Sort Fields list. This is done to show that the detail records will be sorted within the group. Group field sorting is done before detail record sorting. You can sort in ascending or descending order on each field. This expert does not sort groups.

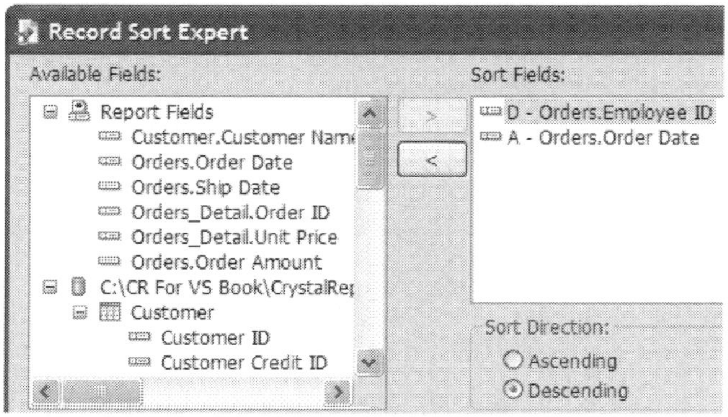

Figure 9-7 Record Sort Expert dialog box

> In addition to clicking on a field in the Available Fields list and clicking the arrow button to add it to the Sort Fields list, you can also drag fields to the Sort Fields list.

There are three ways to open the Record Sort Export dialog box, as discussed below.

① Click the **RECORD SORT EXPERT** button on the Crystal Reports - Main toolbar.
② Crystal Reports ⇒ Report ⇒ Record Sort Expert.
③ Right-click on a blank space on the report, then select Report ⇒ Record Sort Expert.

What I found interesting is that if you click on a group field in the Sort Fields list, all of the buttons become disabled on the dialog box. I suspect that this is because Crystal Reports is trying to protect you from changing the group order. Don't worry. If you need to change the order of the groups, you can change them on the design window by dragging them or you can use the Group Expert.

> The order that fields are added to the **SORT FIELDS** list on the Record Sort Expert is the order that the records will be sorted in. If you discover that the fields are in the wrong order in the Sort Fields list, click on the field that is not in the correct place, then click the Up or Down arrow buttons, to move the field to the correct location.

Summary Information

This is the third task that has to be completed when groups are created. One reason that groups are created is to make the report easier to read. Another reason groups are created is to provide summary information for fields in the Details section of each group on the report.

These summary calculated fields are usually placed in the Group Footer section of the report. Summary fields can also be placed in the Group Header section. Students have asked me how it is possible that summary fields that are in the Group Header section contain accurate totals. The answer is somewhat beyond the scope of this book, but I will answer the question because it may help you understand and allow you to use summary fields in the Group Header section with confidence, when needed.

Crystal Reports actually builds (processes) the entire report before it is displayed or printed. This means that values for summary fields, regardless of where they are placed on the report, are calculated before the report prints.

The two types of calculations that you can perform on text (string) data is counting records in a group and determining the frequency of records in the group. These summary calculations are often also placed in the Report Footer section to create what is known as a grand total or report total. Summary fields are similar to **RUNNING TOTAL** fields. Summary fields that are in the Report Header or Footer section are not dependant on groups. You can create summary calculation fields in the Report Header and Footer if the report does not have any groups. Summary fields in the Report Header and Footer contain totals for all records on the report.

Instead of having to manually count the number of orders that are printed on a report for each customer, a calculated field can be added to the report that would count the number of orders and display the number on the report.

To create a group summary field, the report must have at least one group. If you select the option to create a summary field and the report does not have a group, you will be prompted to create a group. If you place the same summary field in different sections of the report it will produce different total amounts, which is what should happen.

There are three ways to open the Insert Summary dialog box shown in Figure 9-8 **AFTER** you have selected the field that you need to create a summary field for, as discussed below. If the field that you need to create a summary calculation for is not on the report, you have to select option two or three below.

① Right-click on a field or blank space on the report and select Insert ⇒ Insert Summary.
② Click the **SUMMARY** button on the Crystal Reports - Insert toolbar.
③ Crystal Reports ⇒ Insert ⇒ Summary.

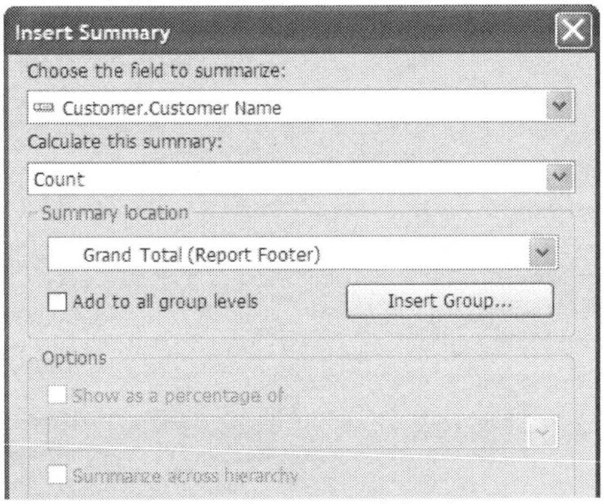

Figure 9-8 Insert Summary dialog box

There are two categories of summary calculations that you can create, as discussed below.

① The **TEXT** field summary calculation options are explained in Table 9-4. Text fields can only use the calculation options in Table 9-4.
② The **NUMERIC** field summary calculation options are explained in Table 9-5. They can also be used with currency fields. Numeric fields can also use the calculation options in Table 9-4.

Text Summary Calculation Options	
Calculation	**Description**
Count	Counts the detail records. By default, if the field being used to count on is **NULL**, it will not be included in the count. Select the **CONVERT DATABASE TO NULL VALUES TO DEFAULT** option on the Report Options dialog box if you need null values to be counted. Duplicate values in the field will also be counted. This may not be what you want.
Distinct Count	Counts all of the unique values in the selected field.

Table 9-4 Text summary calculation options explained

Text Summary Calculation Options	
Calculation	**Description**
Maximum	Finds the highest value in the field.
Minimum	Finds the lowest value in the field.
Mode	Finds the most frequently used value in the field.
N^{th} Largest, N is:	Is used to select a number and calculate the Nth largest value in the group. An example would be if you wanted to find out what the third largest (N^{th} largest) order amount (N) is in the group. (2)
N^{th} Most Frequent, N is:	Is used to select a number and calculate the Nth most frequently occurring value in the selected field. An example would be if you wanted to find out which product was ordered the most in the group, you would enter a 1 in this field. This is similar to the Mode function, but it is not limited to the frequent occurrences. (2)
N^{th} Smallest, N is:	Is used to select a number and calculate the Nth smallest occurring value. An example would be if you wanted to find out what the fifth (N^{th} smallest) smallest order amount (N) is in the group. You would enter a 5 in this field. (2)

Table 9-4 Text summary calculation options explained (Continued)

(2) The N is a value.

Numeric Summary Calculation Options	
Calculation	**Description**
Average	Finds the average value of all of the values in the field.
Correlation With	Finds the relationship between the selected field and another field in the database or on the report. (3)
Covariance With	Finds the difference (often called the variance) between the selected field and another field in the database or on the report. (3)
Median	Finds the middle value of all the values in the field.
Mode	Finds the most frequently used value in the field.
P^{th} percentile, P is:	Is used to select a percent (the P is value) between 0 and 100 and calculates that percentile of the values in the field.
Population Standard Deviation	Calculates how far from the mean (the average) each value in the selected field deviates.
Population Variance	Divides the sum of the number of items in the population. The result is the population variance.
Sample Standard Deviation	Calculates the mean (the average) value for the data in the sample.
Sample Variance	Calculates the square root of the standard deviation of the sample.
Sum	Adds the values in the selected field to get a total.
Weighted Average With	Calculates the average by the number of times the value is in the selected field. You can also adjust the average by selecting another field. (3)

Table 9-5 Numeric summary calculation options explained

(3) This summary type requires two fields. One that is used as the basis of the summary (this is the field that you select at the top of the Insert Summary dialog box). The other field is used for comparison. When this summary type is selected, the drop-down list illustrated in Figure 9-9 is displayed. This is where you select the second field that is discussed above.

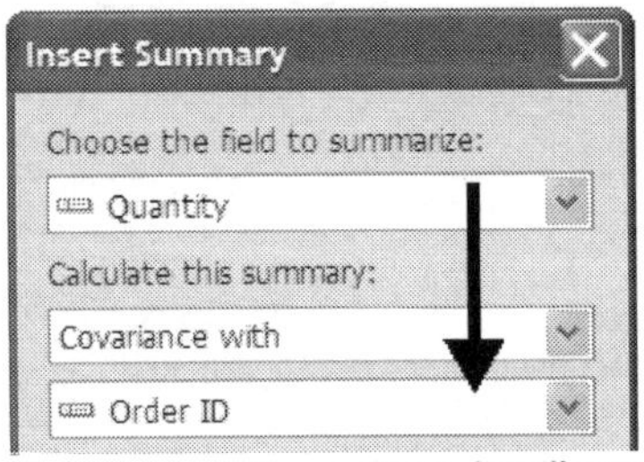

Figure 9-9 Drop-down list illustrated

Date and Boolean fields can only be used in the following types of calculations: Count, distinct count, maximum, minimum, mode, Nth largest, Nth most frequent and Nth smallest.

In addition to the summary options that you read about in Tables 9-4 and 9-5 above, the summary options in Table 9-6 are also available. They are located at the bottom of the Insert Summary dialog box.

Option	Description
Summary Location	Is used to select the section of the report where you want to place the summary field. The good thing is that you are not limited to the options in the drop-down list. You can manually copy or move the summary field to another section of the report.
Add to all group levels	If checked, this option will add the summary field to all existing group levels on the report. This means that you no longer have to create the same summary field manually for every group section that needs the summary field.
Show as a percentage of	Calculates a comparison of the percent of one group that is part of a larger group. If selected, this option is used to select the group or total that you want the comparison to be based on. For example, this option can calculate the percent of sales for June compared to the sales for the entire year. The result would display what percent (out of 100%) the sales in June accounted for, compared to the sales for the entire year. This option is not available for all types of calculations. (4)
Summarize across hierarchy	On reports that have hierarchical groups (groups that have parent/child relationships), an identical summary field will be added to all subgroups under the primary hierarchical group. An example of a report that could have hierarchical groups would be one that displays a list of department managers (the parent group) and the employees (the child group) that are in each department.

Table 9-6 Summary options explained

(4)

Percentage summaries cannot be placed in the Report Footer section.

Headings are not automatically created for group summary fields like they are for fields in the Details section. By default, summary fields are usually placed in a section below the field that it is summarizing. One exception would be if the summary field is placed in the Group Header section.

If all of the summary calculation options seem a little confusing right now don't worry, you will only see options in the drop-down list that are available for the field type that you select to create the calculation for.

> Many of the exercises in this chapter will have you create a title for the report or a title for a field. When you see the phrase "Create a title", that means to add a text object to the report and type in the specified text. Report titles should be placed in the Page Header section unless stated otherwise. They should also be centered across the report.

Summary Field Limitations

While summary fields allow you to create a variety of totals, counts and averages, there are some things that you should be aware of, as discussed below.

① Summary fields cannot be placed in the Details section.

② Summary field calculations include suppressed records, which means that detail records that meet the selection criteria, but do not appear on the report are included in the calculation.

Creating Groups

The reports that you modify in this chapter will show you how to apply a variety of group and sorting options effectively. The name of each exercise describes how the data will be grouped. You will also learn more formatting techniques. As you will see, the more data that you add to a report, the more the report needs to be formatted.

Exercise 9.1: Group Customer Information By Region

In this exercise you will modify a report to include the following group and sorting options. These options also allow you to create totals for the group.

① Group the data by the Region field and sort the group in ascending order.

② Create a count of detail records in each group.

③ Sort the detail records in each group in ascending order by the Postal Code field.

1. Save the Chapter 9 Customer Info report as `E9.1 Customer info by region`.

2. Open the Insert Group dialog box. Open the first drop-down list and select the **REGION** field from the Customer table.

Notice that a **GROUP HEADER** and **GROUP FOOTER** section have been added to the report, as illustrated in Figure 9-10.

If you also wanted to group this report on a second field, you would see a second set of Group Header and Footer sections, as shown in Figure 9-11.

The report should look like the one shown in Figure 9-12.

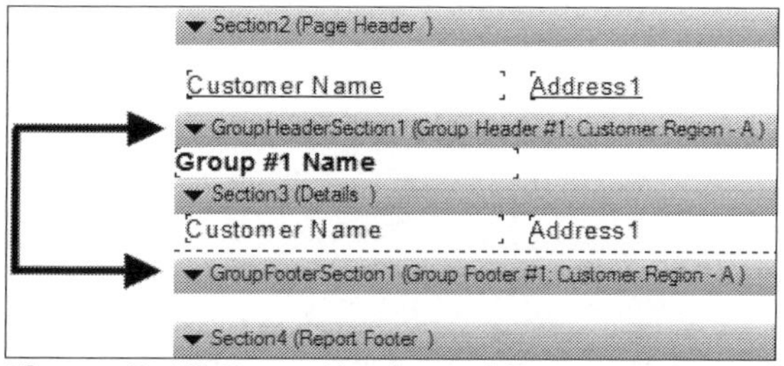

Figure 9-10 Group Header and Footer sections added to the report

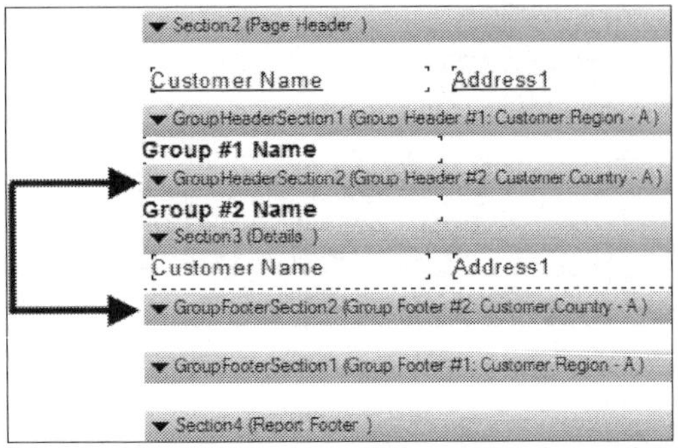

Figure 9-11 Two sets of Group Header and Footer sections

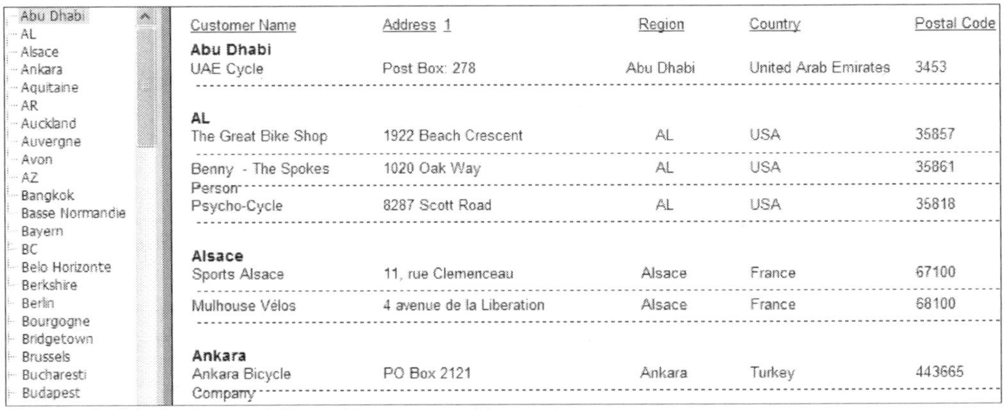

Figure 9-12 Customer information grouped by region

Notice that the group name is bold on the report. This makes it easier to know where each group starts. If you look in the Group Tree section on Figure 9-12 above, you will see all of the groups that the report has. If you scroll down the Group Tree and click on the **PA** group, that section of the report will be displayed, as shown in Figure 9-13.

Figure 9-13 Customers in the PA region

By default, group name fields are added to the Group Header section of the report. If at some point you decide that you do not want the group name to automatically be added to the Group Header section, you can turn the **INSERT GROUP NAME WITH GROUP** option off on the Layout tab on the Options dialog box. If you turn this option off and then need to add a group name to a specific report, you can, without turning this option back on.

Sort The Detail Records

As you can see in Figure 9-12 shown earlier, the detail records in each group are not sorted on any field. Unless you specify a sort order, the detail records will appear in the report based on the order they are retrieved from the database. In this part of the exercise you will sort the detail records by the Postal Code field.

1. Open the Record Sort Expert dialog box and click on the Postal Code field in the **AVAILABLE FIELDS** list, then click the **>** button. Select the **ASCENDING** sort order, if it is not already selected. Figure 9-14 shows the sort options that should be selected.

Notice that the group information for the report is the first entry in the **SORT FIELDS** section of the Record Sort Expert dialog box shown in Figure 9-14.

This is done to outline the sort order for the entire report.

The first way that the report will be sorted is by group.

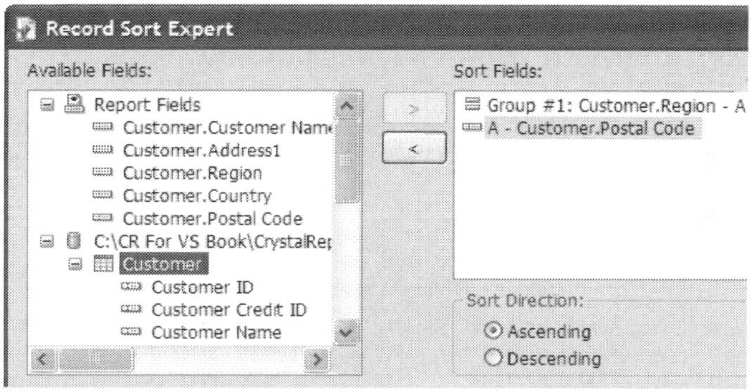

Figure 9-14 Report sort options

Remember that the group is sorted in ascending order, which is denoted by the **A** at the end of the group field. If the field was sorted in descending order, you would see a **D** at the end of the field.

If you need to sort a report by a persons name and the name is in two fields, you should sort on the last name field first, then sort on the first name field.

The detail records in each group will be sorted in ascending order by the Postal Code field.

If you wanted to sort on other fields in the group you can do that also, as shown in Figure 9-15.

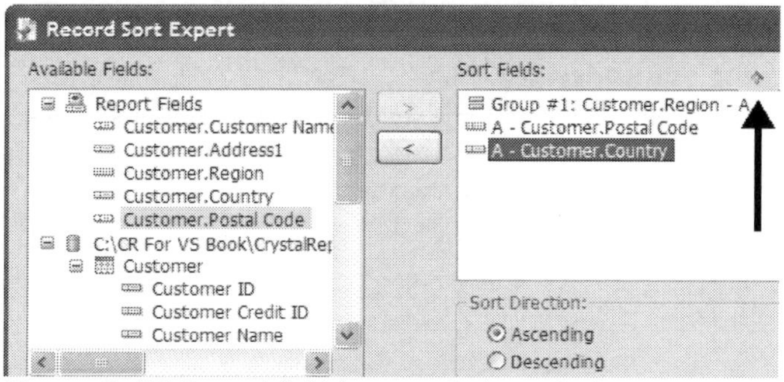

Figure 9-15 Second field in group to be sorted on

In this example, adding the Country field means that within each group, the detail records would be sorted by Postal Code first and then within each Postal Code in the group, the records would be sorted by Country. In reality, these sort options would produce strange results. It is shown here for illustration purposes only.

A better way to sort on these two fields would be to sort on the Country field first in each group, because there are several Postal Codes within each Country. If you wanted to sort on the Country field first instead of the Postal Code field, you would click on the Country field, then click the **UP** arrow. This would move the Country field up, as shown in Figure 9-16.

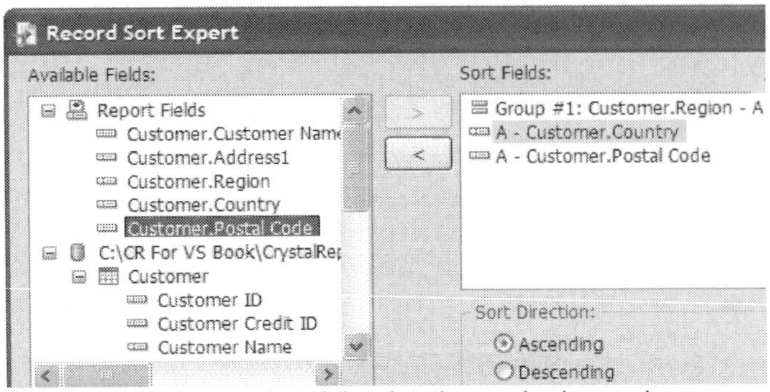

Figure 9-16 Sort order of the detail records changed

> When you make changes to groups or sorting options, you should refresh the data because you may not have all of the data based on the modified sorting and grouping options that have been selected.

2. Preview the report. Go to the PA group. You should see the records shown in Figure 9-17. Notice the different order of the detail records in this version of the report, compared to the order of the detail records in the report shown earlier in Figure 9-13. Leave the report open to complete the next part of the exercise.

PA				
Tek Bikes	8018 Meacon Crescent	PA	USA	19144
Backpedal Cycle Shop	743 Three Rivers Way	PA	USA	19178
Rocky Roadsters	1430 Hastings Boulevard	PA	USA	19440
Insane Cycle	5198 Argus Place	PA	USA	19442
Clean Air Transportation Co.	1867 Thurlow Lane	PA	USA	19453

Figure 9-17 Report with detail record sort order added

Count Summary Field Overview

Creating summary fields is the third step in the grouping and sorting process. In this part of the exercise you will create a summary field that will count the number of detail records in each group.

Create The Count Summary Field

1. On the Insert Summary dialog box open the first drop-down list and select the Customer ID field.

2. Open the second drop-down list and select **COUNT**. You should see all of the options that were discussed earlier in Tables 9-4 and 9-5 for Customer ID field because it is a numeric field.

3. Open the **SUMMARY LOCATION** drop-down list and select the Group 1 option.

   Figure 9-18 shows the summary options that you should have selected. The summary field should be in the Group Footer section.

   The report should look like the one shown in Figure 9-19. The number in bold below the dotted lines is the count field that you just created.

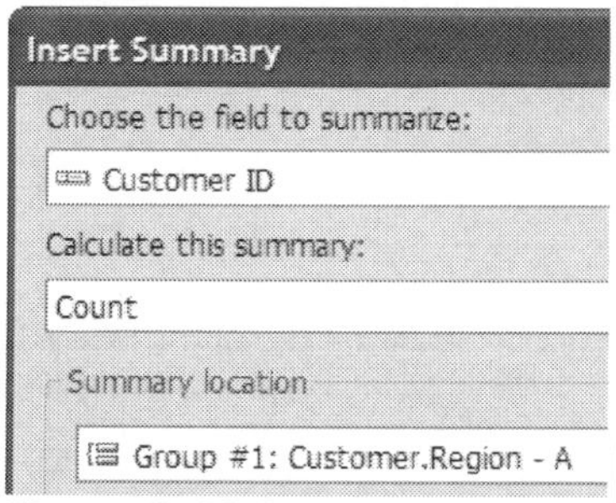

Figure 9-18 Summary options

Customer Name	Address1	Region	Country	Postal Code
Abu Dhabi				
UAE Cycle	Post Box: 278	Abu Dhabi	United Arab Em	3453
1				
AL				
Psycho-Cycle	8287 Scott Road	AL	USA	35818
The Great Bike Shop	1922 Beach Crescent	AL	USA	35857
Benny - The Spokes Person	1020 Oak Way	AL	USA	35861
3				
Alsace				
Sports Alsace	11, rue Clemenceau	Alsace	France	67100
Mulhouse Vélos	4 avenue de la Libération	Alsace	France	68100
2				

Figure 9-19 Report with the summary field added

When used with detail level fields, summary functions like Average and Count will not include records when the detail level field is null because null fields do not contain anything, which is different then an empty string or a zero.

For example, if you were creating a summary field that counts on the city field and some records did not have any data in the city field and the database was set to use **NULL VALUES**, records that fall into this category would print on the report, but would not be included in the count summary calculation.

Often, this may not be what you want to happen. If this is the case, checking the **CONVERT DATABASE NULL VALUES TO DEFAULT** option on the Report Options dialog box will automatically convert the null values in the database to an empty string for string fields or zero for numeric fields. Selecting this option will include records in the count or average summary calculation. If you want this to be the default option for all reports, check the same option on the Reporting tab on the Options dialog box.

Modify The Report

The report would look better if the following changes were made.

① Add a report title, print date and page number.
② Change the Postal Code heading to Zip Code.
③ Change the Address1 heading to Address.
④ Delete the Region field from the Details section of the report. The field is not needed in this section because it is the field that the report is grouped on.
⑤ Create a title for the summary field that you created.
⑥ Create a grand total for the number of customers that are displayed on the report. Place this field in the Report Footer section.
⑦ Rearrange the fields in the Details section so that the report is easier to read.

Add A Report Title, Print Date And Page Number

1. Make the Page Header section longer, so that you will have room to add the report titles. Move all of the headings in the Page Header section down.

2. Create a report title in the Page Header section and type `Customer Information Grouped By Region` in the object. Make the font size 16 and make the title bold.

3. Create a second report title and type `Sorted By Zip Code` in the object. Change the font size to 14 and make the title bold.

4. Center both of these titles across the page.

5. Add the Print Date special field to the Page Header section below the second report title on the left, then add the Page N of M special field across from the Print Date field on the right. Right align the Page Number field.

Change The Field Headings And Delete Fields

1. Change the Address1 field heading to `Address`, then change the Postal Code field heading to `Zip Code`.

2. Delete the Region field.

3. Move the Address field and heading over to the right and make the Customer Name field wider.

Create A Title For The Summary Field

1. Create a title for the summary field in the Group Footer section and type `Total # of customers in region -` in the object. Right align the title.

2. Move the summary field over and place the field title that you just created before it, then remove the bold from the summary field and left align the field.

3. Make the Group Footer section a little longer so that there will be more blank space on the report before the next group prints.

Create A Grand Total Summary Field

Grand totals are also known as **RUNNING TOTALS** because they keep a total for all of the detail records that are included on the report. Earlier in this chapter you learned how to create group summary totals, which are also known as **SUBTOTALS**. The difference between a group summary total and a running total is that a running total field cannot be summarized.

Another difference between group summary total fields and running total fields is that group summary total fields are automatically reset to zero each time a new group is started, as shown earlier in Figure 9-19. Running Total fields have the option of being reset to zero.

Grand or running total fields that are placed in the Report Footer section include all of the records in the report, regardless of which group the detail records are in. Earlier in this chapter, I stated that depending on the section of the report that the summary field is placed in, you will get different results. The summary field that you will copy to the Report Footer section in this exercise will demonstrate this.

1. Copy the summary field in the Group Footer section to the Report Footer section.

2. Create a title for the summary field in the Report Footer section and type `Grand Total # of customers on this report.` Start this title at the two inch mark. Move the grand total field to the right of the title.

> You could create another summary field by using the Insert Summary dialog box, just like the one you created for the Group Footer section and place it in the Report Footer section. I find it easier to copy the field and place the second field in the section that I need it in.

Rearrange The Fields

1. Move the fields in the Details section to the right so that the Customer Name field starts at the half inch mark.

2. Delete the dotted line in the Details section. The report layout should look like the one shown in Figure 9-20.

   Page 1 of the report should look like the one shown in Figure 9-21. The end of the report on the last page should look like the one shown in Figure 9-22. The total number of pages in the report depends on the spacing that you have in each section of the report. Adjust the spacing if necessary, so that it is readable.

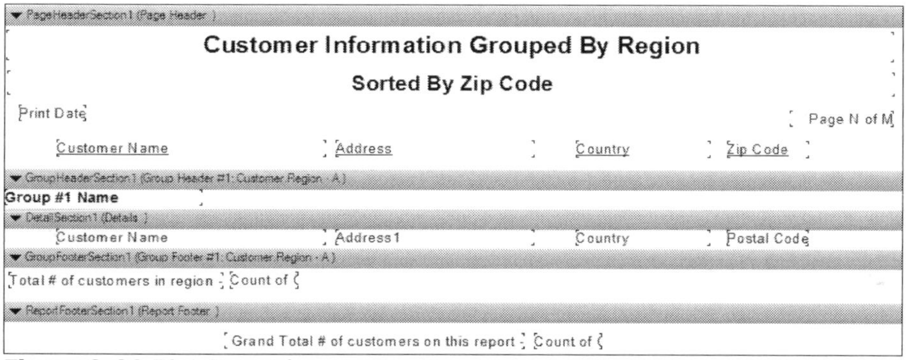

Figure 9-20 E9.1 Report layout

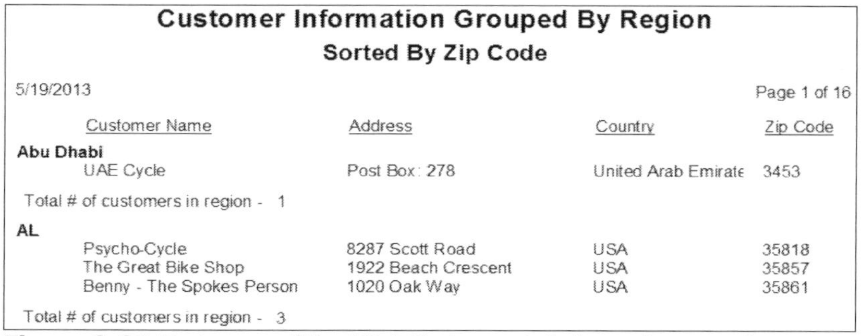

Figure 9-21 First page of the E9.1 Customer info by region report

Figure 9-22 Last page of the E9.1 Customer info by region report

3. If you open the Field Explorer and click on the plus sign in front of the **GROUP NAME FIELDS** option, you will see the Region group that you created, as illustrated in Figure 9-23.

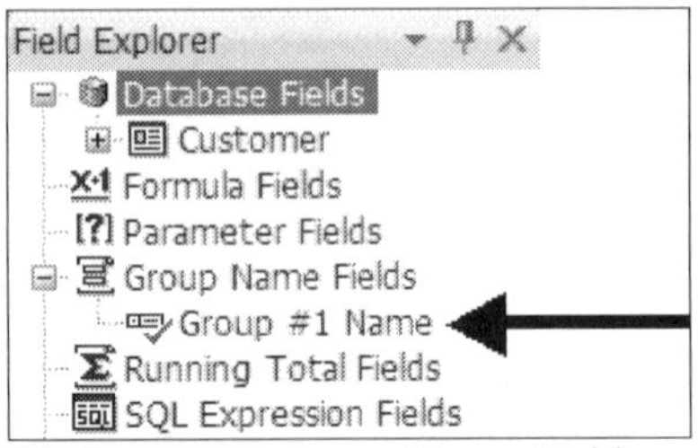

Figure 9-23 Group Name Fields section of the Field Explorer illustrated

You can drag a group name field from the **GROUP NAME FIELDS** section of the Field Explorer onto the report. If you prefer to keep the data in the Group Header or Footer section visible, but not display it on the report, you can suppress the section.

Exercise 9.2: Group Orders By Customer

In this exercise you will modify a report to include the following group and sorting options.

① Group on the Customer Name field and sort the group in ascending order.
② Sort the detail records in each group in ascending order by Order Date.
③ Provide a count of detail records for each customer in each group.
④ Create a total amount per customer based on the order amount field. This will let the person reading the report know the total amount of the orders placed by each customer.

These options will create counts and totals for the group. The changes that you will make to the report will place all of the orders for each customer together. This will make the report more effective, because you will be able to see all of a customers orders in one place. In Exercise 9.1, you created a group based on a field that was not being printed on the report. Groups are often created on fields that are printed on the report, but it is not a requirement.

1. Save the E8.3 report as `E9.2 Orders by customer`.

2. Open the Select Expert. Change the Order Date criteria to 6/24/2011.

3. On the Insert Group dialog box open the first drop-down list and select the Customer Name field, then click OK. The report should look like the one shown in Figure 9-24.

Customer Name	Order Date	Ship Date	Order Amount	Order ID	Unit Price
Alley Cat Cycles					
Alley Cat Cycles	2/19/2012 12:00:00AM	2/22/2012 12:00:00AM	$8,819.55	2,735	$2,939.85
Alley Cat Cycles	10/27/2011 12:00:00AM	11/6/2011 12:00:00AM	$2,699.55	2,272	$899.85
Alley Cat Cycles	1/31/2012 12:00:00AM	2/3/2012 12:00:00AM	$9,290.30	2,664	$455.86
Alley Cat Cycles	1/31/2012 12:00:00AM	2/3/2012 12:00:00AM	$9,290.30	2,664	$2,792.86
Alley Cat Cycles	9/28/2011 12:00:00AM	9/30/2011 12:00:00AM	$2,559.63	2,157	$313.36
Alley Cat Cycles	9/28/2011 12:00:00AM	9/30/2011 12:00:00AM	$2,559.63	2,157	$539.85
Alley Cat Cycles	2/19/2012 12:00:00AM	2/22/2012 12:00:00AM	$8,819.55	2,735	$2,939.85
Backpedal Cycle Shop					
Backpedal Cycle Shop	12/18/2011 12:00:00AM	12/19/2011 12:00:00AM	$6,226.05	2,507	$2,939.85
Backpedal Cycle Shop	11/16/2011 12:00:00AM	11/18/2011 12:00:00AM	$10,798.95	2,358	$2,939.85

Figure 9-24 Orders grouped by customer

Sort The Detail Records

As you can see in Figure 9-24 above, the report is now grouped by customer. The detail records in each group are not sorted. Because orders are entered into the database in the order that they are received, they are often already in date order. There are exceptions to this, including orders that may get changed some how during the ordering process.

Other exceptions that have to be accounted for include how the tables are linked and how the database sends the records to Crystal Reports. To be on the safe side, it is best to control the sort order. In this exercise that means that you should sort the records by the Order Date field to ensure that they are in date order, if that is what the requirement of the report calls for.

1. On the Record Sort Expert dialog box, add the Order Date field to the Sort Fields list.

2. Select the ascending sort order, if it is not already selected.

Total Summary Fields Overview

In this part of the exercise you will create a summary field that will create a total dollar amount of orders for each customer. You will also create a count to show the number of orders for each customer.

> The default summary type is **SUM** for numeric fields.
> The default summary type is **MAXIMUM** for Boolean, date and string fields.

Create The Total Summary Field

This summary field will create a total dollar amount of orders for each customer.

1. On the Insert Summary dialog box open the first drop-down list and select the Order Amount field, then open the second drop-down list and select **SUM**.

2. Open the Summary Location drop-down list and select the Group 1 option. The order amount summary field should be in the Group Footer section.

Create The Count Summary Field

This summary field will create a count of the number of orders for each customer.

1. On the Insert Summary dialog box open the first drop-down list and select the Order ID field in the Orders table, then open the second drop-down list and select **COUNT**.

2. Open the Summary Location drop-down list and select the Group 1 option. The count summary field should be in the Group Footer section.

Create The Distinct Count Summary Field

The distinct count summary will only count the information in a field once. If there are 20 orders for one customer, the distinct count calculation will only count that customer once. This will let you create a count for the total number of customers that are on the report.

1. On the Insert Summary dialog box open the first drop-down list and select the Customer Name field, if it is not already selected, then open the second drop-down list and select **DISTINCT COUNT**.

2. Open the Summary Location drop-down list and select the **GRAND TOTAL (REPORT FOOTER)** option, if it is not already selected. The distinct count only needs to appear once, at the end of the report. The distinct count summary field should be in the Report Footer section. The report should look like the one shown in Figure 9-25. As you can see, the report needs a little work.

Customer Name	Order Date	Ship Date	Order Amount	Order #	Unit Price
Alley Cat Cycles					
Alley Cat Cycles	09/28/2011	09/30/2011	$2,559.63	2157	$313.36
Alley Cat Cycles	09/28/2011	09/30/2011	$2,559.63	2157	$539.85
Alley Cat Cycles	10/27/2011	11/06/2011	$2,699.55	2272	$899.85
Alley Cat Cycles	01/31/2012	02/03/2012	$9,290.30	2664	$455.86
Alley Cat Cycles	01/31/2012	02/03/2012	$9,290.30	2664	$2,792.86
Alley Cat Cycles	02/19/2012	02/22/2012	$8,819.55	2735	$2,939.85
Alley Cat Cycles	02/19/2012	02/22/2012	$8,819.55	2735	$2,939.85
			$44,038.51	**7**	

Figure 9-25 Orders by customer report

If you view the last page of the report you will see the number 78. This is the distinct count summary field that you just created, which shows how many customers are on the report. In the next part of this exercise you will create a title for this field.

Modify The Report

The report would look better if the following changes were made.

① Add a report title, print date and page number.

② Create titles for the summary fields.

③ Create a grand total field and title for the Order Amount field and for the grand total count of order summary field. Place these fields in the Report Footer section.

④ Remove the time from the Order Date and Ship Date fields.

⑤ Add a line above all of the summary fields.

⑥ Rearrange the fields in the Details section so that the report is easier to read.

1. Create a report title in the Page Header section and type `Customer Orders` in the object. Change the font size to 16 and make the title bold. Center the title across the page.

> If a report has selection criteria, it is a good idea to incorporate the selection criteria in the report. Doing this lets the reader know what criteria the report is using. This report will print records for orders that were placed after a specific date and have a specific minimum order amount. How, or if you incorporate this information is up to you and the requestors of the report. Keep in mind that business decisions are based off of the data in reports, so providing as much helpful and useful information as possible is a good thing.

2. Add the Print Date special field to the Page Header section below the report title on the right. Add the Page N of M special field to the Page Footer section in the right corner and right align this field.

3. Copy both of the summary fields in the Group Footer section and place them in the Report Footer section.

> If you select both fields before you select the **COPY** command, you can copy both fields at the same time.

4. Create the field titles in Table 9-7 for the summary fields. The section column in the table refers to the section in the report where the title should be placed. Make all of the titles bold.

Summary Field	Section	Title
Order Amount	Group Footer	Total $ amount of orders -
Order ID	Group Footer	Total # orders -
Customer Name	Report Footer	Total # of customers on this report -
Order Amount	Report Footer	Grand Total $ amount of all orders -
Order ID	Report Footer	Grand Total # of orders -

Table 9-7 Field titles for Exercise 9.2

If I know that the report needs several field titles with the same formatting, I create one and then copy it and just change the text. Over time, you will find a process that works best for you.

I usually right align titles for calculated fields, when the title is placed to the left of the calculated field. Doing this reduces the amount of white space between the title and the calculated field. When I do this, I also left align the corresponding calculated field to further reduce the space between the field and the title. The other option is to drag the calculated field into the text object.

5. Remove the time from the Order Date and Ship Date fields.

6. Delete the Customer Name field. Delete the Record Number field from the Report Footer section. Remove the bold from the Group Name field.

Group Name objects can be formatted like any other object in the report.

7. Change the Order ID heading to `Order #`, then format the Order ID and Order ID count summary fields to display as a whole number without a comma.

8. Add a line to the bottom of the Group Footer section. Change the size of the line to 0.5 pt. Leave the report open to complete the next part of the exercise.

Add A Line Above The Summary Fields

1. Move the summary fields in the Group Footer section down, so that you have room to add the line.

2. Right-click on the Order Amount summary field in the Group Footer section and select **FORMAT OBJECT**. On the Border tab, open the **TOP** drop-down list, select **SINGLE**.

The advantage of using the line option on the Border tab for a field is that if you move or resize the field, the line is automatically re-adjusted. You can also use the **LINE** tool to draw a line. If you use the Line tool and you move or resize the field, you will also have to move or resize the line.

3. Rearrange the fields so that they look like the layout shown in Figure 9-26.
The first page of the report should look like the one shown in Figure 9-27.
The Report Footer section on the last page should have the totals shown in Figure 9-28.

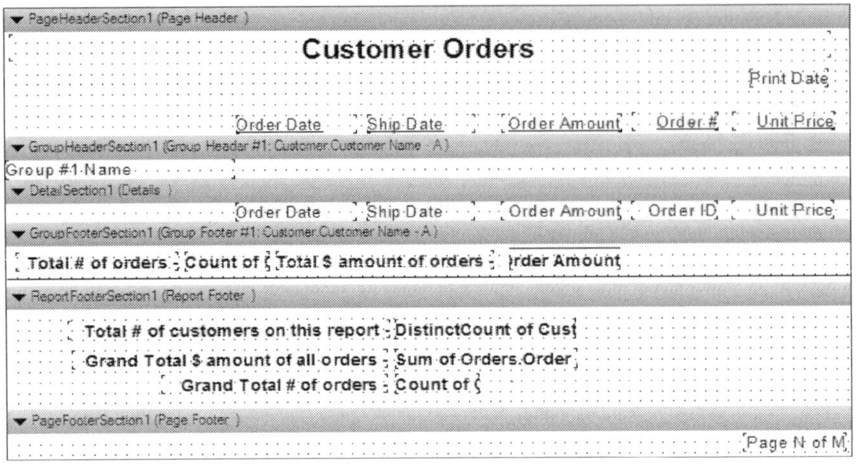

Figure 9-26 E9.2 Report layout

Customer Orders

5/19/2013

	Order Date	Ship Date	Order Amount	Order #	Unit Price
Alley Cat Cycles					
	09/28/2011	09/30/2011	$2,559.63	2157	$313.36
	09/28/2011	09/30/2011	$2,559.63	2157	$539.85
	10/27/2011	11/06/2011	$2,699.55	2272	$899.85
	01/31/2012	02/03/2012	$9,290.30	2664	$455.86
	01/31/2012	02/03/2012	$9,290.30	2664	$2,792.86
	02/19/2012	02/22/2012	$8,819.55	2735	$2,939.85
	02/19/2012	02/22/2012	$8,819.55	2735	$2,939.85
Total # of orders - 7		**Total $ amount of orders -**	**$44,038.51**		
Backpedal Cycle Shop					
	07/02/2011	07/04/2011	$3,479.70	1802	$1,739.85
	08/15/2011	08/19/2011	$3,415.95	1972	$479.85
	08/15/2011	08/19/2011	$3,415.95	1972	$764.85
	08/15/2011	08/19/2011	$3,415.95	1972	$53.90

Figure 9-27 Page 1 of the E9.2 Orders by customer report

Total # of customers on this report - 78
Grand Total $ amount of all orders - $ 4,015,868.71
Grand Total # of orders - 724

Figure 9-28 Last page of the E9.2 Orders by customer report

If you see **###'s** in a field, make the field wider.

Exercise 9.3: Group Orders By Shipping Method

In this exercise you will modify a report to include the following group and sorting options. These options also allow you to create totals for the group.

① Group on the Ship Via field and sort the groups in ascending order.
② Sort the detail records in ascending order on the Order Date field.
③ Create a count of orders in each ship via group.
④ Create a total per customer in each ship via group.

This report currently only displays orders between $2,000 and $5,000. In order to get a count of detail records for each group and a total per customer, two groups need to be created. To get an accurate count of orders for each shipping method in 2011, the existing selection criteria needs to be deleted and new criteria has to be created.

Create The Ship Via And Customer Name Groups

1. Save the Chapter 9 Shipping Info report as `E9.3 Orders by shipping method`.

2. On the Insert Group dialog box open the first drop-down list, select the **SHIP VIA** field, then click OK.

3. On the Insert Group dialog box open the first drop-down list and select the **CUSTOMER NAME** field, if it is not already selected, then click OK.

   You should have two groups in the report layout, as shown in Figure 9-29.

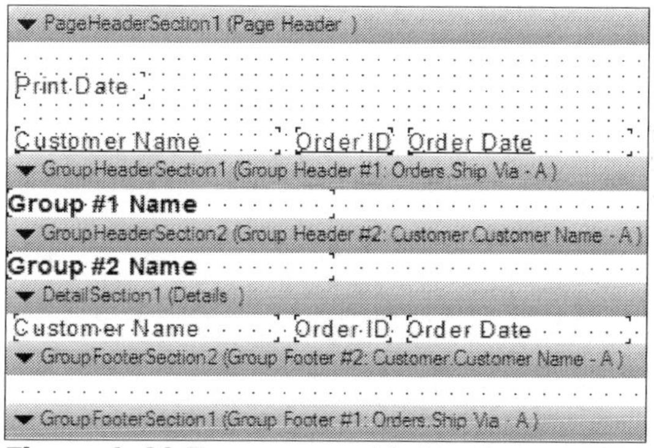

Figure 9-29 Two groups added to the report

4. On the Record Sort Expert dialog box, add the Order Date field to the Sort Fields list. Select the Ascending sort order, if it is not already selected.

Change The Selection Criteria

The report that this one is based off of, has selection criteria that is not needed in the report that you are modifying now. This report needs criteria to only display records from 2011.

1. Open the Select Expert and delete all of the current criteria.

2. Create criteria to only include orders placed in 2011.

Create The Summary Fields

This report requires two summary fields: a count of orders and a total dollar amount of orders per customer.

Create The Order ID Count Summary Field

This count summary field will create a total number of orders per customer. It will also be copied to the Report Footer section to create a grand total number of orders on the report.

1. On the Insert Summary dialog box open the first drop-down list and select the Order ID field. Open the second drop-down list and select Count.

2. Open the Summary Location drop-down list and select the Group 2 option. This will place the summary field in the customer name Group Footer section.

Create The Order Amount Summary Field

This summary field will create a total dollar amount per customer. It will also be copied to the Report Footer section to create a grand total order amount on the report.

1. On the Insert Summary dialog box open the first drop-down list and select the Order Amount field, then open the second drop-down list and select Sum.

2. Open the Summary Location drop-down list and select the Group 2 option. The report should look like the one shown in Figure 9-30.

> Summary fields are available in the **FORMULA WORKSHOP**. They are not available in the Field Explorer.

5/19/2013

Customer Name	Order ID	Order Date	Order Amount	Ship Via	First Name	Last Name
FedEx						
Alley Cat Cycles						
Alley Cat Cycles	2,207	10/11/2011	$72.00	FedEx	Janet	Leverling
Alley Cat Cycles	2,301	10/31/2011	$1,664.70	FedEx	Michael	Suyama
Alley Cat Cycles	2,361	11/17/2011	$389.65	FedEx	Robert	King
	3		**$2,126.35**			
Backpedal Cycle Shop						
Backpedal Cycle Shop	1,311	02/19/2011	$6,233.05	FedEx	Robert	King
Backpedal Cycle Shop	1,802	07/02/2011	$3,479.70	FedEx	Anne	Dodsworth
Backpedal Cycle Shop	2,198	10/08/2011	$93.50	FedEx	Janet	Leverling
	3		**$9,806.25**			
BBS Pty						
BBS Pty	1,776	06/25/2011	$5,913.60	FedEx	Margaret	Peacock
BBS Pty	2,067	09/03/2011	$51.60	FedEx	Michael	Suyama
	2		**$5,965.20**			

Figure 9-30 E9.3 Orders by shipping method report

Modify The Report

The report would look better if the following changes were made.

① Add a report title and page number.
② Create titles for the summary fields.
③ Create a grand total field and title for the order amount and count of orders summary fields. Place the fields in the Report Footer section.
④ Rearrange the fields in the Details section so that the report is easier to read.

1. Create a report title in the Page Header section and type `2011 Orders By Shipping Method` in the object. Change the font size to 16 and make the title bold. Center the title across the page.

2. Move the Print Date field below the report title on the right, then add the Page N of M field to the Page Footer section in the right corner. Right align the field. Delete the Page Number field in the Page Footer section.

3. Add the image6.jpg file to the upper left corner of the Page Header section.

4. Change the Order ID field heading to `Order #`. Format the Order ID field to display as a whole number without a comma.

5. Delete the Customer Name and Ship Via fields. Remove the bold from the Group 2 Header field. Remove the bold from the summary fields in the Group 2 Footer section.

6. Move the First Name and Last Name fields over to the left. Delete the Last Name field header. Change the First Name field header to `Salesperson`. Center this header over the two name fields in the Details section.

7. Copy both of the summary fields in the Group 2 Footer section and place them in the Group 1 Footer and Report Footer sections.

8. Add a line under the totals in the Group 1 and 2 Footer sections. Change the line in the Group 1 Footer section to dotted. Change the size of the line in the Group 2 Footer section to 0.5.

9. Create the field titles in Table 9-8 for the summary fields.

Summary Field	Section	Title
Order Amount	Group 1 Footer	Total order amount for customers -
Order ID Count	Group 1 Footer	Total # of orders for customers
Order Amount	Group 2 Footer	Total order amount for customer -
Order ID Count	Group 2 Footer	Total # of orders for customer -
Order Amount	Report Footer	Total order amount for all customers -
Order ID	Report Footer	Total # of orders for all customers -

Table 9-8 Field titles for Exercise 9.3

10. Copy the Group 1 Header field and place the copy in the Group 1 Footer section, then remove the bold from the field in the Group 1 Footer section.

11. Create a title for the Group 1 Footer section and type `Totals For:` in the object. Create a title for the Report Footer section and type `Report Grand Totals:` in the object. Make both objects bold.

12. Arrange the fields so that they look like the layout shown in Figure 9-31. Page 1 should look like the one shown in Figure 9-32.

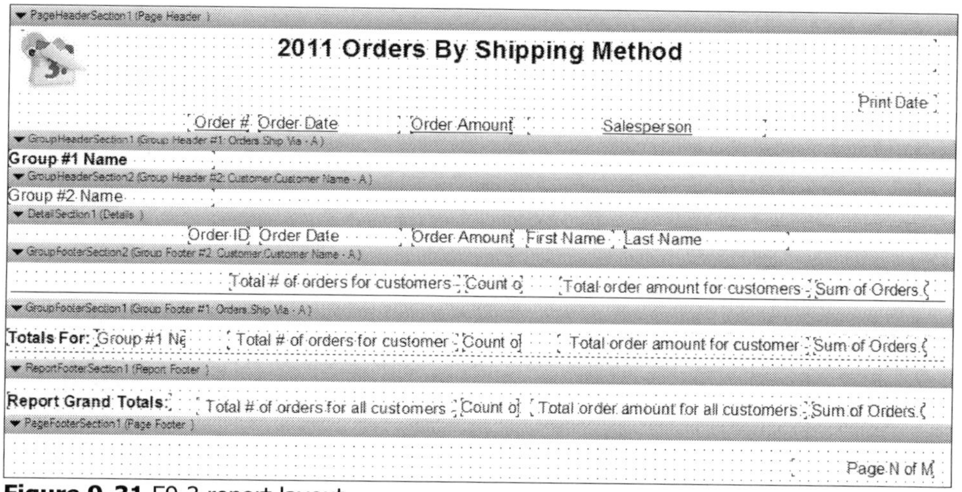

Figure 9-31 E9.3 report layout

2011 Orders By Shipping Method

5/22/2013

	Order #	Order Date	Order Amount	Salesperson	
FedEx					
Alley Cat Cycles					
	2207	10/11/2011	$72.00	Janet	Leverling
	2301	10/31/2011	$1,664.70	Michael	Suyama
	2361	11/17/2011	$389.65	Robert	King
	Total # of orders for customers - 3			Total order amount for customers - $ 2,126.35	
Backpedal Cycle Shop					
	1311	02/19/2011	$6,233.05	Robert	King
	1802	07/02/2011	$3,479.70	Anne	Dodsworth
	2198	10/08/2011	$93.50	Janet	Leverling
	Total # of orders for customers - 3			Total order amount for customers - $ 9,806.25	
BBS Pty					
	1776	06/25/2011	$5,913.60	Margaret	Peacock
	2067	09/03/2011	$51.60	Michael	Suyama
	Total # of orders for customers - 2			Total order amount for customers - $ 5,965.20	

Figure 9-32 Page 1 of the E9.3 Orders by shipping method report

13. Open the FedEx option in the Group Tree. Click on the company Yue Xiu Bicycles. You should see the page of the report shown in Figure 9-33. Notice the totals for the shipping method for FedEx. The bottom of the last page should look like the one shown in Figure 9-34.

Yue Xiu Bicycles					
	3148	06/20/2011	$2,939.85	Nancy	Davolio
	Total # of orders for customers - 1			Total order amount for customers - $ 2,939.85	
Totals For: FedEx	Total # of orders for customer - 271			Total order amount for customer - $ 495,054.99	

Figure 9-33 FedEx information on the E9.3 Orders by shipping method report

Yokohama Biking Fans					
	3174	06/25/2011	$33.90	Nancy	Davolio
	Total # of orders for customers - 1			Total order amount for customers - $ 33.90	
Totals For: UPS	Total # of orders for customer - 255			Total order amount for customer - $ 540,760.37	
Report Grand Totals:	Total # of orders for all customers - 1,562			Total order amount for all customers - $ 2,861,205.48	

Figure 9-34 Last page of the E9.3 Orders by shipping method report

CREATING CUSTOM GROUPS

After completing the exercises in this chapter you will be able to create and use the following types of group functionality:

- ☑ Create percent calculations
- ☑ Create a custom group name
- ☑ User defined sort order
- ☑ Use the Group Expert
- ☑ User defined groups

CHAPTER 10

Custom Groups Overview

In the previous chapter you learned how to create basic groups. While the group functionality that you learned about will handle a large percent of your grouping needs, there will be times when you need to modify something about the group.

When you find that you cannot quite figure out how to use the group options that you learned about in the previous chapter to create the groups that you need, you can create what I call custom groups. That is the focus of this chapter.

Exercise 10.1: Change The Group Order

The E9.3 report that you modified is grouped on two fields: Ship Via and Customer Name. If after viewing the report you decide that the groups should be in the opposite order, meaning that the first group should be the Customer Name, follow the steps below.

1. Save the E9.3 report as `E10.1 Change group order.`

2. Open the Group Expert. Click on the Ship Via group on the right, then click the down arrow button. Click OK.

Notice that Group Header 1 is now grouped on the Customer Name field. This is now the first field that the report will be grouped on, as shown in Figure 10-1. Refer back to Figure 9-32. If you look at the last page of the report, you will see that the report grand totals are the same, but in the E10.1 report, the totals for the shipping method are per customer.

2011 Orders By Shipping

5/20/2013

	Order #	Order Date	Order Amount	Salesperson	
7 Bikes For 7 Brothers					
Parcel Post					
	3054	05/26/2011	$53.90	Janet	Leverling
Totals For: Parcel Post	Total # of orders for customer - 1			Total order amount for customer - $ 53.90	
	Total # of orders for customers - 1			Total order amount for customers - $ 53.90	
Against The Wind Bikes					
Purolator					
	3055	05/26/2011	$479.85	Michael	Suyama
Totals For: Purolator	Total # of orders for customer - 1			Total order amount for customer - $ 479.85	
	Total # of orders for customers - 1			Total order amount for customers - $ 479.85	

Figure 10-1 Page 1 of the E10.1 Change group order report

If you open the Alley Cat Cycles group in the Group Tree you will see options for different types of shipping methods, as shown in Figure 10-2. This means that this company has deliveries from each of these shipping methods. You will see totals for each shipping company if you click on it in the Group Tree. If you go to the next page of the report, you will see the totals shown in Figure 10-3. These are the grand totals for the company.

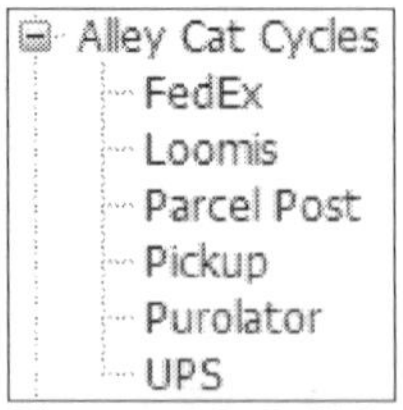

Figure 10-2 Shipping method options for a group

	Order #	Order Date	Order Amount	Salesperson
	2153	09/27/2011	$43.50	Margaret Peacock
	2455	12/06/2011	$43.50	Margaret Peacock
Totals For: UPS	Total # of orders for customer - 5		Total order amount for customer - $ 1,817.65	
	Total # of orders for customers - 21		Total order amount for customers - $ 25,781.75	

Figure 10-3 Totals for a shipping method

Custom Group Names

So far, the group names used in the reports have come from a field that the report is grouped on. In Crystal Reports there are options that let you customize the group name, as discussed below.

① Use a different field as the group name.
② Create a custom group name.
③ Create a user defined group name.
④ Create a formula to display the group name.

Use A Different Field As The Group Name

The custom group name option allows you to use one field to create the group and a different field to display as the group name. In Exercise 9.2, the report is grouped on the Customer Name field.

If that report was grouped on the Customer ID field instead, the group name would be displayed, as shown in Figure 10-4.

If you selected the options shown in Figure 10-5 on the Options tab for the Customer ID group field, the report would look like the one shown in Figure 10-6.

	Order Date	Ship Date	Order Amount	Order #	Unit Price
1					
	09/01/2011	09/02/2011	$4,078.95	2054	$329.85
	09/01/2011	09/02/2011	$4,078.95	2054	$539.85
	09/01/2011	09/02/2011	$4,078.95	2054	$899.85
	01/26/2012	01/26/2012	$2,939.85	2640	$2,939.85
	04/09/2012	04/16/2012	$5,549.40	2900	$329.85
	04/09/2012	04/16/2012	$5,549.40	2900	$1,739.85
2					
	07/21/2011	07/27/2011	$3,526.70	1883	$1,739.85
	07/21/2011	07/27/2011	$3,526.70	1883	$23.50
	08/06/2011	08/14/2011	$5,879.70	1941	$2,939.85
	10/19/2011	10/19/2011	$8,819.55	2242	$2,939.85
	04/26/2012	05/01/2012	$3,185.42	2969	$726.61
	04/26/2012	05/01/2012	$3,185.42	2969	$899.85
	04/26/2012	05/01/2012	$3,185.42	2969	$832.35
3					
	09/16/2011	09/24/2011	$5,545.42	2112	$14.50
	09/16/2011	09/24/2011	$5,545.42	2112	$296.87

Figure 10-4 Report grouped by the Customer ID field

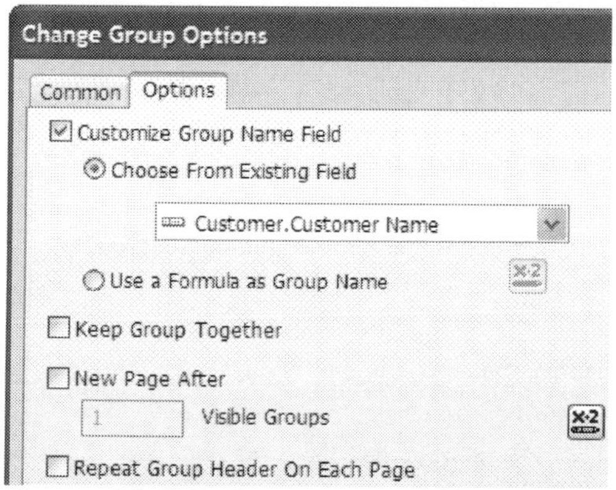

Figure 10-5 Options to use a different field as the group name

	Order Date	Ship Date	Order Amount	Order #	Unit Price
City Cyclists					
	09/01/2011	09/02/2011	$4,078.95	2054	$329.85
	09/01/2011	09/02/2011	$4,078.95	2054	$539.85
	09/01/2011	09/02/2011	$4,078.95	2054	$899.85
	01/26/2012	01/26/2012	$2,939.85	2640	$2,939.85
	04/09/2012	04/16/2012	$5,549.40	2900	$329.85
	04/09/2012	04/16/2012	$5,549.40	2900	$1,739.85
Pathfinders					
	07/21/2011	07/27/2011	$3,526.70	1883	$1,739.85
	07/21/2011	07/27/2011	$3,526.70	1883	$23.50
	08/06/2011	08/14/2011	$5,879.70	1941	$2,939.85
	10/19/2011	10/19/2011	$8,819.55	2242	$2,939.85
	04/26/2012	05/01/2012	$3,185.42	2969	$726.61
	04/26/2012	05/01/2012	$3,185.42	2969	$899.85
	04/26/2012	05/01/2012	$3,185.42	2969	$832.35
Bike-A-Holics Anonymous					
	09/16/2011	09/24/2011	$5,545.42	2112	$14.50

Figure 10-6 Report using a different field as the group name

Exercise 10.2: Group Orders By Month

In this exercise you will modify a report to include the following group and sorting options. These options also allow you to create totals and counts so that the records will be grouped by the month the orders were placed.

① Group on the Order Date field.

② Sort the detail records in ascending order on the Order Date field.

③ Provide a count of orders per month.

The goal of this exercise is to create a report that displays all of the orders from 2011 and have a subtotal for each month. In order to create a subtotal of orders for each month, the report needs to be grouped on the Order Date field. When you group on a date or date/time field, the Insert Group dialog box will display the option, **THE SECTION WILL BE PRINTED**. This option is used to create the group by month, day, quarter, year and more.

Create The Order Date Group

1. Save the Chapter 10 Group Orders report as `E10.2 Orders by month`.

2. On the Insert Group dialog box open the first drop-down list and select the **ORDER DATE** field.

   Open the last drop-down list and select **FOR EACH MONTH**. Figure 10-7 shows the group options that should be selected.

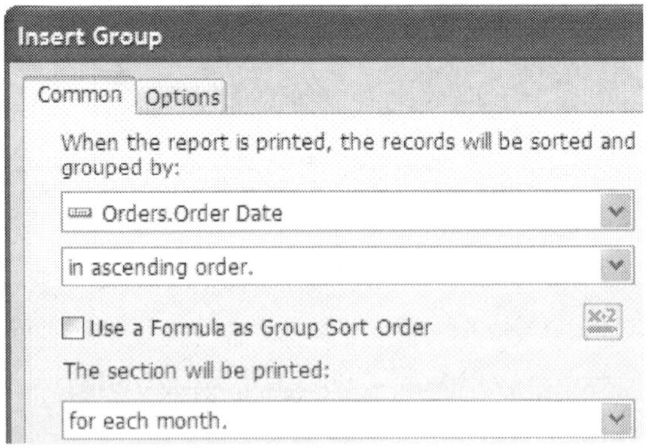

Figure 10-7 Group options

Sort The Detail Records

1. On the Record Sort Expert, add the Order Date field to the Sort Fields list.

2. Select the Ascending sort order, if it is not already selected. The detail records and groups will be sorted in order date.

Select The Records

In this part of the exercise you will create criteria to select all of the orders in 2011.

1. Click on the Order Date field in the Details section.

2. Open the Select Expert and select the **IS BETWEEN** operator, then type `01/01/2011` in the first field. Type `12/31/2011` in the last field.

Create The Order ID Count Summary Field

This count summary field will create a total for the number of orders per month. It will also be copied to the Report Footer section to create a grand total of orders for the entire report.

1. Add the Order Amount field in the Orders table after the Order ID field.

2. On the Insert Summary dialog box, open the first drop-down list and select the Order ID field in the Orders table, then open the second drop-down list and select **DISTINCT COUNT**. Open the Summary Location drop-down list and select the Group 1 option.

Create The Order Amount Summary Field

This summary field will create a total dollar amount per month. It will also be copied to the Report Footer section to create a grand total order amount.

1. Delete the Product ID, Unit Price and Quantity fields from the report.

2. On the Insert Summary dialog box open the first drop-down list and select the Order Amount field, then open the second drop-down list and select **SUM**. Open the Summary Location drop-down list and select the Group 1 option.

Create Percent Calculations

Percent calculations are very useful when you have the need to show what percent each group on the report represents in comparison to the grand total value on the report. For example, on a report that shows the sales for an entire year, there could be a percent calculation by month on the Order Amount field. This would tell the person that reads the report, the percent of sales each month represents for the year. Another example on a yearly sales report would be the percent of sales each salesperson had per month, per year or both.

> You can only create percent calculations on summary fields that have a numeric value. This means that if you are creating a count summary of customers based on the Customer Name field which is a text field, you can create a percent calculation, because the count calculation field is a numeric value.

Each percent calculation on a report requires its own percent summary calculation field. The process of creating a percent summary calculation starts off the same as the calculations that you have already created in this chapter. The options to create percent calculations are at the bottom of the Insert Summary dialog box. To create a percent calculation check the **SHOW AS A PERCENTAGE OF** option, then select the group or total that you want the percent comparison based on.

> If you need a total field and a percent calculation field that are based off of the same field, you have to create two summary calculation fields: one for the total amount and one for the percent.

In the previous part of the exercise you created the Order Amount summary field. Now you will create the Order Amount percent calculation field.

1. On the Insert Summary dialog box open the first drop-down list and select the Order Amount field, then open the second drop-down list and select **SUM**.

   Open the Summary Location drop-down list and select the Group 1 option, then check the **SHOW AS A PERCENTAGE OF** option.

   Figure 10-8 shows the summary options that should be selected.

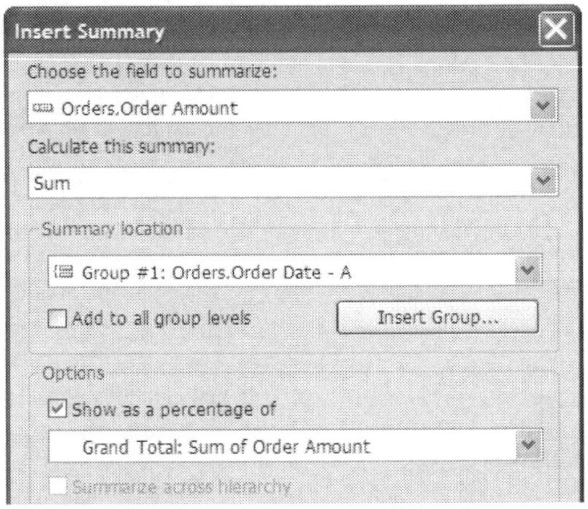

Figure 10-8 Insert Summary dialog box options

2. Move the percent summary field over to the right. On my report, it is currently on top of the Order Amount summary field that you just created. The third page of the report should look like the one shown in Figure 10-9. Notice that the percent summary field is already formatted with a percent sign.

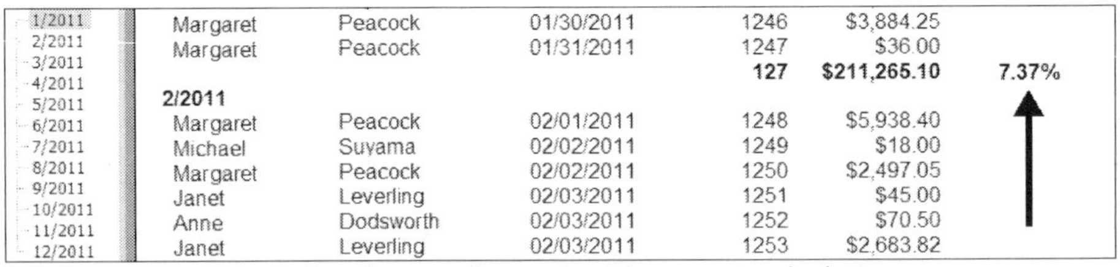

Figure 10-9 E10.2 Orders by month report with percent calculation

How To Check Or Edit Summary Fields

Sometimes reports will have more than two or three summary fields and you may not remember what each summary field is calculating. If a summary field is not producing the output that you think it should, it is possible that you selected an option that you should not have. If either of these is the case, all is not lost. You do not have to delete the field and start over. You can follow the steps below.

1. Right-click on the percentage summary field and select **CHANGE SUMMARY OPERATION**, as illustrated in Figure 10-10. You will then see the dialog box shown in Figure 10-11. You can make any changes that are necessary.

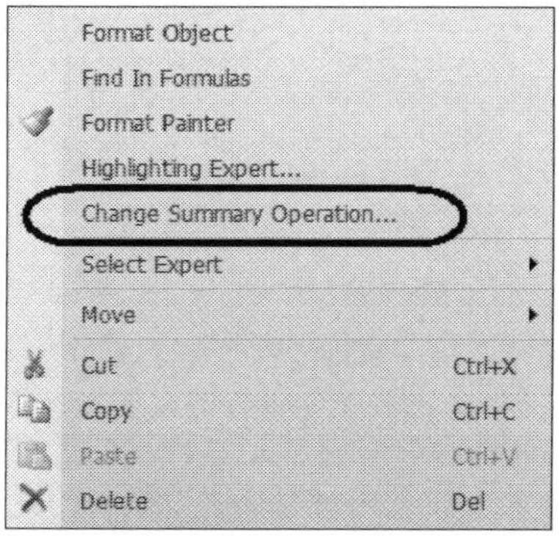

Figure 10-10 Change Summary Operation option illustrated

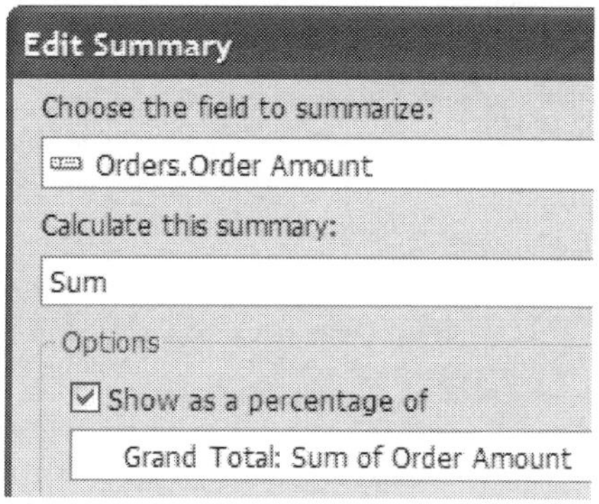

Figure 10-11 Edit Summary dialog box

The Edit Summary dialog box is almost identical to the Insert Summary dialog box. The difference is that you cannot change the location of the summary field. If you need to move a summary field from one section of the report to another, you will have to do it manually.

Modify The Report

The report would look better if the following changes were made.

① Add a report title.
② Create titles for the summary fields.
③ Create a grand total field and title for the order amount and count of orders summary fields. Place the fields in the Report Footer section.
④ Rearrange the fields in the Details section so that the report is easier to read.

1. Create a report title in the Page Header section and type `2011 Orders By Month` in the object. Make the font size 16 and place the title above the field headings.

2. Change the Order ID field heading to `Order #` and center the Order ID field.

3. Delete the Last Name field heading. Change the First Name field heading to `Salesperson`. Center this heading over the two name fields in the Details section.

4. Format the Order ID field in the Group 1 Footer section to display as a whole number without a comma.

5. Copy the Order ID and Order Amount summary fields in the Group 1 Footer section and place the copies in the Report Footer section.

6. Add a line under the totals in the Group 1 Footer section. Change the size of the line to 0.5.

7. Create the field titles in Table 10-1 for the summary fields.

Summary Field	Section	Title
Order Amount	Group 1 Footer	Total order amount for the month -
Order ID Count	Group 1 Footer	Total # orders for the month -
Order Amount Percent	Group 1 Footer	Percent of yearly sales -
Order Amount	Report Footer	Total order amount for the year -
Order ID	Report Footer	Total # orders for the year -

Table 10-1 Field titles for Exercise 10.2

8. Copy the Group 1 Header field and place the copy in the Group 1 Footer section. Remove the bold from the field in the Group 1 Footer section.

9. Create a title for the Group 1 Footer section and type `Totals For:` in the object. Create a title for the Report Footer section and type `Report Grand Totals:` in the object.

10. Add the Page N of M special field to the upper right corner of the report.

11. Arrange the fields so that they look like the layout shown in Figure 10-12. Leave the report open to complete the next part of the exercise.

When you preview the report you will see the months in the Group Tree section of the report. If you click on the 1/2011 group, as illustrated in Figure 10-13, you will see the orders that were placed in January. Later in this chapter you will change the group name to display the name of the month instead of the month number. The Percent of yearly sales field lets you know that the orders in January represent 7.37% of the total sales in 2011.

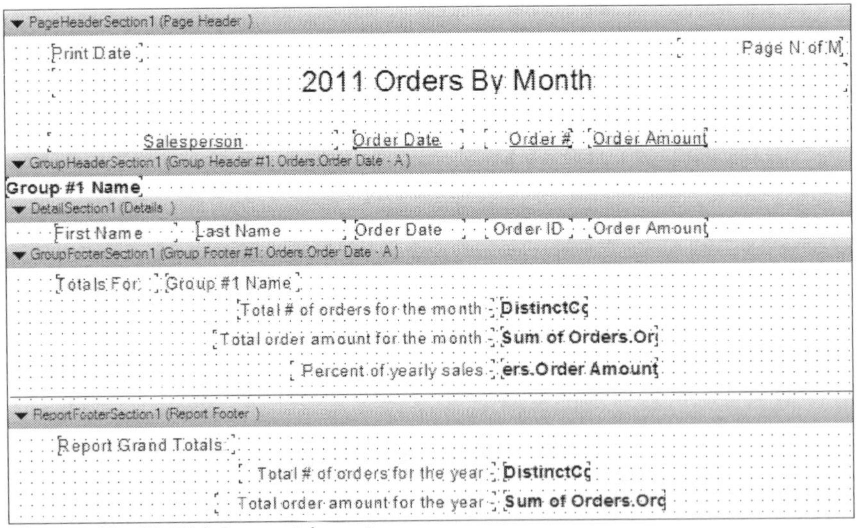

Figure 10-12 E10.2 report layout

1/2011
2/2011
3/2011
4/2011
5/2011
6/2011
7/2011
8/2011
9/2011
10/2011
11/2011
12/2011

5/20/2013 Page 3 of 29

2011 Orders By Month

Salesperson		Order Date	Order #	Order Amount
Robert	King	01/27/2011	1233	$139.48
Michael	Suyama	01/27/2011	1234	$1,723.22
Anne	Dodsworth	01/27/2011	1235	$1,642.05
Janet	Leverling	01/27/2011	1236	$989.55
Robert	King	01/27/2011	1237	$998.35
Robert	King	01/28/2011	1238	$1,024.01
Robert	King	01/28/2011	1239	$101.70
Robert	King	01/28/2011	1240	$3,635.34
Robert	King	01/28/2011	1241	$4,849.86
Michael	Suyama	01/29/2011	1242	$2,993.75
Michael	Suyama	01/29/2011	1243	$128.20
Janet	Leverling	01/30/2011	1244	$24.00
Michael	Suyama	01/30/2011	1245	$3,419.25
Margaret	Peacock	01/30/2011	1246	$3,884.25
Margaret	Peacock	01/31/2011	1247	$36.00

Totals For: 1/2011

Total # of orders for the month - **127**

Total order amount for the month - **$ 211,265.10**

Percent of yearly sales - **7.37%**

Figure 10-13 January orders

How To Create A Custom Group Name

The report would look better if the group name displayed the actual month name instead (January, February, March, etc.). The Format Editor has an option that you can use to display the month name. You could create a formula to accomplish this task, but using the Format Editor is easier. The steps below show you how to create a custom group name.

1. Right-click on the **GROUP 1 NAME** field in the Group Header section, then open the Format Editor. Click the **CUSTOMIZE** button on the Date and Time tab.

2. Open the **ORDER** drop-down list and select Date. Figure 10-14 shows the option that you should have selected.

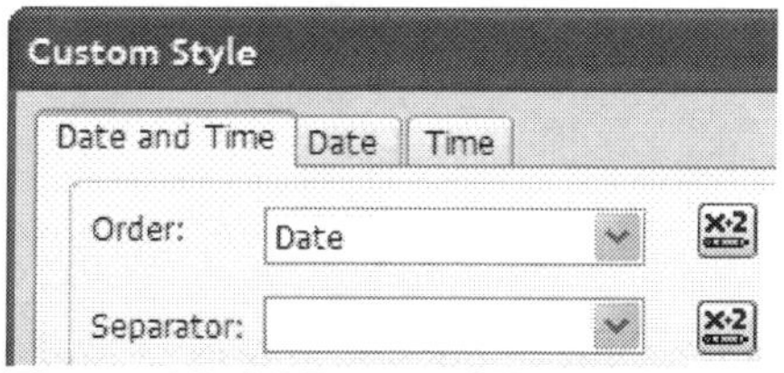

Figure 10-14 Date and Time tab options

3. On the Date tab open the Month drop-down list and select **MARCH**, then select **NONE** for the Day and Year options.

   Figure 10-15 illustrates the options that you should have selected.

   Click OK twice, to close both dialog boxes.

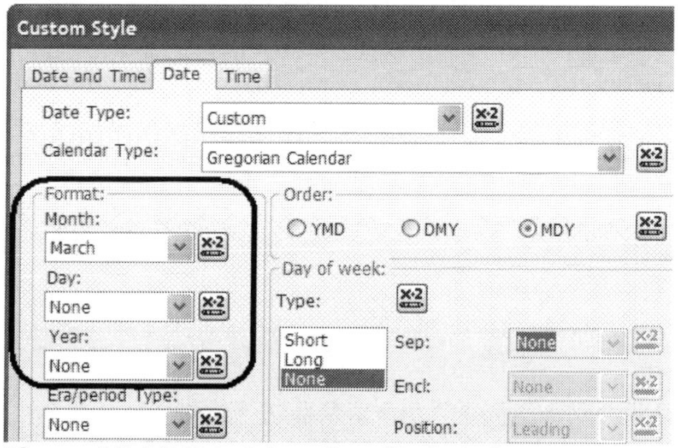

Figure 10-15 Date tab options illustrated

4. Format the Group Name field in the Group Footer section to have the same formatting as the one in the Group Header section.

5. View the last page of the report. The totals for December and the report grand totals should look like the ones shown in Figure 10-16.

   Leave the report open to complete the next exercise.

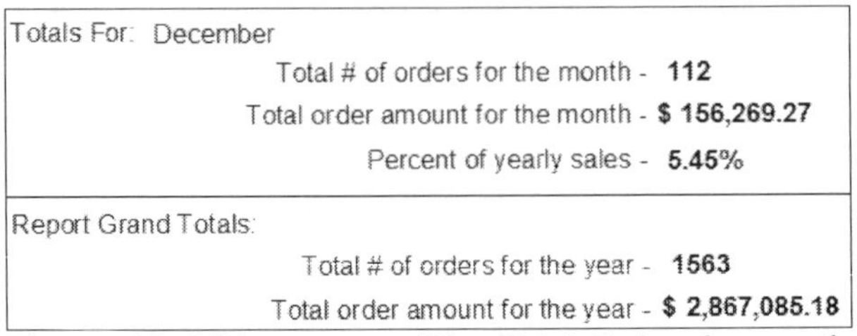

Figure 10-16 Last page of the E10.2 Orders by month report

Exercise 10.3: Create Selection Criteria On Summary Fields

GROUP SELECTION is similar to record selection. The difference is that group selection is done on summary fields, instead of fields in the Details section. If a report is grouping the orders by state, each state would include an order total amount.

In Exercise 10.2 you created a report that grouped the orders by month. At the end of each month are summary calculations for the total number of orders and total order amount for the month. In this exercise you will learn how to create selection criteria on group summary fields. The report that you created in Exercise 10.2 displays data for every month in 2011. In this exercise you will use the Select Expert to modify that report to only display months where the total monthly sales is greater than $250,000.

1. Save the E10.2 report as `E10.3 Monthly total orders over 250K`.

2. Right-click on the Sum of Orders field in the Group Footer section and select, Select Expert ⇒ Group.

3. Open the drop-down list and select **IS GREATER THAN OR EQUAL TO**, then type `250000` in the second field.

4. Change the report title to `2011 Monthly Total Orders Over $250,000`.

As shown in Figure 10-17, the first page of the report is for June. Notice that all of the groups are still visible in the Group Tree. If you click on the 02/2011 option in the Group Tree, you will not see the data for February. That is because the monthly total for February is less than $250,000. I don't know about you, but I would prefer that the only options that appear in the Group Tree are the ones that meet the criteria. This happens because of the way Crystal Reports processes data. Remember that the Group Header information is processed before the totals for the summary calculations in the Group Footer are processed. This is why all of the months appear in the Group Tree.

Figure 10-17 E10.3 Monthly total orders over 250K

Using The Group Expert

All of the groups that you have created in this chapter were created using the Insert Group dialog box. You can also create and edit groups using the Group Expert shown in Figure 10-18.

There are two ways to open the Group Expert as discussed below.

① Right-click on the Group Header or Footer section bar and select Group Expert.

② Crystal Reports ⇒ Report ⇒ Group Expert.

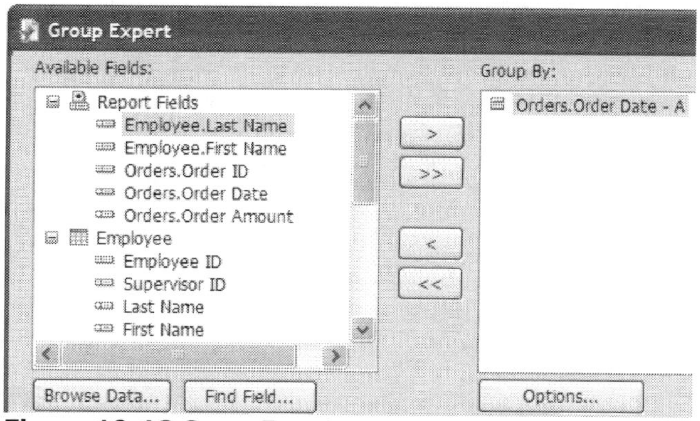

Figure 10-18 Group Expert

The **OPTIONS** button on the Group Expert opens the Change Group Options dialog box shown in Figure 10-19. It is similar to the Insert Group dialog box shown earlier in Figure 10-7.

One benefit of using the Group Expert is that you can create all of the groups for the report without having to re-open a dialog box to create each group. Another benefit is if you need to see the data in a field, you can click the Browse Data button.

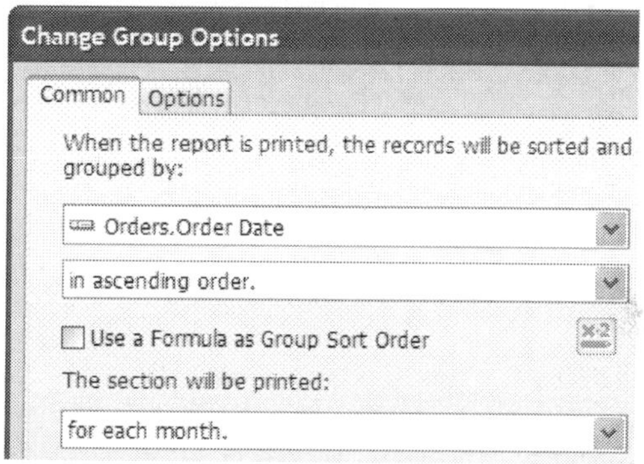

Figure 10-19 Change Group Options dialog box

User Defined Groups

Earlier in this chapter you learned about the User defined sort order. In Exercise 10.2 you learned how to create a custom group name. Custom group names are used to rename existing group names. Custom groups must be based on a single field in the report. User defined groups are similar to custom group names. The major difference is that the user defined group name is free form. In addition to being able to create a free form group name, you can create custom groups. Below are examples of user defined groups.

① Orders placed between the first and the 15th of the month.

② Group customers based on their year to date sales (Example Gold, Bronze and Silver levels).

③ Create sales territories and associate states to a territory (Example Northeast, Southeast and Midwest).

Creating Custom Groups

There are four steps to creating a user defined group as discussed below.

① Select the field that you want to create the user defined group for, then select the option, **IN SPECIFIED ORDER** in the second drop-down list on the Common tab of the Insert Group dialog box. Once this option is selected, other tabs (the Specified Order and Others tabs) will appear on the dialog box.

② Type in the name for the first group name that you need in the **NAMED GROUP** drop-down list shown in Figure 10-20, then click the **NEW** button.

③ The **DEFINE NAMED GROUP** dialog box is similar to the Select Expert. One difference is that each tab on the Define Named Group dialog box is for the same field. User defined groups cannot use parameter fields and the formula cannot be modified. You would type in the criteria for the user defined group, as shown in Figure 10-21. The other difference is that these filters or selection criteria use the **OR** operand, meaning that the detail record can meet the criteria for filter 1 or filter 2 or filter 3.

④ Click OK and repeat steps 2 and 3, until you have created all of the user defined groups that the report needs.

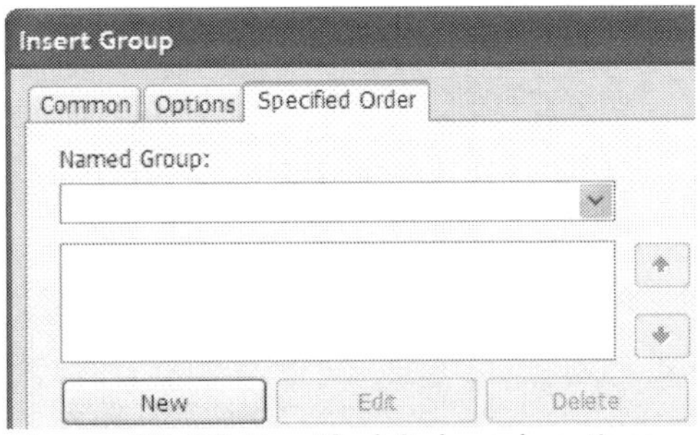

Figure 10-20 Specified Order tab options

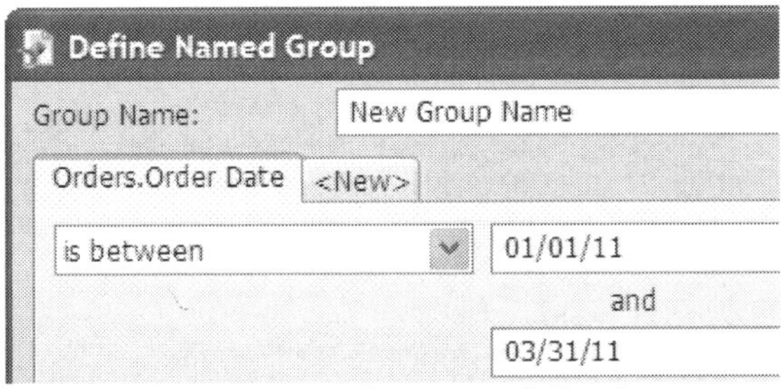

Figure 10-21 Criteria for a user defined group

If you wanted to group orders by specific order date ranges like 1/1/11 to 1/15/11, 2/1/11 to 2/15/11 and 3/1/11 to 3/15/11, you would create three named groups, for example, Jan 2011, Feb 2011 and Mar 2011. For each named group you would select the Order Date field, the operator Is between and the date range for the named group. The report would show the three groups and the detail records that have an order date that falls into one of the three date ranges.

If one group or all groups need additional criteria, click on the New tab and add the next piece of criteria for the group.

You can only add criteria for the same field. For example, if you also wanted to see orders for 1/15/11 to 1/25/11, you would add this criteria on the New tab shown in Figure 10-22.

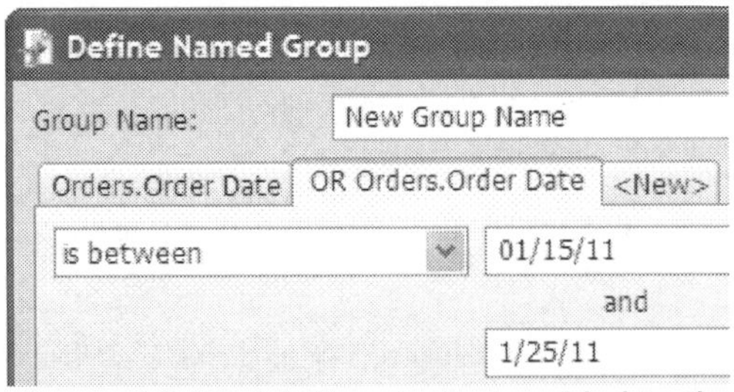

Figure 10-22 Additional criteria added to the named group

The criteria for each group name is joined using the **OR** operand. This means that as long as the record meets one of the sets of criteria for the group name, it will appear on the report.

The options on the Others tab, which you will learn about in the next exercise are used to select what you want to do with the records that do not meet the criteria for any of the named groups.

Exercise 10.4: Create A Report With User Defined Group Names

In this exercise you will modify the E9.1 report to include the following region user defined groups: CA, IL and PA.

1. Save the E9.1 report as `E10.4 User defined groups.`
2. Right-click on the Group Header section bar and select **GROUP EXPERT**, then click the Options button.
3. Select the option **IN SPECIFIED ORDER** in the second drop-down list on the Change Group Options dialog box. You should now see the **SPECIFIED ORDER** tab.
4. Select CA, IL and PA in the **NAMED GROUP** drop-down list. Make sure that the states are in the order shown in Figure 10-23.

   If they are not in the order shown, use the up and down arrow buttons to put the states in the order shown.

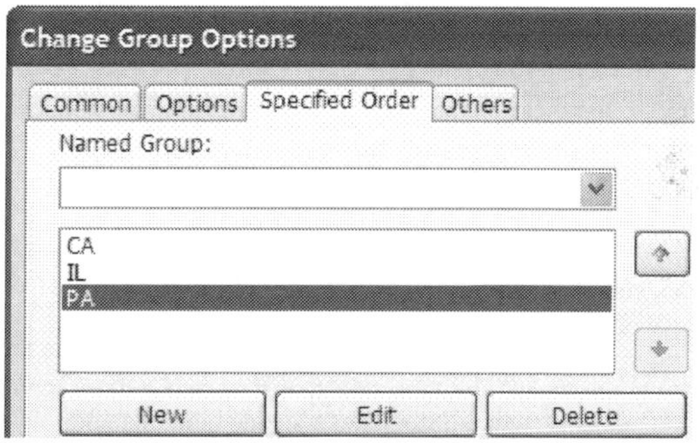

Figure 10-23 Change Group Options dialog box

5. On the **OTHERS** tab select the option **DISCARD ALL OTHERS**, as shown in Figure 10-24.

Selecting the Discard all others option means that records that are not in any of the groups listed on the Specified Order tab will not appear on the report.

The **PUT ALL OTHERS TOGETHER, WITH THE NAME** option, will put all of the records that do not meet the criteria on the Specified Order tab in the report under a new group name that you enter on the field below the option. This group will appear at the end of the report.

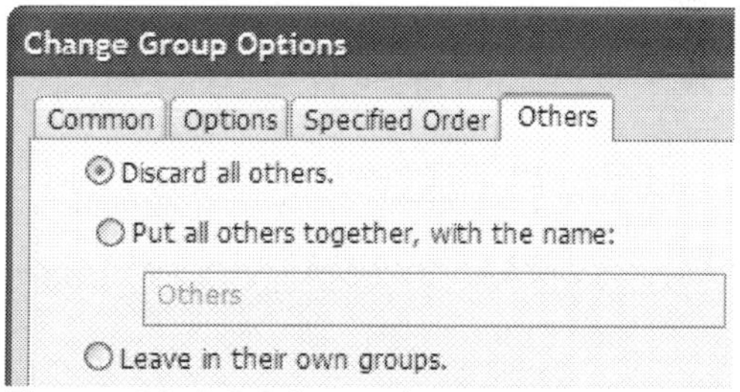

Figure 10-24 Others tab options

6. Preview the report. You should only see the CA, IL and PA groups in the Group Tree, as shown in Figure 10-25. Leave the report open to complete the next exercise.

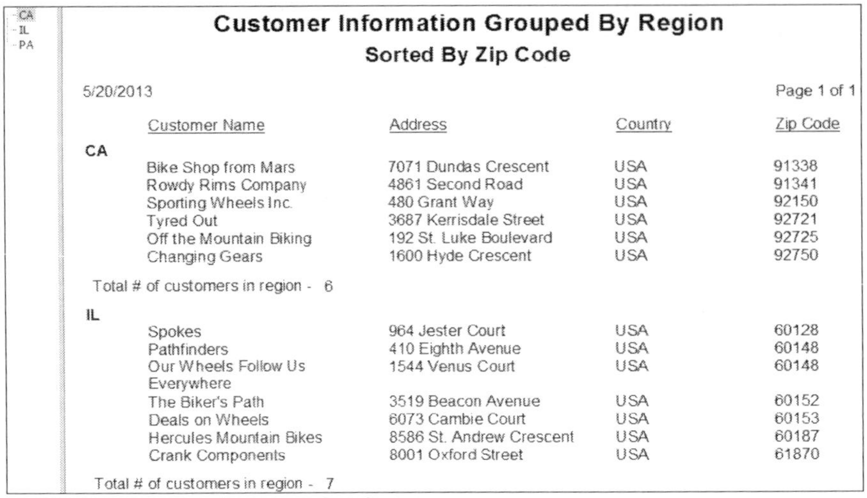

CA
IL
PA

Customer Information Grouped By Region

Sorted By Zip Code

5/20/2013 Page 1 of 1

	Customer Name	Address	Country	Zip Code
CA				
	Bike Shop from Mars	7071 Dundas Crescent	USA	91338
	Rowdy Rims Company	4861 Second Road	USA	91341
	Sporting Wheels Inc.	480 Grant Way	USA	92150
	Tyred Out	3687 Kerrisdale Street	USA	92721
	Off the Mountain Biking	192 St. Luke Boulevard	USA	92725
	Changing Gears	1600 Hyde Crescent	USA	92750
Total # of customers in region - 6				
IL				
	Spokes	964 Jester Court	USA	60128
	Pathfinders	410 Eighth Avenue	USA	60148
	Our Wheels Follow Us Everywhere	1544 Venus Court	USA	60148
	The Biker's Path	3519 Beacon Avenue	USA	60152
	Deals on Wheels	6073 Cambie Court	USA	60153
	Hercules Mountain Bikes	8586 St. Andrew Crescent	USA	60187
	Crank Components	8001 Oxford Street	USA	61870
Total # of customers in region - 7				

Figure 10-25 E10.4 User defined groups report

Exercise 10.5: Create A Report With Custom Group Names

In the previous exercise, the User Defined Group report displayed the two character state name. In this exercise you will modify that report so that the state names are spelled out.

1. Save the E10.4 report as `E10.5 Custom group name`.

2. Right-click on the Group Header report section and select **GROUP EXPERT**, then click the Options button.

3. Delete all of the Named Groups on the Specified Order tab.

4. Click the **NEW** button, then type `California` in the Group Name field.

   Open the first drop-down list and select **IS EQUAL TO**, then select CA from the second drop-down list. You should have the options selected that are shown in Figure 10-26.

Figure 10-26 Defined Name Group options for CA

5. Repeat step 4 above for IL and PA. Leave the Change Group Options dialog box open when you are finished.

6. On the **OTHERS** tab, select the option **PUT ALL OTHERS TOGETHER, WITH THE NAME**, then type `All Other States`, as shown in Figure 10-27.

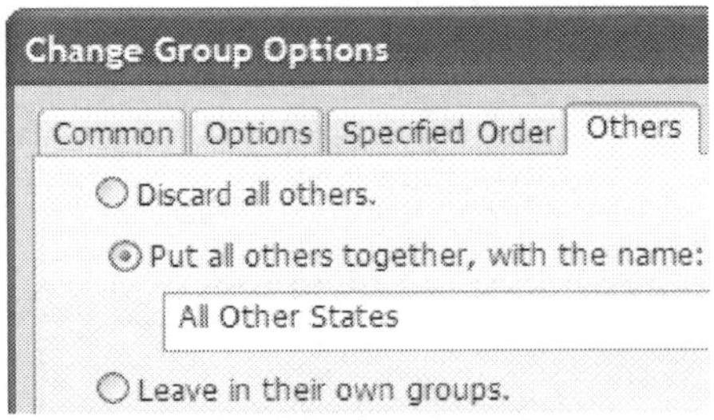

Figure 10-27 Others tab options

The report should look like the one shown in Figure 10-28. Notice that the state names are spelled out in the Group Tree and on the report. Also notice that there is a new group called **ALL OTHER STATES** in the Group Tree. This group contains all of the records that meet the selection options for the report, but are not in CA, IL or PA.

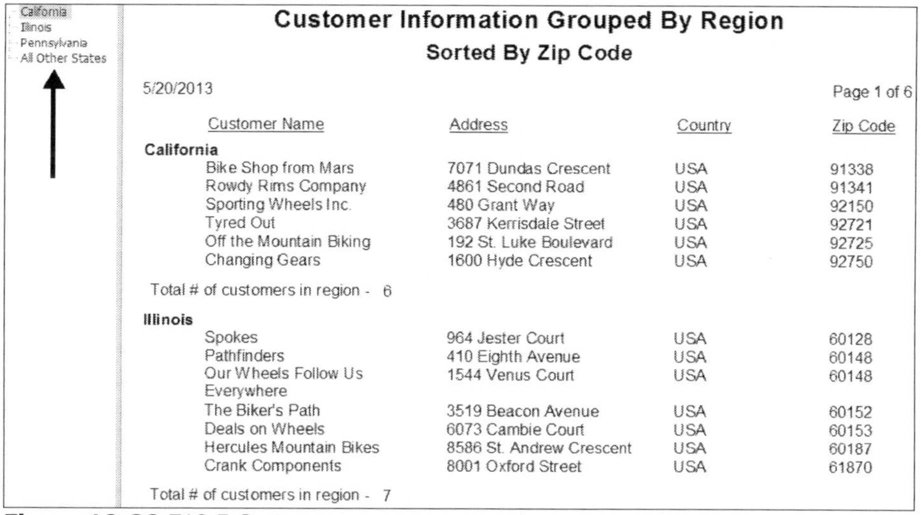

Customer Information Grouped By Region

Sorted By Zip Code

5/20/2013 Page 1 of 6

Customer Name	Address	Country	Zip Code
California			
Bike Shop from Mars	7071 Dundas Crescent	USA	91338
Rowdy Rims Company	4861 Second Road	USA	91341
Sporting Wheels Inc.	480 Grant Way	USA	92150
Tyred Out	3687 Kerrisdale Street	USA	92721
Off the Mountain Biking	192 St. Luke Boulevard	USA	92725
Changing Gears	1600 Hyde Crescent	USA	92750
Total # of customers in region - 6			
Illinois			
Spokes	964 Jester Court	USA	60128
Pathfinders	410 Eighth Avenue	USA	60148
Our Wheels Follow Us Everywhere	1544 Venus Court	USA	60148
The Biker's Path	3519 Beacon Avenue	USA	60152
Deals on Wheels	6073 Cambie Court	USA	60153
Hercules Mountain Bikes	8586 St. Andrew Crescent	USA	60187
Crank Components	8001 Oxford Street	USA	61870
Total # of customers in region - 7			

Figure 10-28 E10.5 Custom group name report

USING THE REPORT CREATION WIZARDS

In the last few chapters, all of the reports that you created were created from scratch. I figured that I would give you a break in this chapter from creating reports from scratch.

Chapter 4 provided an overview of how to create reports and charts using a wizard. In this chapter you will learn more about the wizards. After completing the exercises in this chapter you will be able to:

- ☑ Understand the options on the common wizard screens
- ☑ Know the types of reports that wizards can create
- ☑ Create reports using the Standard Report Wizard
- ☑ Use the Mail Label wizard

CHAPTER 11

Report Wizard Overview

Now that you have used several report creation and modification features and were able to see the completed reports, many of the options on the wizard screens will hopefully make more sense. Selecting the wrong option in the wizard or not selecting an option that you need will cause you to have to fix the report manually. That's okay though, as wizards can be used as a starting point for a report that you can modify as needed.

I think that it is important to understand sorting, grouping and summary options before using a wizard to create a report. One reason that I think this is important is because many of the wizard screens are scaled down versions of an expert screen. This is why this chapter comes after chapters that had you create reports from scratch that demonstrated how to sort, group and summarize records.

Table 11-1 explains the type of report that each wizard creates. As you will see, they have a core set of common screens. Table 11-2 lists the screens and illustrates the screens that are unique to a specific report wizard.

Wizard	Type Of Report It Creates . . .
Standard	A variety of reports because it is a generic report wizard. It is similar to creating a report from scratch.
Cross-Tab	Reports that look like spreadsheets.
Mail Label	Reports in a column layout, which can be used to create any size mailing label that you need.

Table 11-1 Report Wizards explained

Screen	Standard	Cross-Tab	Mail Label
Data	X	X	X
Link	X	X	X
Fields	X		X
Grouping	X		
Summaries	X		
Group Sorting	X		
Record Selection	X	X	X
Report Style	X	X	
Cross-Tab		X	
Grid Style		X	
Label			X

Table 11-2 Report wizard screens

You should be familiar with many of the wizard screens because in Exercise 4.1 you created a report using a wizard that selected options on every screen of the Standard Wizard. This was done to demonstrate all of the options in the wizard. The reports that you create with wizards in this chapter will be more focused. Many of the reports that you will create in this chapter are reports that you have already created from scratch or modified. The reason for this is two-fold:

① So that you will be able to determine which method (by wizard or by scratch) is better suited for a specific type of report.
② So that you can decide which way you like best.

The wizards are designed to make what may seem like a complicated task, a little easier to complete. What you may not realize is that there is often more going on behind the scenes of a wizard then you realize. By that I mean, wizards can have default options that you may not be aware of. In Exercise 11.6 you will see an example of this.

Unless you are very familiar with the data that is being used to create the report, you or the person using the report may not know that the data on the report is not 100% accurate. I personally try not to use wizards because of this. I may reconsider using wizards if there was documentation that thoroughly explains the inner workings and defaults that you can't see.

Common Wizard Screens

As you saw above in Table 11-2, several of the report wizards use the same screens. The majority of reports that you will create with a wizard will be created using the Standard wizard. This section will explain the purpose and features of the screens that provide the foundation for many of the wizards.

Some of the wizard screens including the Record Selection, Chart and Cross-Tab have less functionality then the "Expert" that it was taken from. If you find that there is a task that you can't complete using the wizard, check the options on the Expert to see if there is an option that will help you complete the task.

I would like to have the ability to preview the report before the wizard creates it. This would let you know how "close" you are to getting the output that you want. If you make a mistake or leave something out, you would not have to start all over again because you could click the Back button and fix the mistake or add what you need, because you could see what the report would look like before clicking the Finish button, which closes the wizard dialog box.

Data Screen

Figure 11-1 shows the Data screen. This is the first screen that wizards use. This screen is used to select the data sources that are needed to create the report. The Data screen provides the same functionality as the Database Expert.

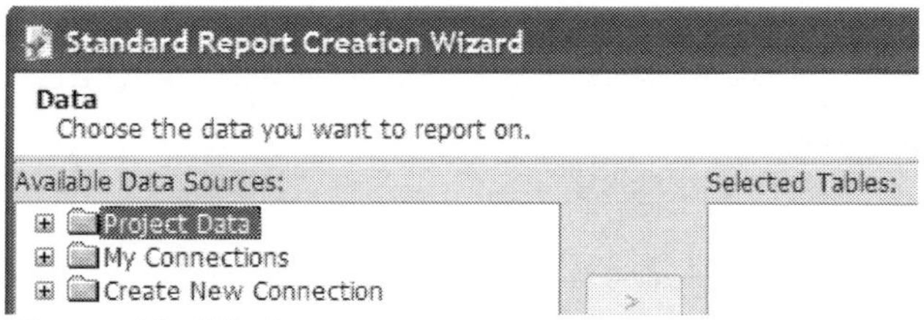

Figure 11-1 Data screen

Fields Screen

Figure 11-2 shows the Fields screen. This is where fields are selected for the report. The fields that are selected on this screen will be placed in the Details section of the report.

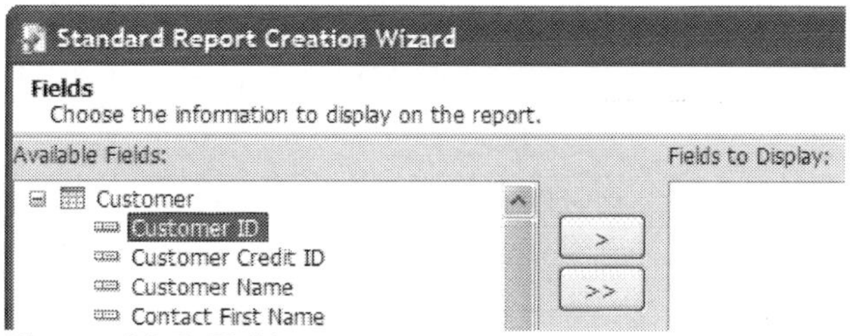

Figure 11-2 Fields screen

Grouping Screen

Figure 11-3 shows the Grouping screen. The options on this screen are used to select the fields to group the data by. Creating groups is optional.

Grouping options if selected, will create the Group Header and Footer sections of the report. This screen is the equivalent of the Insert Group dialog box.

You cannot sort the detail records on this wizard screen.

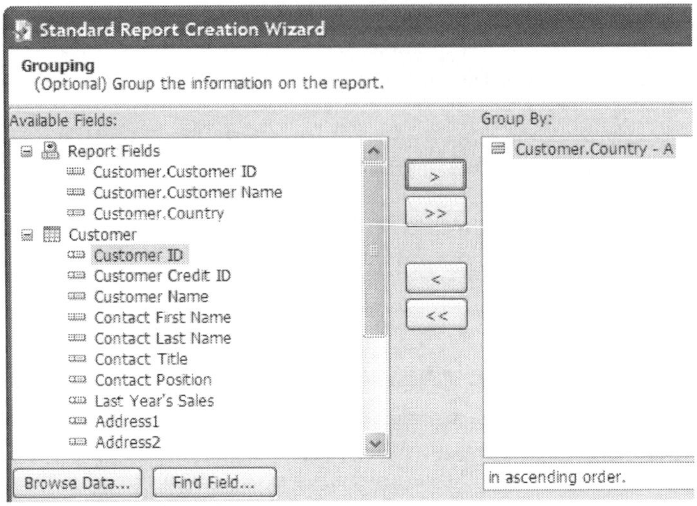

Figure 11-3 Grouping screen

If you need to sort records in a report that does not have a group, you will have to do that through the Record Sort Expert, after the report has been created with the wizard.

Keep in mind that when you create a group using the wizard, the field(s) that are being grouped on, are automatically moved to the left most fields on the report.

Summaries Screen

The Summaries screen is only available if at least one field is being grouped on. By default, the numeric fields that you select on the Grouping screen are automatically added to the **SUMMARIZED FIELDS** list, as shown in Figure 11-4.

This may not be what you want. You can remove the field from the Summary Fields list if the report does not have a need to create a total for it.

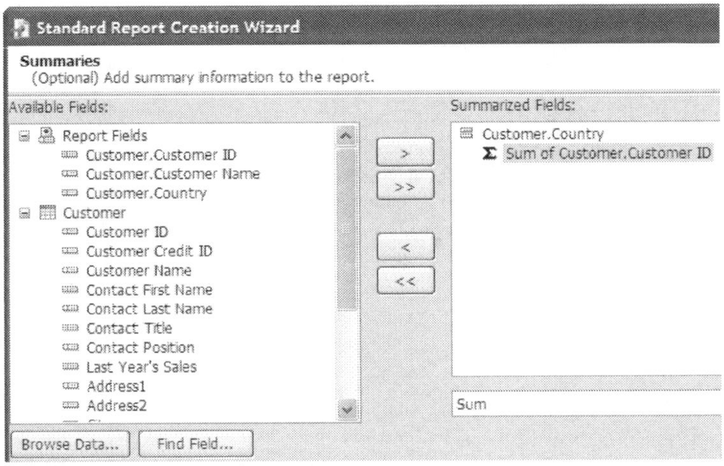

Figure 11-4 Summaries screen

The fields in the Summarized Fields section will automatically have grand total fields created and placed in the Report Footer section of the report.

The Summaries screen is the equivalent of the Insert Summary dialog box. If you do not need a summary field for a field that is in the Summarized Fields section, click on the summary field that is not needed, then click the **<** button. If you need to add a field to summarize on, select it here.

Group Sorting Screen

The Group Sorting screen is only available if at least one field was selected on the Grouping and Summaries screens.

Figure 11-5 shows the options that can be selected as needed to change the order of the groups based on the value from the selection on the Summaries screen.

The Group Sorting screen is a scaled down version of the Group Sort Expert.

There are three group ordering options that you can select from, as discussed below.

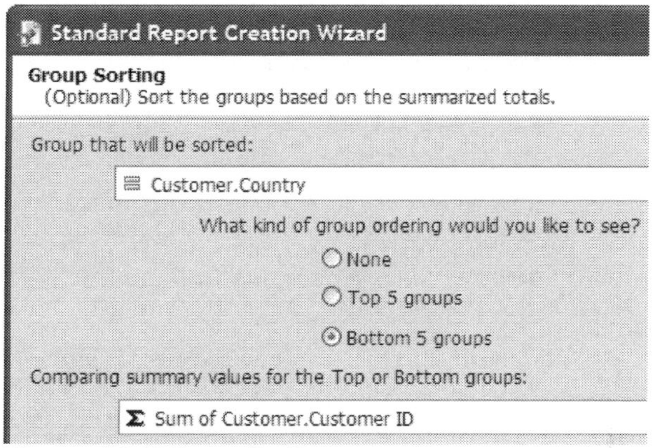

Figure 11-5 Group Sorting screen

① **NONE** This is the default group ordering option. This option will leave the group order the way it is. Most of the time, this is the option that you want.

② **TOP 5 GROUPS** This option will only print the five groups that have the highest value in the field that is being grouped on. The other groups will not print on the report.

③ **BOTTOM 5 GROUPS** This option will only print the five groups that have the lowest value in the field that is being grouped on. The other groups will not print on the report.

If the Top 5 groups or Bottom 5 groups option is selected, the **COMPARING SUMMARY VALUES FOR THE TOP OR BOTTOM GROUPS** option is enabled. This option is used to select the summarized field to base the sort on. The options available in the drop-down list come from the summary fields created on the Summaries screen.

Top and Bottom N reports, commonly known as Top N reports, allow you to show the first N or bottom N records in a group. Instead of displaying all orders in a certain date range, you could only show the largest 5 orders in the date range. The wizard does not allow you to select the value of N. It always uses five. If you use the Group Sort Expert to create a Top or Bottom N report, you can select the value of N, by typing it in or using a parameter field to get the value of N each time the report is run. You can use the Group Sort Expert to edit a Top N report that was created with a wizard.

Chart Screen

The options shown in Figure 11-6 are used to add a chart to the report. Adding a chart is optional.

In order to add a chart, the report has to have at least one group. Compared to the Chart Expert, the options and chart types on the Chart screen are limited, which means that most of the time you will have to modify the chart after the wizard creates it.

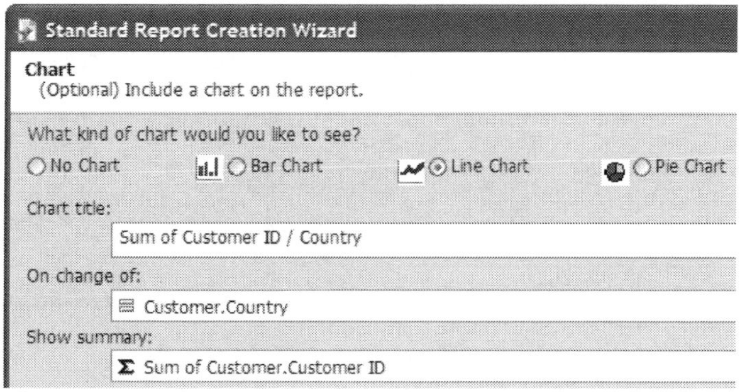

Figure 11-6 Chart screen

The other major drawback to creating a chart using a report wizard is that you have to create the chart from fields that will print on the report. The Chart Expert can create a chart with fields that will not be printed on the report. Once you select a chart type in the wizard, the three options discussed below are available to help customize the chart.

① **CHART TITLE** The information in this field will be printed above of the chart.

② **ON CHANGE OF** This option defaults to a field that the report is being grouped on.

③ **SHOW SUMMARY** This option defaults to the summary field for the field that is in the On Change Of field.

Record Selection Screen

The options shown in Figure 11-7 are used to create selection criteria like you can on the Select Expert. Selecting options on this screen is optional. After the report is created, you can open the Select Expert and view the criteria that is created on the Record Selection screen.

The difference is that you cannot see the formula that is created from the wizard screen.

You can view it after the report is created with the wizard by opening the Select Expert. This will let you edit the formula if necessary. Like the Select Expert, you can create as many filters as you need.

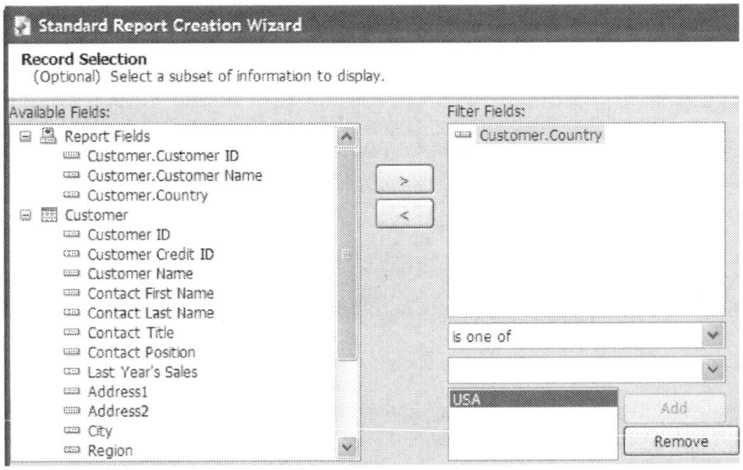

Figure 11-7 Record Selection screen

Report Style Screen

The options shown in Figure 11-8 are used to apply a style which is similar to a template to the report. Applying a style to a report is optional.

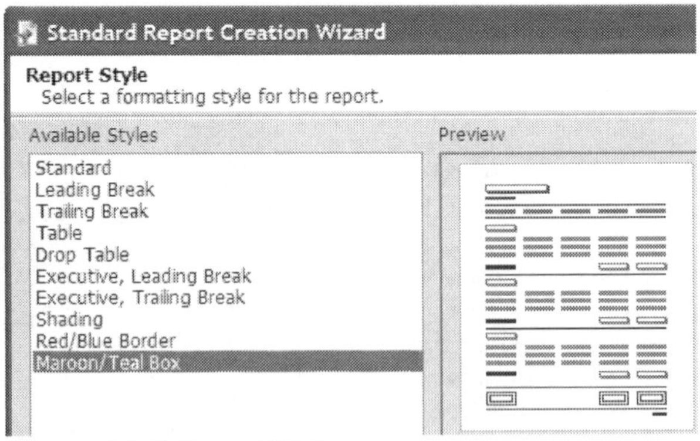

Figure 11-8 Report Style screen

Exercise 11.1: Create The Region = OH Or FL List Report

List reports are one of the easiest types of reports to create. In Chapter 9 you learned how to select records. In this exercise you will select options on the wizard that will filter the data in the customers table to retrieve customers that are in OH or FL.

1. Create a new report and save it as `E11.1 Region = OH or FL list`.
   Open the Standard report wizard and add the Customer table, then click Next.

2. Add the following fields: Customer Name, Address1, Region, Country and Postal Code, then click Next.

3. Click Next on the Grouping screen because this report does not have any grouping requirements.

4. On the Record Selection screen, add the Region field to the **FILTER FIELDS** list. Open the drop-down list and select **IS ONE OF**, then open the next drop-down list and select **OH** or you can type it in. Open the same drop-down list that you just used and select **FL** or you can type it in. Figure 11-9 shows the filter options that should be selected.

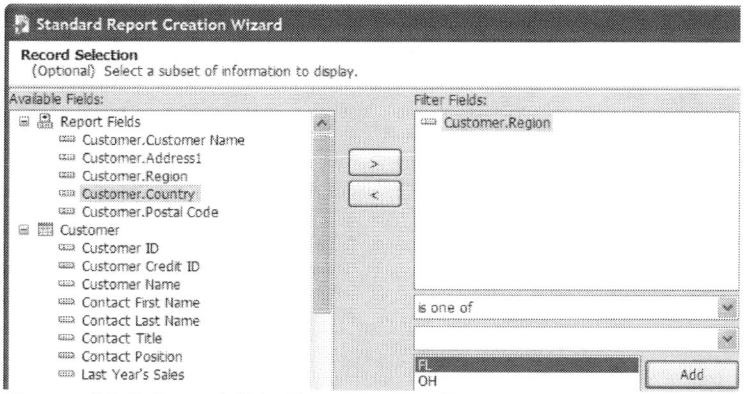

Figure 11-9 Record Selection screen options

5. The report does not require a report style. Click **FINISH**. Your report should look like the one shown in Figure 11-10. Notice that a date field was automatically added to the report.

5/20/2013

Customer Na	Address	Region	Country	Postal Code
Bike-A-Holics Anonymous	7429 Arbutus Boulevard	OH	USA	43005
Wheels and Stuff	2530 Bute Avenue	FL	USA	34666
Uni-Cycle	1008 Kerr Street	OH	USA	43042
Extreme Cycling	1925 Glenaire Avenue	FL	USA	34638
Karma Bikes	1516 Ohio Avenue	OH	USA	43092

Figure 11-10 E11.1 Region = OH or FL list report

Exercise 11.2: Create The Order Date And Order Amount Report

In this exercise you will create a report that selects criteria on fields in different tables. You will create a filter that will select records that have an order date greater than or equal to 6-24-11 and has an order amount greater than 2499.99.

1. Create a new report and save it as `E11.2 Order Date GTE 6-24-2011 Order Amount GT 2499.99`. Open the Standard report wizard and add the Customer, Orders and Orders Detail tables, then click Next.

2. The reason that you see the **LINK** screen is because more than one table is being used to create the report. The default links between the tables are correct. Click Next.

3. Add the following fields: Customer Name, Order Date, Ship Date, Order Amount, Order ID and Unit Price, then click Next.

4. Click Next on the Grouping screen because this report does not have any grouping requirements.

5. Add the Order Date field to the **FILTER FIELDS** list. Open the drop-down list and select **IS GREATER THAN OR EQUAL TO**. Open the next drop-down list and select 6/24/2011 or you can type in the date.

6. Add the Order Amount field to the **FILTER FIELDS** list, click on it, then open the drop-down list and select **IS GREATER THAN**. Type `2499.99` in the next drop-down list, then click Finish. Your report should look like the one shown in Figure 11-11.

5/20/2013

Customer Na	Order Date	Ship Date	Order Amou	Order ID	Unit Price
Furia	1/14/2012 12:00:00AM	1/17/2012 12:00:00AM	$2,996.65	2,600	$14.50
Furia	1/14/2012 12:00:00AM	1/17/2012 12:00:00AM	$2,996.65	2,600	$21.15
Furia	1/14/2012 12:00:00AM	1/17/2012 12:00:00AM	$2,996.65	2,600	$2,939.85
Rad Bikes	1/14/2012 12:00:00AM	1/16/2012 12:00:00AM	$7,445.57	2,601	$2,939.85
Rad Bikes	1/14/2012 12:00:00AM	1/16/2012 12:00:00AM	$7,445.57	2,601	$2,939.85
Rad Bikes	1/14/2012 12:00:00AM	1/16/2012 12:00:00AM	$7,445.57	2,601	$1,565.87

Figure 11-11 E11.2 Order Date GTE 6-24-2011 and Order Amt GT 2499.99 report

Exercise 11.3: Create A Group Report

In this exercise you will create a report that groups records by the product that was ordered.

1. Create a new report and save it as `E11.3 Orders grouped by product name.` Open the Standard report wizard and add the Orders Detail and Product tables, then click Next. The reason that you are adding the Product table is so that you can print the name of the product instead of the Product ID number that is in the Orders Detail table.

2. Click Next on the Link screen because the link options do not need to be changed.

3. Add the following fields: Product Name, Quantity and Order ID, then click Next.

4. Add the Product Name field to the Group By list. The default sort order for the group will cause the Product Names to be sorted in ascending order.

5. No other options need to be selected. Click Finish. Your report should look like the one shown in Figure 11-12.

Active Outdoors Crochet
Active Outdoors Lycra Gl
Descent
Endorphin
Guardian "U" Lock
Guardian ATB Lock
Guardian Chain Lock
Guardian Mini Lock
Guardian XL "U" Lock

5/20/2013

Product Name	Quantity	Order ID
Active Outdoors Crochet Glove		
Active Outdoors Crochet Glove	2	1,326
Active Outdoors Crochet Glove	1	1,891
Active Outdoors Crochet Glove	1	1,850

Figure 11-12 E11.3 Orders grouped by product name report

Exercise 11.4: Create A Summary Report

The report that you just created lets you see how many orders for each product there are. If you wanted to know how many customers ordered a specific product you would have to manually count the detail records in each group. You can add a count summary field to the report that will display the total number of orders for each product. In this exercise you will create a report that has a count summary field.

1. Repeat the first four steps in Exercise 11.3. Save the report as `E11.4 Product summary`.

2. Click Next on the Grouping screen, instead of clicking the Finish button.

As you can see in Figure 11-13, two summary fields were automatically added to the Summarized Fields section.

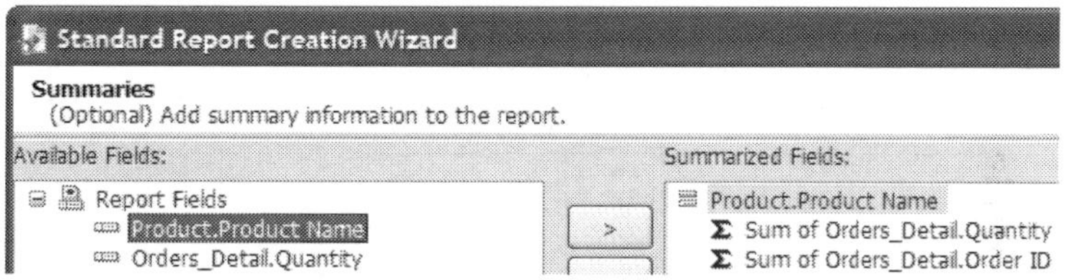

Figure 11-13 Group and summary options

You need to remove the fields in the Summarized Fields section that are not needed. To count the number of orders for each product, you can use the Order ID field or the Product Name field because each will print in the Details section of the report. The Quantity summary field is not needed.

3. Remove the Quantity summary field.

4. Click on the Sum Order ID field, then open the drop-down list and select Count. You should have the options selected, that are shown in Figure 11-14. Click Finish. Figure 11-15 shows the total number of orders for the first product on the report.

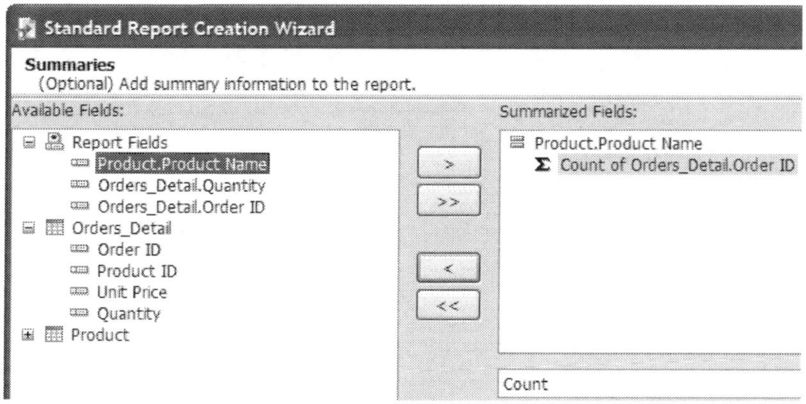

Figure 11-14 Modified summary options

Active Outdoors Crochet Glove	2	1,810
Active Outdoors Crochet Glove	1	2,122
Active Outdoors Crochet Glove	1	1,737
Active Outdoors Crochet Glove	**165**	

Figure 11-15 Total number of orders for the first product on the report

Exercise 11.5: Create The Orders By Customer Report

The report that you will create in this exercise is similar to the Orders by customer report that you created in Exercise 9.2.

1. Create a new report and save it as `E11.5 Orders by customer`. Open the Standard report wizard and add the Customer, Orders and Orders Detail tables. Click Next, then click Next on the Link screen.

2. Add the following fields: Customer Name, Order Date, Ship Date, Order Amount, Order ID and Unit Price, then click Next.

3. Add the Customer Name field to the **GROUP BY** list, then click Next.

4. Click on the Order ID field in the Summarized Fields list and select **COUNT** from the drop-down list, then remove the Unit Price field from the Summarized Fields section.

5. Click on the Order ID field in the **AVAILABLE FIELDS** list, then click the **>** button. This will let you create another summary for the Order ID field.

6. With the second Order ID field still selected, open the drop-down list and select **DISTINCT COUNT**.

   Figure 11-16 shows the Summarized Field options that should be selected.

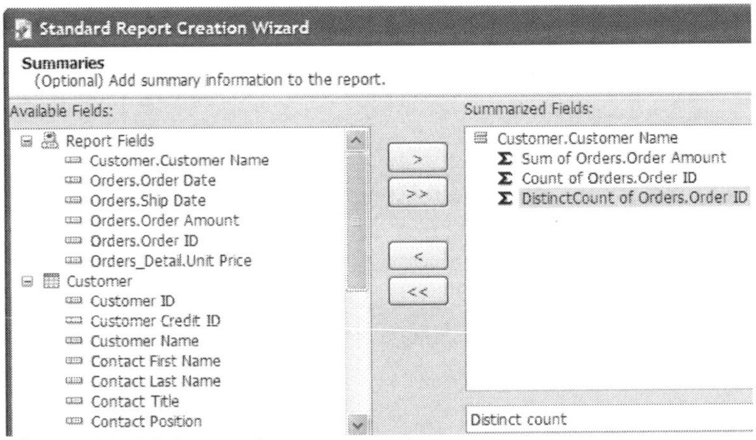

Figure 11-16 Summaries screen options

7. Click Next. Click Next again because none of the options on the Group Sorting screen are needed for this report. Click Next again because none of the options on the Chart screen are needed for this report.

8. Add the Order Date field to the Filter Fields list. Open the drop-down list and select **IS GREATER THAN OR EQUAL TO**, then open the next drop-down list and select 6/24/2011 or you can type it in.

9. Add the Order Amount field to the Filter Fields list then click on it. Open the drop-down list and select **IS GREATER THAN**, then type `2499.99` in the next drop-down list and click Finish. Your report should look like the one shown in Figure 11-17. Have you noticed that you can't create a title for the report in the wizard?

Customer Name	Order Date	Ship Date	Order Amou	Order ID	Unit Price
Alley Cat Cycles					
Alley Cat Cycles	2/19/2012 12:00:00AM	2/22/2012 12:00:00AM	$8,819.55	2,735	$2,939.85
Alley Cat Cycles	10/27/2011 12:00:00AM	11/6/2011 12:00:00AM	$2,699.55	2,272	$899.85
Alley Cat Cycles	1/31/2012 12:00:00AM	2/3/2012 12:00:00AM	$9,290.30	2,664	$455.86
Alley Cat Cycles	1/31/2012 12:00:00AM	2/3/2012 12:00:00AM	$9,290.30	2,664	$2,792.86
Alley Cat Cycles	9/28/2011 12:00:00AM	9/30/2011 12:00:00AM	$2,559.63	2,157	$313.36
Alley Cat Cycles	9/28/2011 12:00:00AM	9/30/2011 12:00:00AM	$2,559.63	2,157	$539.85
Alley Cat Cycles	2/19/2012 12:00:00AM	2/22/2012 12:00:00AM	$8,819.55	2,735	$2,939.85
Alley Cat Cycles	**$44,038.51**	**7**	**4**		

Figure 11-17 E11.5 Orders by customer report

Exercise 11.6: Create A Top N Report

In previous exercises in this chapter you created reports that grouped data. By default, the groups are sorted on the value in the group field. For example, in Exercise 11.5 the orders were grouped by the values (the actual customer names) in the summary customer name field.

There is another way to sort groups on a report. Just like you can filter detail records, you can filter groups. One way to explain Top N reports is that this sort method is sorting the groups based on the value of a group summary field instead of the values in the group by field. Top N reports do not display all of the groups. They only display the number of groups that N has. Top N reports rank the groups based on the summary field values. For example, if N=7, only the seven highest groups based on the value of the summary field would be displayed on the report.

> The grand totals that appear on a report when the top five or bottom five group sorting option is used, are not the real totals for the detail records on the report. They are the totals for all records that meet the other report criteria before the top five or bottom five group sort option is applied. This happens when the **INCLUDE OTHERS** option on the Group Sort Expert dialog box is not checked. If you do not want to use the Include Others option, create a running total field instead of the summary grand total field.

In this exercise you will create a report that will display the top five days in June 2011 with the largest daily order totals. You will also create a pie chart that displays the top five order days.

1. Create a new report and save it as `E11.6 Top 5 order days in June 2011`. Open the Standard report wizard, then add the Customer and Orders tables and click Next. Click Next on the Link screen.

2. Add the following fields: Customer Name, Order ID, Order Amount and Order Date, then click Next.

3. Add the Order Date field to the **GROUP BY** list, then click Next.

4. Remove the Order ID field from the Summarized Fields list, then click Next.

5. On the Group Sorting screen, select the **TOP 5 GROUPS** option, then click Next.

6. On the Chart screen, select the Pie chart option. In the Chart Title field type `Top 5 Order Days In June 2011`, then click Next.

7. On the Record Selection screen, add the Order Date field to the Filter Fields list. Open the drop-down list and select **IS BETWEEN**, then type `6/1/2011` in the next drop-down list. In the last drop-down list type `6/30/2011`. Figure 11-18 shows the options that should be selected.

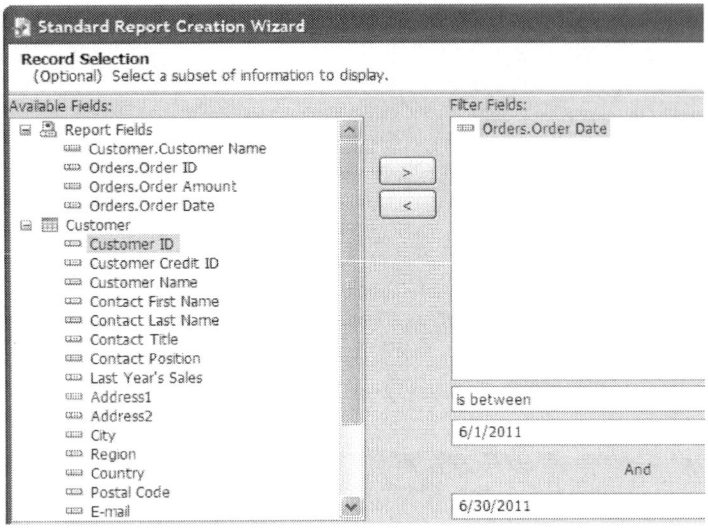

Figure 11-18 Record Selection options

8. Click Finish. Your report should look like the one shown in Figure 11-19. You will only see detail information for the top five order days. Leave the report open to complete the next exercise.

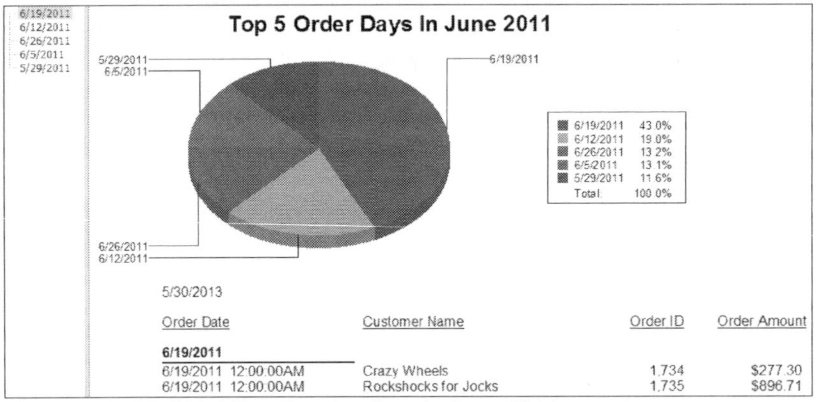

Figure 11-19 E11.6 Top 5 order days in June 2011 report

As you can see, one of the dates in the Group Tree and chart legend is in May. If you click on that link, you will see orders for June. No, I did not lead you astray. This is one of the features of the wizard that does not work as intended and is why many report designers tend to stay away from the report wizards. There are options that are preset that you don't know about, that can produce unexpected results. If you plan to use this wizard on a regular basis for something other then a basic report, hopefully you see how important it is to understand the data that the report should produce. That should lead you in the direction of how to fix any problem that the wizard creates.

Exercise 11.7: How To Fix The E11.6 Top 5 Order Days Report

When I looked at the data in the report, I noticed that each of the five groups actually had more than one days worth of data. Each group actually had a weeks worth of data, even though I was expecting to only see data for one day in each group. Because the data is grouped on the Order Date field, I realized that the wizard must have a group default set to weekly. I opened the Group Expert and sure enough, the option was set to weekly.

This is an example of how a wizard will produce unexpected results. What scares me is that I get the feeling that because the majority of people that use wizards use them without questioning the results, this is something that could easily be missed. What would be helpful on the Standard wizard would be if the Group Sorting wizard screen had an option to select how you want the data to be grouped, by day, week, month, year etc. After looking at the options on the Group Sort Expert, I noticed that it did not have this option either, so because the Group Sorting wizard screen is a subset of the Group Sort Expert, it made a little sense.

Even though the wizard produces results that you may not want, I do not know about you, but I can do without this type of "help" from a wizard. The best advice that I can give you if you insist on using a wizard is after the wizard creates the report, open each corresponding expert for a screen that you selected options on in the wizard and look at the options. While this is good advice, if you think for a minute, you will realize that even that advice would not have helped you detect this error because options from the Group Expert are not used in this wizard. The good news is that this report can be fixed by following the steps below.

1. Save the E11.6 report as `E11.7 Fixed Top 5 order days in June 2011.`

2. Open the Group Expert, then click the **OPTIONS** button. You will see the Change Group Options dialog box. In the last drop-down list you will see that the option **FOR EACH WEEK** is selected.

3. Open **THE SECTION WILL BE PRINTED** drop-down list and select **FOR EACH DAY**, as shown in Figure 11-20.

   As you can see, knowing about this option would allow you to create a variety of reports just by changing this option.

   The report should look like the one shown in Figure 11-21. You should now see five days in June (opposed to four as shown earlier in Figure 11-19) in the Group Tree section of the report. All of the detail records in each group should have the same order date.

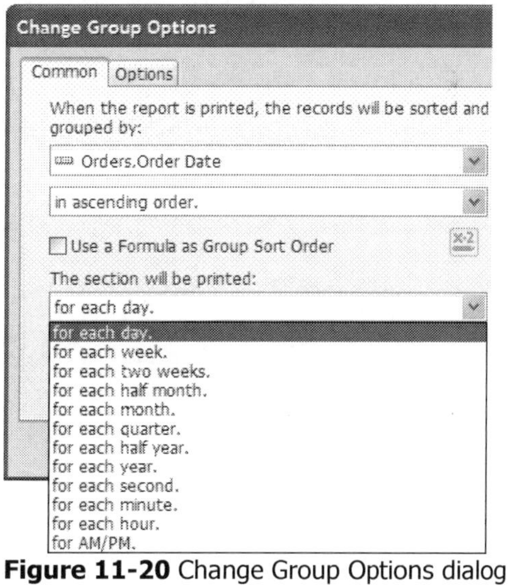

Figure 11-20 Change Group Options dialog box

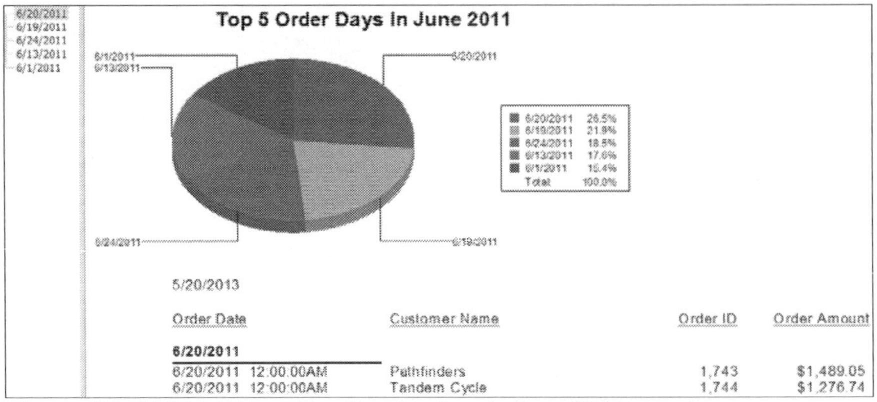

Figure 11-21 E11.7 Fixed Top 5 order days in June 2011 report

Exercise 11.8: Use The Mail Label Report Wizard

This wizard is used to create a column layout report which many people use to print labels. You can use this wizard to create other types of columnar reports besides mailing labels. In this exercise you will learn how to create a report that can be used to print labels. The report will print shipping labels for customers that placed an order in June 2011, that are in the US. Many of the screens in this wizard are the same as the ones that you have used in the Standard report wizard.

1. Create a new report and save it as `E11.8 Customer labels for June 2011`. Open the Mail Label report wizard and add the Customer and Orders tables, then click Next twice.

2. Add the following fields: Customer Name, Address1, Address2, City, Region and Postal Code, then click Next.

3. Open the **MAILING LABEL TYPE** drop-down list and select Avery 5163. Figure 11-22 shows the options that should be selected. The Mailing Label Type drop-down list has the **USER-DEFINED LABEL** option, that is used to create a custom size label.

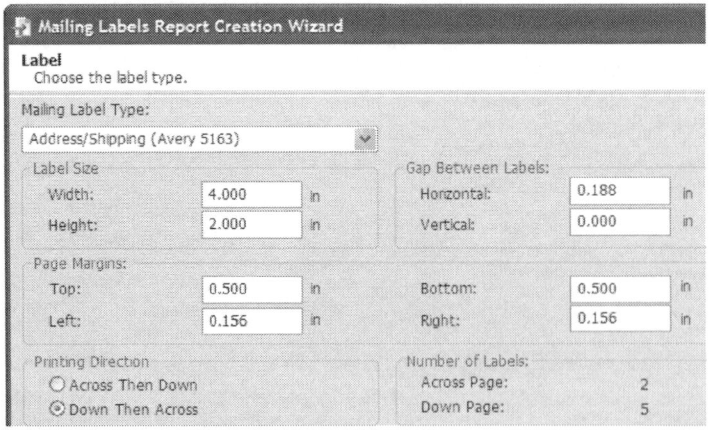

Figure 11-22 Label screen options

4. Click Next and add the Country field to the Filter Fields list. Open the drop-down list and select **IS EQUAL TO**, then open the next drop-down list and select USA or type it in.

5. Add the Order Date field to the Filter Fields list, then click on the field in the list. Open the drop-down list and select **IS BETWEEN**, then type `6/01/2011` in the first drop-down list.

6. Type `6/30/2011` in the last drop-down list. Click Finish. Your report should look like the one shown in Figure 11-23.

   Because the date criteria is for a month, you see duplicate customer names.

   More than likely, the labels would be printed daily, which means that you would not see duplicate customer names in the labels unless a customer placed more than one order on the same day.

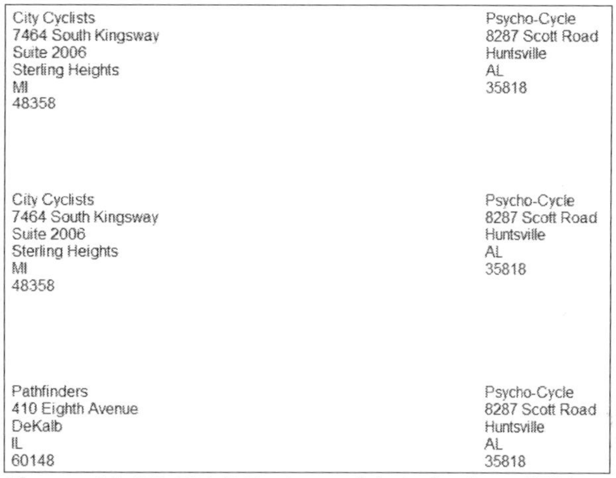

Figure 11-23 E11.8 Customer labels for June 2011 report

> This label report uses two address lines. What many people do is modify the label layout and put both address fields on the same line. That is not a requirement for this exercise.

7. Make the City, Region and Postal Code fields smaller.

   Move the Region and Postal Code fields up next to the City field.

   The report should look like the one shown in Figure 11-24.

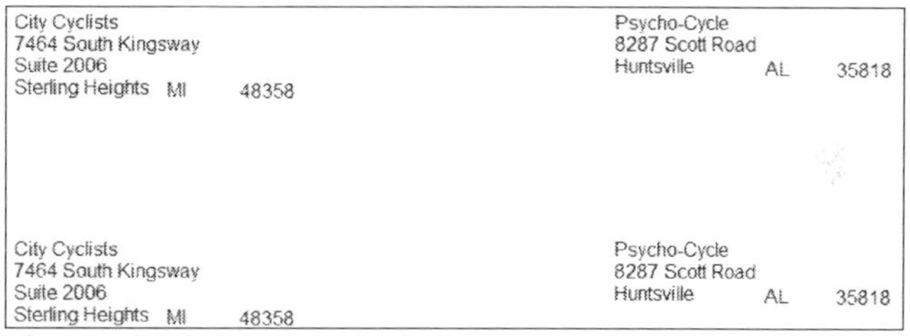

Figure 11-24 Modified label layout

EXPORTING REPORTS

After completing the exercises in this chapter you will be able to create the following export file types: PDF, Excel and CSV.

CHAPTER 12

Export Format Options

Crystal Reports supports over 20 formats that reports can be exported to. Some export formats save the report in a better format then others in terms of the formatting and layout. Other export formats are better suited for data. Many of the formats are installed when Crystal Reports is installed. Exporting reports is a two step process, as explained below.

① Select the **EXPORT** format. This option determines the format that the exported report will be saved in.
② Select the **DESTINATION**. This option determines where the report will be saved.

There are two ways to open the Export dialog box shown in Figure 12-1, as explained below.

① Click the **EXPORT** button on the Report Navigation toolbar on the preview window.
② Right-click on the report in preview mode and select Export.

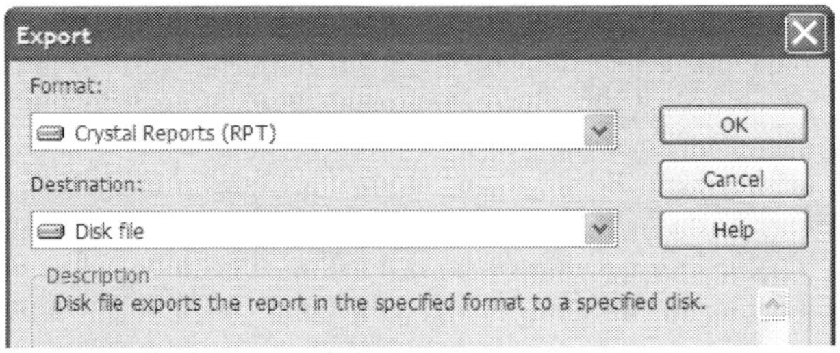

Figure 12-1 Export dialog box

Figure 12-2 shows the export format options. Reports can be exported to more than one format if needed. Some export formats are better suited for certain types of reports then others in terms of formatting and layout. For example, some Word and Excel export format options are better suited for reports that may need to be edited by the end-user.

Table 12-1 explains the export format options. Some of the formats in the table do a better job of duplicating the report then others. I have noticed that sometimes reports that are exported to Excel get shifted a little.

If the data does not need to be edited by the person using the exported report, the best format to use is PDF because it retains all of the formatting that you see when the report is viewed in Crystal Reports.

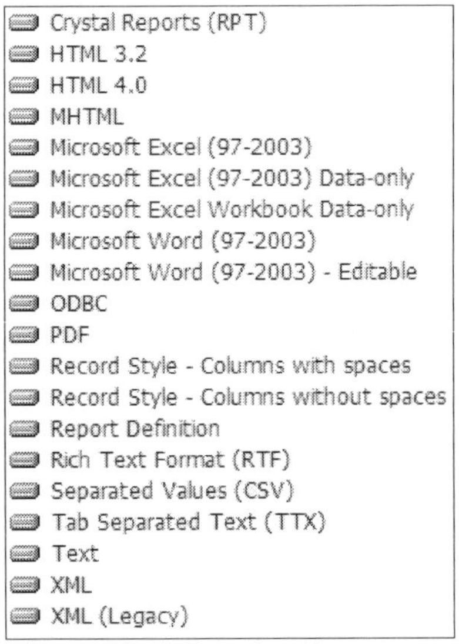

Figure 12-2 Export options

Format	Select This Format If You Want To . . .
Crystal Reports (RPT)	View the report with the current data in Crystal Reports or the Crystal Reports viewer.
HTML 3.2	Display the report on the Web in a browser that does not support HTML 4.0 or higher. It does not maintain the exact layout that the report has. By today's standards, browsers that cannot use anything higher than HTML v3.2 are considered obsolete. (1) (2)

Table 12-1 Export format options explained

Format	Select This Format If You Want To . . .
HTML 4.0	Display the report on the Web. This format can be read by web browsers that support HTML v4.0 or higher. This format has better formatting capabilities then the HTML v3.2 format because it preserves the formatting by using DHTML. (1) (2)
MHTML	Send an HTML file in an email message or to save a web page and its objects like pictures in a single file.
Excel (97-2003)	Export the report to Excel and keep as much of the formatting as possible. This format will not include any formulas from the report, just the result of the formulas. It has a limit of 256 columns in Excel. Boxes and lines are not exported in this format. (3) (4)
Excel (97-2003) Data-Only	Export the report to Excel. Don't select this format if the report has charts or maps that you also need to export. Any data that is suppressed will not be exported. The majority of formatting is exported. (3) (4)
Excel Workbook Data Only (.xlsx)	Save the report in the Excel 2007 (or higher) .xlsx file format. (3) (4)
Word (97-2003)	Create an RTF document. Report objects are placed in text frames. The majority of formatting is retained. RTF stands for Rich Text Format.
Word (97-2003) - Editable	Create an RTF document. It allows the user to edit the report in Microsoft Word. Text formatting is retained. All of the layout may not be retained. (3)
ODBC	Export the report to any ODBC compliant database.
PDF	Create a PDF file, which is one of the most popular export formats because it can be read by both PC and MAC computers. If you want the report to retain its formatting and layout after it is exported, select this format. True Type fonts are embedded. (3) (5)
Record Style - Columns with spaces	Export the report data to an ASCII fixed length format like text, with spaces between columns. (3) (5) (6)
Record Style - Columns without spaces	Export the report data to an ASCII fixed length format like text, without spaces between columns. (3) (5) (6)
Report Definition	Create a report that contains a description of the reports design. This includes the sections, selection criteria, object formats, groups and more. This export format is usually for technical people. It does not export the data in the report. It exports information about the report.
Rich Text Format (RTF)	Export the report to RTF format, which retains the formatting of the report including graphics. Select this option if the report will be opened in a word processor other than Word.
Separated Values (CSV)	Create a comma delimited file. CSV stands for Comma Separated Values. This format is similar to the two Record Style formats discussed above. The difference is that in this format the fields are separated by a comma. This is often called a "Comma Delimited" file. Reports with any of the following cannot be exported to this format: Subreports in the Page Header or Footer section, Cross-tab or OLAP grids. (3) (5) (7)
Tab Separated Text (TTX)	Export the report in text format and keep the layout. This format is similar to the Separated Values format because it separates the fields. The difference is that the fields are separated by tab spaces, instead of commas. (5) (7)
Text	Create a plain text file. (3) (7)

Table 12-1 Export format options explained (Continued)

Format	Select This Format If You Want To . . .
XML	Create an XML file from the data in the report using the Crystal XML Schema for the data exchange. Style sheets can be applied to the XML file so that the data can be used in another application or on the web. XML stands for Extensible Markup Language. (3)
XML (Legacy)	Use an older Crystal Reports XML Schema to produce an XML file. The XML option above should be used.

Table 12-1 Export format options explained (Continued)

(1) Left justified is the only justification that will work.
(2) This export file format creates more than one file if the report has images.
(3) This export file format has the ability to save the report export options selected with the report. Doing this means that the person running the report does not have to select any export options. [See Default Export Options, later in this chapter]
(4) This export file format does not merge cells. Some summary functions like SUM and COUNT are exported.
(5) The drill down feature and hyperlinks will not work with this report format.
(6) This export format is often used to move data into older applications. Only data from the details and group sections are exported.
(7) This export format does not retain any formatting like bold, italic or underline.

Export Destination Options

In addition to selecting an export format, a destination for the report also has to be selected. The destination options that are available by default are discussed in Table 12-2. Some of the options may not be installed. You may have other options in addition to the ones in the table.

Option	Description
Disk File	This option is used to select a folder, either on a hard drive or on a server (which is also known as a Network drive), where the exported report will be placed. This destination option does not automatically open the application associated with the export file type.
Exchange Folder	Allows the exported report to be placed on a public or private Exchange mail server.
Lotus Domino	Exports the report to a Lotus Domino database. This requires that the form already be created in the Lotus database before the export is run. (8)
Lotus Domino Mail	Is used to send the exported report as an attachment to a Lotus email message. (8)
MAPI	Is used to send the exported report as an attachment to a MAPI compliant email. To use this option, email software like Outlook has to be installed and configured on your computer.

Table 12-2 Export destination options explained

(8) To use this option, the appropriate Lotus mail client software must be installed and configured on your computer.

Application Export Destination Option
This option was in prior versions of Crystal Reports for Visual Studio. It was removed in the developer version of Crystal Reports.

Export Formatting Tips

I have found that by making sure that the export format tips listed below are followed, the exported file, regardless of the format, will look more like the report does in Crystal Reports.

① Make sure that all of the data fields in the same column have the same alignment (left or right). This is especially important for number and currency fields. If the fields in the same column have a different alignment option, some fields may appear in a different column in the exported report.

② All objects in the same column should be attached (snapped) to the same guideline.

③ Remove any space that is not needed in each section of the report by moving all of the objects in each section up, as much as possible.

Report Export Formats

The exercises in this chapter will show you how to create some of the more popular report export formats. To demonstrate the differences between the export format output options, you will use the same report to create all of the export formats covered in this chapter.

The E10.2 Orders by month report is the report that you will use to create all of the export reports in this chapter. You should open this report and then open the Export dialog box shown earlier in Figure 12-1, prior to starting each exercise, unless instructed otherwise. Save each exported report in the folder that you created for this book.

For all of the exercises in this chapter, select the **DISK FILE OPTION** in the Destination drop-down list on the Export dialog box, as shown earlier in Figure 12-1, then click OK.

Exercise 12.1: Create A PDF Export File

This export file type will create a PDF file of the report. End-users that need to open reports in this file type will need to have the Adobe Acrobat Reader installed. This software is free and can be downloaded from http://www.adobe.com/products/acrobat/readstep2.html.

You do not have to download and install any other software that is shown on this web page for the Acrobat Reader software to work. This export file type can also be opened and viewed with Adobe Acrobat, which is the full version of the software that is used to create PDF files.

1. Select the PDF format.

The dialog box shown in Figure 12-3 is used to select whether you want to include all or some of the pages from the report in the PDF export file that you are about to create.

If you were going to send each sales rep their stats for the month, from the report, you would enter the corresponding page numbers in the From and To fields in the dialog box.

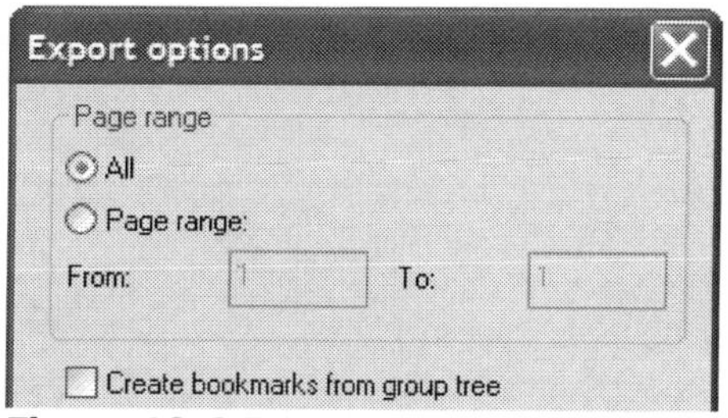

Figure 12-3 Export page range options

If the report has **PARAMETER FIELDS**, you would not have to do this to get a specific sales reps stats.

The **CREATE BOOKMARKS FROM GROUP TREE** option if checked, will create bookmarks (similar to hyperlinks) in the PDF file for each group in the Group Tree. This will make it easier for the person reading the PDF version of the report to find specific information.

2. Check the Create bookmarks from group tree option.

   Click OK to include all of the pages. You will see the dialog box shown in Figure 12-4.

   This dialog box is used to select where you want to store the export file.

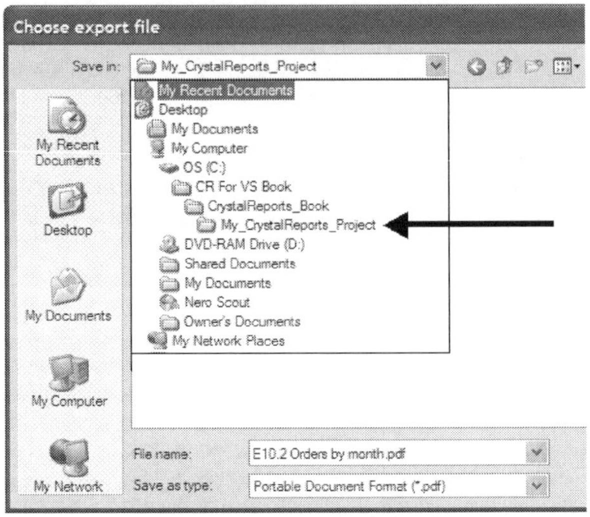

Figure 12-4 Choose Export File dialog box

3. Navigate to your project folder, as illustrated above in Figure 12-4.
   Type `E12.1 Orders by month exported PDF file` as the file name at the bottom of the dialog box, then press Enter or click the Save button.

You will see the dialog box shown in Figure 12-5. This dialog box lets you know that the export file is being created and how many records will be exported. When the export is complete, you can open the PDF file in either the Adobe Acrobat Reader or Adobe Acrobat.

The exported PDF file should look similar to the one shown in Figure 12-6.

Figure 12-5 Exporting Records dialog box

When the export is complete, you can open the PDF file in either the Adobe Acrobat Reader or Adobe Acrobat.

The exported PDF file should look similar to the one shown in Figure 12-6.

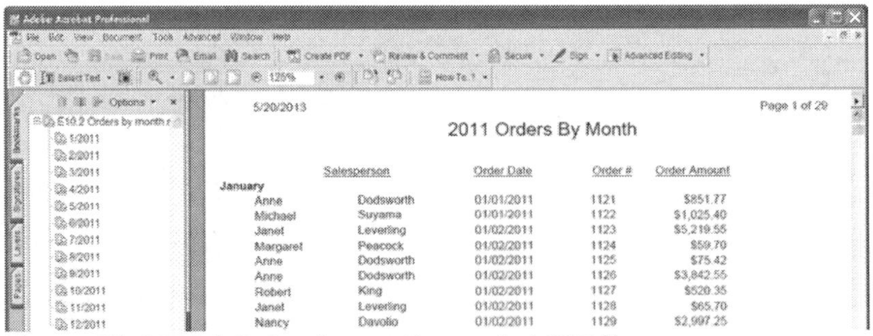

Figure 12-6 E12.1 Orders by month exported PDF file

The bookmarks shown on the left side of Figure 12-6 are the groups on the report. Like the report, you can click on the group and the corresponding section of the report will be displayed.

Exercise 12.2: Create An Excel (97-2003) Export File

This export file type copies the data in the report to an Excel spreadsheet. To open this exported file type, Microsoft Excel needs to be installed. As you read in Table 12-1, there are three Excel export formats. Each of the Excel export format options provide a slightly different output of the data. You will use two of the export options so that you can see the differences.

1. Select the first Excel (97-2003) format, then click OK. You will see the dialog box shown in Figure 12-7.

   As you can see, there are several options that you can select, which will determine how the data will be formatted in Excel.

   Table 12-3, at the end of this exercise, explains the options.

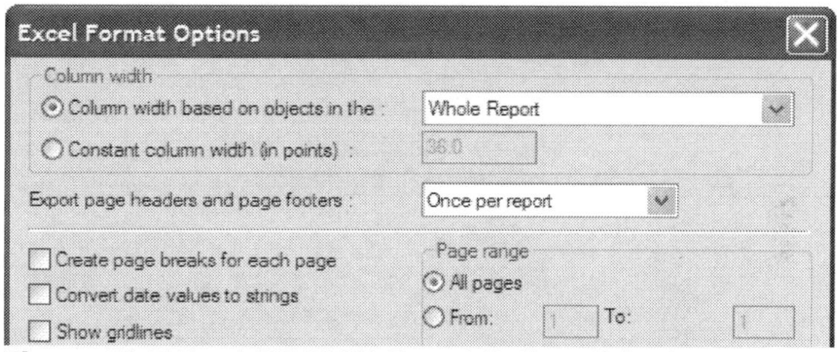

Figure 12-7 Excel (97-2003) Format Options dialog box

2. Select the **SHOW GRIDLINES** option shown above in Figure 12-7, then click OK.

3. Save the spreadsheet as `E12.2 2011 Orders by month exported file`.

   When the export is complete, open the file in Excel and you will see the report shown in Figure 12-8.

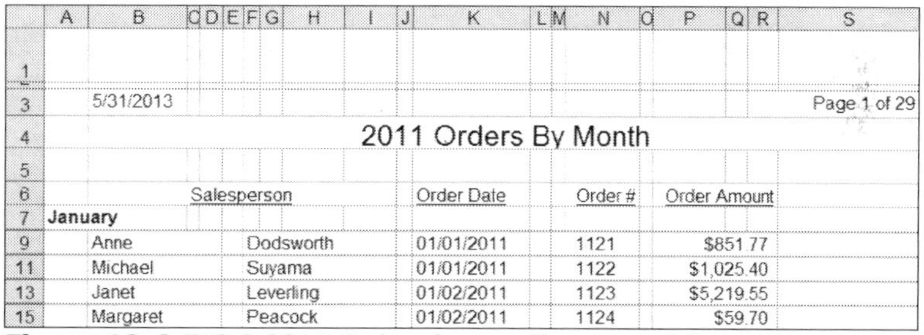

Figure 12-8 E12.2 2011 Orders by month exported Excel file

4. Scroll down to row 261, then click in the cell illustrated in Figure 12-9, the Total # of orders for the month. It may be a different cell then the one shown.

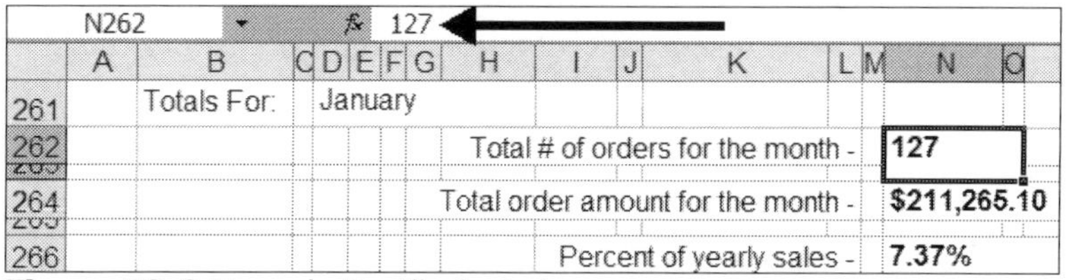

Figure 12-9 Formula Bar illustrated

If you look in the Formula Bar at the top of the spreadsheet shown above in Figure 12-9, you will not see the summary calculation (formula). One reason to use this export format is if you do not want the end-user to be able to change or see the formulas. For other end-users, it would be helpful if the formulas that are used in the report were also exported. You will learn how to export formulas in the next exercise.

Option	Description
Column Width	These options are used to select the column widths in Excel. ① The **COLUMN WIDTH BASED ON OBJECTS IN THE** option is used to select the column width in Excel based on a section in the report. ② The **CONSTANT COLUMN WIDTH (IN POINTS)** option is used to select a free form column width.
Export page headers and page footers	This option is used to select whether or not the information in the Page Header and Footer sections on the report will be exported to Excel. If the Page Header and Footer information is exported, the options in the drop-down list determine where the header and Footer information will be placed in the Excel file. ① **ONCE PER REPORT** causes the header information to be placed at the top of the first page and the footer information to be placed at the bottom of the last page. ② **ONCE PER PAGE** causes the header and Footer information to print on each page of the spreadsheet.
Create page breaks for each page	If selected, page breaks will be added to the spreadsheet in the same place they would appear in Crystal Reports. This may cause the report to break someplace other then at the end of the printed page in Excel. If you want the page breaks to happen automatically in Excel, do not check this option.
Convert date values to strings	If selected, this option will keep the date formatting in Crystal Reports when the report is exported to Excel. If this option is not checked, the formatting for the date fields will come from the date formatting options in the copy of Excel that the exported file is opened in. This means that if different people have different date settings in their copy of Excel, the dates in the spreadsheet will appear differently.
Show Gridlines	If selected, this option forces gridlines to appear in the spreadsheet.
Page range	These options are used to select how many pages of the report will be exported.

Table 12-3 Excel (97-2003) export format options explained

Exercise 12.3: Create An Excel (97-2003) Data Only Export File

As you noticed in the previous exercise, the formulas were not included in the spreadsheet. To have the formulas included in the spreadsheet, you have to select the Excel Data-only export format.

If the **DETAILS** option was selected in the Column Width drop-down list on the Excel Format Options dialog box instead of the **WHOLE REPORT** option shown earlier in Figure 12-7, the spreadsheet would look the way that many Excel users are use to seeing it. They would just have to turn the **GRIDLINES** option on.

1. Select the **EXCEL (97-2003) DATA-ONLY** format. You will see the dialog box shown in Figure 12-10. The typical and minimal options pre-select some options on the bottom portion of the Excel Format Options dialog box for you. Table 12-4 explains the Excel format options.

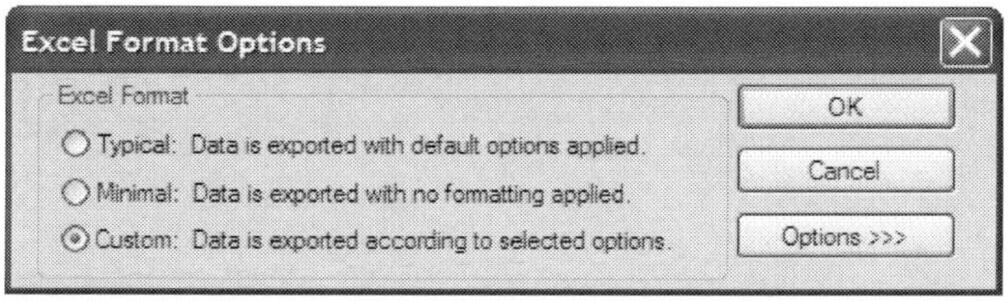

Figure 12-10 Top section of the Excel Format Options dialog box

Format	What Is Pre-Selected . . .
Typical	The most common options in the bottom section of the dialog box, which are shown in Figure 12-10.
Minimal	The basic options shown in Figure 12-11, to export the report without any formatting options.
Custom	This option lets you select the export options.

Table 12-4 Excel Format Options dialog box options explained

Changing an option after selecting the typical or minimal option changes the format to custom.

The pre-selected options shown in Figures 12-11 and 12-12 can be used as a starting point. You can select one of these options and then add or remove options as needed.

This may be helpful if one of these export formats has a few of the options already selected that you need. Selecting one of these options and then making changes to it may save you some time.

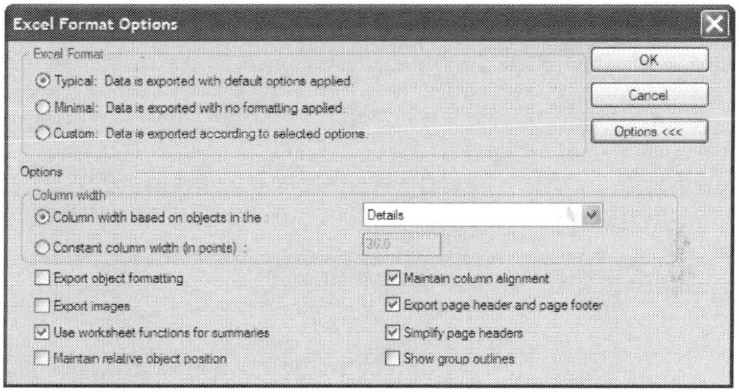

Figure 12-11 Typical format pre-selected default options

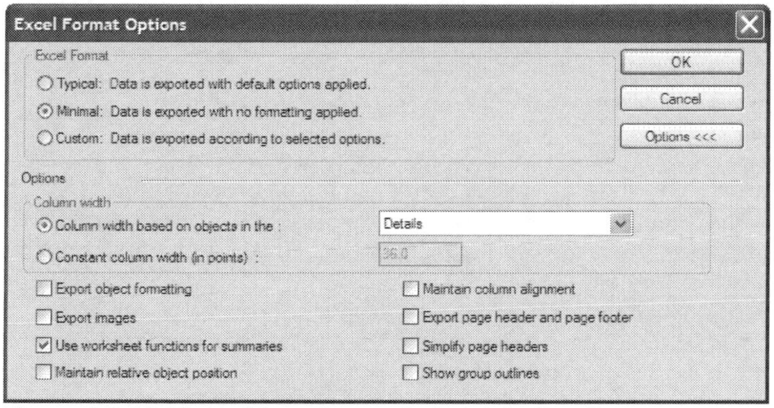

Figure 12-12 Minimal format pre-selected default options

2. Click the **OPTIONS** button. You will see the options shown in Figure 12-13.

   Table 12-5, at the end of this exercise, explains the options.

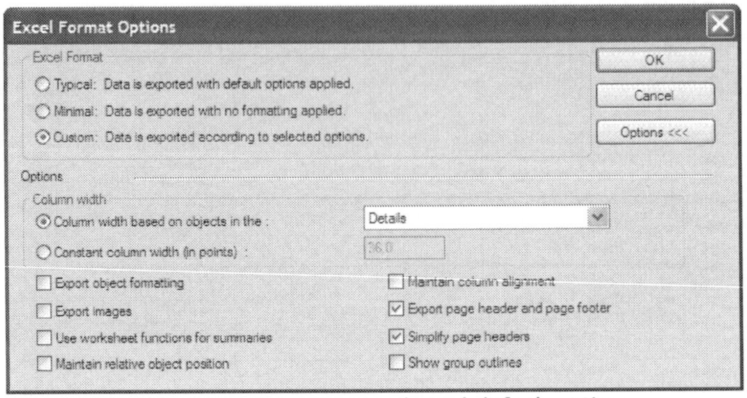

Figure 12-13 Custom format pre-selected default options

3. Check the option **USE WORKSHEET FUNCTIONS FOR SUMMARIES**, then click OK. Save the exported file as `E12.3 Orders by month data only exported file`.

4. Open the E12.3 Orders by month data only spreadsheet in Excel. Scroll down to row 130 and click in cell F130, then look in the Formula Bar. You will see the equivalent of the summary calculation that was created in the report, as illustrated in Figure 12-14.

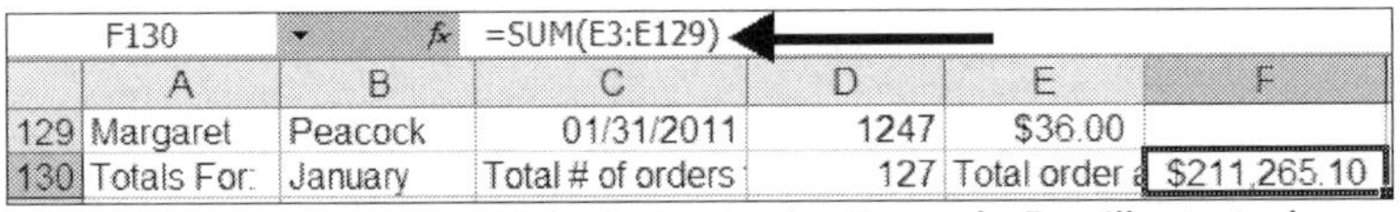

Figure 12-14 Summary calculation in the Formula Bar illustrated

Option	Description
Column Width	These options are used to select the column widths in Excel. ① The **COLUMN WIDTH BASED ON OBJECTS IN THE** option is used to select the column width in Excel based on a section in the report. ② The **CONSTANT COLUMN WIDTH (IN POINTS)** option is used to select a free form column width.
Export object formatting	Check this option to export as much of the formatting that is in the report as possible.
Export images	Check this option to export any images that are in the report.
Use worksheet functions for summaries	Check this option if you want Crystal Reports to try and convert summary fields to Excel functions. If a matching function is not found, the summary field will be exported as a number without the formula.
Maintain relative object position	Check this option if you want Crystal Reports to add rows and columns as needed to keep objects in the spreadsheet in the same location and position that they are in the report.
Maintain column alignment	Check this option to force summary fields to appear in the correct column in Excel. By default, the export process ignores blank spaces to the left of fields, which causes fields to be shifted.
Export page header and page footer	Check this option if you want the information in the Page Header and Footer sections to be exported.

Table 12-5 Excel data only export options explained

Option	Description
Simplify page headers	Check this option if you only want the last row of the Page Header section to be exported. Usually the last row of the Page Header section contains the field headings.
Show group outlines	Check this option if the report has groups that you want to use with the Group and Outline features in Excel.

Table 12-5 Excel data only export options explained (Continued)

Exercise 12.4: Create A Separated Values (CSV) Export File

In this exercise you will export the report to a CSV file.

1. Select the **SEPARATED VALUES (CSV)** format.

The options on the dialog box shown in Figure 12-15 are used to select how you want the data from the report to be exported. The options that you select depend on how the data will be used.

The **ISOLATE REPORT/PAGE SECTIONS** option if checked, will export the report and Page Header and Footer sections of the report as separate records.

The **ISOLATE GROUP SECTIONS** option if checked, will export the group header and Footer sections of the report as separate records.

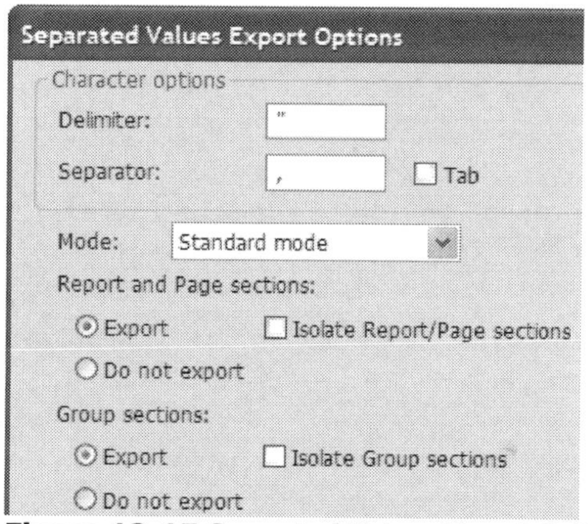

Figure 12-15 Separated Values Export Options dialog box

2. For this exercise, the default options are fine. Save the file as `E12.4 Exported CSV file`. This file can be opened in Excel.

ODBC Export Format

If you select the ODBC export format, the destination option is not enabled on the Export dialog box. This is because this format exports the data from the report to a table. When you click OK on the Export dialog box, you will see the dialog box shown in Figure 12-16.

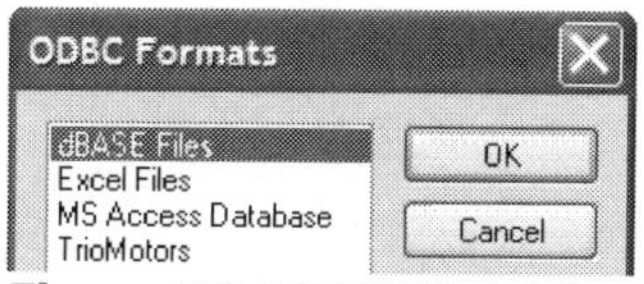

Figure 12-16 ODBC database format options

You may be prompted to install the DLL. Select the ODBC format that you want to export the report to, then click OK. You will then see the Select Database dialog box. Enter the name for the table that you will export the data to, then click OK. The table will be created in the format that you selected and the report data will be exported to it.

CREATING FORMULAS AND USING FUNCTIONS

After completing the exercises in this chapter you will be able to:

- ☑ Understand the difference between formulas and functions
- ☑ Know what the formula syntax rules are
- ☑ Select a Syntax Editor
- ☑ Use the Formula Workshop
- ☑ Customize the Formula Editor window
- ☑ Use the Workshop Tree
- ☑ Understand the formula evaluation order
- ☑ Create numeric formulas
- ☑ Create string formulas
- ☑ Use functions in string formulas
- ☑ Create date formulas
- ☑ Use the Truncate function

CHAPTER 13

Formulas And Functions Overview

Formulas and functions are some of the most powerful features in Crystal Reports. Ironically, many people that are first learning Crystal Reports think that formulas and functions are one of the most dreaded features because there is math and logic involved <smile>. If you fall into this category, hopefully this chapter will help you overcome some of the fear.

As part of the report design process, you learned that not all fields that are needed for a report exist in tables. You learned how to create summary fields which are not stored in tables. While summary fields provide a quick way to create totals, that is about as far as they go.

For example, summary fields will not let you add two fields together, nor can you multiply a field in a table by a constant value, like calculating the sales tax for an order. When you have exhausted all other math related options, it is time to turn to formulas and functions. Formulas are created in the Formula Workshop, which you will learn about in this chapter.

Actually, you have two options for creating formulas: The Formula Workshop and writing SQL Expressions. This type of field is what would be placed in the SQL Expression Fields section of the Field Explorer. If you are already freaking out about creating formulas, don't worry because this book does not cover SQL. The focus of this book is using the Formula Workshop because you would need to learn the version of SQL that works with the database that you are using for the reports.

What Is The Difference Between Formulas And Functions?

This is one of the questions that I am asked a lot. Formulas are calculations or some type of data manipulation that you create. Functions are built-in formulas or procedures that have already been created. If there is a built-in function that meets your needs, use it because there is no point to reinventing the wheel, as they say. If you have created or used formulas or functions in spreadsheet software, you are already familiar with the basics of using them in Crystal Reports.

Formula Overview

Formulas are used to create new fields. If you need to include data on a report that is not stored in tables, many times you will need to create a formula to get the data. An example of this would be the line item total on an order report. Line item information is not stored in an Order Detail table, but the price and quantity ordered are stored in the table. These are the fields that you would use to create the formula to calculate the line item total. A line item total is sometimes referred to as the **EXTENDED PRICE**. Formulas allow you to create the following types of calculations, comparisons, manipulations and much more.

① Solve math problems
② Convert data from one format to another
③ Compare or evaluate data
④ Combine two or more text fields into one field
⑤ Combine text and data fields

You may be thinking or asking why all of this information is not stored in tables. There are many reasons including the following, why data that falls into these categories is not stored in tables.

① It would take a lot of hard drive or server space to store all of the data for these fields.
② Applications that share data have slightly different data needs, which means that some tables would have empty fields.

③ Some data is only needed once or the data changes constantly, so it is more efficient to calculate it when it is needed.

④ The more data that has to be written (added or changed) to a table, the slower the application will run. This "slowness" is often referred to as a performance issue.

Syntax Rules

Formulas have rules (also known as syntax rules) that have to be followed. Basically, the rules require that items be placed in a certain order, so that the formula will work. Table 13-1 provides the rules for Crystal Syntax, that if followed, will make learning how to write formulas easier. The items listed below are the parts of the formula.

Item	Syntax
//	The double slash is used to add comments to a formula. This is helpful when you need to document the formula. (1)
Case Sensitive	Formulas are not case sensitive.
Hard Returns	Pressing the Enter key to continue the formula on another line to make the formula easier to read is acceptable. The one time that this will cause an error is if there is a hard return between quotation marks in a formula.
Operators	Placing a space before or after an operator is acceptable, but is not required. Many people include spaces to make the formulas easier to read. The spaces are ignored when the formula is executed. The operators are similar to the ones that you learned about in Chapter 8. The difference is that symbols are used in formulas instead of words. = < > + - are some of the operators that you can use when creating formulas.
Fields	They must be surrounded by braces. For example, {Table.Field Name}.
Functions	Each function requires at least one argument. Each argument must be followed by a comma, except the last one. Arguments must be entered in this format: FunctionName (Argument 1, Argument 2).
Numbers	Numbers must be entered without any formatting. 5600 or 56000 is correct. 5,600 or 56,000.00 is incorrect.
Text	Text must be entered inside of quotation marks. Examples: "Help" would be printed as Help. ' "Help" ' would be printed as "Help". Notice the difference in the output when different types of quotes are used.

Table 13-1 Syntax rules explained

(1) Comments should be added to formulas to explain the purpose of the formulas and to provide documentation. If the comment needs more than one line, each line must start with two slashes, otherwise Crystal Reports will treat the line as part of the formula, which will generate a syntax error. You may think that you will remember what the formula does six months from now, but it may take you a minute or so to remember. I have learned that it is easier to add comments to formulas and give them a descriptive name when they are first created.

Functions

Functions are prewritten, built-in formulas or procedures. The functions that Crystal Reports supports have been thoroughly tested and from what I can tell, they are error free. However, this does not mean that if there is bad data in a table that you won't have a problem with the function. If you do not follow the syntax rules or fill in the arguments correctly when using the function, you will get an error.

Crystal Reports has over 300 functions that you can use. Sum, Average, Count and Distinct Count are functions that you have already learned how to use. Many of the Special Fields are also functions, as are the Document Properties that you learned about. You can also create your own functions. This chapter covers some of the more popular functions that you may have a need to use.

Syntax Language And Editors

You can select the syntax language that you want to use. If you are already familiar with one, by all means continue to use it. If you have used a previous version of Crystal Reports, you may already be familiar with Crystal Syntax. You can create formulas and incorporate functions in both languages and both languages can be used in the same report. The good thing is that you do not have to be a programmer to create formulas or use functions in the Formula Workshop. Each language has its own rules for control structures, functions and other syntax. Figures 13-1 and 13-2 show the same formula using different syntax editors. In order to create a formula, you need to select one of the following languages:

① **Crystal Syntax** This language is included in every version of Crystal Reports and is the default language that is selected when Crystal Reports is installed. The formulas that you viewed at the bottom of the Select Expert dialog box are written in Crystal Syntax, unless you changed the default language to Basic Syntax prior to working on the exercises in this book. Some say that Crystal syntax is more user-friendly than Basic syntax. The exercises in this book use Crystal Syntax.

② **Basic Syntax** If you have developed applications in Visual Basic, you will find this syntax language familiar. The main difference that you will notice between Visual Basic and Basic Syntax is that the Basic Syntax language has extensions for creating reports.

```
// This formula combines the Supplier ID and Supplier Name field
ToText ({Supplier.Supplier ID}, 0) + " - " + {Supplier.Supplier Name}
```

Figure 13-1 Formula using Crystal Syntax

```
'This formula combines the Supplier ID and Supplier Name field
formula = ToText ({Supplier.Supplier ID},0)+ " - " + {Supplier.Supplier Name}
```

Figure 13-2 Formula using Basic Syntax

Statements

Depending on the environment that you work in, you may hear the term "Statement" and have a different interpretation of what a statement is then the context that I will present it in. That's fine, I just don't want you to think that either interpretation is incorrect. You may have also heard the term **EXPRESSION**. I believe that the terms statement and expression mean the same thing, but some will argue that there is a difference. Formulas in Crystal Reports and other software tools as well, consider a statement a combination of fields, operators, functions and other variables that provide an answer or value. I think of statements in Crystal Reports as sentences. Formulas have at least one statement.

Control Structures

This is how Crystal Reports processes a formula. The process starts at the beginning of the formula and moves from one statement to the next. Control structures evaluate expressions or conditions. The result of this evaluation is known as the **RETURN VALUE**. Formulas must return a value. The result of the last statement executed in the formula contains the result value. It is important to note that the last statement executed may not be the last physical line of code in the formula. Types of control structures include **WHILE DO/DO WHILE**, **SELECT CASE STATEMENTS** and **IF STATEMENTS**, which are also known as If Then Else statements.

Formula Workshop

The Formula Workshop shown in Figure 13-3 is the tool that you will use to create and manage formulas. You can also work with record and group selection formulas in the Formula Workshop. Notice that it does not have any menus. Depending on how you open the Formula Workshop, you will either see the Formula Editor or the Formula Expert. If you do not like the toolbars at the top of the window, you can move them. Each section of the Formula Workshop is explained below.

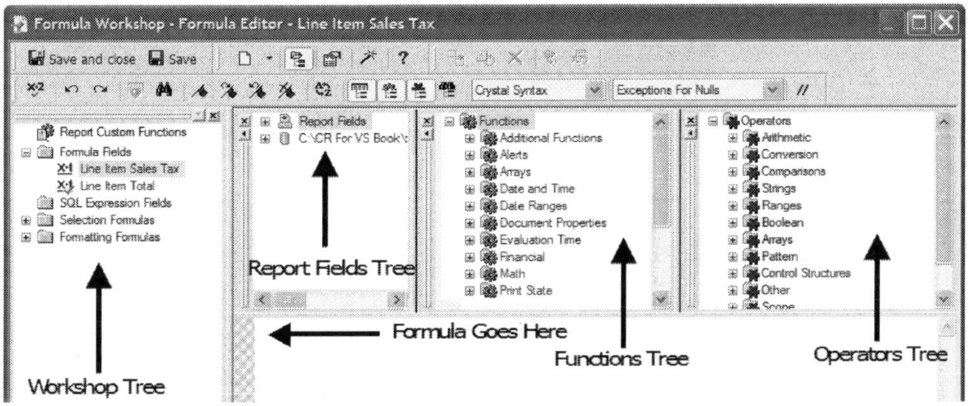

Figure 13-3 Formula Workshop

General Toolbar

Figure 13-4 shows the General toolbar. Table 13-2 explains the buttons on the toolbar.

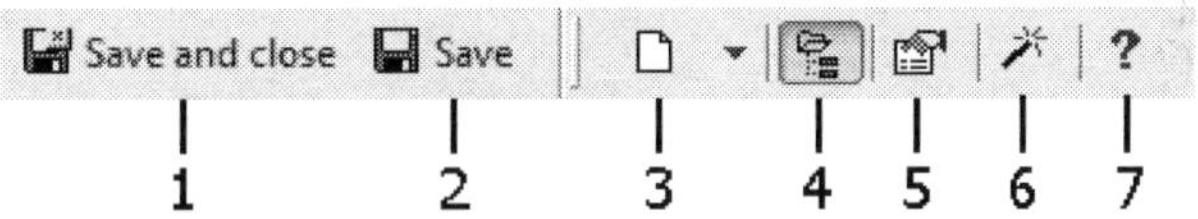

Figure 13-4 General toolbar

Button	Description
1	Closes the Formula Workshop after prompting you to save changes if necessary. (2)
2	Saves the formula and leaves the Formula Workshop open. (2)
3	The New button is used to create a new formula based on the category selected from the drop-down list shown in Figure 13-5. If a formula is open prior to clicking this button, the syntax is checked and the current formula is saved.
4	The Show/Hide Workshop Tree button displays or hides the Workshop Tree.
5	The Toggle Properties Display button toggles between displaying the Custom Function Editor and Custom Function Properties dialog box. Custom functions and formulas (where possible) are displayed in the selected mode until this button is clicked again.
6	The Use Expert/Editor button toggles between the Formula Editor and the Formula Expert. Use the Formula Expert to create a formula based on a custom function. This button is not available when creating a custom function.
7	Opens the online help for the Formula Workshop, Formula Editor or Formula Expert, depending on which is currently displayed or where the insertion point is.

Table 13-2 General toolbar buttons explained

(2) When you save the changes, the formula, custom function or SQL Expression is checked for errors.

The **RECORD SELECTION FORMULA** option is used to create a formula to select data that will appear on the report based on records.

The **GROUP SELECTION FORMULA** option is used to create a formula to select which groups will appear on the report.

The **SAVED DATA SELECTION FORMULA** option is used to create a formula to filter the data that has already been saved with the report.

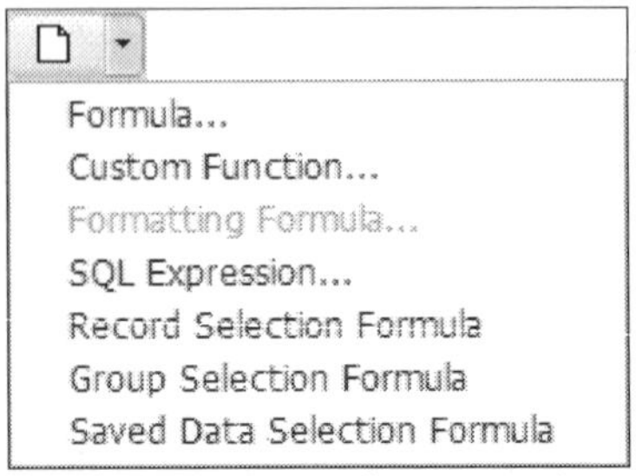

Figure 13-5 New button options

Expression Editor Toolbar

Figure 13-6 shows the Expression Editor toolbar. Table 13-3 explains the buttons on the toolbar.

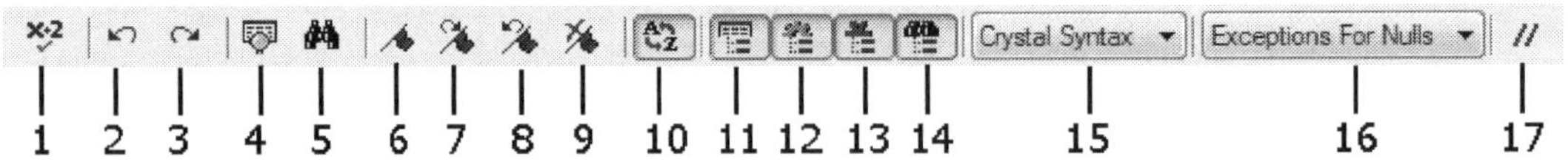

Figure 13-6 Expression Editor toolbar

Button	Description
1	The Check button tests the syntax of the formula or custom function and identifies syntax errors.
2	The Undo button undoes the last action made to the formula.
3	The Redo button redoes the last action made to the formula.
4	The Browse Data button is used to view the data in a field. (3)
5	The Find or Replace dialog box shown in Figure 13-7 searches the formula, fields, functions or operators, for words or expressions. You can also replace text in formulas using this dialog box.
6	The Bookmark button inserts a bookmark in the current line of the selected formula. Click the button again to remove the bookmark. Bookmarks are used to mark a line of code as important. The bookmark feature is helpful in long formulas when you have to go from one part of the formula to another.
7	The Next Bookmark button places the insertion point at the next bookmark in the formula.
8	The Previous Bookmark button places the insertion point at the previous bookmark in the formula.
9	The Clear All Bookmarks button deletes all bookmarks in the current formula.
10	Sorts the options in the Report Fields, Functions and Operators trees in alphabetical order or returns them to their original order.
11	Displays or hides the Report Fields tree. (3)
12	Displays or hides the Functions tree.
13	Displays or hides the Operators tree.
14	Displays or hides the Find results window shown in Figure 13-8. This window displays the results of the search on the Find dialog box.

Table 13-3 Expression Editor toolbar buttons explained

Button	Description
15	Is used to select **CRYSTAL SYNTAX** or **BASIC SYNTAX** as the formula syntax editor.
16	Is used to select **EXCEPTIONS FOR NULLS** or **DEFAULT VALUES FOR NULLS** as the method for handling null values in the data. Fields in a formula that have a null value will return invalid data or generate an error. Selecting the Default values for nulls option will replace data that has a null value, with the default value for the field type. String fields are changed to an empty string. Numeric fields are changed to zero. If you don't know how or do not want to write code to test for nulls or check for errors, select this option.
17	Is used to add comments to a formula. Commented lines are not evaluated as part of the formula. I type the // into the Formula section when typing the formula because I find it faster then clicking this button.

Table 13-3 Expression Editor toolbar buttons explained (Continued)

(3) This button is not available for custom functions.

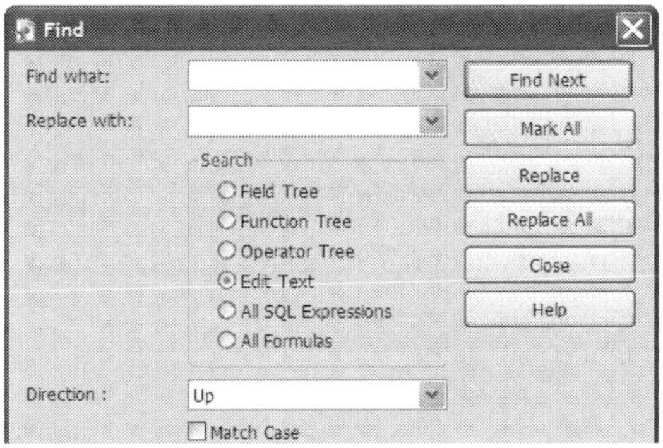

Figure 13-7 Find dialog box

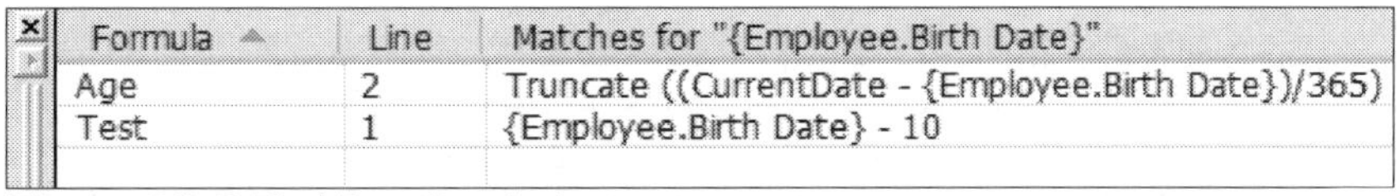

Figure 13-8 Find Results window

The **FIND IN FORMULAS** shortcut menu option is used if you need to find out if a field is used in a formula. Right-click on the field in the Workshop tree, Report Fields tree, Functions tree, the field in the report or in the Field Explorer and select Find in formulas. If the field is being used in a formula, the Formula Workshop will open and display all of the formulas that use the field.

How To Open The Formula Workshop

Like many other tools in Crystal Reports, there is more than one way to open the Formula Workshop, as explained below.

① Click the **FORMULA WORKSHOP** button on the Expert Tools toolbar.

② Report ⇒ Formula Workshop.

③ Right-click on a formula or SQL Expression field in the design window, then select Edit.

④ Right-click on a formula or SQL Expression field in the Field Explorer, then select New or Edit.

⑤ Click on a formula or SQL Expression field, then click the **NEW** button on the Field Explorer toolbar.

⑥ Click the **FORMULA** button on any tab of the Format Editor dialog box.

⑦ Open the Select Expert, click the Show Formula button, then click the **FORMULA EDITOR** button.

Workshop Tree

This section of the Formula Workshop contains all of the formulas that are in the report. Items under the Selection Formulas folder are the ones that you have created with the Select Expert.

As you saw earlier in Figure 13-3, the Workshop Tree contains several sections called **NODES** or **CATEGORY** folders that formulas can be saved in. In addition to being able to create formulas, you can also rename and delete formulas, just like you can in the Field Explorer. Each of the categories in the Workshop Tree are explained below.

① **Report Custom Functions** If you create a function or copy a function from the repository into the report, this is where it would be stored. The functions in this category can be used by any formula in your report. Custom functions are used just like the built-in functions that come with Crystal Reports.

② **Formula Fields** The formulas in this category are same ones that are in the Field Explorer in the Formula Fields, Parameter Fields, Running Total Fields and Group Name Fields sections.

③ **SQL Expression Fields** The formulas in this category are the same expression fields that are in the SQL Expression Fields section of the Field Explorer. If you create a new expression or modify an existing expression, the SQL Expression Editor will open in the Formula Workshop instead of the Formula Editor. The options in the Report Fields Tree, Functions Tree and Operators Tree will change and display the options that are available for the type of database that the report is using. It has been reported that the SQL Expression Editor may not reflect all of the operators and functions that are really available for certain database types.

④ **Selection Formulas** The formulas in this folder are the formulas that are created when you use the Select Expert or the selection formula options on the Report menu. You can also create selection formulas in the Formula Workshop. If you click on the Group Selection option, the **GROUP SELECTION FORMULA EDITOR** will open. If you click on the Record Selection option, the **RECORD SELECTION FORMULA EDITOR** will open. If you click on the Saved Data option, the **SAVED DATA SELECTION FORMULA EDITOR** will open. The only difference that you will notice with these editors is that the title bar of the Formula Workshop, will display the name of the editor.

⑤ **Formatting Formulas** This category has a folder for each section of the report. All of the objects from each section of the report are listed here. Formatting formulas, like changing the color, font or font size for objects on the report are stored in this category.

Workshop Tree Toolbar

Figure 13-9 shows the Workshop Tree toolbar. Table 13-4 explains the buttons on the toolbar.

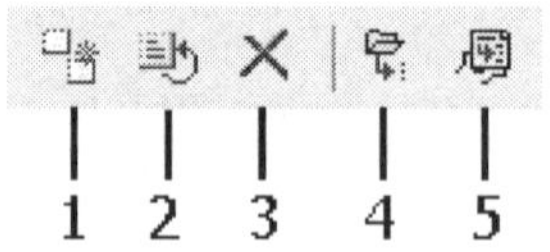

Figure 13-9 Workshop Tree toolbar

Button	Description
1	Duplicates the formula selected in the Formula Fields section of the Workshop Tree.
2	Renames the selected formula, custom function, or SQL Expression.
3	Deletes the selected formula, custom function, or SQL Expression.
4	Expands the selected node(s) in the Workshop Tree.
5	The Show Formatting Formulas button displays or hides all of the report objects in the Formatting Formulas folder or only the objects that have a formatting formula.

Table 13-4 Workshop Tree toolbar buttons explained

Formula Editor

The Formula Editor is in the Formula Workshop. The contents of each of the trees in the Formula Editor change to show the options that are available for the type of database that the report is based on. The Formula Editor is used to create formulas by double-clicking on the functions, operators and fields that you need to include in the formula. The Formula Editor can create at least 90% of the formulas that you need. The Formula Editor contains the three trees discussed below. You may want to open some of the categories (nodes) in each tree to become familiar with the options.

① The **Report Fields Tree** displays all of the fields that are on the report, including groups, summary fields, running totals, parameters, formulas and the tables that the report uses. This tree is similar to the Field Explorer. You can use any of these fields in a formula.
② The **Functions Tree** contains built-in functions. The functions are divided into categories, which may make it easier to find the function that you need.
③ The **Operators Tree** contains the operators (logical and mathematical) that you can use to create formulas. The operators are grouped by type to make them easier to find. Operators use symbols instead of words.

When you first open the Formula Workshop, you will not see the Formula Editor. You can do either of the following to open the Formula Editor.

① Select an option in a folder under the Formula Fields, SQL Expression Fields or Selection Formulas in the Workshop Tree.
② Select one of the formula or function options on the New button drop-down list, shown earlier in Figure 13-5.

If you open the Formula Editor using the **FORMULA EDITOR** button on the Select Expert, Crystal Syntax is the only programming language that you can use.

Formula Text Section

In addition to the three trees, the blank section, which is called the Formula Text section, below the trees is where you type in the formula. I refer to this area as the formula section. Depending on the field selected in the Workshop Tree, the Formula Editor can change to a different editor, because each formula type has its own editor. By default, the font is automatically color coded as follows:

① Green represents comments that you type in.
② Blue represents reserved words like functions.
③ Black represents constants and variables.

Formula Editor Shortcut Keys

Like word processors, the Formula Editor has shortcut key functionality including the following:

- ☑ Ctrl+C Copy the formula.
- ☑ Ctrl+X Delete the selected content.
- ☑ Ctrl+V Paste the selected content.
- ☑ Ctrl+A Select all of the content in the Formula Text section.
- ☑ Ctrl+S Save the formula and close the Formula Workshop.

Using Auto Complete

You can use the **AUTO COMPLETE** feature in the Formula Text section by typing in the first few letters of the function that you need, then press the **CTRL+SPACE BAR** keys. You will see a list that has functions that start with the letters that you typed in, as shown in Figure 13-10. If you type in enough letters to only display the function that you want, the drop-down list will not be displayed. Instead, the function will be filled in for you. If you press the CTRL+Space bar keys before typing any letters, you will see all of the functions in the list.

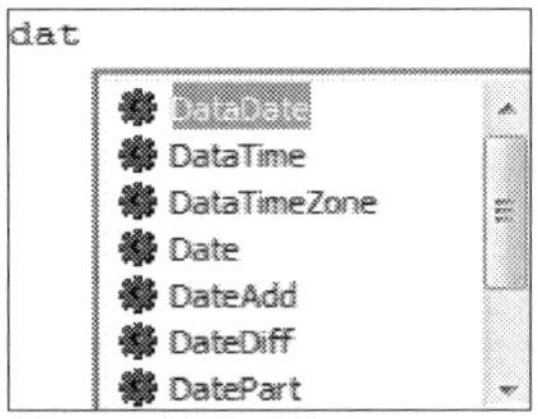

Figure 13-10 Auto complete list of functions in the Formula Text section

To view a list of tables, type a {, as shown in Figure 13-11.

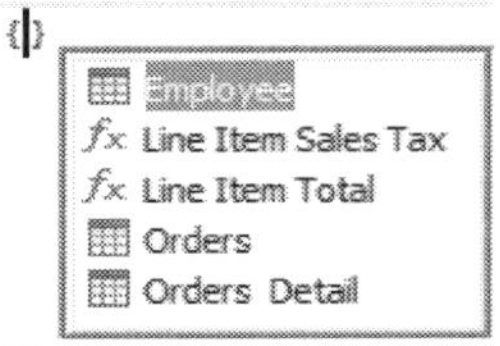

Figure 13-11 Auto complete list of tables in the Formula Text section

Customizing The Formula Editor

You can customize the Formula Editor by doing any or all of the following:

① Resize any of the tree sections by dragging the bar illustrated in Figure 13-12.
② Close a tree by clicking on the ☒ button to the left of the section that you want to close.
③ Expand a tree by clicking on the ◂ button to the left of the section that you want to expand.
④ Make the Formula section longer or shorter by dragging the section bar above it, up or down.

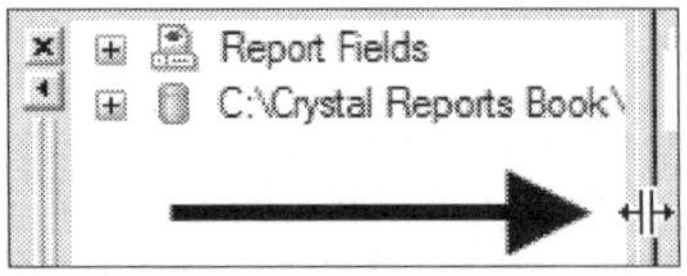

Figure 13-12 Mouse pointer in position to resize a tree

Formula Evaluation Order

Many of the formulas that you will create will use more than one operator. The order that the formula is written in from left to right may not be the order that the formula is calculated or evaluated in. Some operations are processed first, regardless of where they are in the formula. This is known as the **ORDER OF PRECEDENCE**. The formula evaluation order is:

① The portion of the formula that is in parenthesis.
② Exponential.
③ Multiplication and division. (4) (5)
④ Integer division.
⑤ MOD.
⑥ Addition and subtraction. (4)

(4) If the operators (3 and 6 above) are on the same level, they are evaluated from left to right. See the examples below.

Example #1 3 + 4 / (2 + 19) = 3.19
Example #2 3 + (4 / 2) + 19 = 24

The first example calculates the (2+19) first, then divides that by 4 and then adds 3.
The second example calculates the (4/2) first, then adds 3 and then adds 19.

(5) In Crystal syntax, percents are evaluated at the same level as multiplication and division.

You may find it helpful to write the formula on paper and use data in the tables to test the formulas to see if you get the results that you are expecting from the formula. As you saw in the examples above, the same data and operators can produce different results.

I have noticed in the workplace and in classes that I teach that this is one area where many people have a lot of trouble. I think this is because they are not willing to write out the formula and test it prior to opening the Formula Workshop. Yes, I am fully aware that doing this takes more time up front, but experience shows that the more time you spend "preparing", the less time you will spend debugging reports in the future. Trust me, a year from now, you will not remember why you wrote a formula the way that you did <smile>. Keep the following in mind when creating formulas:

① Formulas must have an equal number of left and right parenthesis.
② Arguments must be the same data type.

Formula Naming Conventions

The naming conventions for formulas is free form. You should use as descriptive a name as possible, one that will make sense to you a year from now. The name that you select is what you will see when the formula field is added to the report. Formula names can be up to 256 characters. You can use upper and lower case letters, spaces and the underscore. You should not use characters like the slash, dollar or percent sign in the formula name.

The company that you work for may have naming conventions. You should check to find out. One convention that many companies have is that they do not want spaces in object names. When this is the case, most companies use the underscore in place of spaces in object names.

Create Numeric Formulas

The exercises in this section will teach you how to create numeric formulas.

Exercise 13.1: Create A Formula Field

The report that you will modify displays an order total per customer. As you will see, the order total is not correct. You will create a formula that will calculate the amount for each item. This is known as the line item amount. The formula is Unit Price * Quantity. This will allow the report to have the correct total amount.

1. Save the Chapter 13 Orders by sales rep report as `E13.1 Formula field for line item totals.`

2. Right-click on the **FORMULA FIELDS** option in the Field Explorer, then select **NEW**.

3. Type `Line Item Total` in the dialog box as shown in Figure 13-13, then click OK.

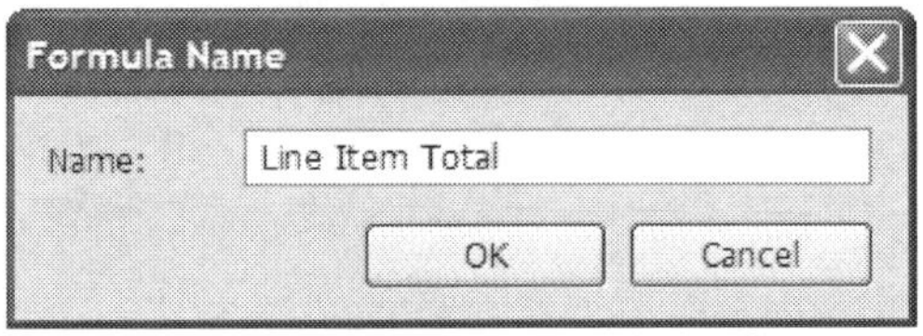

Figure 13-13 Formula Name dialog box

4. In the Report Fields tree, double-click on the Unit Price field in the Orders Detail table.

   You should see the field in the formula section, as shown at the bottom of Figure 13-14.

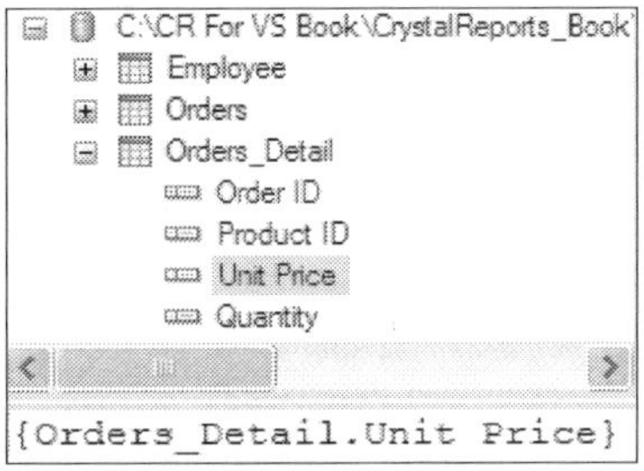

Figure 13-14 Field added to the Formula section

You can also drag the field to the formula section in the Formula Editor.

5. Type a `*` after the Unit Price field, then double-click on the Quantity field.

You can use the **MULTIPLY** Arithmetic operator illustrated in Figure 13-15 instead of typing in the operator.

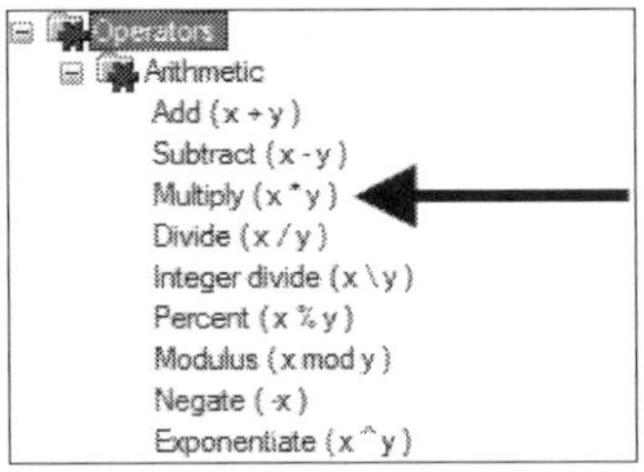

Figure 13-15 Multiply arithmetic operator illustrated

6. Add a blank line above the formula and type the following comment.
   `// This formula calculates the Line Item Total.`

   Your formula should look like the one shown in Figure 13-16.

```
// This formula calculates the Line Item Total
{Orders_Detail.Unit Price} *{Orders_Detail.Quantity}
```

Figure 13-16 Line Item Total formula

Notice that the comment line is a different color then the formula line. This is one way to know that you have entered the comment correctly. Comments do not have to go at the beginning of a formula.

7. Click the **x+2** button on the Expression Editor toolbar. You should see the message shown in Figure 13-17.

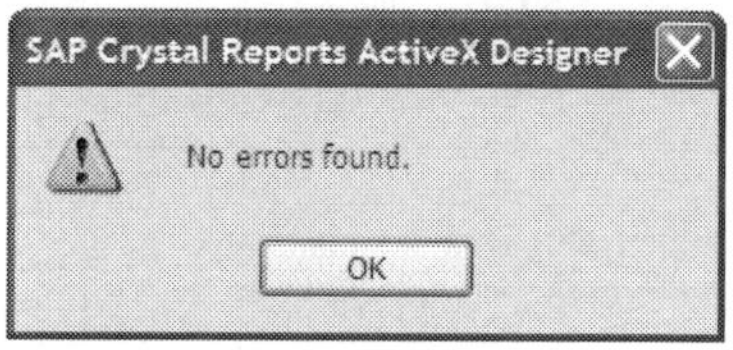

Figure 13-17 No errors found message

The message shown above in Figure 13-17 means that Crystal Reports did not find a syntax error. This does not mean that the formula will produce the results that you are expecting.

Using the **x+2** button is optional because the syntax is automatically checked when you exit the Formula Editor.

If you do not see the message in Figure 13-17, there is an error in your formula. Check to make sure that your formula looks like the one shown earlier in Figure 13-16.

Figure 13-18 shows one error message that you could see. If there is an error, the flashing insertion bar will be at the location in the formula where Crystal Reports thinks the error is.

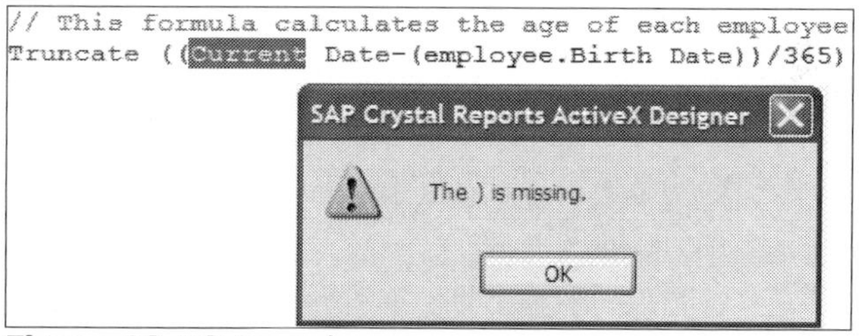

Figure 13-18 Formula error message

The part of the formula where the syntax checker stopped understanding the formula will also be highlighted, as shown above in Figure 13-18. You are not required to fix the error immediately. You can save it as is and work on something else. Just don't forget to come back and fix it.

8. Click OK, then click the **SAVE AND CLOSE** button.

If you need to work on another formula, click the **SAVE** button instead of the Save and close button. Doing this will leave the Formula Workshop open. When you save a formula it becomes a field, which you can then add to the report or use in another formula.

Using Formula Fields In Reports

You can use formula fields in reports, just like you use fields from a table. Formula fields can be placed in any section of the report. You can create counts and summary fields that are based on formula fields. You can also use formula fields as selection criteria.

Add The Line Item Formula Field To The Report

In this part of the exercise you will add the formula field that you just created to the report.

1. Delete the Order Amount field, then move the four fields after the Order Amount field over to the left.

2. Add the Line Item Total field to the report. The report should look like the one shown in Figure 13-19. Leave the report open to complete the next part of the exercise.

Orders By Sales Rep

Salesperson	Order Date	Order ID	Customer #	Product #	Unit Price	Quantity	Line Item Total
1 Nancy Davolio							
2/14/2010							
30							
	02/19/2010	1310	30	1101	$14.50	3	$43.50
	02/19/2010	1310	30	1104	$14.50	1	$14.50
Total order amount for customer - **$ 116.00**							
75							
	02/19/2010	1312	75	302162	$479.85	1	$479.85
	02/19/2010	1312	75	401001	$267.76	1	$267.76
	02/19/2010	1312	75	2202	$41.90	1	$41.90
Total order amount for customer - **$ 2,368.53**							
Daily Totals	# of Orders for the day - **2**						
Total amount of sales for the day - **$ 2,484.53**							

Figure 13-19 E13.1 Formula field for line item totals added to the report

Modify The Total Fields

As you can see, the Total Order Amount for each customer is still not correct. That is because the Total order amount field is adding the values in the Order Amount field. The Total Order Amount field should be adding the values in the Line Item Total formula field. Complete the task below to fix this.

1. Modify the Total order amount for customer, Total amount of sales for the day, Total amount of sales for salesperson and Total amount of sales fields to use the Line Item Total field for the summary, instead of the Order Amount field. (**Hint**: Use the Change Summary option)
   The report should look like the one shown in Figure 13-20.

Orders By Sales Rep

Salesperson	Order Date	Order ID	Customer #	Product #	Unit Price	Quantity	Line Item Total
1 Nancy Davolio							
2/14/2010							
30							
	02/19/2010	1310	30	1101	$14.50	3	$43.50
	02/19/2010	1310	30	1104	$14.50	1	$14.50
Total order amount for customer - **$ 58.00** ←							
75							
	02/19/2010	1312	75	302162	$479.85	1	$479.85
	02/19/2010	1312	75	401001	$267.76	1	$267.76
	02/19/2010	1312	75	2202	$41.90	1	$41.90
Total order amount for customer - **$ 789.51** ←							
Daily Totals	# of Orders for the day - **2**						
Total amount of sales for the day - **$ 847.51** ←							

Figure 13-20 Modified report

Exercise 13.2: Create A Sales Tax Formula

Many orders (or purchases) require sales tax to be collected. This exercise will show you how to create a sales tax formula. You will create a formula that calculates 6% of the Line item total. As you know, not all items are taxable. If all items were taxable, you could create a sales tax formula that used the order total times the sales tax rate. In this exercise, you will modify a report and create a sales tax formula that will use the Line Item Total field instead of the Order Total field.

> In the real world, the product table would have a field that is used to signify if each product is taxable or not. In that case, you would have to create a conditional formula that checked the field to see if the product is taxable. If it is taxable, then calculate the sales tax.

1. Save the E13.1 report as `E13.2 Sales tax formula`.

2. Create a formula field named `Line Item Sales Tax`.

3. Double-click on the Line Item Total formula field in the Report Fields tree, then type `* .06` at the end of the field. Check the formula to make sure that the syntax is correct by clicking the x+2 button.

   Your formula should look like the one shown in Figure 13-21. Click the Save and close button.

```
{@Line Item Total} * .06
```

Figure 13-21 Line Item Sales Tax formula

4. Move all of the fields in the Details section to the left, then add the Line Item Sales Tax field at the end of the Details section.

5. Change the field heading for the Line Item Sales Tax field to `Sales Tax`. Your report should look similar to the one shown in Figure 13-22. Leave the report open to complete the next exercise.

Salesperson	Order Date	Order ID	Customer #	Product #	Unit Price	Quantity	Line Item Total	Sales Tax
1	Nancy Davolio							
2/14/2010								
30								
	02/19/2010	1310	30	1101	$14.50	3	$43.50	$2.61
	02/19/2010	1310	30	1104	$14.50	1	$14.50	$0.87
	Total order amount for customer - **$ 58.00**							
75								
	02/19/2010	1312	75	302162	$479.85	1	$479.85	$28.79
	02/19/2010	1312	75	401001	$267.76	1	$267.76	$16.07
	02/19/2010	1312	75	2202	$41.90	1	$41.90	$2.51
	Total order amount for customer - **$ 789.51**							
Daily Totals	# of Orders for the day - **2**							
	Total amount of sales for the day - **$ 847.51**							

Figure 13-22 E13.2 Sales tax formula report

Exercise 13.3: Create A Summary Formula

All of the summary fields that you have created so far in this book were based off of fields in a table. In this exercise you will create a summary field that is based off of a formula field.

1. Save the E13.2 report as `E13.3 Summary formula`.

2. Right-click on the Line Item Sales Tax formula field and select Insert ⇒ Summary.

3. Select the Average summary type, then select the Group 2 Orders Date summary location as the section to place the field in and click OK. You will see the average sales tax amount for the daily totals, as illustrated in Figure 13-23. If you want, you can add a title for the field so that the person reading the report knows what the number is.

75								
	02/19/2010	1312	75	302162	$479.85	1	$479.85	$28.79
	02/19/2010	1312	75	401001	$267.76	1	$267.76	$16.07
	02/19/2010	1312	75	2202	$41.90	1	$41.90	$2.51
Total order amount for customer - **$ 789.51**								
Daily Totals	# of Orders for the day - **2**				Average Sales Tax **$ 10.17**			
	Total amount of sales for the day - **$ 847.51**							

Figure 13-23 E13.3 Summary formula report

Exercise 13.4: Create A Weekly Salary Formula

In this exercise you will create a formula that will calculate each employees weekly salary. The annual salary field is stored in the Employee table. You will use this field to calculate the weekly salary.

1. Save the Chapter 13 Employee List report as `E13.4 Employee list with weekly salary formula`.

2. Create a formula field named `Weekly Salary`.

3. Double-click on the Salary field in the Employee table, then drag the **DIVIDE (X/Y)** Arithmetic operator to the formula section.

4. Type `52` after the slash. Your formula should look like the one shown in Figure 13-24.

```
{Employee.Salary} / 52
```

Figure 13-24 Weekly Salary formula

5. Delete the Region field, then add the Weekly Salary formula field before the Salary field. The report should look like the one shown in Figure 13-25. Leave the report open to complete the next part of the exercise.

First Name	Last Name	Address1	Weekly Salary	Salary
Steven	Buchanan	14 Garrett Hill	$961.54	$50,000.00
Robert	King	Edgeham Hollow	$711.54	$37,000.00
Anne	Dodsworth	7 Houndstooth Rd.	$673.08	$35,000.00
Michael	Suyama	Coventry House	$576.92	$30,000.00

Figure 13-25 E13.4 Employee list with weekly salary formula report

Use A Formula Field As Selection Criteria

Earlier you learned that you can use a formula field as selection criteria. In this part of the exercise you will use the Weekly Salary formula field to only display employees that have a weekly salary between $500 and $750.

1. Create selection criteria for the Weekly Salary formula field to select records where the weekly salary is between $500 and $750.

2. The report should look like the one shown in Figure 13-26. There should be five records on the report.

First Name	Last Name	Address1	Weekly Salary	Salary
Robert	King	Edgeham Hollow	$711.54	$37,000.00
Anne	Dodsworth	7 Houndstooth Rd.	$673.08	$35,000.00
Michael	Suyama	Coventry House	$576.92	$30,000.00
BC				
Margaret	Peacock	4110 Old Redmond Rd.	$673.08	$35,000.00
Janet	Leverling	722 Moss Bay Blvd.	$634.62	$33,000.00

Figure 13-26 Formula field used as selection criteria

Create String Formulas

The exercises in this section will teach you how to create formulas that use String (text) fields or literals. String formulas can be used to convert date and numeric fields to text, select specific portions of a field and trim fields. A common string formula that is used is one that will concatenate (combine) the first and last name fields. Names are usually stored in two or more fields in a table. There are several string formula operators and functions that you can use, as explained in Tables 13-5 and 13-6.

Operator	Description
+ or &	These are known as concatenation operators. They are used to combine text fields. The plus sign requires that all arguments be string fields. Crystal Reports will automatically convert every argument to a string when the ampersand (&) operator is used.
[ ]	Subscript operators are used to select specific characters from a text field.
" " or ' '	Quotes will treat the text inside of them as a literal. If a string or text field contains numeric data and you need to use it in a formula, you have to put the numeric data in quotes.

Table 13-5 String operators explained

Date/Time literals must be in one of these formats: #6/24/2011# or #June 24, 2011#.

Keep in mind that while the + (plus sign) operator allows you to join text and data fields, it does not add a space between the fields that are being joined. You have to type + " " + to add a space between the fields that you are joining. There is a space between the quotes in the syntax above.

Function	What It Does . . .
ChrW(x)	Returns the character that represents the Unicode value of (x).
Is Null	Checks to see if a field has a value. It is often used with the If...Then... Else operator. If the function is used alone, it returns a value of True or False (Boolean).
Length (str)	Counts the number of characters in a string. It is used to determine the length of the value in a field.
Lower Case (str)	Converts the text to all lower case letters. Use **LOWERCASE** for Crystal Syntax. Use **LCASE** for Basic Syntax.
Picture (str, picture)	Is used to format a string field. This is similar to the "mask" feature that some database software packages support.

Table 13-6 String functions explained

Function	What It Does . . .
To Text	Is used to convert non text fields like Date, Number and Currency to a text string. This function can have multiple arguments, as shown in Figure 13-27. The only argument that requires a value is X.
Trim (str)	Removes spaces before and after the data in a string argument. Use **TRIMLEFT** if you only want to remove spaces on the left of the string argument. Use **TRIMRIGHT** if you only want to remove spaces on the right of the string argument.
Upper Case (str)	Converts the text to all upper case letters. Use **UPPERCASE** for Crystal Syntax. Use **UCASE** for Basic Syntax.

Table 13-6 String functions explained (Continued)

```
⊟ ToText
      ToText (x)
      ToText (x, y)
      ToText (x, y, z)
      ToText (x, y, z, w)
      ToText (x, y, z, w, q)
```

Figure 13-27 To Text functions

Exercise 13.5: Combine Two String Fields

Earlier in this chapter you modified a report that displayed the first and last names. The report would look better if the employee first and last names were closer together. This produces the same result as dragging one field into another as you learned earlier in the book. One reason that you would create a formula field to combine the name fields is if you only needed to combine fields when a certain condition was met. Another reason to create a formula field to combine fields is if there is a possibility that at least one of the fields is null.

1. Save the E13.1 report as `E13.5 Combine string fields`.

2. Create a formula field named `Employee Full Name`, then add the First Name field from the Employee table to the formula section.

3. Click after the First Name field and type `+ " " +`
   This will add a space after the First Name. Make sure that there is a space between the quotes, then add the Last Name field to the formula.

4. Add a blank line above the formula, then type `// This formula combines 2 fields`. The formula should look like the one shown in Figure 13-28.

```
//This formula combines 2 fields
{Employee.First Name}+" "+{Employee.Last Name}
```

Figure 13-28 String formula

Add The Employee Full Name Formula Field To The Report

1. Delete the First and Last name fields in the Group Header 1 section. Add the Employee Full Name field in place of the two fields that you just deleted.

2. Create a field title in the Page Header section. Type `Employee` in the field, then underline it. Place it above the Employee Full Name field. The report should look like the one shown in Figure 13-29. Leave the report open to complete the next exercise.

	Employee	Order Date	Order ID	Customer #	Product #	Unit Price	Quantity	Line Item Total
1	Nancy Davolio							
2/14/2010								
30								
		02/19/2010	1310	30	1101	$14.50	3	$43.50
		02/19/2010	1310	30	1104	$14.50	1	$14.50
	Total order amount for customer - **$ 58.00**							

Figure 13-29 E13.5 Combine string fields report

Exercise 13.6: Use The Subscript Operator

The subscript operator is used to extract specific characters in a field based on their position in the field. In Exercise 13.5 you learned how to combine the first and last name fields. If you needed to modify that formula to only display the first letter of the first name, you would use the subscript operator. The subscript [1] means to select the first character in the field from the left. Subscript [3] means to select the third character in the field, from the left. In this exercise you will add the subscript operator to an existing formula.

1. Save the E13.5 report as `E13.6 Subscript.`

2. Right-click on the Employee Full Name field in the report and select **EDIT FORMULA**. Modify the Employee Full Name formula so that it looks like the one shown in Figure 13-30.

```
// This formula combines 2 fields and only uses the first letter
// of the First Name field
{Employee.First Name}[1]+" "+{Employee.Last Name}
```

Figure 13-30 Subscript formula

The report should look like the one shown in Figure 13-31.

Notice that only the first letter of the first name is displayed.

	Employee	Order Date
1	N Davolio ←	
2/14/2010		
30		
		02/19/2010
		02/19/2010

Figure 13-31 E13.6 Subscript report

Exercise 13.7: Combine A Text And Numeric Field

In the reports that you have created with totals, you created a text object for the title of the summary field. If you had trouble either getting the text object and total field to line up or getting the two fields to be close together, this exercise will show you how to combine these fields using a formula, which means that you will not have to align the field and text object.

1. Save the E9.1 report as `E13.7 Combine text and numeric fields.`

2. Create a formula field named `Total Field.`

3. Add the comment `This formula combines text with a numeric field.`

4. Type `"Total # of customers in region - "` in the formula section.

5. Open the **STRINGS** operators node, then drag the **CONCATENATE (X&Y)** operator illustrated on the right in Figure 13-32, to the formula.

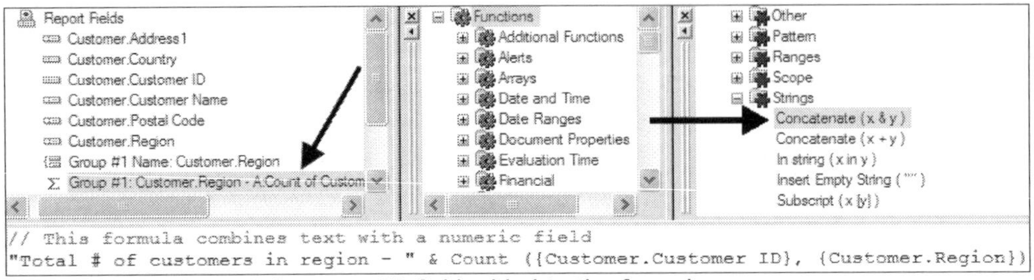

Figure 13-32 Group 1 Customer ID field added to the formula

6. Add the Group 1 Customer ID field illustrated on the left, above in Figure 13-32 to the formula.

Add The Total Formula Field To The Report

1. Delete everything in the Group Footer section.

2. Add the Total Field formula field to the Group Footer section, then make it wider. The report should look like the one shown in Figure 13-33. Notice that there is a decimal point in the number. To format the number to not display the decimal point, change the formula shown above in Figure 13-32 to the one shown in Figure 13-34.

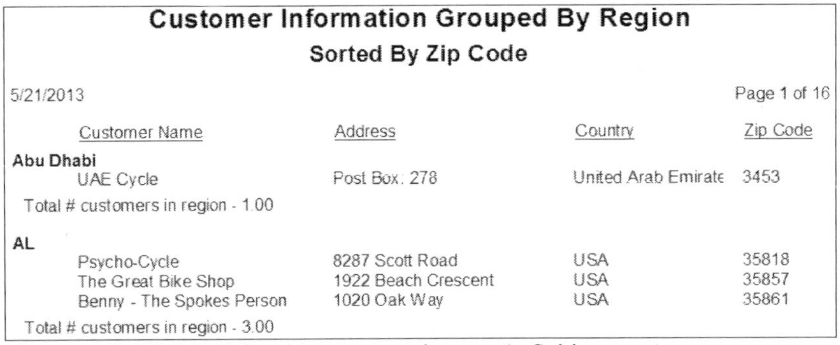
Customer Information Grouped By Region

Sorted By Zip Code

5/21/2013 Page 1 of 16

Customer Name	Address	Country	Zip Code
Abu Dhabi			
UAE Cycle	Post Box: 278	United Arab Emirate	3453
Total # customers in region - 1.00			
AL			
Psycho-Cycle	8287 Scott Road	USA	35818
The Great Bike Shop	1922 Beach Crescent	USA	35857
Benny - The Spokes Person	1020 Oak Way	USA	35861
Total # customers in region - 3.00			

Figure 13-33 E13.7 Combine text and numeric fields report

```
"Total # customers in region - " &
ToText(Count ({Customer.Customer ID}, {Customer.Region}),0)
```

Figure 13-34 Formula to format the number to not display the decimal point

Use Functions In String Formulas

You may have the need to combine data that is stored in different data types or format data differently then it is stored in the table. The next two exercises will show you how to incorporate functions in string formulas.

Exercise 13.8: Use The Picture Function

The phone numbers in the Supplier table are stored in the format shown in Figure 13-35.

Notice that there are also international phone numbers in the table. When you want to print US phone numbers, they will look better if they are printed like this **(555) 555-5555**.

In this exercise you will use the Picture function to format US phone numbers in the Supplier table.

Figure 13-35 Phone numbers stored in the table

1. Create a new report and save it as `E13.8 Picture function`. Add the Supplier table, but do not add any fields to the report.

2. Create selection criteria to only display US suppliers on the report.

3. Create a formula field named `Supplier Phone`, then add the comment `This formula formats the Phone Number field` to the formula.

4. Open the **ADDITIONAL FUNCTIONS** category in the Functions tree, then open the **SAMP1** category and double-click on the **PICTURE** function illustrated in Figure 13-36.

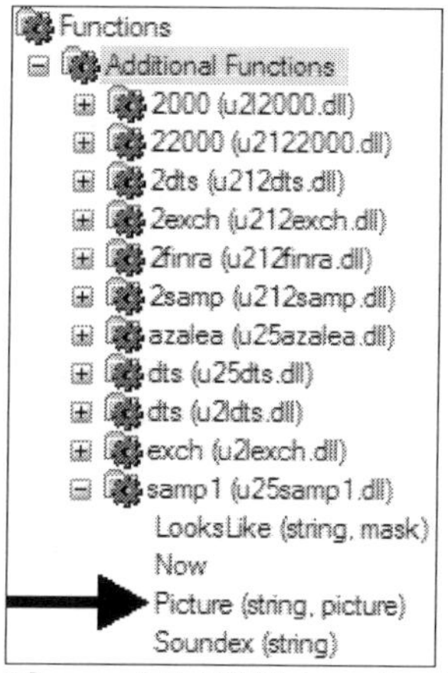

Figure 13-36 Picture function illustrated

5. Double-click on the Phone field in the Supplier table in the Report Fields tree, then click after the comma in the formula and type `"(XXX)XXXXXXX"`. Your formula should look like the one shown in Figure 13-37. Leave the Formula Workshop open to complete the next part of the exercise.

```
// This formula formats the Phone Number field
Picture ({Supplier.Phone},"(XXX)XXXXXXX")
```

Figure 13-37 Phone number formula

> The brackets { } in a formula are used for data fields. The parenthesis ( ) are used to control the order that the formula is evaluated in.

In Figure 13-35 shown earlier, you saw the phone numbers that are stored in the Supplier table. All of the phone numbers will not work with the mask that you just created in the formula, which is why you created selection criteria to only display US suppliers. In order to be able to accommodate international phone numbers, the formula would have to be modified to also use the **LENGTH** function and have another mask to accommodate phone numbers of a different length. This is known as conditional formatting.

Use The ToText Function

The ToText function is one of the more popular functions. It is used to convert dates, numbers and more to a string/text field. In this part of the exercise you will combine the Supplier ID and Supplier Name fields. In order to combine a numeric and string field, you have to convert the numeric field to text. The ToText function will let you do this.

1. Click the New button on the toolbar and type `Supplier ID & Name` as the formula name.
2. Add the comment `This formula combines the Supplier ID and Supplier Name fields.`
3. Open the Strings category in the Functions tree, then double-click on the ToText (x,y) function.
4. Click inside of the parenthesis if necessary, then add the Supplier ID field to the formula.
5. Click after the comma in the formula and type a zero. The zero means that the number should not display any decimal places if there are any in the field.
6. Click outside of the formula on the right and type `+ " - " +`, then add the Supplier Name field. Your formula should look like the one shown in Figure 13-38.

```
// This formula combines the Supplier ID and Supplier Name fields
ToText ({Supplier.Supplier ID},0 )+" - "+{Supplier.Supplier Name}
```

Figure 13-38 Supplier ID and Name formula

7. Add both of the formula fields to the Details section of the report. The report should look like the one shown in Figure 13-39.

Supplier ID & Name	Supplier Phone
1 - Active Outdoors	(503) 555-9931
2 - Triumph	(313) 555-5735

Figure 13-39 E13.8 Picture function report

Using The Ampersand To Concatenate Strings
In the exercise that you just completed, you used the ToText function and the plus sign operator to concatenate string fields. The benefit of using the ToText function with the plus sign is that you can control the formatting. If you do not need to control the formatting, use the ampersand operator instead of the plus sign.

Formatting Strings With A Mask

In Exercise 13.8 you formatted a phone number field with the Picture function, which used a mask to format the field. Masks use characters including d, m and y as placeholders for the data, which determines how the data will be formatted when it is converted to a string. Table 13-7 lists some of the mask placeholders that are used for date fields. Table 13-8 provides placeholder examples for the date 6/1/12.

Placeholder	Description
d	Day of the month in numeric format without a leading zero.
dd	Day of the month in numeric format with a leading zero if necessary.
dddd	Name of the day spelled out.
M	Month in numeric format without a leading zero.
MM	Month in numeric format with a leading zero if necessary.
MMMM	Name of the month spelled out.
y or yy	Last two digits of the year.
yyyy	Four digit year.

Table 13-7 Placeholder options explained

Mask	Displays
dd, MM, yy	01, 06, 12
MMMM dd yyyy	June 01 2012
dddd MMMM d, yyyy	Wednesday June 1, 2012
M, d, yy	6, 1, 12

Table 13-8 Mask options

Using Date Formulas

Table 13-9 provides an overview of some of the date functions. The exercises in this section will show you how to create some of the more popular date formulas using functions.

Function	What It Does . . .
CurrentDate	Uses the system date on your computer.
DateAdd	Is used to increment a date field by intervals, including days, weeks, months and years.
DateDiff	Calculates the difference between the start and end dates in the function. (6)
Day	Extracts the day from a Date or Date/Time field and returns a whole number.
Month	Extracts the month from a Date or Date/Time field and returns a whole number.
ToText	Formats any or all parts of a date field. This function also allows you to convert a date field to a text value.
Year	Extracts the year from a Date or Date/Time field and returns a whole number.

Table 13-9 Date functions explained

(6)

> The **DATEDIFF** function has arguments that are used to determine how to calculate the difference between two date fields. The most common arguments are:
> **D** calculates the difference in days
> **M** calculates the difference in months
> **YYYY** calculates the difference in years

Exercise 13.9: Create A Date Formula To Calculate The Order Processing Time

In this exercise you will create a formula to find out how long it is between the day an order is placed and when the order was shipped. This is known as the order processing time.

1. Save the Chapter 8 Order Date report as `E13.9 Calculate order processing time`.

2. Create a formula field named `Delay In Days To Ship`.

3. Expand the Date and Time function category, then expand the **DATEDIFF** category and double-click on the first DateDiff function.

4. Type `"d"` before the first comma in the formula.

5. Add the Order Date field to the formula after the first comma, then add the Ship Date field to the formula after the second comma. Your formula should look like the one shown in Figure 13-40.

```
DateDiff ("d",{Orders.Order Date} ,{Orders.Ship Date})
```

Figure 13-40 Delay in days to ship formula

Add The Delay In Days To Ship Formula Field To The Report

1. Remove the time from the Order Date and Ship Date fields. Make these fields smaller, then move all of the fields after the Order Date field, to the left.

2. Add the Delay In Days To Ship formula field to the end of the Details section and format it so that it does not have any decimal places. The report should look like the one shown in Figure 13-41.

Customer Name	Order Date	Ship Date	Order ID	Unit Price	Quantity	Delay In Days To Ship
City Cyclists	12/02/2010	12/10/2010	1	$41.90	1	8
Deals on Wheels	12/02/2010	12/02/2010	1,002	$33.90	3	0
Deals on Wheels	12/02/2010	12/02/2010	1,002	$1,652.86	3	0
Warsaw Sports, Inc.	12/02/2010	12/05/2010	1,003	$48.51	3	3
Warsaw Sports, Inc.	12/02/2010	12/05/2010	1,003	$13.78	3	3
Bikes and Trikes	12/02/2010	12/02/2010	1,004	$274.35	3	0

Figure 13-41 E13.9 Calculate order processing time report

A zero in the Delay In Days To Ship field means that the order was shipped within 24 hours of when it was placed. When using Date/Time fields, depending on the time an order was placed and shipped, the Ship Date could be the next day and still have a zero in the Delay In Days To Ship field because the order was shipped in less than 24 hours.

Exercise 13.10: Calculate A Persons Age

One of the more popular date functions is used to calculate a persons age if you have their date of birth. In this exercise you will create an employee birthday list report. You will create a formula to calculate the age of the employees. Earlier in this chapter, I listed four reasons why certain types of data are not saved in a table. A persons age is a good example of the type of data that should not be saved in a table. The reason is because the age changes every year. This would mean that the field would have to be updated once a year on each persons birthday. This is why it is best to calculate the age, each time the report is run.

1. Create a new report and save it as `E13.10 Calculate age formula`.
   Add the following fields from the Employee table: Position, Birth Date and Hire Date.

2. Remove the time from the Birth Date and Hire Date fields.

If you need to use the same formula in more than one report, you can copy it from one report and paste it in another report.

3. Create a formula field named `Employee Name`. Create a formula to combine the first and last name fields.

4. Create a formula field named `Age`. Add the **CURRENT DATE FUNCTION** in the Date and Time category to the formula, then type a - (minus sign). Add the Birth Date field to the formula.

Modify The Report

1. Add the Employee Name formula field to the beginning of the Details section, then add the Age formula field after the Birth Date field.

2. Sort the report by the Last Name field. The report should look like the one shown in Figure 13-42. You will see different numbers in the Age column because it is calculated based on the date the report was run.

Employee Name	Position	Birth Date	Age	Hire Date
Justin Brid	Marketing Director	10/08/1977	13,009.00	01/01/1994
Steven Buchanan	Sales Manager	03/04/1975	13,958.00	09/13/1992
Laura Callahan	Inside Sales Coordinator	01/09/1974	14,377.00	01/30/1993
Nancy Davolio	Sales Representative	12/08/1972	14,774.00	03/29/1991

Figure 13-42 Age field added to the report

Modify The Age Formula

As you can see, the age formula did not return the age in the format that you expected. The age shown on the report is in days, not years. This is because the Current Date function calculates in days. The formula will have to be modified so that the age is displayed in years.

1. Right-click on the Age formula field in the Field Explorer and select Edit Formula.

You may be thinking that the only thing that you have to do is click after the Birth Date field in the formula and type /365 and the age would be converted to years.

Just adding this to the formula will not calculate the age in years. Instead, you will see the message shown in Figure 13-43.

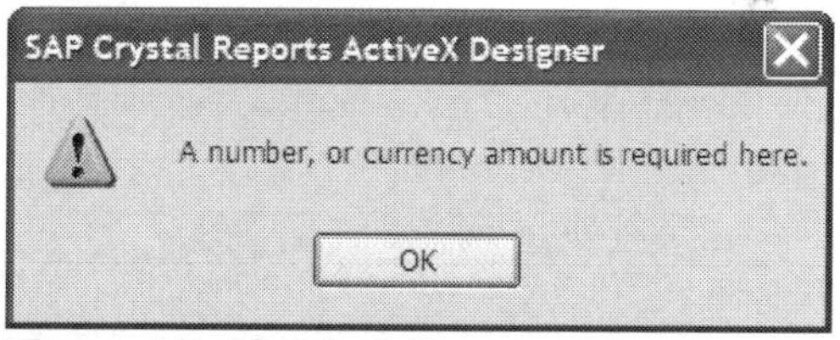

Figure 13-43 Calculation warning message

> The reason that you will see this message is because you are trying to divide the Birth Date field which is a Date or Date/Time field by 365, which is a numeric field. As you learned earlier, arguments must be the same data type to use them in a formula. This is not the case in this formula.

Another reason that this formula will not work is because of the formula evaluation order. The evaluation order must be forced in this formula. The way to force it is by adding parenthesis around the portion of the formula that has to be evaluated first. The order needed is to force the Birth Date to be subtracted from the Current Date **BEFORE** the division takes place.

2. Type parenthesis around the formula, then type `/365` after the last parenthesis.

Use The Truncate Function

When you previewed the report you saw that the age field has a decimal place. The decimal place represents part of the year. This is not what you want. The Truncate function will remove that portion of the data.

1. Add the comment `This formula calculates the employees age.`

2. Expand the Math function category, then expand the Truncate category.

3. Click at the beginning of the formula, then double-click on the Truncate (x) function.

> **TRUNCATE(X)** truncates a field. **TRUNCATE (X, #PLACES)** determines how many decimal places to keep before truncation occurs.

4. After the truncate function, you will see parenthesis. Delete the right parenthesis and add it to the end of the formula. Your formula should look like the one shown in Figure 13-44.

```
// This formula calculates the employee age
Truncate ((CurrentDate-{Employee.Birth Date})/365)
```

Figure 13-44 Age formula

5. Format the Age field on the report so that it does not have any decimal places. The bottom half of the report should look like the one shown in Figure 13-45.

Employee Name	Position	Birth Date	Age	Hire Date
.		.		
.		.		
Robert King	Sales Representative	05/29/1972	39	11/29/1992
Janet Leverling	Sales Representative	08/30/1971	39	02/27/1991
Xavier Martin	Marketing Associate	11/30/1975	35	01/15/1994
Caroline Patterson	Receptionist	09/11/1979	31	05/15/1993
Margaret Peacock	Sales Representative	09/19/1973	37	03/30/1992
Laurent Pereira	Advertising Specialist	12/09/1970	40	02/01/1994

Figure 13-45 E13.10 Calculate age formula report

> You will see different ages for all of the employees, then those shown in the figures. This will happen if you run the report after an employees birthday has past. For example, I ran the report shown above in Figure 13-45 in early August 2011. I ran the report shown in Figure 13-46 the end of September 2011. Notice that the age for some employees has changed. That is because some people had a birthday since I ran the report shown above.

Employee Name	Position	Birth Date	Age	Hire Date
.		.		
.		.		
Robert King	Sales Representative	05/29/1972	39	11/29/1992
Janet Leverling	Sales Representative	08/30/1971 →	40	02/27/1991
Xavier Martin	Marketing Associate	11/30/1975	35	01/15/1994
Caroline Patterson	Receptionist	09/11/1979 →	32	05/15/1993
Margaret Peacock	Sales Representative	09/19/1973 →	38	03/30/1992
Laurent Pereira	Advertising Specialist	12/09/1970	40	02/01/1994

Figure 13-46 E13.10 Calculate age formula report run almost two months later

CONDITIONAL FORMATTING

After completing the exercises in this chapter you will be able to use the following tools and techniques to format fields and sections in a report.

- ☑ Use the Highlighting Expert
- ☑ Apply conditional formats to fields
- ☑ Create If Then Else statements
- ☑ Suppress fields and sections

CHAPTER 14

Overview

Chapter 7 covered basic formatting techniques. In Chapter 13 you learned that data could be formatted or manipulated using formulas and functions. The techniques covered in those two chapters will handle a large percent of your report formatting needs. What you may have noticed is that the formatting that you have learned to create so far, is applied to every detail or every group record. There will be times when the report does not need or require the same formatting to be applied to every detail record.

Conditional Formatting Tips

There are formatting techniques that you can use that will give you the option of applying the formatting only if a condition is met. This is known as **CONDITIONAL FORMATTING**. Examples of conditional formatting include the following:

① Highlighting records when the data in one field is greater than a constant value.
② Highlighting records with a specific color that have data missing in a field.
③ Check the value or length of a field and apply different formatting, depending on the value or length of the field.
④ Print a background color on every other detail record on the report.
⑤ Formatting one field with a border based on the value in another field.

The formatting techniques covered in Chapter 7 are known as **ABSOLUTE FORMATTING** because they are applied to every occurrence of the object. Conditional formatting starts off as absolute formatting, but goes a step further by setting up criteria to determine when the formatting should be applied.

> Conditional formatting is created using the Format Editor. Conditional formatting overrides absolute formatting that is created with the Format Editor. You can set the "on" and "off" properties conditionally.

There are two types of properties that conditional formatting can be applied to. The property type determines the type of conditional formula that has to be created. When you create a formula for an option, this is known as conditional formatting because the formula will turn the option on and off. Boolean formulas are used for on-off options in conditional formatting. When creating conditional If...Then...Else statements, keep the following in mind.

① **ON-OFF** properties like the Can Grow option or any option that has a check box on the Format Editor. On-off properties require **BOOLEAN** formulas. Check box formatting options are either on or off. This means that you do not have to type the entire If...Then...Else statement. Crystal Reports will enable the format option if the test returns a true value. If the formula returns a false value, the formatting is not enabled.
② **MULTIPLE CHOICE** properties like the border line style option, which is a drop-down list on the Line tab of the Format Editor is an example. Multiple choice properties require If Then Else or Select Case statements. Drop-down list and Text Box formatting options can have more than one choice. For this type of conditional formatting, you have to type the entire If...Then...Else statement to specify what you want to happen if the test is true and if the test is false.

Highlighting Expert

The Highlighting Expert is used to easily create and apply font, background and border conditional formatting to fields on a report without having to create a formula. It is a scaled down version of the Format Editor. The downside is that it does not have a lot of options like the Format Editor has. The Highlighting Expert is used to bring attention to certain values on the report by changing at least one of the following:

- ☑ Font style
- ☑ Font color
- ☑ Background color
- ☑ Border style

> Conditional formatting that is created by the Highlighting Expert cannot be modified in the Formula Editor.

An example of when to use the Highlighting Expert dialog box, shown in Figure 14-1, would be if you wanted to highlight the order amount if it is more than $1,000. To open the dialog box, right-click on the field that needs to meet a condition and select Highlighting Expert.

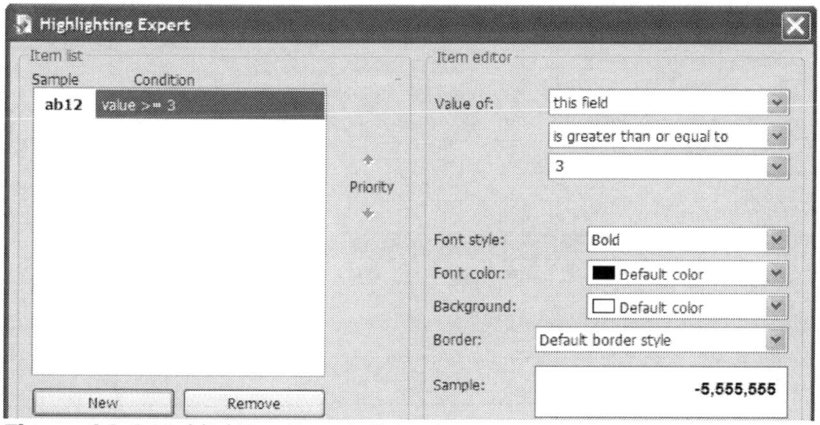

Figure 14-1 Highlighting Expert dialog box

As shown above in Figure 14-1, the Highlighting Expert has the following two sections:

① **Item List** Displays the conditional formatting formulas created by the Highlighting Expert for the field that is selected. The **CONDITION** column displays the formula that will create the formatting.

② **Item Editor** Is used to create and view the conditional formatting formulas. The **SAMPLE** section displays the highlighting that will be applied.

Item List Section Options

① The **PRIORITY** buttons are used to change the order that the highlighting will be applied. Priority is important when there are multiple conditions set for the same field. For example, if you want to set the background of a date field to green if it is greater than 1/1/09 and another condition to place a border around the same date field if the date is greater than 6/24/10. If the date is 1/24/11, which of the two formatting conditions should be applied to the date field? If the greater than 1/1/09 is the first condition, all of the records that are greater than 1/1/09 would have a green background applied, even if the date is greater than 6/24/10. In some instances, multiple conditions can conflict. This is why setting a priority is important. It is how Crystal Reports resolves the conflicts.

② The **REMOVE** button will delete the highlighting criteria that is displayed in the Item List.

Item Editor Section Options

① The **VALUE OF** drop-down list contains the fields, formulas and functions that are on the report or that are connected to the report, as shown in Figure 14-2.

These are the fields that you can use to create the conditions for.

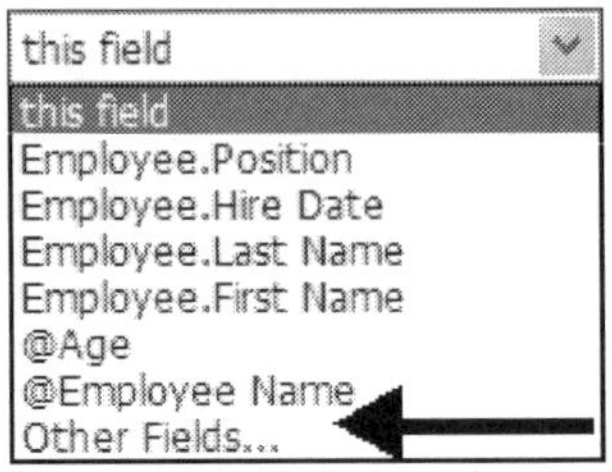

Figure 14-2 Field selection drop-down list

The **THIS FIELD** option in the Value of field lets you use the field that was selected before the Highlighting Expert was opened. Selecting a different field then the one that was selected prior to opening the Highlighting Expert means that you want to apply the formatting to the field selected prior to opening the Highlighting Expert, but you want the condition to be set based on the value in a different field.

The last option in the drop-down list, **OTHER FIELDS** opens the Choose Field dialog box, which is used to select another field from any data source connected to the report, to use to create highlighting criteria for.

② The **COMPARISON** drop-down list is the second field in the Item Editor section.

It contains the selection criteria options shown in Figure 14-3. You can use these operators to select which records will be highlighted.

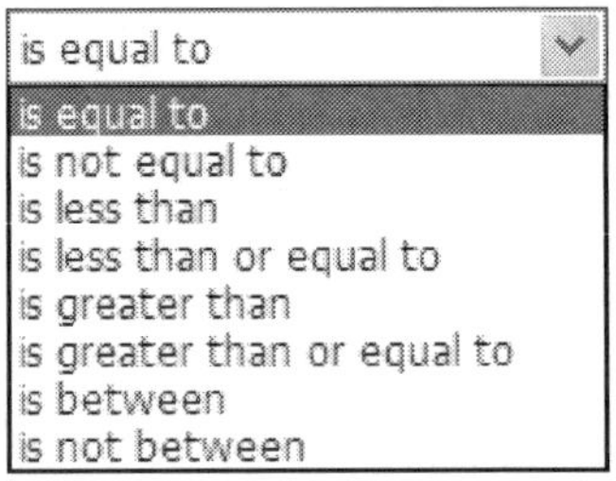

Figure 14-3 Comparison drop-down list operators

③ The **COMPARE TO** drop-down list is the third field from the top. It displays the values in the field that you select in the Value of drop-down list. This is like the Browse Data dialog box. You can also type in the value that you want.

> The Highlighting Expert does not work with **PARAMETER FIELDS**. The Highlighting Expert can only compare data in a table to set the conditional formatting.

The Highlighting Expert is similar to the Select Expert. One difference that I noticed is that the Highlighting Expert does not have as many operators as the Select Expert.

Create Reports That Highlight Data

The first two exercises in this chapter show you how to highlight data using the Highlighting Expert.

Exercise 14.1: Use The Background Highlighting Option

In this exercise you will modify a report to highlight the background of the Delay In Days To Ship field for orders that were not shipped in two days or less.

1. Save the E13.9 report as `E14.1 Highlight shipping time conditionally.`

2. Right-click on the Delay In Days To Ship formula field in the report and select **HIGHLIGHTING EXPERT**, then click the **NEW** button on the Highlighting Expert dialog box.

3. Open the Comparison drop-down list and select **IS GREATER THAN OR EQUAL TO**, then type a `3` in the field below.

4. Select **GRAY** as the background color.

   You should have the options selected that are shown in Figure 14-4.

   The report should look like the one shown in Figure 14-5.

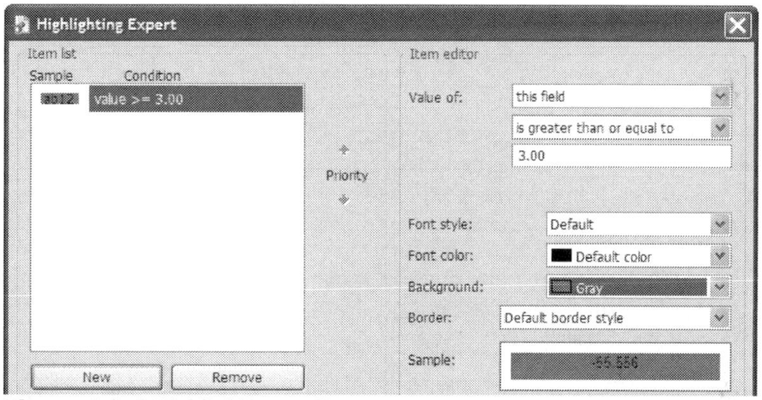

Figure 14-4 Highlighting options

Customer Name	Order Date	Ship Date	Order ID	Unit Price	Quantity	Delay In Days To Ship
City Cyclists	12/02/2010	12/10/2010	1	$41.90	1	8
Deals on Wheels	12/02/2010	12/02/2010	1,002	$33.90	3	0
Deals on Wheels	12/02/2010	12/02/2010	1,002	$1,652.86	3	0
Warsaw Sports, Inc.	12/02/2010	12/05/2010	1,003	$48.51	3	3
Warsaw Sports, Inc.	12/02/2010	12/05/2010	1,003	$13.78	3	3
Bikes and Trikes	12/02/2010	12/02/2010	1,004	$274.35	3	0

Figure 14-5 E14.1 report with conditional field background highlighting

Exercise 14.2: Use One Field To Highlight Another Field And Set A Priority

The Highlighting Expert allows you to create more than one highlighting condition per field. In this exercise you will create two conditions for the same field and set a priority for the conditions. You will create the following conditions:

① Make the quantity bold if it is greater than or equal to three.

② Italicize the quantity if the unit price is greater than $500.

Create The Quantity Is Greater Than Condition

1. Save the E13.9 report as `E14.2 Use multiple highlight conditions.`

2. Right-click on the Quantity field and select Highlighting Expert, then click the New button.

3. Open the Comparison drop-down list and select **IS GREATER THAN OR EQUAL TO**, then type `3` in the field below.

4. Select the bold Font style. Leave the Highlighting Expert dialog box open to complete the next part of the exercise.

Create The Unit Price Is Greater Than Condition

1. Click the New button, then open the Value of drop-down list and select the Unit Price field.

2. Open the Comparison drop-down list and select **IS GREATER THAN**, then type `500` in the next field.

3. Select the Bold Italic font style, then select red as the font color. Leave the Highlighting Expert dialog box open to complete the next part of the exercise.

Set The Priority

There could be a lot of records that meet both of the conditions that you just created. Unless it doesn't matter which order the conditions are applied to the field, you should set a priority. In this exercise, the most important criteria is for the Unit Price field.

1. Click on the Unit Price condition in the **ITEM LIST**, then click the (Priority Up) button. You should have the options selected that are shown in Figure 14-6. The report should look like the one shown in Figure 14-7. I added the words red and bold to the report to indicate what you should see on your report.

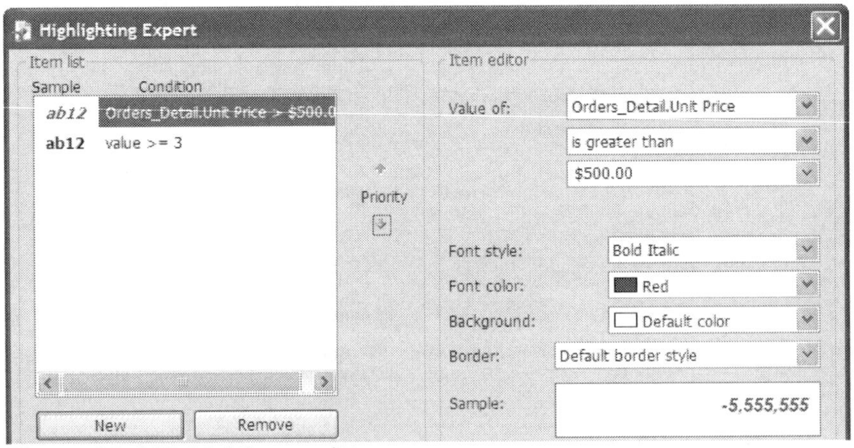

Figure 14-6 Highlighting conditions

Customer Name	Order Date	Ship Date	Order ID	Unit Price	Quantity	Delay In Days To Ship
City Cyclists	12/02/2010	12/10/2010	1	$41.90	1	8
Deals on Wheels	12/02/2010	12/02/2010	1,002	$33.90	Bold **3**	0
Deals on Wheels	12/02/2010	12/02/2010	1,002	$1,652.86	Red ***3***	0
Warsaw Sports, Inc.	12/02/2010	12/05/2010	1,003	$48.51	Bold **3**	3

Figure 14-7 E14.2 Use multiple conditions to highlight a field report

Highlighting Expert Limitations

Despite being relatively easy to use, there are some features in Crystal Reports in my opinion, that could be improved. You should be aware of the following two facts about the Highlighting Expert.

① Formulas created by the Highlighting Expert override formulas in the Formula Workshop.

② Formulas created by the Highlighting Expert are not accessible or visible in the Formula Workshop. This means that you cannot see the formulas created by the Highlighting Expert and can easily forget that they exist.

> Any formula that you can create with the Highlighting Expert can be created in the Formula Editor. It is easier to maintain formulas if they are all in the same place. Take from this what you will.

If...Then...Else Statements

This is one of the most used lines of programming code. This statement is used to set different options based on what you need to happen when the data is evaluated. The syntax below is for an If Then Else statement:

If **EXPRESSION/CONDITION** Then **TRUE STATEMENTS**
Else
FALSE STATEMENTS

Parts Of The If Then Else Statement Explained

① The **Expression/Condition** must evaluate to true or false.

② The **True Statements** will execute if the Expression/Condition is true.

③ The **Else** part of the statement is optional. If the Else clause is not included and the Expression/Condition is false, nothing will happen, which may be what you want. By "nothing happens", I mean that the If statement will default to the value for the data type. For example, if Field A is greater than 95, then textfield5 = "Great Job". If the variable "textfield5" was not declared to have a specific default value, the default value for a text field data type is " " (null), which is what would be displayed if Field A is not greater than 95.

④ The **False Statements** will execute if the Expression/Condition is false.

The plain English translation is: **IF** Choice A meets this condition, **THEN** do X, **ELSE** do Y.
Walk through the examples in Table 14-1 to gain a better understanding of If Then Else statements. Fill in the column on the right based on the numbers in the Choice A column.

If Choice A is greater than 25, then Field B = 100, else Field B = 0.

Choice A	What Does Field B =
26	
1	
25	

Table 14-1 If Then Else examples

It may help to understand If...Then...Else statements if you think of them as a true or false test question. In the example above, the test question can be worded as "Is Choice A greater than 25?" There are two possible answers:

① Yes, it is (True). If it is, Field B would be set to 100.

② No, it isn't (False). If it isn't, Field B would be set to 0.

How Did You Do?

Table 14-2 contains the answers for the second column in Table 14-1. The third column explains the answer.

Choice A	Field B =	Reason
26	100	The answer is 100 because 26 is greater than 25.
2	0	The answer is 0 because 1 is less than 25.
25	0	The answer is 0 because 25 is not greater than 25.

Table 14-2 If Then Else answers for Table 14-1

To complicate If statements even more, there can be multiple true and false statements in the same If Then Else statement. When this is the case, they have to be enclosed in parenthesis, otherwise Crystal Reports will stop processing the statement after the first semi-colon, which often will produce a syntax error. If Then Else statements with multiple true and false statements are known as **NESTED IF STATEMENTS**.

Conditional Formatting Warnings

You should be aware of the following when creating conditional formatting:

① If a field has formatting that is created with the Highlighting Expert and with conditional formatting, the Highlighting Expert formatting takes precedence. If the conditional formatting does not change the formatting created by the Highlighting Expert, the conditional formatting will be applied.

② Conditional formatting overrides absolute formatting, even if the result of the conditional formatting is false.

③ Keep in mind that Crystal Reports does not require the "Else" part of an If Then Else statement.

④ If absolute and conditional formatting are applied to a field and the If Then Else statement for the conditional formatting does not have an Else clause and the conditional formatting does not return a "True" value, neither the conditional formatting or the absolute formatting is applied.

⑤ In addition to If Then Else statements you can also use **SELECT CASE** statements, as long as the formatting property is in the Function Tree.

As you can see, it can be difficult to apply both absolute and conditional formatting to the same field. Even with the best intentions and code, you can get unexpected results. There are two things that you can do to help ensure that you get the output that you need when you have to combine absolute and conditional formatting. I have found the second option below to be more effective, but if the first option fits your needs, you should use it.

① Use the "Else" clause on If statements or the **DEFAULT** clause on Select Case statements.

② Use the "Else" clause with the **DEFAULTATTRIBUTE** function. To do this, select the default (absolute) option on the Format Editor dialog box and use the DefaultAttribute as the Else part of the If statement. For example, if you need to set the default value for a field to green on the Format Editor, use the following If Then Else statement.

```
If {Employee.Salary}/52 <= 750
  Then crRed
    Else
      DefaultAttribute
```

This formula will display salaries that are less than or equal to $750 in red and the other salaries in green if the salary field is set to green on the Format Editor.

> Formulas are created because the report needs an action to be taken based on the result. Sometimes you always need an action to be taken, regardless of the outcome of the formula. In those cases, you would put what you want to happen in place of the **DEFAULTATTRIBUTE FUNCTION** in the formula. Use the DefaultAttribute function when you do not want to change the property. It is not a requirement to use this function.

> Unless stated otherwise, when instructed to open a category, the category is in the Functions tree.

IsNull Function

The formula shown in Figure 14-8 is often used to combine two address fields. This formula is fine as long as there is data in both address fields. Unless the fields are required to be filled in on a data entry form, you cannot be 100% sure that they will contain data. The second address field is an example of a field that can have null values because all addresses do not require two fields.

```
{Employee_Addresses.Address1} + " " +{Employee_Addresses.Address2}
```

Figure 14-8 Address fields combined

While the Employee Addresses table only has a few records, you could manually check to see if both address fields have data before creating the formula. If the table had two million records, checking them manually probably is not a good idea and could be quite time consuming. There are two options discussed below that you can use to prevent a formula from failing, if a field is null (empty).

① The **ISNULL** function is used to test a field to see if it is null. If it is, you can make a decision on what to do. To make this decision you need to use the If Then Else statement with the IsNull function.

② Enable the **CONVERT DATABASE NULL VALUES TO DEFAULT** option on the Options dialog box. Enabling this option will convert null values to zero for numeric fields or blank for string fields. "Blank" is different than Null.

> While Crystal Reports supports the **CONVERT DATABASE NULL VALUES TO DEFAULT** option, not all databases support it. If you want to use this option, you need to make sure that the database that you are working with supports it. If you can't or don't want to confirm whether or not a database supports this feature, you can use the **ISNULL** function. I personally find it easier to use the IsNull function all the time, so that I can "see" what is going on.

Exercise 14.3: Use The If Then Else Statement And IsNull Function

In this exercise you will create a formula that will combine the two employee address fields and check the Address2 field to see if it is null. The majority of the time, the second address field will be the one that will not have data. On the rare occurrence that the first address field is null, you would want the formula to fail so that the field would be blank on the report. Hopefully, the person reading the report will notice this and fix the data. You can also write code that will print a message in the combined address field if either of the address fields is empty.

> The **ISNULL** function has to be placed inside the If Then Else statement because the check that it will perform on the Address2 field is the first part (the test question) that the If Then Else statement evaluates. In "plain" English the formula that you will create is:
>
> **If** the Address2 field does not have any data
> **then** set the Full Address field (the formula field name) to only use the Address1 field
> **else** set the Full Address field to use the Address1 field and the Address2 field.

1. Save the Chapter 13 Employee List report as `E14.3 If Then Else Statement`.

2. Create a formula field named `Full Address`.

3. Open the **CONTROL STRUCTURES** category in the Operators tree, then double-click on the **IF X THEN Y ELSE Z** statement illustrated in Figure 14-9.

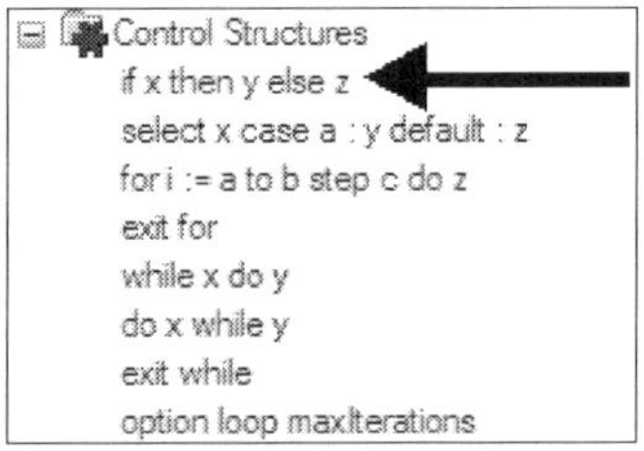

Figure 14-9 If Then Else statement illustrated

4. Open the **PRINT STATE** function category, then double-click on the **ISNULL** function illustrated in Figure 14-10.

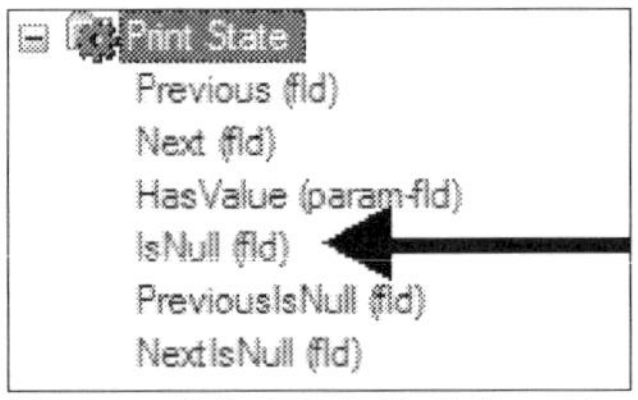

Figure 14-10 IsNull function illustrated

5. With the flashing insertion point between the parenthesis in the formula, double-click on the Address2 field in the Report Fields tree. This is the question part of the **IF** statement.

6. Click after the word **THEN** in the formula and double-click on the Address1 field, then press Enter. The word **ELSE** should be on the next line. This is the "true" part of the question, meaning that this is what you want to have print if the Address2 field is null.

7. Click after the word **ELSE** and add the Address1 field, then type `+ " " +`.

8. Add the Address2 field. If you want to add a comment to the formula, you can. The formula should look like the one shown in Figure 14-11.

```
// This formula checks to see if the Address2 field is null
if IsNull ({Employee_Addresses.Address2}) then {Employee_Addresses.Address1}
else {Employee_Addresses.Address1}+" "+{Employee_Addresses.Address2}
```

Figure 14-11 If Then Else and IsNull formula

9. Delete the Address1 field from the report. Add the Full Address formula field in its place and change the title to `Address`. The report should look like the one shown in Figure 14-12.

First Name	Last Name	Address	Region	Salary
Steven	Buchanan	14 Garrett Hill		$50,000.00
Robert	King	Edgeham Hollow		$37,000.00
Anne	Dodsworth	7 Houndstooth Rd.		$35,000.00
Michael	Suyama	Coventry House		$30,000.00
Bas-Rhin				
Justin	Brid	2 impasse du Soleil	Bas-Rhin	$75,000.00
Xavier	Martin	9 place de la Liberté	Bas-Rhin	$50,000.00
Laurent	Pereira	7 rue Nationale	Bas-Rhin	$45,000.00

Figure 14-12 E14.3 If Then Else Statement report

Exercise 14.4: Using Nested If Statements

Formulas that contain more than one If statement are known as **NESTED IF** statements. You can have as many If statements in a formula as you need. In this exercise you will create a Nested If statement to give customers a different discount on their next order based on the total amount of their last order.

1. Save the Chapter 14 Customer Discount report as `E14.4 Nested If Statement`.

2. Create a formula field named `Order Discount`, then add the If Then Else statement to the formula.

3. Add the Order Amount field, then type `>=10000`.

4. Click after the word **THEN** and type `"10% discount"`.

5. Copy the formula and paste it twice.

6. Change the middle Order Amount line of code to `>=5000`, then change the discount to `15%`. Change the last Order Amount line of code to `>=2500`, then change the discount to `20%`.

7. Click after the last **ELSE**, press Enter and type `"25% discount"`. Your formula should look like the one shown in Figure 14-13.

```
if {Orders.Order Amount} >=10000 then "10% discount" else
if {Orders.Order Amount} >=5000 then "15% discount" else
if {Orders.Order Amount} >=2500 then "20% discount" else
"25% discount"
```

Figure 14-13 Order Discount formula

Because the Order Amount field is evaluated for each record, it will only match one of the If statements when the statement is set up correctly. If the Order Amount is $3,000, the formula will stop processing after the third statement. If the Order Amount is $6,500, the formula will stop processing after the second statement.

The order that you place the criteria values in is very important. If the statements were in a different order, the formula would not return the correct result because it is possible that the order amount would meet the criteria of another statement. For example, if the >=2,500 portion of the statement was above the >=10,000 portion of the statement and the order amount is $6,500, the formula would stop processing after the first If statement because $6,500 is >=2,500. That is not the outcome that you want though. You really want the $6,500 order to receive a 15% discount.

The rule of thumb is to put the criteria in high to low order. The option after the last else statement is the "catch all" statement. Sometimes, this will be an error message. In the example above, the customer would receive a 25% discount off of their next order if their last order was less than $2,500. In this example, the company is going to offer larger discounts to customers that placed smaller orders in hopes of having them place a larger order the next time that they place an order.

8. Add the Order Discount formula field to the report after the Ship Via field. The report should look like the one shown in Figure 14-14.

Customer Discount Report

Customer Name	Order ID	Order Date	Order Amount	Ship Via	Order Discount
City Cyclists	1	12/02/2010	$41.90	UPS	25% discount
Deals on Wheels	1002	12/02/2010	$5,060.28	Pickup	15% discount
Deals on Wheels	1002	12/02/2010	$5,060.28	Pickup	15% discount
Warsaw Sports, Inc.	1003	12/02/2010	$186.87	UPS	25% discount
Warsaw Sports, Inc.	1003	12/02/2010	$186.87	UPS	25% discount
Bikes and Trikes	1004	12/02/2010	$823.05	Pickup	25% discount

Figure 14-14 E14.4 Nested If Statement report

Suppressing Fields And Sections

There are times when there is no need to print the same data over and over again on a report. Sometimes not repeating the same data makes the report easier to read. There are also times when you will need to suppress a section of the report. Like the Highlighting Expert, fields and sections in a report can be suppressed based on a condition. These conditions are created using Boolean formulas.

Exercise 14.5: Suppressing Fields

In this exercise you will learn how to suppress fields by creating a conditional formula for a field that has a salary greater than $50,000.

1. Save the Chapter 13 Employee List report as `E14.5 Suppress salary GT 50000`.

2. Right-click on the Salary field and select Format Object.

   On the Common tab, check the **SUPPRESS** option illustrated in Figure 14-15.

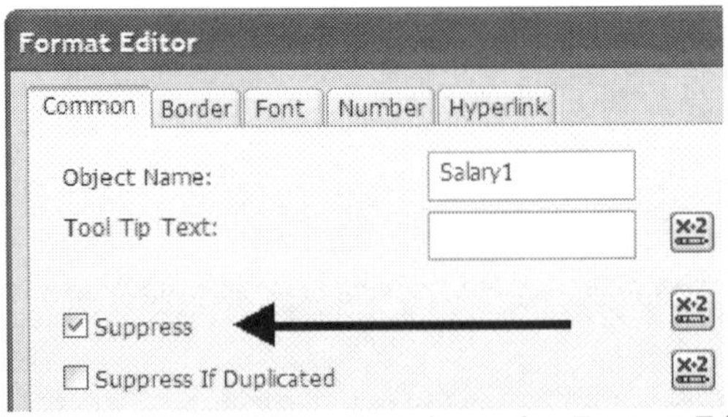

Figure 14-15 Common tab on the Format Editor

> As you see in Figure 14-15 above, most of the options have the button shown in Figure 14-16. This button will open the **FORMAT FORMULA EDITOR**. The default color for the Formula button is blue, which means that the option does not have a formula. If the button is red, it means that the option does have a formula. You will also notice that the pencil on the button is in a different position when the option has a formula, as shown in Figure 14-17. Formatting formulas that you create with the Section Expert or Format Editor will be applied whether or not the property option that it is attached to is checked. As long as the Formula button is red, the formula will be applied.

Figure 14-16 Blue formula button

Figure 14-17 Red formula button

3. Click the **FORMULA** button for the Suppress option. You will see the Formula Workshop. Create a formula to suppress the salary if it is greater than $50,000. Add a comment that explains what the formula does.

4. Notice that the button across from the **SUPPRESS** option now has red text. Click OK to close the Format Editor. Notice that the Salary field is grayed out in the design window. This lets you know that this field will not always print on the report because of the suppression criteria. The report should look like the one shown in Figure 14-18. If your report does not look like the one shown, make sure that your formula looks like the one shown in Figure 14-19. You can refer back to Figure 14-12 to see what the report looks like without the conditional formatting.

First Name	Last Name	Address1	Region	Salary	
Steven	Buchanan	14 Garrett Hill		$50,000.00	
Robert	King	Edgeham Hollow		$37,000.00	
Anne	Dodsworth	7 Houndstooth Rd.		$35,000.00	
Michael	Suyama	Coventry House		$30,000.00	
Bas-Rhin					
Justin	Brid	2 impasse du Soleil	Bas-Rhin		← Suppressed
Xavier	Martin	9 place de la Liberté	Bas-Rhin	$50,000.00	
Laurent	Pereira	7 rue Nationale	Bas-Rhin	$45,000.00	
BC					
Andrew	Fuller	908 W. Capital Way	BC		← Suppressed
Albert	Hellstern	13920 S.E. 40th Street	BC		← Suppressed
Laura	Callahan	4726 - 11th Ave. N.E.	BC	$45,000.00	

Figure 14-18 E14.5 Suppress salary GT $50000 report

```
// This formula will suppress the salary if it is > 50000
{Employee.Salary} >50000
```

Figure 14-19 Suppression formula

Comparison Conditional Formatting

You can use one field for the comparison criteria and a different field to apply the conditional formatting to. You will learn how to do this in the next three exercises.

Exercise 14.6: Compare Customer Averages

The report that you will modify currently prints the average order amount for each customer and the average order amount for all of the customers on the report. In this exercise you will modify the report to display a message if a customers average order amount is greater than the average order amount for all customers on the report. If the average order amount is less, no message will print. In order to print a message based on a condition, the formula has to use the **DISPLAY STRING** option on the Format Editor.

> If you open the Formula Workshop from the Format Editor dialog box, you cannot create a different type of formula. You also cannot modify or delete existing formulas.

1. Save the Chapter 14 Customer Order Averages report as `E14.6 Display string conditional formatting`.

2. Right-click on the Average Order Amount field in the Group Footer section and select Format Object.

3. On the Common tab, click the Formula button for the **DISPLAY STRING** option, then double-click on the If Then Else statement.

4. After the word **IF**, add the Group 1 Average Order Amount field, then type `>=` after the field.

5. Add the Report Area:Avg Of Orders.Order Amount field, then press Enter.

6. Click after the word **THEN** and add the ToText(x) function.

7. Add the Group 1 Avg of Orders.Order Amount field inside of the ToText(x) function. Click outside of the parenthesis and type `+ " ** Above report average",` then press Enter.

8. Copy the ToText portion of the formula and paste it after the **ELSE** clause, then type `+ " "` at the end of the formula. Your formula should look like the one shown in Figure 14-20.

```
if Average ({Orders.Order Amount}, {Customer.Customer Name})>=Average ({Orders.Order Amount})
then ToText (Average ({Orders.Order Amount}, {Customer.Customer Name}))+" ** Above report average"
else ToText (Average ({Orders.Order Amount}, {Customer.Customer Name}))+" "
```

Figure 14-20 Customer average comparison formula

9. Make the Average Order Amount field in the Group Footer section wider. Left align the field. The first page of the report should look like the one shown in Figure 14-21. The last page of the report should look like the one shown in Figure 14-22. Notice that there is no message next to the customer shown. This is because the customer average amount is less than $5,625.32, which is the average order amount for the report. Leave the report open to complete the next exercise.

	Order Date	Ship Date	Order Amount	Order #	Unit Price
Alley Cat Cycles					
	01/08/2011	01/08/2011	$5,879.70	1151	$2,939.85
	09/28/2011	09/30/2011	$2,559.63	2157	$313.36
	09/28/2011	09/30/2011	$2,559.63	2157	$539.85
	10/27/2011	11/06/2011	$2,699.55	2272	$899.85
	01/31/2012	02/03/2012	$9,290.30	2664	$2,792.86
	01/31/2012	02/03/2012	$9,290.30	2664	$455.86
	02/19/2012	02/22/2012	$8,819.55	2735	$2,939.85
	02/19/2012	02/22/2012	$8,819.55	2735	$2,939.85
Total # of orders - 8		Total $ amount of orders -	$ 49,918.21		
		Average order amount for customer -	$6,239.78 ** Above report average		
Aruba Sport					
	06/05/2011	06/08/2011	$5,879.70	3079	$2,939.85
Total # of orders - 1		Total $ amount of orders -	$ 5,879.70		
		Average order amount for customer -	$5,879.70 ** Above report average		

Figure 14-21 Page 1 of the E14.6 Display string conditional formatting report

Yue Xiu Bicycles					
	06/20/2011	06/20/2011	$2,939.85	3148	$2,939.85
Total # of orders - 1		Total $ amount of orders -	$ 2,939.85		
		Average order amount for customer -	$2,939.85		

Total # of customers on this report - 102
Grand Total # of orders - 1,142
Grand Total $ amount of all orders - $ 6,424,118.58
Average order amount for all customers - $ 5,625.32

Figure 14-22 Last page of the E14.6 Display string conditional formatting report

Exercise 14.7: Font Color Conditional Formatting

In the previous exercise you compared the customer average amount to the average amount for the report. Detail records that are below the report average were not formatted. It may be helpful to change the color of customers that have an average less than the report average.

1. Save the E14.6 report as `E14.7 Font color conditional formatting`.

2. Right-click on the Average Customer Order Amount field in the Group Footer section and select Format Object. On the Font tab, click the Formula button for the **COLOR** option.

The formula that you need to create to change the font color is the opposite of the formula that you created in the previous exercise. Rather than type the formula in again, you can copy the formula that you created in the previous exercise and change it as needed.

3. Open the **FORMATTING FORMULAS** folder in the Workshop Tree.

   Under the Avg Of Order Amount1 section you should see the **DISPLAY STRING** formula, as illustrated in Figure 14-23.

   Click on the Display String formula and select (highlight) the formula up to the first ToText function, then press the **CTRL+C** keys.

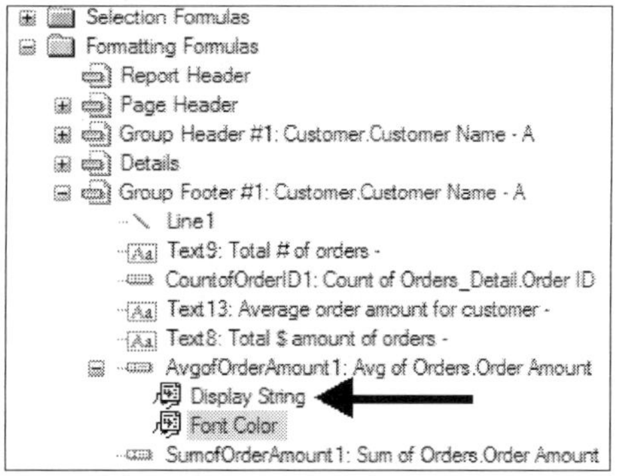

Figure 14-23 Formatting Formulas folder

4. Click on the Font Color formula in the Workshop Tree, then scroll to the end of the comments and paste the formula in by pressing the **CTRL+V** keys.

5. Change the >= to <=, then type `crRed` after the word **THEN**.

6. View the last page of the report. You should see some customer average dollar amounts in red. If you do not see the color red on the last few pages of the report, compare your font color formula to the one shown in Figure 14-24.

```
if Average ({Orders.Order Amount}, {Customer.Customer Name})<=Average ({Orders.Order Amount})
then crRed
```

Figure 14-24 Font color formula

Exercise 14.8: Suppress Currency Formatting

Every detail record on the E14.6 report prints the dollar sign for the Order Amount field. The report may look better if the dollar sign only printed for the first detail record for the customer. In this exercise you will create conditional formatting to suppress the dollar sign on any record other than the first one for each customer.

1. Save the E14.6 report as `E14.8 Suppress currency formatting`.

2. Right-click on the Order Amount field in the Details section and select Format Object. Click the Customize button on the Number tab. Click on the **CURRENCY SYMBOL** tab.

3. Click the Formula button for the **ENABLE CURRENCY SYMBOL** option and add the If Then Else statement to the Formula section.

4. Click after the word **IF**, then add the **ONFIRSTRECORD** function, which is under the Print State category.

5. Type the word `or`, then press the space bar.

6. Add the Customer Name field, then type `<> Previous`.

7. Press the space bar. Add the Customer Name field again, then press Enter.

8. Delete the word **ELSE** and add the **CRFLOATINGCURRENCYSYMBOL** function, which you can copy from a few lines above in the formulas comments.

9. Add two left parenthesis in front of the first Customer Name field and one parenthesis after the field. Add two left parenthesis in front of the second Customer Name field and three after the field. You may want to add a comment so that when you look at the formula later, you will know what it does. The report should look like the one shown in Figure 14-25. As you can see, the dollar sign for the Order Amount field only prints on the first detail record for each customer. If your report does not look like the one shown, compare your formula to the one shown in Figure 14-26.

	Order Date	Ship Date	Order Amount	Order #	Unit Price
Alley Cat Cycles					
	01/08/2011	01/08/2011	$5,879.70	1151	$2,939.85
	09/28/2011	09/30/2011	2,559.63	2157	$313.36
	09/28/2011	09/30/2011	2,559.63	2157	$539.85
	10/27/2011	11/06/2011	2,699.55	2272	$899.85
	01/31/2012	02/03/2012	9,290.30	2664	$2,792.86
	01/31/2012	02/03/2012	9,290.30	2664	$455.86
	02/19/2012	02/22/2012	8,819.55	2735	$2,939.85
	02/19/2012	02/22/2012	8,819.55	2735	$2,939.85
Total # of orders - 8		**Total $ amount of orders -**	**$ 49,918.21**		
		Average order amount for customer -	**$6,239.78 ** Above report average**		

Figure 14-25 E14.8 Suppress currency formatting report

```
// This formula will suppress the dollar sign on all detail records
// in each group, except for the first record
  if OnFirstRecord or ({{Customer.Customer Name}}<> Previous ({{Customer.Customer Name}})))
  then crFloatingCurrencySymbol
```

Figure 14-26 Dollar sign suppression formula

Formula Wrap Up

So how did you do creating If Then Else statements? Hopefully, you did okay. The reason that I am asking is because if you can understand and create If Then Else statements, you are well on your way to becoming a Crystal Reports power report writer. If you are curious about other statements that you can use, check out the following in the Help file: For Loop and my favorite, the Select Case statement.

Select Case Statement

Select Case is similar to If Then Else. I personally find the Select Case statement easier to read and understand, especially easier then Nested If statements. For example, the following Select Case statement provides the same logic as the Nested If statement shown earlier in Figure 14-13.
For whatever reason, I find this easier to read and understand.

```
Select {Orders.Order Amount}
    Case Is >= 10000: "10% discount"
    Case Is >= 5000: "15% discount"
    Case Is >= 2500: "20% discount"
    Default: "25% discount";
```

Boolean Formulas

You learned that Boolean fields have values of true/false or yes/no. **BOOLEAN EXPRESSIONS** return a value of true or false. In Chapter 7 you learned how to format a Boolean field. Earlier in this chapter I said that one way to understand If Then Else statements is to think of them as a true or false question. A Boolean formula is the test question portion of an If Then Else statement. Boolean formulas do not have to be created on Boolean fields. The value that a Boolean formula returns is either true or false. You can then format the result of the Boolean formula like you did in Exercise 7.4.

In Exercise 14.5 you created a formula that would suppress the salary if it was greater than $50,000. A Boolean formula could have been used to accomplish the same result. Figure 14-20 shown earlier, shows the formula. The difference would be the values printed in the salary field in the E14.5 report. Instead of printing the salary for some records and nothing for other records, as shown earlier in Figure 14-20, the values **TRUE** or **FALSE** would have printed as shown in Figure 14-27.

First Name	Last Name	Address1	Region	Salary > 50K
Steven	Buchanan	14 Garrett Hill		False
Robert	King	Edgeham Hollow		False
Anne	Dodsworth	7 Houndstooth Rd.		False
Michael	Suyama	Coventry House		False
Bas-Rhin				
Justin	Brid	2 impasse du Soleil	Bas-Rhin	True
Xavier	Martin	9 place de la Liberté	Bas-Rhin	False
Laurent	Pereira	7 rue Nationale	Bas-Rhin	False

Figure 14-27 Boolean Suppression Formula report

USING THE SECTION EXPERT

After completing the exercises in this chapter you will be able to use the Section Expert to format fields and sections in a report. You will also learn the following techniques:

- ☑ Create page breaks
- ☑ Reset page numbers
- ☑ Suppress a section of the report
- ☑ Use the row color formula
- ☑ Create odd and even page headers

CHAPTER 15

The Section Expert

The Section Expert has been modified. A new tab has been added and the page and orientation options were moved to the new tab. So far, all of the formatting techniques that you have used changed individual objects on the report. You can use the Section Expert to format an entire section of the report, similar to how the Format Editor is used to format fields. You can also create formulas for many of the options on the Section Expert, which is shown in Figure 15-1.

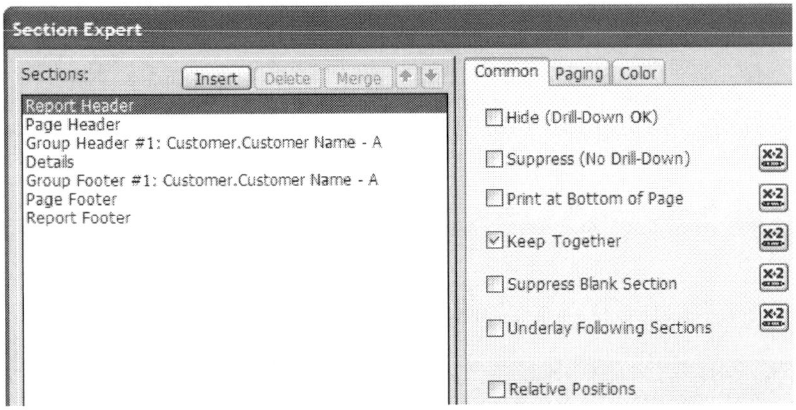

Figure 15-1 Section Expert

With section formatting, you can make the following types of changes to a report.

① Force each group to start at the top of a new page.
② Change the line spacing in the Details section to something other than single spacing.
③ Create page breaks.
④ Conditionally suppress a section of the report.

How To Open The Section Expert

① Right-click on the section bar and select Section Expert, as shown in Figure 15-2. If there is more than one of the same section, for example Page Header a and Page Header b, you will see the shortcut menu shown in Figure 15-3, which has additional options. Table 15-1 explains the options on the section shortcut menu that you may not be familiar with.

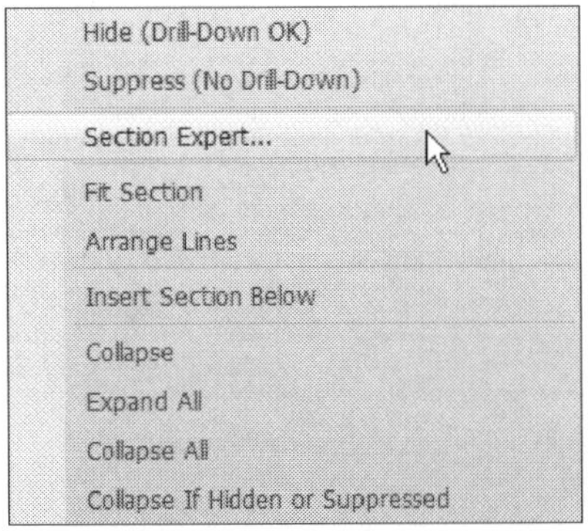

Figure 15-2 Section shortcut menu

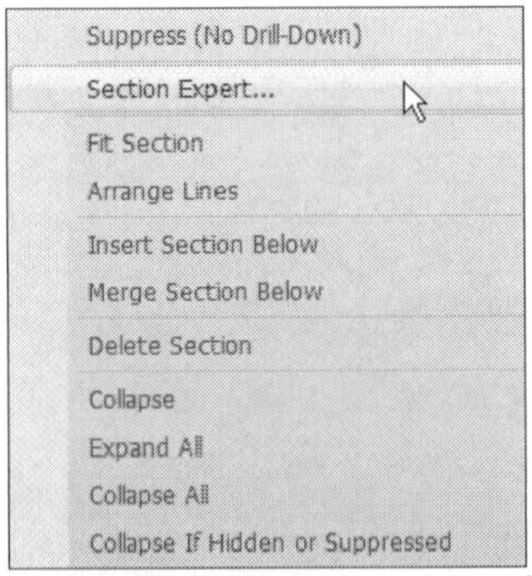

Figure 15-3 Multiple section shortcut menu

② Right-click on a blank space of the report, then Report ⇒ Section Expert.

③ Crystal Reports ⇒ Report ⇒ Section Expert.

Option	Description
Fit Section	Removes vertical unused space from a section. This option is not available on the header or Footer subsection (a).
Arrange Lines	Adds a guideline to the selected report section.
Merge Section Below	Moves the fields in the section below to the selected section, then deletes the section below. This option is not available on the last header or footer subsection.
Delete Section	Deletes the selected section of the report.

Table 15-1 Section shortcut menu options explained

The advantage to using the first option above to open the Section Expert is that the section will already be selected on the left side of the Section Expert dialog box when it is opened.
Table 15-2 explains the formatting section options on the Common tab. The options on this tab are available for most sections.
Table 15-3 explains the options on the Common tab that are only available for a specific section of the report.
Table 15-4 explains the options on the Paging tab. The options on this tab are used to select the orientation, format page numbers and page breaks.
Table 15-5 explains the options on the Color tab.
Table 15-6 explains the options on the Layout tab, which is only available when the **FORMAT MULTIPLE COLUMNS** option for the Details section is selected.

Common Tab

Option	Description
Hide (Drill-Down OK)	Hides the section when the report is printed. The section can be viewed on the Preview tab. If the section that this option is applied to is part of a higher level group and the group is drilled-down on, the objects in the section will be visible on the Drill-down tab. This option is not available for subsections.
Suppress (No Drill-Down)	The section that this option is applied to will not be printed, does not allow drill-down and cannot be viewed on the Preview tab, even if a higher level section is drilled-down on. This option is also available for subsections.
Print at Bottom of Page	Forces the section to be printed as close to the bottom of the page as possible, even if the detail records stop printing half way down the page.
Keep Together	Keeps the data for a record in the Details section together on the same page when printed. The exception is if the Details section has a memo or multi-line field. This option is sometimes confused with the Keep Group Together option on the Group Expert dialog box. These options produce different results.
Suppress Blank Section	Prevents the section from printing when all of the objects in the section are blank. This option saves space on the page.

Table 15-2 Common tab section formatting options explained

Option	Description
Underlay Following Sections	Causes the section to print in the same location that the section below it will print. This option will allow charts or images to print next to the section that follows.
Relative Positions	Locks an object next to another object like a cross-tab or OLAP grid. If the cross-tab grows, the object will be repositioned so that it remains aligned with the grid object.

Table 15-2 Common tab section formatting options explained (Continued)

If all of the detail sections have the Hide or Suppress option checked, the result is a Summary report.

Section	Option	Description
Details	Format With Multiple Columns	Displays data in columns similar to a newspaper layout. When checked, a tab named **LAYOUT** will open, as shown in Figure 15-5. The options on the Layout tab are used to select the size of the columns, as explained in Table 15-5.
Page Footer	Clamp Page Footer	This option removes white space from the bottom of the report. If the Page Footer section is empty, selecting this option removes the white space from the Page Footer, which will provide more space on the page for the other sections of the report. This option is also helpful when a report is viewed online.
Page Footer	Reserve Minimum Page Footer	Select this option to reduce the space set aside for the Page Footer section on reports that have more than one Page Footer section. This provides more space for other data on the printed page.

Table 15-3 Section specific common tab formatting options explained

Paging Tab

Option	Description
New Page Before	Forces a page break before the section. This option is not available for the Report Header and Page Header sections. (1)
Reset Page Number After	Resets the page number back to one after the section has printed. This option also resets the Total Page Count special field.
New Page After	Forces a page break after the section or after a specific number of records have printed. (1)
Orientation	Is used to select the orientation (portrait or landscape) for a section of the report, as shown at the bottom of Figure 16-2. Figure 16-3 shows the options on the Paging tab for the Details section. The orientation option is not available for the Page Header and Footer sections.

Table 15-4 Paging tab options explained

(1) This option is often used to force each group to start on a new page.

Formatting options that are not available for the section of the report that is selected are not enabled. For example, in Figure 15-4, the **NEW PAGE BEFORE** option is not enabled for the Report Header section.

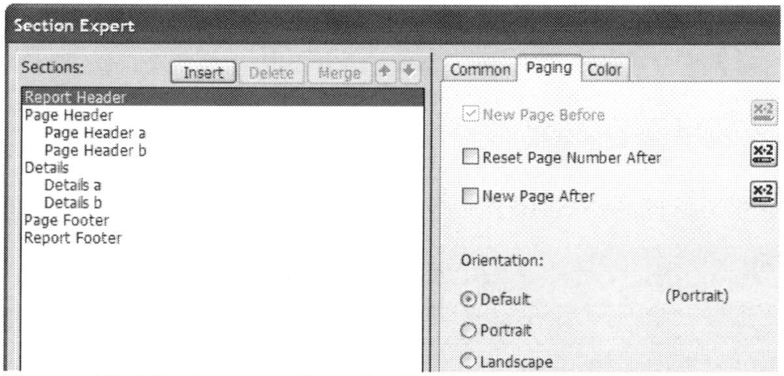

Figure 15-4 Paging tab options for the Report Header section

The New Page After option shown in Figure 15-5, for the Details section, has the following options:

The **END OF SECTION** option forces a page break after the section is printed.

The **VISIBLE RECORDS** option is used to select the number of records that will print (in the Details section) before the page break for the group occurs.

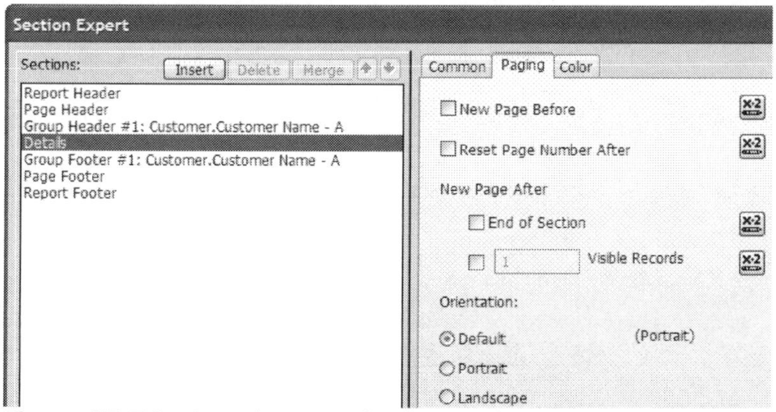

Figure 15-5 Paging tab options for the Details section

Color Tab

Figure 15-6 shows the options on the Color tab.

The options are explained in Table 15-4.

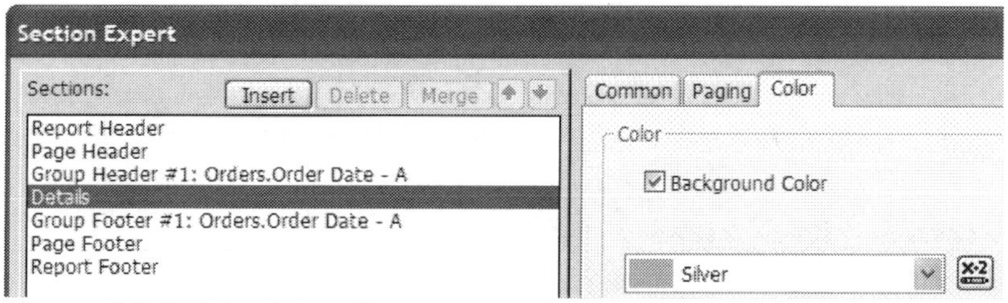

Figure 15-6 Color tab options

Option	Description
Background Color	Enables the Color option.
Color	This option is used to select a color for the background of the section. This is different then the formatting that objects in the section have.

Table 15-5 Color tab options explained

Layout Tab

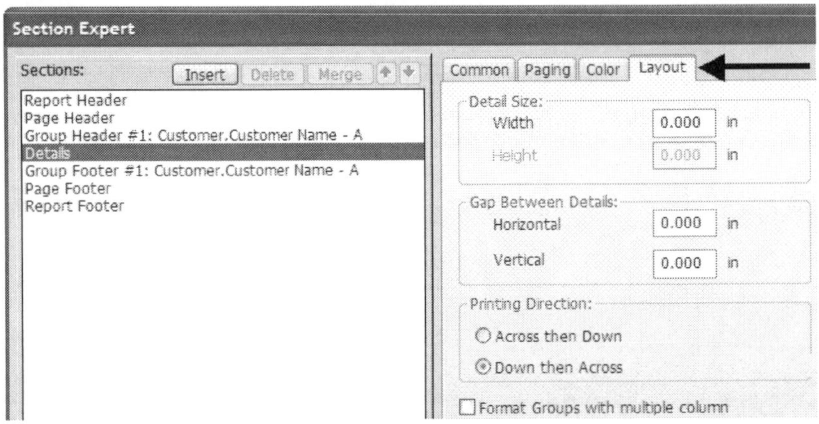

Figure 15-7 Layout tab options

Option	Is Used To . . .
Detail Size	Select the height and width size of each column in the Details section.
Gap Between Details	Select the amount of space between the rows and columns. The **HORIZONTAL** option is for the space between columns. The **VERTICAL** option is for the space between rows.
Printing Direction	Select how the rows and columns in the Details section are printed. The **ACROSS THEN DOWN** option prints row by row. The **DOWN THEN ACROSS** option prints column by column.
Format Groups with multiple column	Apply the same options (as those selected above in this table) to the Details section of groups that have multiple columns.

Table 15-6 Layout tab options explained

Exercise 15.1: Create Page Breaks

Page breaks are one of the most used section formatting techniques. While the concept appears straight forward, it can be tricky and can produce unexpected results. In this exercise you will add a page break to a report that prints orders by month. The objective is to force a page break when the month of the actual close date changes in the Group Header section of the report.

1. Save the E10.2 report as `E15.1 Report with a page break.`

2. Open the Section Expert, then click on the Group Header section. On the Paging tab check the **NEW PAGE BEFORE** option.

3. Preview the report. As you can see, the New Page Before option did not work as intended.

Using Pages Breaks With More Than One Group

In reports that have two or more groups, the page break options work differently, as illustrated below.

1. Save the E10.1 report as `E15.1A Page break with two groups.`

2. Apply the New Page Before option on the Paging tab to the Group Header #1 section. Preview the report.

You should see that the first page of the report is blank. More than likely, having the first page break occur before the detail records for the first group are printed on the report, is not what you had in mind. If you applied the New Page Before option to the Group Header #2 section, the first page will display the header information and the group name, but no detail records.

Exercise 15.2: Conditionally Format A Page Break

As you saw in the second part of the previous exercise, selecting the **NEW PAGE BEFORE** option did not accomplish what you thought it would. In this exercise you will fix this problem. The problem with only selecting a page break option is that it causes a page break before any data prints.

Hopefully you are asking yourself what is different about the first group of data. You may have looked through the functions to see if there is a function that you can use. If you have looked for a function, you won't find any that are specifically for sections on a report or for page breaks. You could create your own formula, but what would you write? You may have to think outside of the box on this one.

In case you are thinking that you could use the **NEW PAGE AFTER** option for the Group Header section, this option would cause the detail records to start on a different page, but the Group Header information would remain on the previous page, as shown in Figure 15-8.

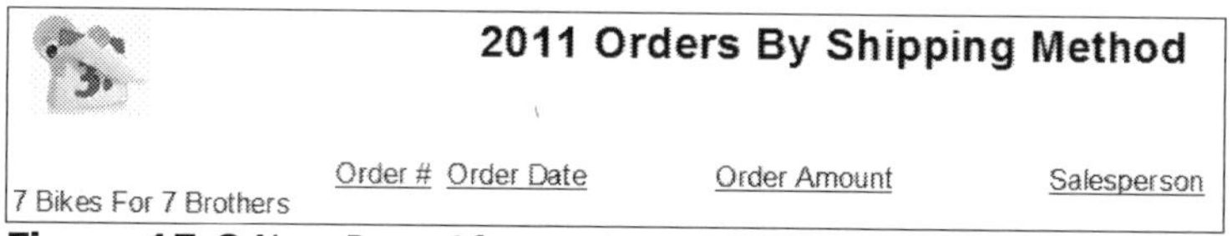

Figure 15-8 New Page After option enabled for the Group Header section

I know what you are thinking: Use the **NEW PAGE AFTER** option on the Group Footer section. That will give you the desired output of having each group start on a new page. The downside is that if the report has data in the Report Footer section, it will not print on the same page as the last Group Footer section of information. The information in the Report Footer section will be forced to a new page.

If the report that you are creating does not have data in the Report Footer section or you want the information in the Report Footer section to print on a page by itself, using the New Page After option on the Group Footer section will work.

In Chapter 14 Exercise 14.8, you used the **ONFIRSTRECORD** function. You could create a formula to check if the group contains the first record in the report. If it does, do not force a page break. This will work because only one group on the report will contain the first record on the report. It just so happens that the first record is in the first group, which is the group that currently has a page break before it. Creating a formula to not force a break on the first record will cause the formatting, in this case a page break, to be disabled on the first group. This is what you want to have happen.

1. Save the E15.1A report as `E15.2 Conditional page break.`

2. Open the Section Expert, then select the Group Header #1 section. On the Paging tab, click on the Formula button for the New Page Before option.

3. Type `Not` and press the space bar, then add the OnFirstRecord function, or you can type the function in.

4. Preview the report. The first group (7 Bikes), should be on page 1 of the report. If you click on any of the companies in the Group Tree, you will see that the data for the group starts on a new page. If you look at the last page of the report, you will see that the Report Footer information is not on a page by itself.

Using The New Page After Option To Format A Page Break
Earlier, the idea of using the New Page After option was discussed as a way to force a page break. Adding the **NOTONLASTRECORD** function to the New Page After option on the Group Footer section will force each group to start on a new page, just like the exercise that you just completed.

Exercise 15.3: Resetting Page Numbers

Depending on the type of report that you create, you may have the need to have the page number reset after a certain condition has been met. A report that you may need this for is one that will be distributed to more than one person. An example of this would be a report like a monthly order report by sales rep. Resetting the page number to one when orders for a different sales rep prints, would allow the report to be distributed to each rep and have the page numbers make sense to each rep. Can you imagine receiving a report that started on page 75? You may think that you were missing pages. Using the **RESET PAGE NUMBER** section formatting option would prevent that from happening. In this exercise you will learn how to use this option.

1. Save the Chapter 15 Monthly orders by sales rep report as `E15.3 Reset page number.`

2. Move the page number field from the Page Footer section to the Page Header section.

3. Create a page break formula that does not cause a page break on the first record of the report, for the Group Header section.

4. On the Section Expert on the Paging tab, check the **RESET PAGE NUMBER AFTER** option for the Group Footer section.

5. The first page of the report should start on page 1. In the Group Tree, click on Group 3. You will see that the page number is 1. If you go to the next page, it will be page 2, even though the physical page is page 9. This is what should happen. Leave the report open to complete the next exercise.

Exercise 15.4: Using The Change Group Dialog Box Options

If you look at the second page for any group in the report that you just modified, you will notice that the Group Header information (the Salespersons name) only prints on the first page of each group.

Figure 15-9 shows the second page of the first group. The report would look better if the group name printed on every page. Options on the **CHANGE GROUP** dialog box will let you force the Group Header information to print on every page.

Salesperson	Order Date	Order ID	Product ID	Unit Price	Quantity
	11/17/2011	2362	303221	$329.85	2
	11/17/2011	2362	201201	$832.35	3
	11/15/2011	2356	6401	$12.00	2

Figure 15-9 Second page of the first group on the E15.3 Reset page number report

1. Save the E15.3 report as `E15.4 Use Repeat Group Header option.`

2. Right-click on the Group Header section bar and select **GROUP EXPERT**, then click the Options button.

3. On the Options tab, check the **REPEAT GROUP HEADER ON EACH PAGE** option, shown in Figure 15-10.

   This option will cause the Group Header information to print on every page of the report.

   If you go to any page after the first page of a group, you will see the Group Header information, just like it is on the first page of each group. Leave the report open to complete the next exercise.

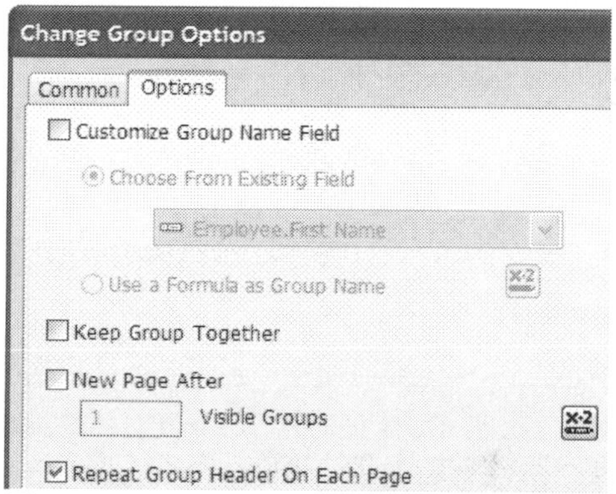

Figure 15-10 Change Group Options dialog box

How The Change Group Options Work

If checked, the **CUSTOMIZE GROUP NAME FIELD** option is used to create the name for the group as you want it to appear in the Group Header section, or a different section if you copy or move the Group Header field to it.

Do not check this option if you only want to display the data that is in the field that is being grouped on.

The purpose of the **KEEP GROUP TOGETHER** option shown above in Figure 15-10 is to force all records that are in the same group to print on the same page. If this option is checked and the first group on the report does not fit on the first page, the group will start printing on the second page and the first page of the report will be blank. If this happens, clear the **RESPECT KEEP GROUP TOGETHER ON FIRST PAGE** option on the Report Options dialog box.

The Keep Group Together option if checked, will cause all of the group sections (the Group Header, Group Footer and Details section for the group) to be printed on the same page. If all three sections will not fit on the current page, they will start printing on the next page. This is different then the **KEEP TOGETHER** option on the Section Expert, which only causes the section that the option is applied to, to print on the same page. [See Table 15-2] These options are best suited for reports that do not have a lot of detail records in each group. Groups that have a lot of records may require more than one page, which may result in the report having breaks in unexpected places.

The **USE A FORMULA AS GROUP NAME** option is used to create a formula that will control what appears in the Group Name field. This option is very helpful if you need to change what prints in the group name field based on data that appears in the report or data in a table that is connected to the report.

The **NEW PAGE AFTER** and **VISIBLE GROUPS** options are used to control the number of page breaks after a specific number of groups have printed. If you wanted a page break to occur after every three groups, enter a 3 in the Visible Groups field.

The **REPEAT GROUP HEADER ON EACH PAGE** option will cause the Group Header section to be printed at the top of each page. This will let you know which group the details records and totals are for.

Exercise 15.5: Using The InRepeatedGroupHeader Function

Prior to changing the group options in the previous exercise, it was easy to tell which was the first page for each group in the report. For this report, that is not exactly true because each group starts on page 1, but pretend that the page numbers are not reset. To help make reading the report easier, adding text on the pages in the group, other than the first page would resolve this issue. The **INREPEATEDGROUPHEADER** function is used to add conditional formatting to a Group Header or Footer when the group prints on more than one page.

1. Save the E15.4 report as `E15.5 Use the InRepeatedGroupHeader function`.

2. Add a text object to the right of the Last Name field in the Group Header section, then type `(Continued)` in the object. Change the font size of the text object to 8.

3. Right-click on the text object and select Format Object, then click the Formula button for the Suppress option. Type `Not InRepeatedGroupHeader` in the formula section.

4. View the second page of the report. You should see (Continued) next to the salespersons name, as shown in Figure 15-11.

Salesperson	Order Date	Order ID	Product ID	Unit Price	Quantity
Nancy Davolio	(Continued)				
	11/17/2011	2362	303221	$329.85	2
	11/17/2011	2362	201201	$832.35	3

Figure 15-11 Page 2 of the E15.5 Use the InRepeatedGroupHeader function report

Exercise 15.6: Suppress A Section Of The Report

There will be times when you need to permanently hide a section of a report. Often, this is done (on a second copy of an existing report) when you do not want some users to see certain information on a report. An example that comes to mind is the monthly orders by sales rep report that you modified in Exercise 15.3. Because the goal of this report was to distribute the sections of the report to the appropriate sales rep, there is no reason to display the Report Total information in the Report Footer section. You will learn how to suppress a section of the report in this exercise.

1. Save the E15.3 report as `E15.6 Report footer suppressed`.

2. Right-click on the Report Footer section bar and select the **HIDE (DRILL-DOWN OK)** option. The Report Footer section should look like the one shown in Figure 15-12. On the last page of the report, you should not see the totals in the Report Footer section.

The slanted lines indicate that the section is suppressed.

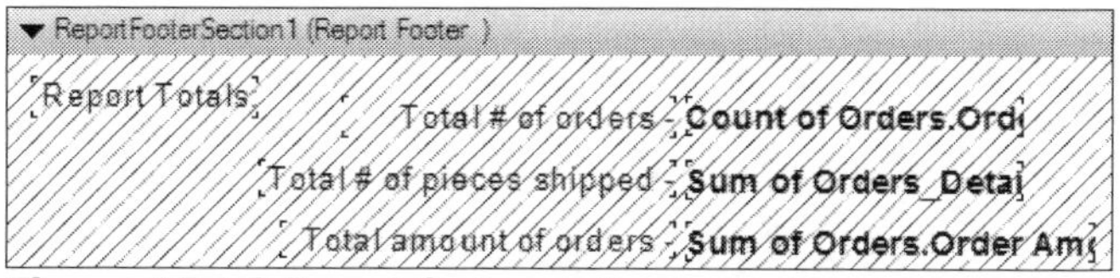

Figure 15-12 Report footer section suppressed

You can also turn the suppression options on or off by selecting the option on the Section Expert dialog box.

Use The Suppress (No Drill-Down) Option

Earlier in this book you learned how to add sections to a report. In the exercise that you just completed, you learned how to suppress a section of the report. If you have the need to create a report that uses more than one address field, often they are placed on separate rows in the Details section. The second address field is often blank, which means that a blank row will print for the records when the second address field is blank, as illustrated in Figure 15-13.

When combined, the Suppress (No Drill-Down) section option and adding a section with conditional formatting, will allow you to suppress a section of the report based on a condition.

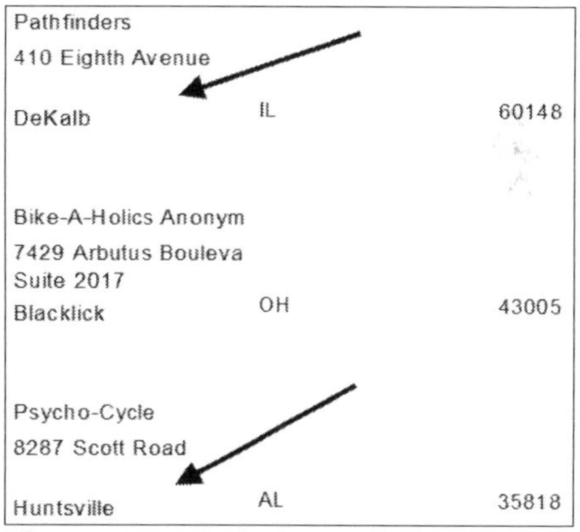

Figure 15-13 Blank row illustrated

You can combine these options and place the second address field in a section by itself, then conditionally hide the section if the second address field is blank.

Remember that if you suppress a field in a section that has other objects, the entire section will be suppressed if the condition is true. Often, this is not what you want. If you move the second address field to its own section of the report as shown in Figure 15-14, you can suppress the section if the address field is blank. This will cause the report to print like the one shown in Figure 15-15 instead of the one shown above in Figure 15-13.

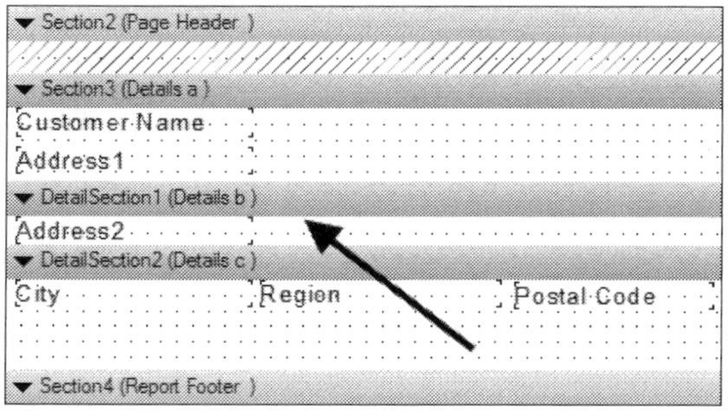

Figure 15-14 Address 2 field in a section by itself

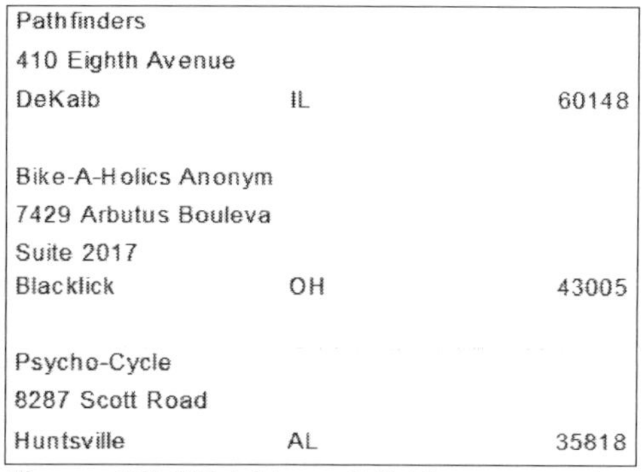

Figure 15-15 Address 2 field suppressed

Exercise 15.7: Suppress A Group

Depending on the amount of data that is displayed on a report, not all users may need to view all of the records. In this exercise you will modify a report to only print groups of data that meet specific criteria. You will modify a customer average report to only print groups that have a group total average amount that is less than $2,500. This report also has record selection criteria that needs to be removed.

Modify The Existing Record Selection Criteria And Total Fields

1. Save the Chapter 14 Customer Order Averages report as `E15.7 Suppress group if avg customer amount LT 2500K`.
   (LT is my abbreviation for less than.)

2. Delete the Order Amount record selection criteria.

3. Change the Order Date selection criteria to only include orders in 2011.

4. Change the Total # of orders field in the Group Footer section to use the Order ID field in the Orders table. Change the summary type to Distinct count.

5. In the Report Footer section change the Grand Total # of orders summary field to Distinct count.

6. Format these two total fields to display whole numbers.

Add The Suppression Criteria

1. Open the Section Expert and add the formula shown in Figure 15-16 to the Suppress (No Drill-Down) option for the Group Header, Details and Group Footer sections.

```
// This formula will suppress groups on the report where the
// average order amount of the customer is less than $2,500
//
// This formula is used on the Group Header, Details and
// Group Footer report sections
  Average ({Orders.Order Amount},{Customer.Customer Name}) <2500
```

Figure 15-16 Suppress group formula

Notice that the Formula Workshop displays the format option Suppress (No Drill-Down) in the title bar, as shown in Figure 15-17.

Figure 15-17 Format Workshop title bar

The first page of the report should look like the one shown in Figure 15-18. Some of the groups (customers) that you should not see on the report are AIC Childrens, Alley Cat Cycles and Belgium Bike Co. You will see these options in the Group Tree.

Figure 15-19 shows the grand totals for the report. The report has suppression criteria to not display a group if the average customer order amount is less than $2,500.

Remember that records that are suppressed are still included in the total fields on the report. Some people consider this a flaw so to speak, of how data is processed. To correct this problem, running total fields should be used instead of summary fields in the Group and Report Footer sections.

	Order Date	Ship Date	Order Amount	Order #	Unit Price
Aruba Sport					
	06/05/2011	06/08/2011	$5,879.70	3079	$2,939.85
Total # of orders - 1		**Total $ amount of orders -**	**$ 5,879.70**		
		Average order amount for customer -	**$ 5,879.70**		
Athens Bicycle Co.					
	06/08/2011	06/18/2011	$8,819.55	3097	$2,939.85
Total # of orders - 1		**Total $ amount of orders -**	**$ 8,819.55**		
		Average order amount for customer -	**$ 8,819.55**		
Backpedal Cycle Shop					
	02/08/2011	02/09/2011	$3,544.20	1279	$12.00
	02/08/2011	02/09/2011	$3,544.20	1279	$1,739.85

Figure 15-18 E15.7 Suppress group if avg customer amount LT 2500K report

Total # of customers on this report -	**256**
Grand Total # of orders -	**1,562**
Grand Total $ amount of all orders -	**$ 5,830,030.25**
Average order amount for all customers -	**$ 2,228.60**

Figure 15-19 Report totals

Exercise 15.8: Using The Color Tab Section Expert Options

One of the more popular uses of the Color tab on the Section Expert is to add a color background to every other detail record on the report. If you have ever seen what is known as "green bar" computer paper, you understand the color effect that you will create in this exercise.

1. Save the Chapter 14 Customer Discount report as `E15.8 Add color to rows.`

2. Open the Section Expert. Select the Details section, then click on the Color tab.

3. Click the Formula button, then type the formula shown at the bottom of Figure 15-20.

   The report should look like the one shown in Figure 15-21.

```
// This formula will print a silver background for all
// even number rows in the details section of the report.
//
// RecordNumber mod 2 will return 0 for even row numbers
// and 1 for odd row numbers
//
// DefaultAttribute is the default row color
//

  If RecordNumber mod 2=0
  then crSilver
  Else DefaultAttribute
```

Figure 15-20 Row color formula

Customer Discount Report

Customer Name	Order ID	Order Date	Order Amount	Ship Via
City Cyclists	1	12/02/2010	$41.90	UPS
Deals on Wheels	1002	12/02/2010	$5,060.28	Pickup
Deals on Wheels	1002	12/02/2010	$5,060.28	Pickup
Warsaw Sports, Inc.	1003	12/02/2010	$186.87	UPS
Warsaw Sports, Inc.	1003	12/02/2010	$186.87	UPS
Bikes and Trikes	1004	12/02/2010	$823.05	Pickup

Figure 15-21 E15.8 Add color to rows report

Some of the options on the Format Editor and Section Expert will be displayed with comments when they are opened in the Formula Workshop, as shown in Figure 15-22. The comments that you see are for the four line style options for the Border tab on the Format Editor. The options in the comments let you know what values you can use in your formula. The row color formula that you just created had a list of colors at the top of the formula, that you could select from to use as the background color.

```
// This conditional formatting formula must return one of the following Line Style Constants:
//
// crSingleLine
// crDoubleLine
// crDashedLine
// crDottedLine
// crNoLine
//
```

Figure 15-22 Default comments for the line style option

How The Row Color Formula Works

Now that you have created the row color formula, knowing how it works will be helpful because you can modify the formula to create other color patterns.

RECORDNUMBER is a special field that counts records in the Details section.

MOD divides one number by another number and returns the remainder, instead of the result of the division.

IF RECORDNUMBER MOD 2=0 means to divide the record number by 2. If the remainder is zero, meaning that if the record number is evenly divisible by two, apply the color to the background of the detail row. You can change this formula to create a background pattern different then every other row, as demonstrated in the examples below.

If the report that you are applying the background row color formatting to has background formatting for objects in the section of the report that will have a background color, you should use **NOCOLOR** for the Else clause instead of using the color white because NoColor produces a result that is similar to being transparent, which is what you want. Using the color white will cause the background color applied to individual fields to produce results that are not always visually appealing. If the report does not have any fields with background color formatting, using the **DEFAULT ATTRIBUTE** is acceptable.

Example #1 The formula, If RecordNumber mod 5 = 0 will shade every fifth row, as shown in Figure 15-23.

Customer Name	Order ID	Order Date	Order Amount	Ship Via
City Cyclists	1	12/02/2010	$41.90	UPS
Deals on Wheels	1002	12/02/2010	$5,060.28	Pickup
Deals on Wheels	1002	12/02/2010	$5,060.28	Pickup
Warsaw Sports, Inc.	1003	12/02/2010	$186.87	UPS
Warsaw Sports, Inc.	1003	12/02/2010	$186.87	UPS
Bikes and Trikes	1004	12/02/2010	$823.05	Pickup
SAB Mountain	1005	12/03/2010	$29.00	Loomis
Poser Cycles	1006	12/03/2010	$64.90	Purolator
Poser Cycles	1006	12/03/2010	$64.90	Purolator
Poser Cycles	1006	12/03/2010	$64.90	Purolator
Spokes	1007	12/03/2010	$49.50	Parcel Post
Clean Air Transportation	1008	12/03/2010	$2,214.94	Purolator
Clean Air Transportation	1008	12/03/2010	$2,214.94	Purolator
Clean Air Transportation	1008	12/03/2010	$2,214.94	Purolator
Extreme Cycling	1009	12/03/2010	$29.00	Loomis
Cyclopath	1010	12/03/2010	$14,872.30	UPS

Figure 15-23 Mod 5 = 0 output

Example #2 The formula, If RecordNumber mod 3 in [1,2] will shade the first two rows out of every three rows, as shown in Figure 15-24. Figure 15-25 shows the formula.

Customer Name	Order ID	Order Date	Order Amount	Ship Via
City Cyclists	1	12/02/2010	$41.90	UPS
Deals on Wheels	1002	12/02/2010	$5,060.28	Pickup
Deals on Wheels	1002	12/02/2010	$5,060.28	Pickup
Warsaw Sports, Inc.	1003	12/02/2010	$186.87	UPS
Warsaw Sports, Inc.	1003	12/02/2010	$186.87	UPS
Bikes and Trikes	1004	12/02/2010	$823.05	Pickup
SAB Mountain	1005	12/03/2010	$29.00	Loomis
Poser Cycles	1006	12/03/2010	$64.90	Purolator
Poser Cycles	1006	12/03/2010	$64.90	Purolator

Figure 15-24 Mod 3 in [1,2] output

```
If RecordNumber mod 3 in [1,2]
  then crSilver
  Else DefaultAttribute
```

Figure 15-25 Mod 3 in [1,2] formula

Example #3 The formula, If RecordNumber mod 10 in [3,5] will shade the third and fifth rows out of every ten rows, as shown in Figure 15-26.

Customer Name	Order ID	Order Date	Order Amount	Ship Via
City Cyclists	1	12/02/2010	$41.90	UPS
Deals on Wheels	1002	12/02/2010	$5,060.28	Pickup
Deals on Wheels	1002	12/02/2010	$5,060.28	Pickup
Warsaw Sports, Inc.	1003	12/02/2010	$186.87	UPS
Warsaw Sports, Inc.	1003	12/02/2010	$186.87	UPS
Bikes and Trikes	1004	12/02/2010	$823.05	Pickup
SAB Mountain	1005	12/03/2010	$29.00	Loomis
Poser Cycles	1006	12/03/2010	$64.90	Purolator
Poser Cycles	1006	12/03/2010	$64.90	Purolator
Poser Cycles	1006	12/03/2010	$64.90	Purolator

Figure 15-26 Mod 10 in [3,5] output

Exercise 15.9: Use The Suppress And Record Number Options

Earlier in this chapter you learned how to use the Suppress (No Drill-Down) option to suppress a section of the report. You also learned that the Record Number special field can be used to control when the formatting is applied. When used together, these two features can be used to conditionally add blank lines to a report. The steps below show you how to conditionally print a blank line in the Details section after every third detail record.

1. Save the E15.7 report as `E15.9 Suppress and Record Number options`, then add another Details section. Make sure that the data is in the first Details section.

2. On the Section Expert, select the Details b section. Check the Suppress (No Drill-Down) option, then click the Formatting button.

3. Type the formula `Remainder(recordumber, 3) <>0`. If you view the data for the Back Pedal Cycle Shop, you will see a blank line after every third record, as illustrated in Figure 15-27.

Backpedal Cycle Shop					
	02/08/2011	02/09/2011	$3,544.20	1279	$12.00
	02/08/2011	02/09/2011	$3,544.20	1279	$1,739.85
	02/08/2011	02/09/2011	$3,544.20	1279	$13.50
→					
	02/19/2011	02/19/2011	$6,233.05	1311	$23.50
	02/19/2011	02/19/2011	$6,233.05	1311	$2,939.85
	02/19/2011	02/19/2011	$6,233.05	1311	$329.85
→					
	03/16/2011	03/21/2011	$31.36	1428	$15.68

Figure 15-27 Blank lines added to report

Exercise 15.10: Create Odd And Even Page Headers

As more and more word processing mail merge documents are being converted to reports, the need for odd and even page headers and footers is becoming more popular in reports. Some of these documents have header and footer information similar to the pages in this book. Documents that fall into this category are also often printed on printers that can print two pages on one sheet of paper automatically on duplex printers.

Earlier in this chapter you learned that the MOD function can be used with a special field to determine an action based on the current record number. Creating odd and even page headers is similar. The difference is that two Page Header sections are needed and each one requires its own conditional MOD formula. These formulas are for the page number to determine if the current page number is odd or even. Each page of the report only needs either the odd page header information or the even page header information. Therefore, each Page Header section has to be suppressed when the other Page Header section prints.

Even page numbers have a remainder of zero. Odd page numbers have a remainder of one.

1. Create a new report and save it as `E15.10 Odd even page headers`. Add the Customer Name and Address fields from the Customer table, as shown below in Figure 15-28.

2. Add another Page Header section, then delete the print date field.

3. In the first Page Header section add a text object, then type `This is the right page header and should have an odd page number` in the object.

4. Add the Page Number field to the right corner of the Page Header a section, then place the text object to the left of the page number field.

5. Copy everything in the Page Header a section to the Page Header b section. Make sure that the field headings in both Page Header sections are lined up with the fields in the Details section.

6. In the second Page Header section change the text object to `This is the left page header and should have an even page number` in the object. Move the Page Number field to the left corner, then place the text object to the right of the page number field. The report layout should look like the one shown in Figure 15-28.

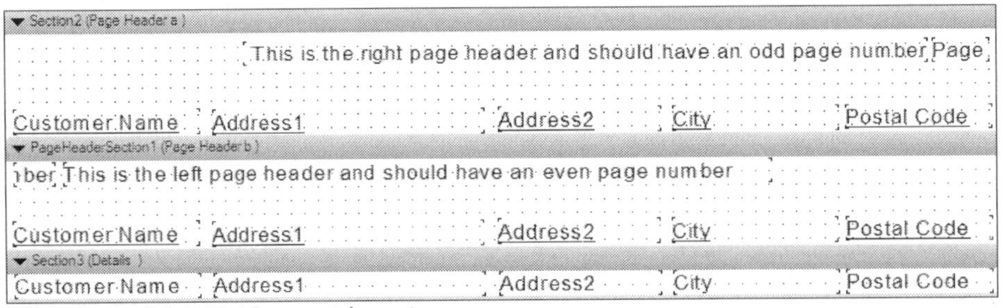

Figure 15-28 E15.10 report layout

7. Add the following formula `PageNumber mod 2 = 0` to the Page Header a Suppress (No Drill-Down) option on the Section Expert. You are adding this to the right Page Header section so that the left Page Header section will be suppressed when the right Page Header information is printed. Because the report does not have any groups, you do not have to check the Suppress (No Drill-Down) option.

8. Add the following formula `PageNumber mod 2 = 1` to the Page Header b Suppress (No Drill-Down) option on the Section Expert. The report should look like the one shown in Figures 15-29 and 15-30.

This is the right page header and should have an odd page number 1

Customer Name	Address1	Address2	City	Postal Code
City Cyclists	7464 South Kingsway	Suite 2006	Sterling Heights	48358
Pathfinders	410 Eighth Avenue		DeKalb	60148

Figure 15-29 E15.10 report - odd page number

2 This is the left page header and should have an even page number

Customer Name	Address1	Address2	City	Postal Code
Feel Great Bikes Inc.	3015 Delta Place	Suite 2601	Eden Prairie	55367
SAB Mountain	Hauptstr. 29		Bern	CH-3006

Figure 15-30 E15.10 report - even page number

Exercise 15.11: Print Symbols Conditionally

In this exercise you will create a report that will print a check mark next to the quantity if it is less than 350. This can be used as a visual reminder of which products need to be reordered. In Exercise 7.3 you learned how to use the Character Map. You will use an image from the Character Map to indicate that a product needs to be reordered.

1. Create a new report and save it as `E15.11 Print symbols conditionally`.

2. Add the Product and Purchases tables to the report. Add the first four fields shown below in Figure 15-31 to the report.

3. Add the title `Reorder Report` to the Page Header section.

4. Create a formula field named `Reorder Product`, then type the formula shown below.

```
// Chr(252) is the character code for a check mark
If {Purchases.Units in Stock} <= 350 Then Chr(252)
```

5. Add the Reorder Product formula field to the report to the right of the Units in Stock field. Select the formula field. Change the font to Wingdings, then change the font size to 12. The report should look like the one shown in Figure 15-31.

Product ID	Product Name	Price (SRP)	Units in Stock	Reorder Product
1,101	Active Outdoors Crochet Glove	$14.50	220	✓
1,102	Active Outdoors Crochet Glove	$14.50	450	
1,103	Active Outdoors Crochet Glove	$14.50	325	✓
1,104	Active Outdoors Crochet Glove	$14.50	265	✓

Figure 15-31 Symbols conditionally added to the report

CREATING CHARTS

Crystal Reports has an expert that you can use to create charts. There are 16 types of charts that you can create, including pie, bar and line. In this chapter you will learn how to create many of the chart types using the Chart Expert.

CHAPTER 16

Charts Overview

In addition to being able to format data in reports, charts are used to present data in a graphical format which often makes the data easier to understand by visually displaying the relationship between the data. Charts also allow data to be presented in formats that text-only reports cannot do as well. For example, charts can show trends over time, relationships or how one set of data compares to another set of data.

You have created basic charts using a report wizard. As you saw, the chart options were very limited. When you need to create or modify charts that require more detail than the wizards provide, you should use the Chart Expert. It is very easy to get carried away when creating charts. Try to create charts that present the data in a meaningful way. Remember that sometimes, less is more. There are four ways to open the Chart Expert as discussed below.

① Click the **CHART** button on the Crystal Reports - Insert toolbar.
② Right-click on the report, then Insert ⇒ Chart.
③ Crystal Reports ⇒ Insert ⇒ Chart.
④ Right-click on an existing chart and select Chart Expert.

Chart Considerations

There are two areas that need to be addressed before you start to create the chart. The two areas are the chart type and the source of the data for the chart. Changing the chart type is easy. If you are not sure which chart type is the most appropriate, with a few mouse clicks, you can try out a few chart types and variations to see which is the best one for the data.

Charts should enhance the ability to understand the data and make it easy to see the differences. The data source for the chart comes from one of the following: records in the Details section of the report, a cross-tab or summary data.

I have taught technical writing classes and one of the assignments had students create three charts to visually present data. Overall, the students did a good job on the charts. However, it was easy to tell which students had never created a chart before, for at least one of the reasons listed below.

① The wrong chart type was selected. Newsflash: Bar charts are not the best option for all types of data, especially data that shows trends or needs to show how data has changed over time.
② The values on the X and Y axes were backwards. Dollar amounts, quantity and percents usually go on the Y axis and time, dates and categories usually go on the X axis.
③ Not understanding the data that the chart will use.

The Chart Expert

This tool is used to create new charts and modify charts. It has wizard like characteristics because you click on the tabs to accomplish different tasks associated with creating and editing a chart. The biggest benefit of using the Chart Expert instead of the chart options on a wizard is that you have a lot of the chart options available from the beginning and the chart does not have to be based on data that will be printed on the report, like the wizards require. The options on each tab are covered in detail in this chapter because not understanding what all of the options are or not knowing where they are, will take you longer to create a chart. As you read about the Chart Expert, you may gain a better understanding of the options if you have the Chart Expert open.

The tabs on the Chart Expert (Type, Data, Axes, Options, Color Highlight and Text) contain options for a variety of features that you can use to make the chart as effective as possible. Keep in mind that not all of these tabs are available for all chart types. The tabs and options are discussed below.

You do not have to create a chart from an existing report. You can select the fields that you need on the Chart Expert.

Type Tab

The options on this tab are used to select what the chart will look like. The chart types that you can select from are shown on the left side of Figure 16-1.

Many of these chart types have variations that you can select, which gives you more chart options. Each chart type is explained in Table 16-1.

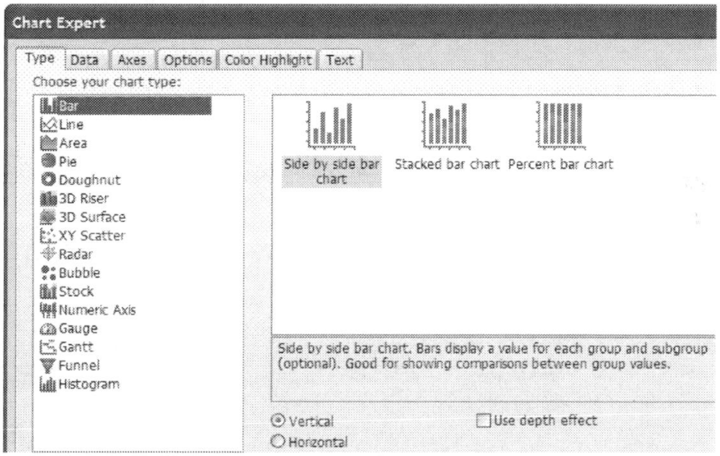

Figure 16-1 Chart Expert Type tab options

Earlier in this book you created a chart using the wizard. If you have created charts in spreadsheet software, you are probably familiar with many of the chart types in Crystal Reports. When selecting the chart type, the most important consideration should be to select the chart type that will best display the data that will be presented in the chart. This is the first thing that you have to do. When you click on the chart type on the left you will see variations of the chart on the right. Click on the chart style (variation) on the right that you want to use. Under the chart variations you will see a description of the chart type.

Chart Type Options

At the bottom of the Type tab shown above in Figure 16-1, you will see one or more of the options discussed below. Some chart types do not have any of these options.

① **VERTICAL** This is the default option. The elements will start at the bottom of the chart, as shown on the right side of Figure 16-1, shown above.
② **HORIZONTAL** If selected, this option will change the direction of the elements on the chart. The bars will start on the left, instead of the bottom, as shown in Figure 16-2.
③ **USE DEPTH EFFECT** If checked, this option will display the chart in 3D format, as shown in Figure 16-3.

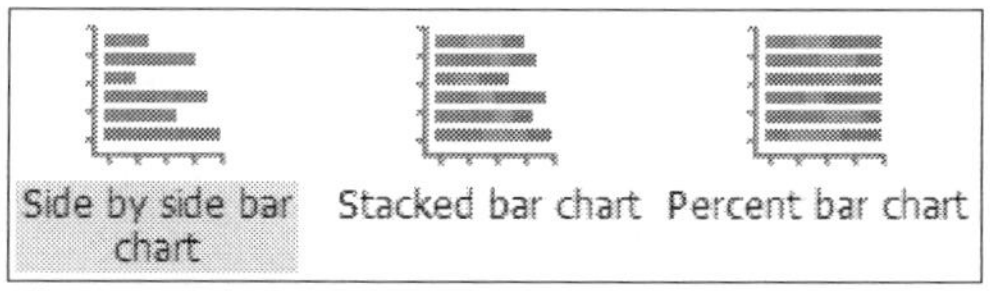

Figure 16-2 Horizontal chart options

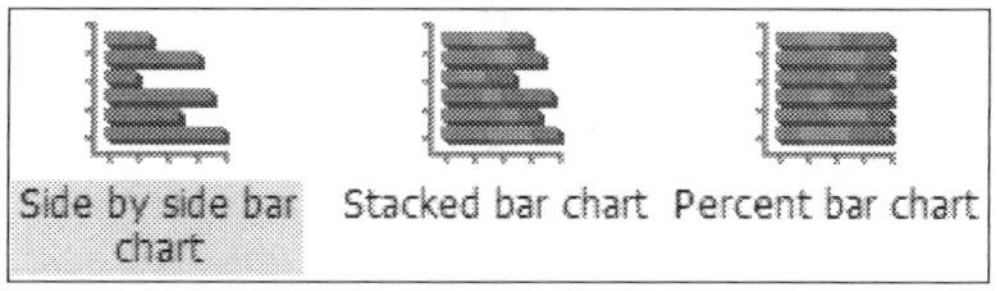

Figure 16-3 Use depth effect options

Chart Type	Description
Bar	Bar charts, as shown in Figure 16-4 show differences between items and relationships between grouped data. This is probably the most used chart type. Stacked bar charts show each item as a percent of the total.
Line	Line charts show trends and changes over a period of time. The markers on the bottom three line chart types indicate the exact values. In Figure 16-5, the data is represented with lines. A good use of **3D LINE CHARTS** is when the data lines cross each other often. This makes a line chart easier to read. (1)
Area	Area charts show how the data has changed over a period of time. Figure 16-6 shows how the four types of income (mail order, store, kiosk and Internet) make up the total income and how the income changes over the months. Area charts are almost identical to stacked line charts. The difference is that area charts are filled in below the trendline. Area charts are probably best suited for a few groups of data. (1)
Pie	Pie charts only show information for one point in time. Figure 16-7 shows the various types of income for July. Each slice of the pie represents the percent for the item. The Multiple pie chart type will create a chart for each group. (2)
Doughnut	This chart type is similar to pie charts. The difference is that there is a hole in the center, which contains the grand total of the data presented in the chart. (2)
3D Riser	This is the 3D version of bar charts that shows data values side by side, separately or stacked. It can display several groups of data in shapes like a pyramid or octagon.
3D Surface	This is the 3D version of area charts. This chart type uses three sets of data. The surface of the chart has a curve and shows trends in relation to time.
XY Scatter	XY Scatter charts show how two values are related (like month of year and order amount) and how a change in one value affects the other value, as shown in Figure 16-8. This chart type is used to show the correlation between the items. The X and Y axis must display numeric data. If data like dates or months can be converted to numeric data, it can be used in this chart type.
Radar	Radar charts compare sets of data relative to a center point and shows how far the data value is from the standard (the center point value). The values that are often used are group subtotals. The data from the X axis is usually plotted in a circle and the Y values are plotted from the center of the circle out.
Bubble	This chart type is similar to XY Scatter charts because it plots individual points. The difference is that bubble charts use different size plot points based on the data value. The larger the data value, the larger the size of the plot point.
Stock	This chart type is similar to bar charts. The difference is that the bars in stock charts do not have to touch the bottom of the chart. This type of chart is often used to display the minimum and maximum of stock prices, where each bar represents a different stock. Stock charts plot the first and last trade of the day or the high and low values for each element.
Numeric Axis	This chart type does not use a fixed X axis value or interval like many other chart types do. You can use a date/time field or numeric value for the X axis. This chart type is another way to create bar, line and area charts.

Table 16-1 Chart types explained

Chart Type	Description
Gauge	This chart type looks like a gauge in a car, as shown in Figure 16-9. The needle in the chart points to the value that is being represented. If there is more than one value or group being represented, a gauge chart is automatically created for each value or group. Multiple needles in one gauge means that there is more than one "On change of" value.
Gantt	This type chart is primarily used to display project management data like the start and end dates of tasks on a project plan. Gantt charts only work with date and date/time fields.
Funnel	This chart type is similar to stacked bar charts because each bar on the funnel shows each item as a percent of the total. The difference is that the bars are in the shape of a funnel. The height of the bar represents the percent of the data. The width of the bar does not represent anything.
Histogram	This chart type places the data into buckets, based on the range that the data falls into and displays a count of the records in each bucket, as shown in Figure 16-10. Usually, you will not see more than eight bars on a histogram chart, regardless of how many ranges (buckets) there really are.

Table 16-1 Chart types explained (Continued)

(1) This chart type requires at least two sets of data.
(2) This chart type only uses one value because it shows how the whole (100%) is divided.

It would be very helpful and a big time saver to me if at least one of the tabs on the Chart Expert would display the chart with the options that are selected, similar to what you see when you use the Chart Options dialog box to modify the chart.

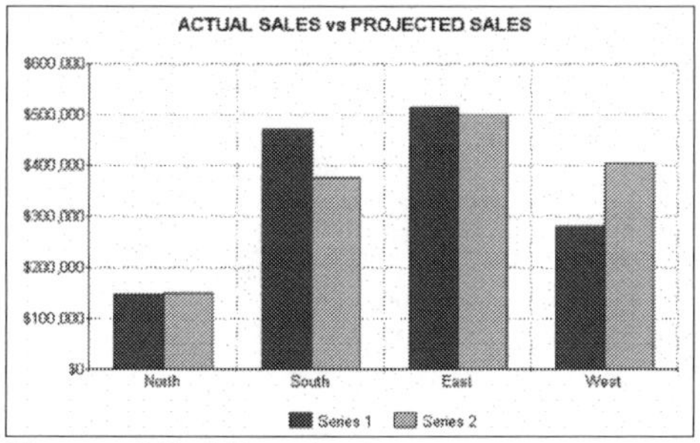

Figure 16-4 Bar chart

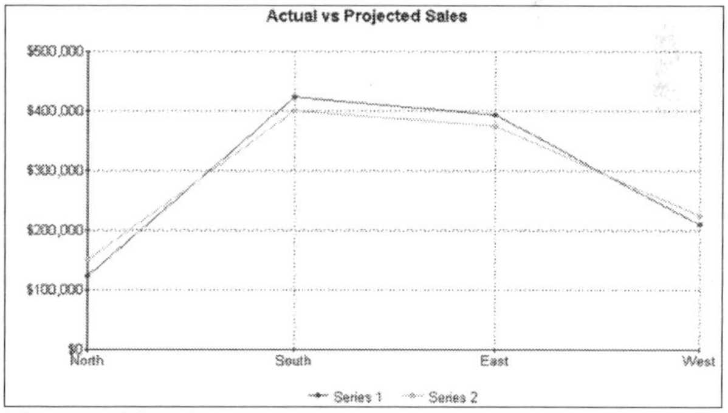

Figure 16-5 Line chart

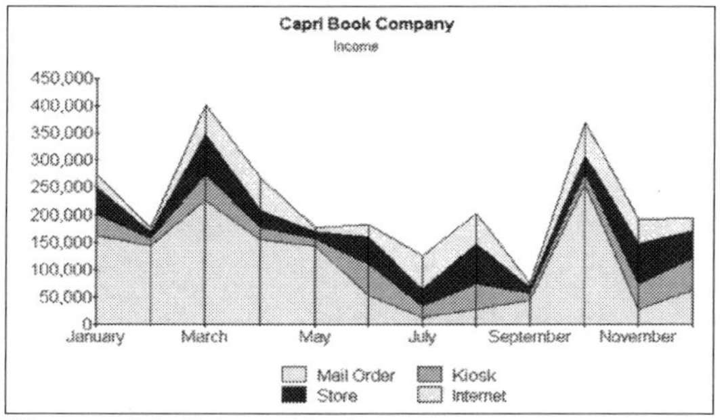

Figure 16-6 Area chart

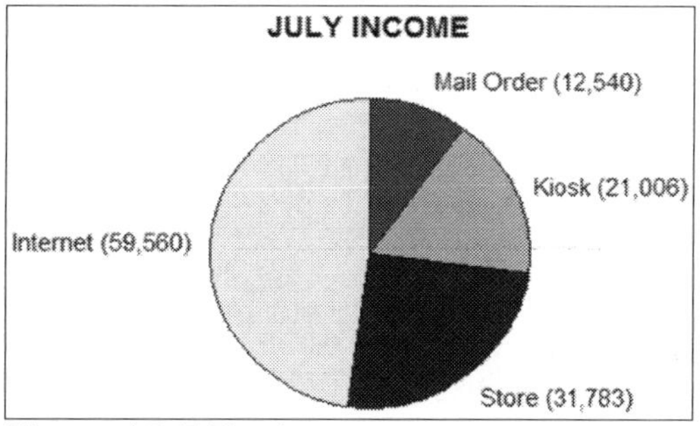

Figure 16-7 Pie chart

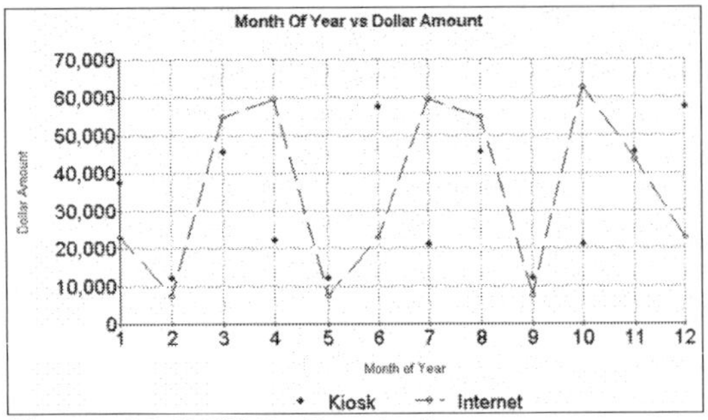

Figure 16-8 XY Scatter chart

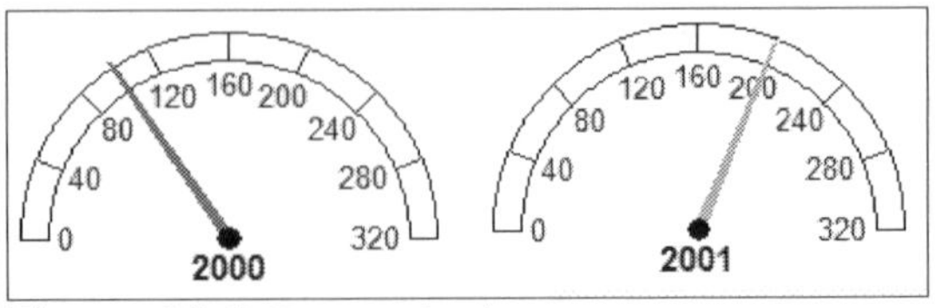

Figure 16-9 Gauge chart

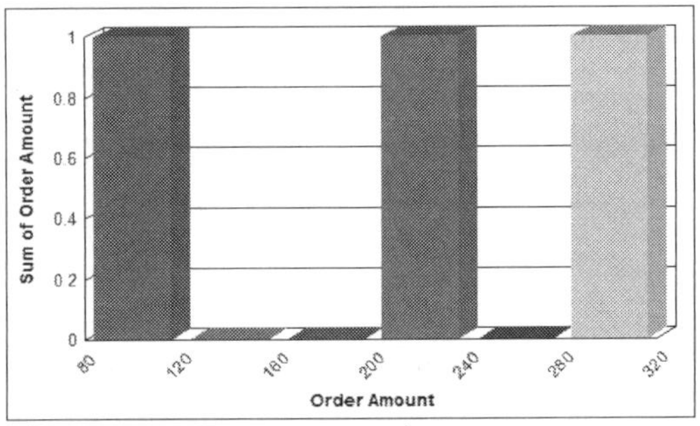

Figure 16-10 Histogram chart

Data Tab

The options on this tab are used to select the source of the data for the chart. This is the second area that needs to be addressed before you create the chart. There are three ways (called layout options) to chart data, as discussed below. Depending on the chart type that was selected, not all of the data layout options will be available.

Each layout type works independently of the others. You can only select one layout type. If you select one and make changes on that screen, then select a different layout type and make changes, the only information that will be saved, will be the layout that you changed last.

All of the layout options have the **ON CHANGE OF** drop-down list. The options in this list are how you decide when a new element (bar, slice of pie, point on a line, etc) will be added to the chart. This option lets Crystal Reports know that when the value in the field(s) listed below this option changes, you want a new element on the chart to be created.

OLAP functionality is not available in Crystal Reports for Visual Studio.

Advanced Layout Options

This layout option is always available. This is probably the most complex layout option because it allows you to create a chart that is not based on data that will print on the report. If you created a report using the Blank Report option and have not added any fields to the report, the options on this tab will let you select the fields for the chart. This is how you would create a report that only has a chart. If you need to a create a chart based on records in the Details section of the report, click on the Advanced layout option on the Data tab. You will see the options shown in Figure 16-10.

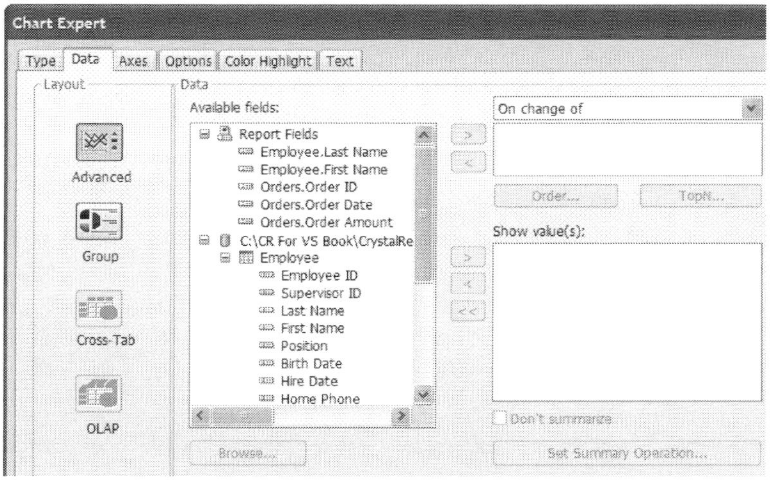

Figure 16-11 Chart Expert Data tab - Advanced options

> When you are working on exercises that use the options on the Advanced tab, you will see this instruction: **ADD THE FIELD TO THE FIRST LIST**. This means to add the field to the list that is under the On Change Of option shown above in Figure 16-10.

> If the report already has groups defined, you can still create an advanced chart because the options on this tab are not affected by the groups that are on the report.

The **AVAILABLE FIELDS** section of the Advanced layout screen contains the fields that are already on the report, including the summary, formula, running total fields, as well as, all of the fields in the tables associated with the report. This section is only available if the On Change of option is selected in the drop-down list on the right.

> The summary and running total fields can only be added to the **SHOW VALUE(S)** list.

The **ON CHANGE OF** option allows you to select up to two fields to group the data in the chart on. This group is not a real group like the ones that you learned how to create earlier in this book. When the value in the field changes a new element is created. Each element on the chart represents one group.

If you wanted to create a chart that displayed the orders by sales rep, you would add the sales rep (Employee Last Name) field to the list box below this drop-down list.

The Order Amount field would be added to the Show Value(s) list to get a total for each sales rep. Figure 16-12 shows this report.

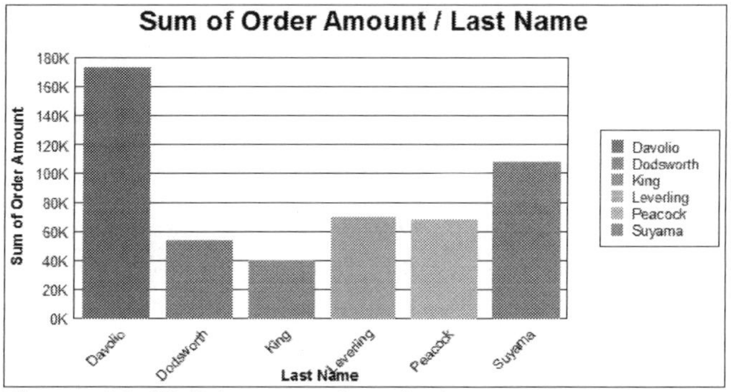

Figure 16-12 Sales rep orders chart

The On Change Of option works like the group option because it summarizes the values in the group. The difference is that the groups in the chart do not have an effect on the report. If you select multiple fields to group on, the data from each group will be displayed (side by side or stacked, based on the chart type that is selected). If the order date was added to the Evaluate option as shown in Figure 16-13, the report would look like the one shown in Figure 16-14.

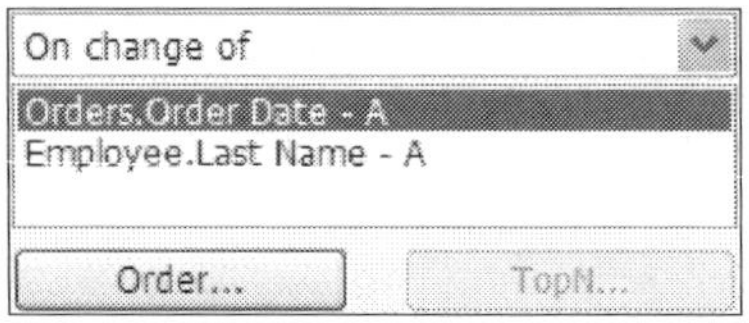

Figure 16-13 On change of options

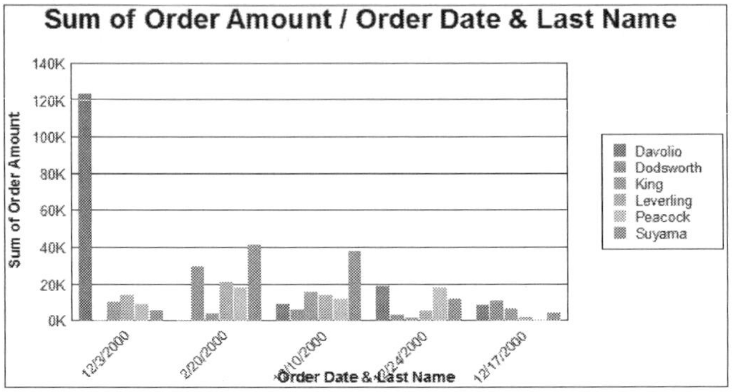

Figure 16-14 Sales rep orders chart with additional options

The first field below the drop-down list is the primary group and determines how the data is grouped. The second field creates the elements in the primary group. In the example shown above in Figure 16-13, the order date field is the primary group. The Employee Last Name field is the secondary group. Putting the fields in this order groups the records by date. Each element in the date group is a different sales rep.

The **FOR EACH RECORD** option in the drop-down list will cause a new element to be added to the chart for every record that would print on the report. If this option is selected, only one field can be added to the box below this drop-down list. If there is not a lot of data in the table that the field that you select is in, it is okay to select this option because the chart will be legible. If there are a lot of records, more than likely it would be hard to read the chart if this option is selected. If this option is selected, fields that are added to the **SHOW VALUE(S)** list will not be summarized, the actual value in the field is what will appear in the chart.

You can reduce the number of records that are used to create the chart by using the Select Expert. If you realize that you need to do this, you can create the selection criteria after the chart has been created. You will learn how to do this later in this chapter.

> Gantt charts have to use the **FOR EACH RECORD** option. A start and end date field must be added to the Show value(s) list.

The **FOR ALL RECORDS** option creates a chart with only one element, which is a grand total for all of the records that are on the report. You cannot add any fields to the box below the drop-down list if this option is selected.

The **SHOW VALUE(S)** list contains the field(s) that the chart will create a summary for. The default calculation type is **SUM**. The actual value or the value from the summary calculation will be used as an element on the chart. Which value is used, is determined by the option selected in the Evaluation option drop-down list.

Table 16-2 explains the type of summary values each of the evaluation options causes to be created. If you add more than one field to this list, the chart will plot a separate line or bar for example, for each field in this list. Each chart type allows at least one field in the Show Value(s) list. In the Orders by sales rep example, if you add the Order Amount field to the Show value(s) list, a total (summary) for each sales rep would be created.

Option	Show Value Summary Type
On change of	Summary for each group.
For each record	Actual value for each record.
For all records	One summary value for the entire report.

Table 16-2 Evaluation options explained

Summary Calculations

Table 16-3 explains the default type of summary calculations that the Show Value option applies to different field types. You can change the summary calculation type by following the steps below.

Field Type	Default Calculation Type
Number	Summary
Currency	Summary
All others	Count

Table 16-3 Default summary calculations

① Click on the field that you want to change the calculation for in the Show value(s) list.

② Click the **SET SUMMARY OPERATION** button shown earlier in Figure 16-11. You will see the Edit Summary dialog box shown in Figure 16-15.

③ The options in the **CALCULATE THIS SUMMARY** drop-down list are the ones that are available for the data type of the field that you are changing. Select the type of calculation that you want.

The **ORDER** button on the Advanced Layout screen opens the Chart Sort Order dialog box shown in Figure 16-16. The options on this dialog box work the same way that the options on the Insert Group dialog box work. These options are used to select the sort order for the element in the chart.

In the orders by sales rep example, if you selected the Order Amount field and then clicked the Order button you would be able to select how you wanted the total order amount for each rep to be displayed. If you were creating a bar chart and wanted to see the sales reps in order from high to low, based on sales, you would select **DESCENDING**.

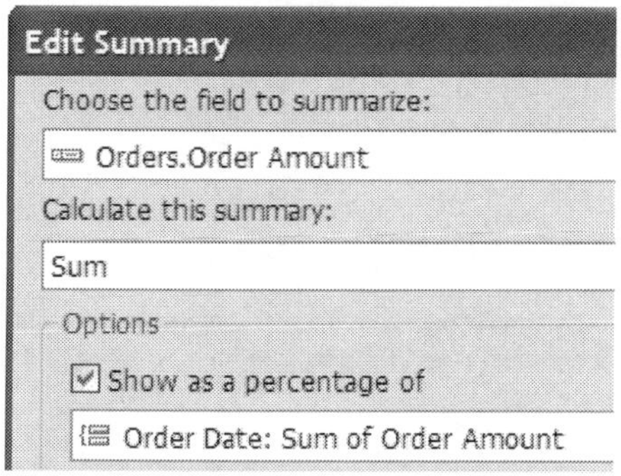

Figure 16-15 Edit Summary dialog box

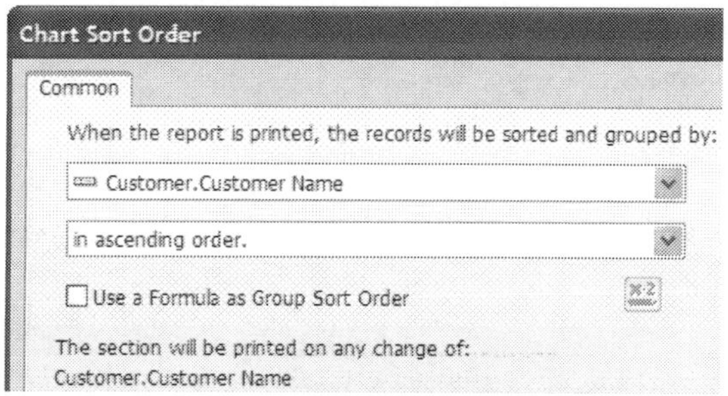

Figure 16-16 Chart Sort Order dialog box

Group Sort Expert

The **TOP N** button on the Advanced Layout screen opens the Group Sort Expert, shown in Figure 16-17.

The options on this dialog box are similar the ones on the **OTHERS** tab on the Change Group Options dialog box.

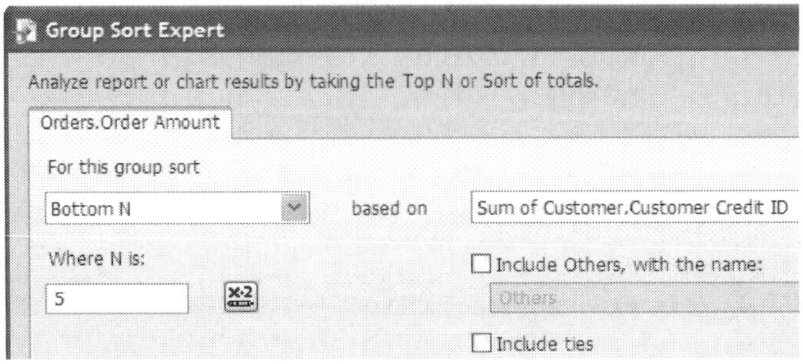

Figure 16-17 Group Sort Expert

If you only wanted to include the top or bottom N records, groups or percents, you would select the options here. The options selected in Figure 16-17 will display the five sales reps that had the lowest number of sales.

If you want to include groups that are not part of the group sort, you can, by checking the appropriate **INCLUDE** options on the right side of the dialog box. If checked, the **INCLUDE TIES** option will include groups that have the same summarized value if they meet the other selection criteria.

Group Layout Options

The group layout options create a chart that is based off of fields in a Group Header or Footer section of the report. This chart layout type is only available if both of the conditions discussed below have been met.

① The chart must be placed in the Report Header or Footer or in a Group Header or Footer section that is on a higher level then the data in the group that the chart will be based on.
② The report has to have one group that has a summary or total field.

The options shown in Figure 16-18 are used to select how the data in the group will be displayed in the chart. The options are explained below.

The options in the **ON CHANGE OF** drop-down list are the fields (that have a summary or total field) that are in a lower level then the section of the report that the chart has been placed in. This option is used to select the group that the chart will be based on.

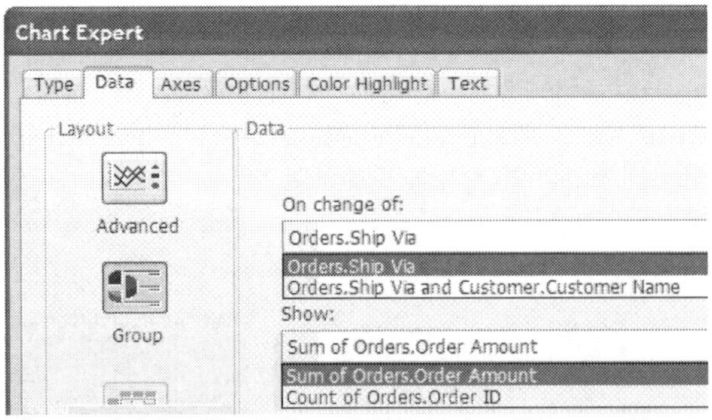

Figure 16-18 Chart Expert Data tab - Group options (On Change Of options for the two groups below the chart)

The Orders by shipping method report that you created in Exercise 9.3 has two groups: The Ship Via group and the Customer Name group. Both of these groups have summary fields. If you put the chart in the Report Header or Footer section, the On Change Of drop-down list will have the options shown above in Figure 16-18.

If the report has three groups with a summary or total field and you place the chart in the first group section, you would see the summary or total fields for the two groups below it.

Just by looking at the options in Figure 16-19, you do not know if the chart is in a report or group section.

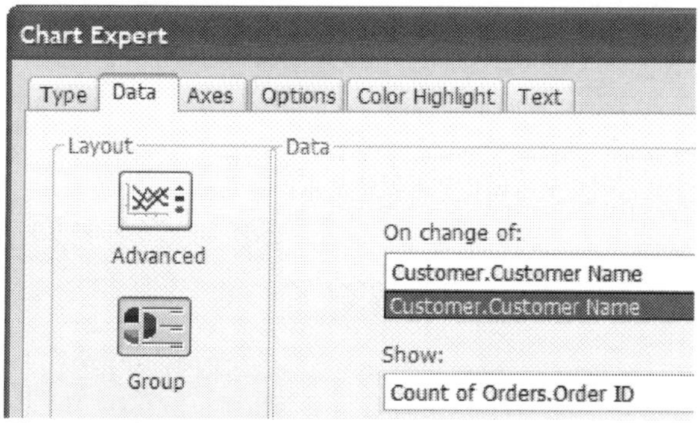

Figure 16-19 On Change Of options for one group below the chart

If you put the chart in the first Group Header or Footer section or the Report Header or Footer section and there is only one group below it that has a summary or total field, you would only see one option in the On Change Of drop-down list, as shown above in Figure 16-19. These are the summary fields in the Group Header or Footer section in the report.

The fields in the **SHOW** drop-down list are the summary and subtotal fields in the group that is selected in the On Change Of field. This is how you select the summary field in the group that will be used in the chart.

Cross-Tab Layout Options

This layout option is only available if the report has a cross-tab object in the same or corresponding section of the report that the chart is placed in. By corresponding section, I mean if the cross-tab that the chart will be based off of is in the Group 2 Footer section, the chart can be placed in the Group 2 Header or Footer section.

The options shown in Figure 16-20 are used to create a chart based on the data in the cross-tab.

Earlier you learned that cross-tab charts cannot be placed in the Details section. If you move the cross-tab object to a different section after a cross-tab chart has been created, the chart will automatically be moved to the new section also.

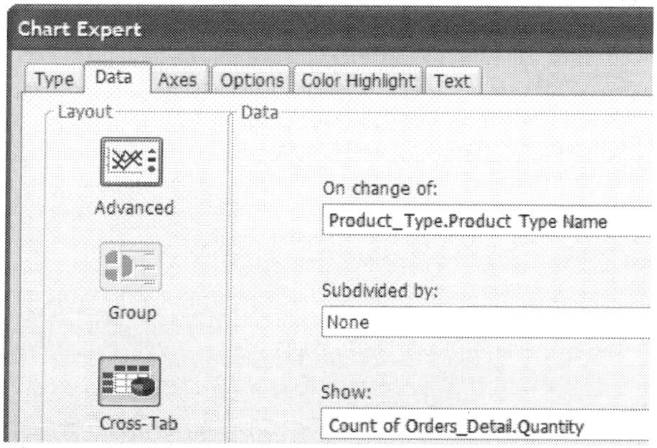

Figure 16-20 Chart Expert Data tab - Cross-Tab options

If the report has more than one cross-tab object, you have to select the cross-tab object that you want to create the chart off of before you open the Chart Expert.

The options in the **ON CHANGE OF** drop-down list are the first fields in the Rows and Columns sections of the Cross-Tab Expert or Wizard, regardless of how many fields each of these sections have. The field selected in this drop-down list is the first (or only) element that will be used as the primary X axis value.

Selecting a field in the **SUBDIVIDED BY** drop-down list is optional, which is why the default option is **NONE.**

The only field that is available in the Subdivided By drop-down list is the one that was not selected in the On Change Of drop-down list above it. Selecting a field will create a second X value, which will add a second series of data to the chart. This will let you create a chart that does a side by side comparison.

Figure 16-21 shows a line chart with the first field in the Row section and the first field in the Column section from the cross-tab selected.

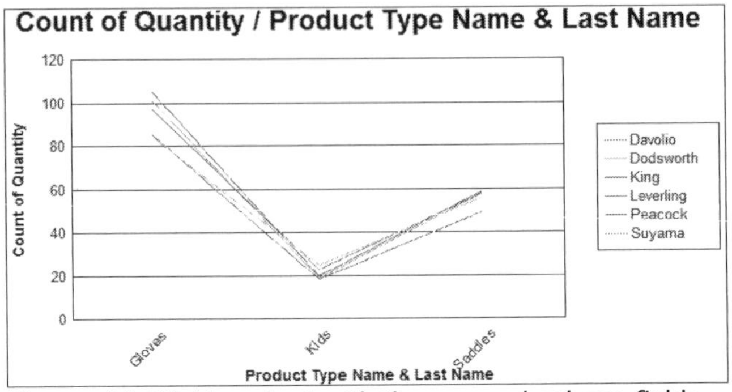

Figure 16-21 Line chart with the row and column fields selected

The options in the **SHOW** drop-down list (shown earlier in Figure 16-20) are the fields that are in the Summary Fields section of the Cross-Tab screen. They are the fields that you select from, to summarize the report on, like the Show Value(s) list on the Advanced Layout screen.

Axes Tab

Depending on the chart type that is selected, you may not see the Axes tab shown in Figure 16-22. You will see this tab if the chart type selected uses the X and Y axis.

For example, bar, line, area and radar charts use the X and Y axis. Pie, Doughnut and Gantt chart types do not.

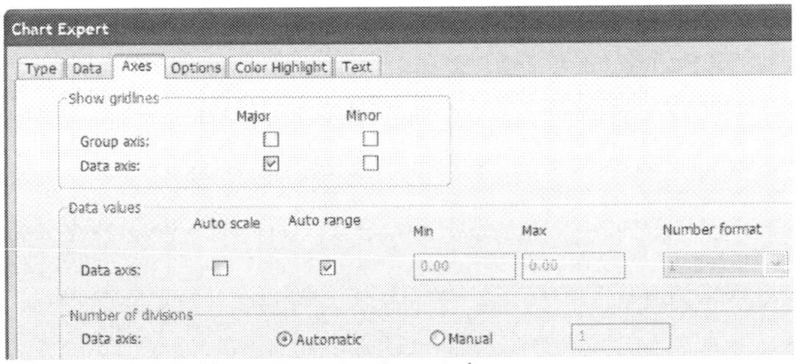

Figure 16-22 Chart Expert - Axes tab

The options on this tab are used to select how the chart will display the data values that you see across the bottom of the chart (the X axis) and on the left side of the chart (the Y axis). If you are creating a 3D chart you can also select the data values for the **Z AXIS**.

If the chart that you are creating needed to display order totals by month, the months would be placed on the X axis because the report is grouped by month and the totals would be placed on the Y axis because they represent the quantity, as shown in Figure 16-23.

If you were creating the same chart, but selected a 3D layout, the chart would look like the one shown in Figure 16-24, which also includes the data axis (the Z axis).

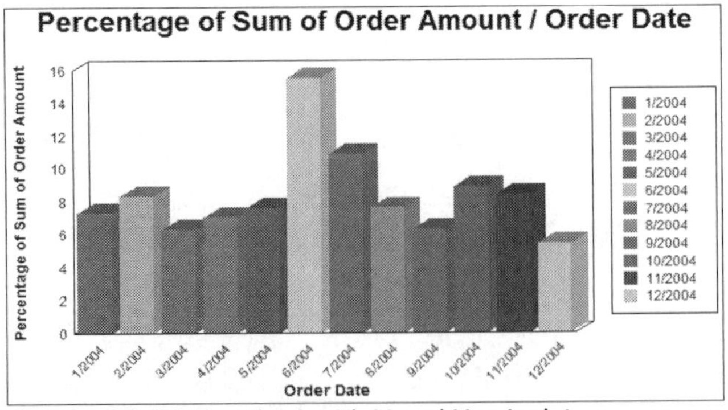

Figure 16-23 Bar chart with X and Y axis data

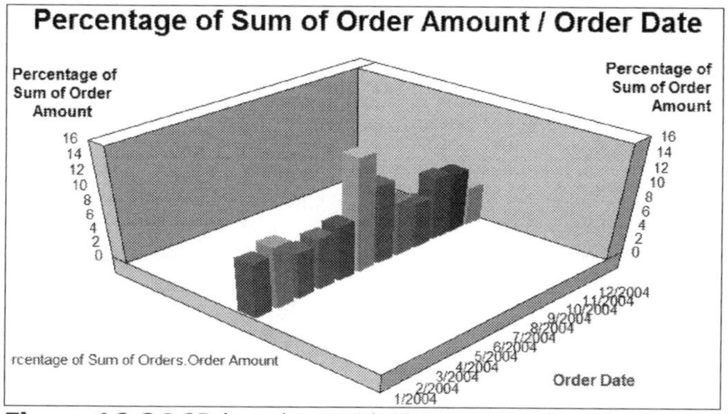

Figure 16-24 3D bar chart with X, Y and Z axis data

Show Gridlines Options

Gridlines make the chart easier to read if the values are close in range. There are horizontal and vertical gridlines. You will see two or three axis options in this section depending on whether the chart is two or three dimensional.

The **GROUP AXIS** option corresponds to the **ON CHANGE OF** field on the Advanced Layout screen on the Data tab.

The **SERIES AXIS** will only appear for three dimensional chart types.

The **DATA AXIS** option corresponds to the **SHOW** field on the Advanced Layout screen on the Data tab.

If checked, the major and minor options will add gridlines to the chart.

The **MAJOR** option will place the gridlines (with labels) on the axis, as shown in Figure 16-25.

The **MINOR** option can only be used with numeric labels and will place the gridlines between the labels on the axis.

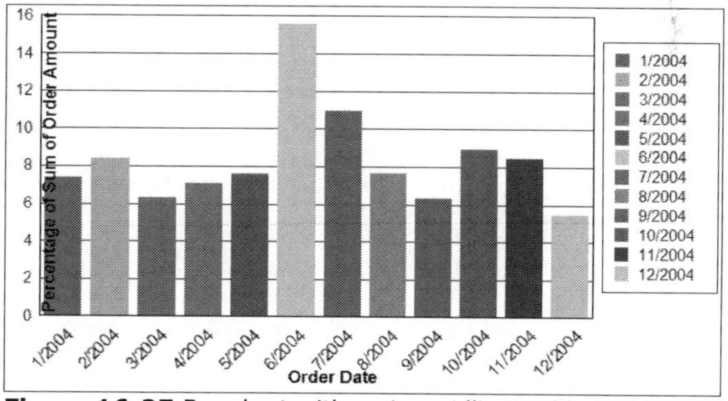

Figure 16-25 Bar chart with major gridlines added

Some chart types will have a gridline on the Group axis whether you select the option or not.

Data Values Options

The options in this section of the Axes tab are used to customize the **VALUES** on the Data axis.

The **AUTO RANGE** option is the default and lets Crystal Reports use the chart values to set the starting and ending values for the Data axis. If you want to customize the values, clear this option and enter the Min, Max and Number formats that you want.

MIN is the lowest value that you want to see on the axis. Usually this is zero, but you may have the need to use a different starting value.

MAX is the highest value that you want to see on the Axis. This value is usually larger than the largest value of the data on the axis.

The danger in changing the Max Value in my opinion is that you would be basing the change on the current values that are displayed on the chart. If the report is run later and for whatever reason has a larger value than the value that you entered in this field, the chart would not capture the largest value, thus making the data on the chart inaccurate.

The **NUMBER FORMAT** option is only available if the Auto Range option is not checked.

The options in the drop-down list shown in Figure 16-26 are used to select the format for the numbers that will be displayed on the chart.

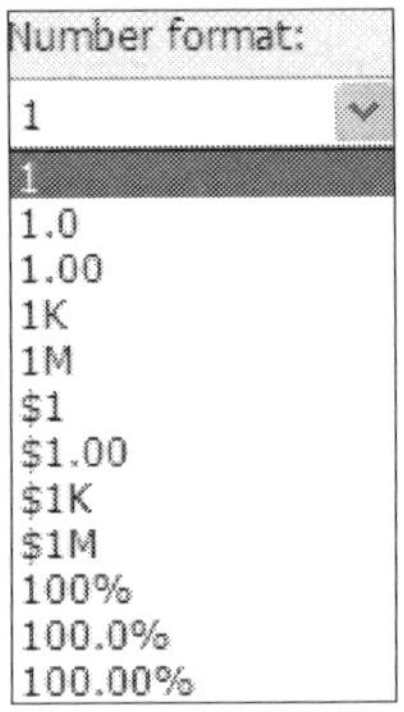

Figure 16-26 Number Format options

If you change the data value options and then recheck the **AUTO RANGE** option, the changes that you made will still be in effect, even though the options are not enabled.

If checked, the **AUTO SCALE** option is used to select the starting numeric value that the chart will use.

Number Of Division Options

The options in this section are used to customize the number of gridlines (intervals) and labels that the data axis will have. Select the **MANUAL** option if you want to set the intervals.

Options Tab

Figures 16-27 to 16-29 show various versions of the Options tab. The options are different depending on the chart type that is selected.

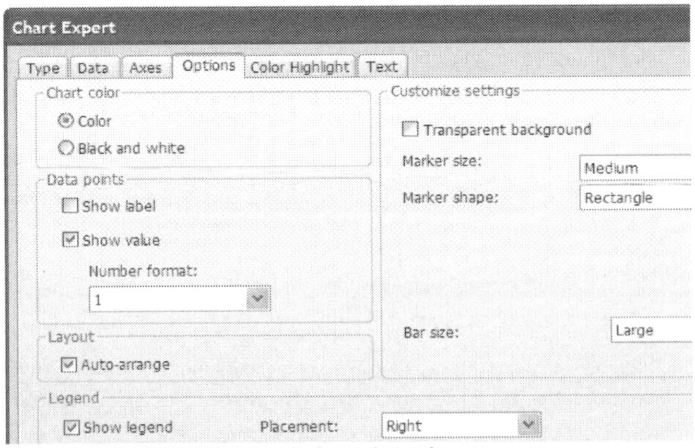

Figure 16-27 Options tab for a bar chart

The **AUTO-ARRANGE** layout option resets the chart to its original size and position.

The options in the **CUSTOMIZE SETTINGS** section are used to select the size and shape for the legend in some chart types or the shape of the markers for bar and line charts.

The **MARKERS** are the points on a chart that are connected by lines. This feature is often used in line charts, as shown earlier in Figure 16-5.

The last size option in this section is used to select the size of the element.

For example, the size of a slice of the pie or the size of the bar, as shown in Figures 16-28 and 16-29.

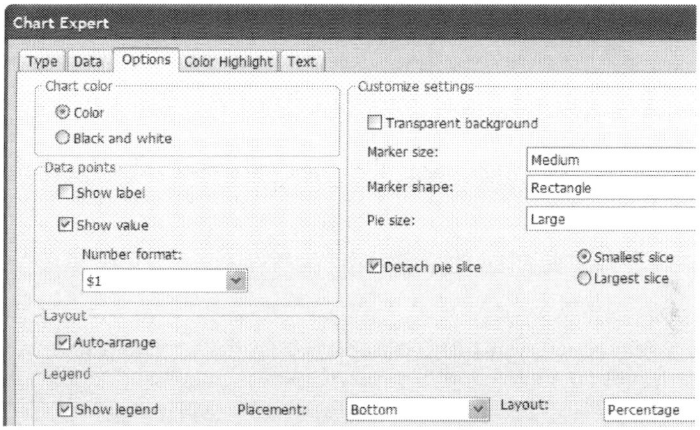

Figure 16-28 Options tab for a pie chart

The options in the **DATA POINTS** section are used to select whether or not labels and values (the actual data) are displayed with the elements.

Each element (slice) in the pie chart shown earlier in Figure 16-7 has a label and value. The value is in parenthesis for illustration purposes in the figure.

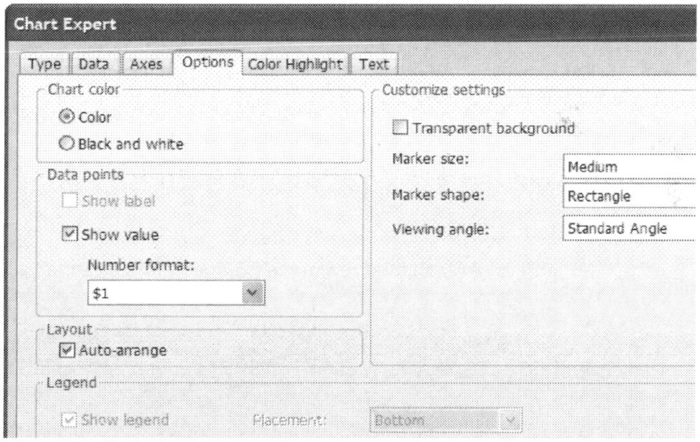

Figure 16-29 Options tab for a 3D Riser chart

The options in the **LEGEND** section are used to turn the legend on and off, as well as, select where you want the legend placed in reference to the chart. The legend is the color coded key that lets you know what the elements on the chart are referencing.

The area chart shown earlier in Figure 16-6 has the legend at the bottom of the chart.
In Figure 16-28 shown earlier, the legend will be placed below the chart. Notice in Figure 16-29 above that the legend options are not enabled. That means that the chart type cannot have a legend. There are also times when a chart looks better without a legend.

Color Highlight Tab

The options on this tab are used to conditionally format the colors for the elements on a chart. The options shown in Figure 16-30 should look familiar because they are similar to the options on the Highlighting Expert.

The difference between them is that the Highlighting Expert works with objects on the report and the options on the Color Highlight tab work with elements on a chart.

The options shown in Figure 16-30 will change the color of the field to Teal if the order date is greater than 6/1/2004.

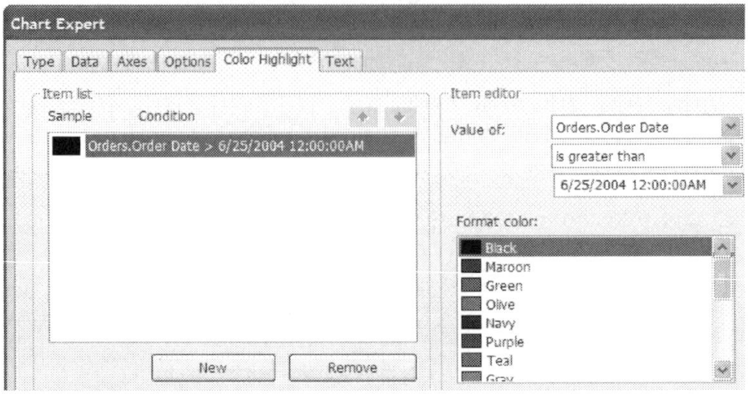

Figure 16-30 Color Highlight tab options

Differences Between The Color Highlight Tab And The Highlighting Expert

Conditional formatting on the Color Highlight tab is not available for all of the chart types. The difference is that the Highlighting Expert works with objects on the report and the options on the Color Highlight tab work with elements on a chart. To display conditional formatting using the Color Highlight tab, line charts have to have data markers. Area charts have to have two "On Change Of" values to display conditional formatting.

> The conditional formatting that you apply to an element does not change if the data for that element changes. For example, if you apply conditional formatting to the bottom section (for example, the mail order section) of the area chart shown earlier in Figure 16-6 and the data changes and the mail order element is no longer on the bottom, the formatting for the mail order element does not change. The new data that is in the bottom section of the area chart will change. In my opinion, conditional formatting usually looks better on charts that are using data that is grouped.

Text Tab

The options on this tab are used to add text to a chart.

As shown in Figure 16-31, the **AUTO TEXT** option is checked for all of the title fields and the text fields are not enabled. This is because Crystal Reports automatically creates many of the titles based on the field names that the chart is being created from.

You saw this when you created charts with the wizards in Chapter 11.

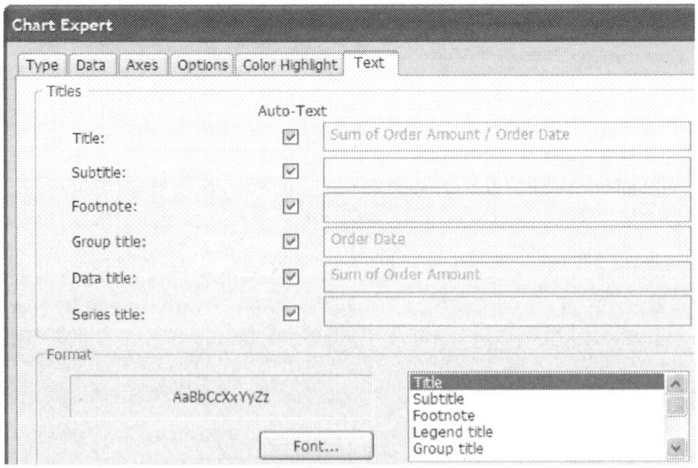

Figure 16-31 Text tab chart options

To change a title, clear the check mark next to the title that you want to change and type in the title that you want. It is not a requirement to have titles.

You can change the font of a title by clicking on the title that you want to change in the **FORMAT** section and then click the Font button. Figure 16-32 shows the font options.

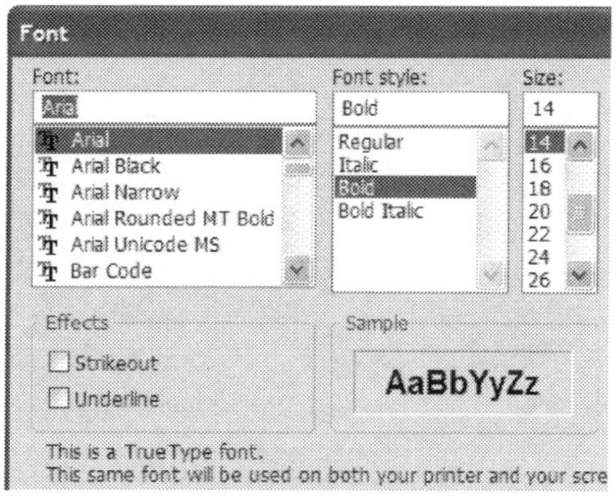

Figure 16-32 Font options

Parts Of A Chart

Charts can contain all or any of the options discussed below. These options can be added or deleted as needed. Figure 16-33 illustrates many of the parts of a chart that have already been discussed in this chapter. The parts of the chart are explained below.

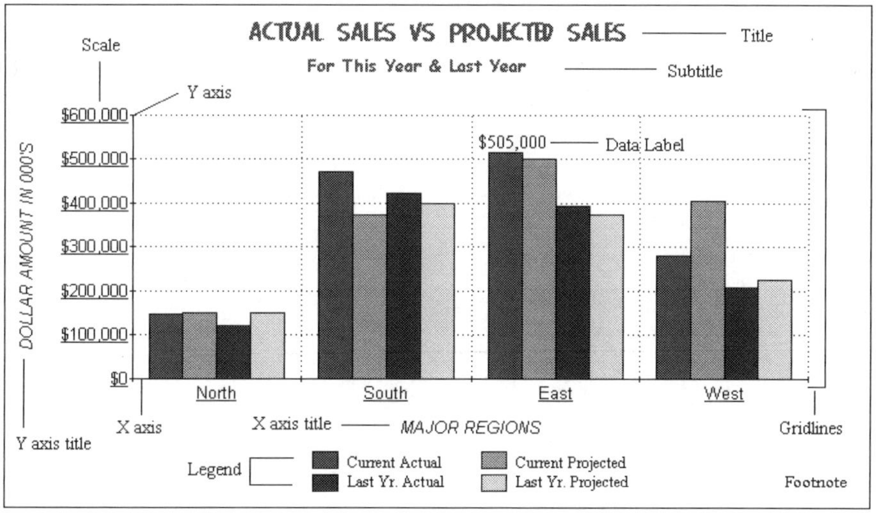

Figure 16-33 Parts of a chart illustrated

Title and **Subtitle** are a description of what type of data the chart is displaying.

X and **Y Axis** represent the vertical (Y) axis and horizontal (X) axis of the chart. The X axis often represents quantities or percents.

Gridlines make the chart easier to read if the values are close in range. You can have horizontal and vertical gridlines.

Scale shows the unit of measurement. The scale range is taken from the data that is displayed on the report. The scale is automatically created for you, but you can change it. Crystal Reports uses the Auto Scale and Auto Range options on the Chart Expert Axes tab to create the scale.

The **Legend** is used to help make the chart easier to read. Legends are color coded representations of different data elements on the chart.

Chart Exercise Tips

① Unless stated otherwise, if the exercises in this chapter do not create a new report, open the Chart Expert after step 1 in each exercise and place the chart in the report header section. If the Report Header section is suppressed, remove the suppression.

② If the instruction to select a chart type says to select the line chart with markers data points for example, you would select the line chart type from the list on the left of the Type tab on the Chart Expert dialog box. You would then click on the icon on the right that has the words markers data points.

③ Some of the options in the instructions may already be selected.

④ If prompted to refresh the data, do so.

When you view a chart on the design tab, you may see fields that you did not select. You will see real data on the preview tab. The chart in the design window does not represent data in the tables that the chart is using. I am telling you this because I do not want you to think that you are losing your mind when you see a chart in the design window that doesn't display what you are expecting.

Exercise 16.1: Create A Bar Chart

1. Save the E11.7 report as `E16.1 Bar chart`.

2. Delete the existing chart. Open the Chart Expert, then select the Side by side bar chart type.

3. On the Data tab, select the Group layout option. Select the Order Date field from the On Change Of drop-down list, then select the Order Amount field in the Show drop-down list.

4. On the Axes tab, add a major gridline to the Group axis option.

5. On the Options tab, select the **SHOW VALUE** Data points option, then change the Number format to $1.

   Place the Legend at the bottom of the chart.

   You should have the options selected that are shown in Figure 16-34.

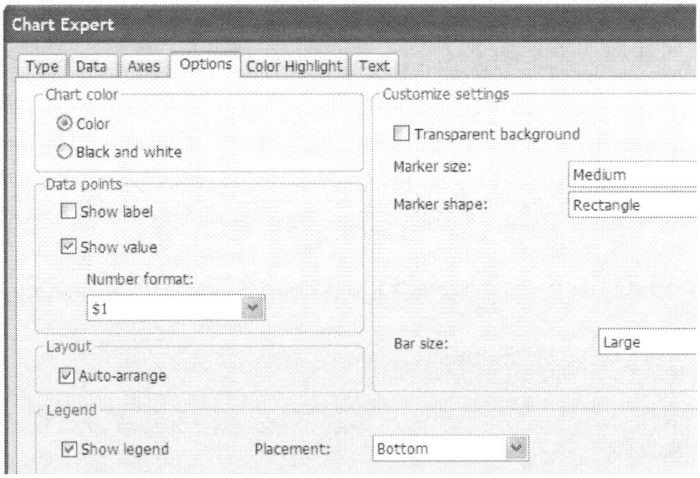

Figure 16-34 Options for the bar chart

6. On the Text tab, change the Title to `Bar Chart.`

   The chart should look like the one shown in Figure 16-35.

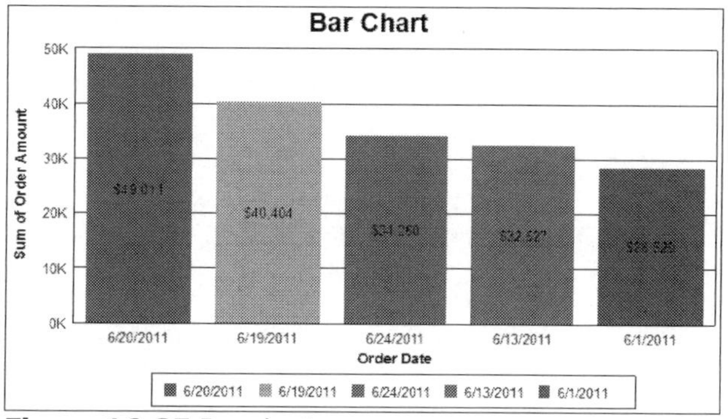

Figure 16-35 Bar chart

Exercise 16.2: Copy A Chart To A Group Section

Earlier you learned that if the same chart is placed in a group section of the report that it will only display data for the group. In this exercise, you will copy the chart that you created in Exercise 16.1 and place the copy in the Group Footer section of the report.

1. Save the E16.1 report as `E16.2 Chart in group footer section.`
2. Open the Section expert, click on the Group Footer section and click the **INSERT** button, then click OK. You should now see a Group Footer 1b section on the report.
3. Right-click on the chart and select Copy. Right-click and select Paste, then click in the Group Footer 1b section.
4. Open the Chart Expert for the chart in the Group Footer 1b section. On the Data tab add the Customer Name field to the first list, then add the Order Amount field to the Show value(s) list.
5. Clear the Show value option on the Options tab.
6. Change the Title to `Chart In Group Footer Section.`
   Change the Subtitle to `Customer Orders By Day.`
   Delete the text in the Group title field. The chart should look like the one shown in Figure 16-36.

At the end of every group on the report you will see a chart that only contains data for the records in that group.

If you didn't want the chart in the Report Header section, you could delete it.

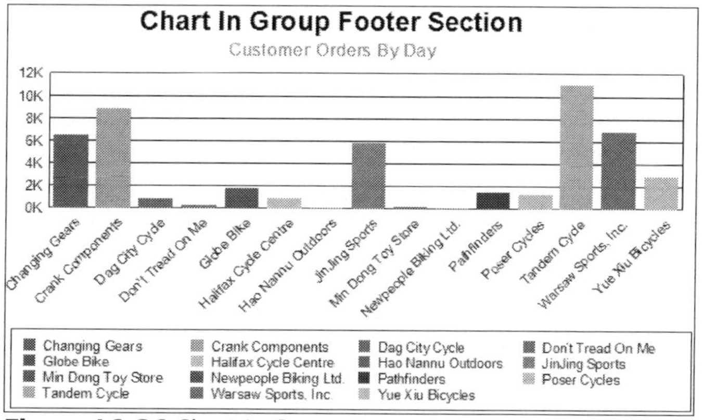

Figure 16-36 Chart in Group Footer section

Exercise 16.3: Create A Line Chart

In this exercise you will create a chart that displays order totals by month for a specific year.

1. Save the E10.2 report as `E16.3 Line chart.`
2. Select the Line chart type with markers at data points, then select the Group layout option on the Data tab.
3. In the Show drop-down list, select the Sum Order Amount field.
4. Place the legend on the right side of the chart. Select the large **MARKER SIZE** and the **DIAMOND** Marker shape.
5. Change the Subtitle to `Line Chart`. The chart should look like the one shown in Figure 16-37.

As you can see, the markers are not diamond shaped. The only option on the Chart Expert that works is the Rectangle option.

To fix this, select the **CHART OPTIONS ⇒ GENERAL** option on the Chart shortcut menu. On the Appearance tab (on the Chart Options dialog box), open the **SHAPE** drop-down list and select the Diamond option.

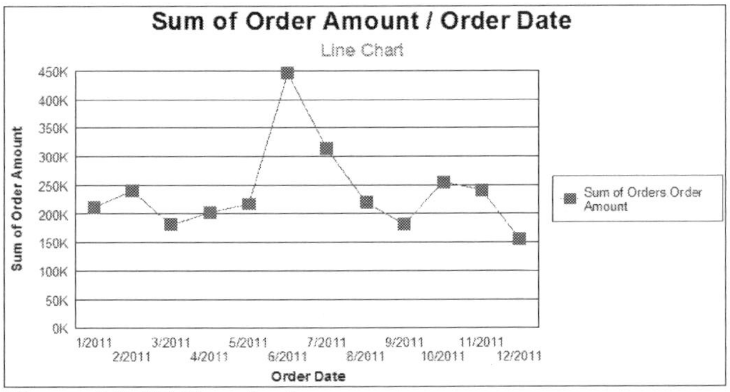

Figure 16-37 Line chart

Exercise 16.4: Create An Area Chart

As mentioned earlier, you can add a chart to a report that does not have any data. You will learn how to do that in this exercise by creating a report that charts the sum of last years sales by region.

1. Create a new report and save it as `E16.4 Area chart`. Add the Customer table.
2. Select the Stacked Area chart type and the Use depth effect option.
3. On the Data tab, add the Region and Customer Name fields to the first list, then add the Last Year's Sales field to the Show value(s) list. You should have the options shown in Figure 16-38.

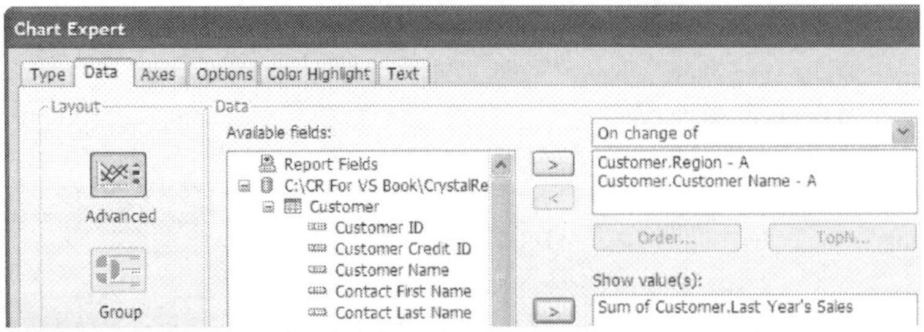

Figure 16-38 Area chart data tab options

4. Add a major gridline to the Group axis option. Change the option to show the legend at the bottom of the chart.

5. Change the Subtitle to `Area Chart`. Delete the Group title. Make the chart at least 6.5 inches wide.

Add The Selection Criteria

In addition to being able to create a report that does not have any other information besides a chart, you can also select the records that you want the chart to be based on.

1. Open the Select Expert. Select the Region field, then click OK.

2. Select the **IS ONE OF** value, then add the following regions: CA, NY, PA and BC.

   The chart should look like the one shown in Figure 16-39.

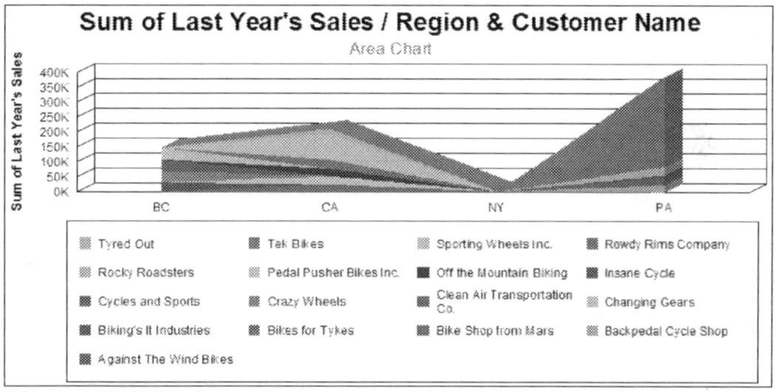

Figure 16-39 Area chart

Exercise 16.5: Detach A Slice Of A Pie Chart

One way to emphasize a slice of a pie chart is to pull it away from the rest of the chart. This is sometimes referred to as "Exploding" a slice of a pie chart.

1. Save the Chapter 16 Pie Chart report as `E16.5 Explode a slice of the pie chart`.

2. Right-click on the chart and select Chart Expert.

3. On the Options tab, check the option **DETACH PIE SLICE**, then select the **LARGEST SLICE** option.

4. Change the Title to `Explode a slice of a pie chart`.

   The chart should look like the one shown in Figure 16-40.

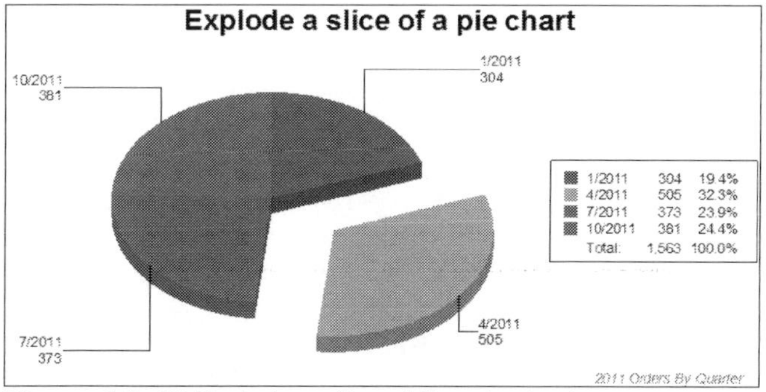

Figure 16-40 Explode a slice of the pie chart

Exercise 16.6: Create A Doughnut Chart

In this exercise you will modify a pie chart to change it to a doughnut chart.

1. Save the Chapter 16 Pie Chart report as `E16.6 Doughnut chart.`

2. Select the Doughnut chart type.

3. Change the Title to `Doughnut Chart.`

   The chart should look like the one shown in Figure 16-41.

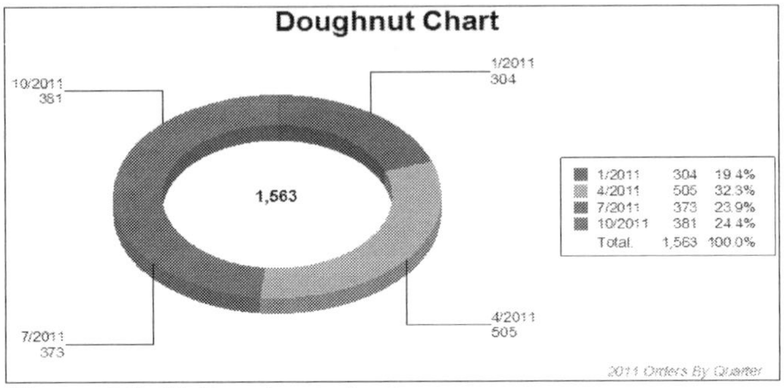

Figure 16-41 Doughnut chart

> You can detach a slice of a doughnut chart, just like you can in a pie chart.

Exercise 16.7: Create A 3D Riser Chart

In this exercise you will create a chart that shows last years sales for three states (regions) that are over a certain dollar amount. In order to do that the report will need selection criteria.

1. Save the E16.4 report as `E16.7 3D Riser chart.`

2. Use the Select Expert to create the criteria shown in Figure 16-42.

```
{Customer.Region} in ["MA", "PA", "WI"] and
{Customer.Last Year's Sales} >= $35000.00
```

Figure 16-42 Selection criteria

3. Select the 3D Riser bar chart type.

4. Display major gridlines for all axes. Show minor gridlines for the Data axis. Clear the Auto Scale option.

5. Change the Title to `3D Riser Chart.`

   Change the Subtitle to `Last Year's Sales >= $35,000.`

   The chart should look like the one shown in Figure 16-43.

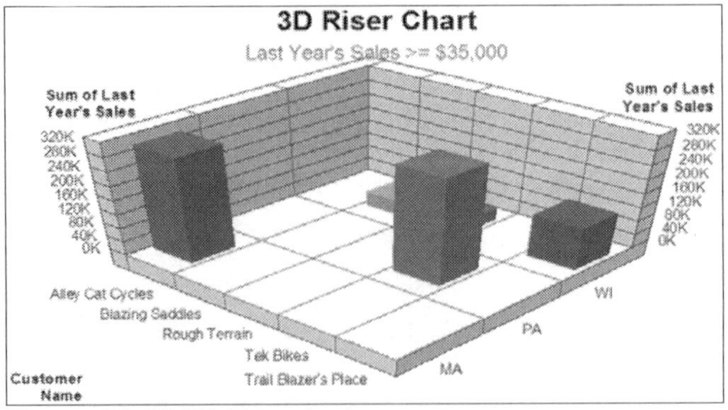

Figure 16-43 3D Riser chart

Exercise 16.8: Create An XY Scatter Chart

In this exercise you will create a chart that plots the number of orders in 2004 by month and total dollar amount.

1. Save the E10.2 report as `E16.8 XY Scatter chart.`
2. Select the XY Scatter chart type, then select the Advanced layout option.
3. Add the Order Date field to the first list, then add the Order ID and Order Amount fields to the Show value(s) list.
4. Click on the Order ID field that you just added, then click the Set Summary Operation button. Change the summary to Distinct count.
5. On the Options tab, change the Marker shape to Rectangle.
6. Change the Title to `XY Scatter Chart.`

   Add the Subtitle `2011 Orders By Month.`

   The chart should look like the one shown in Figure 16-44.

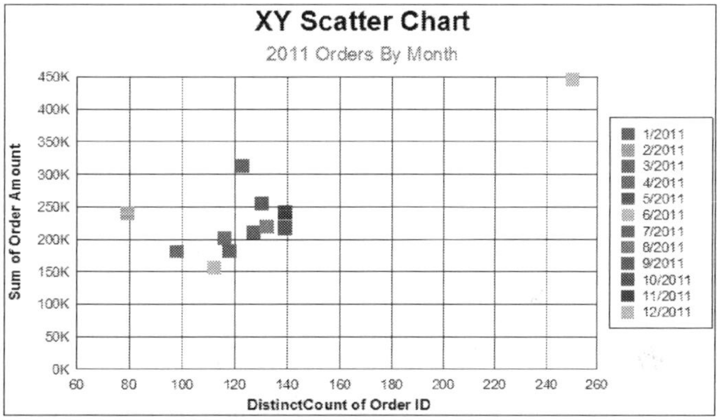

Figure 16-44 XY Scatter chart

Exercise 16.9: Show The Bottom 20% Of Orders

In the exercise that you just completed, the chart plotted the data for all 12 months. If the marketing department wanted to create a campaign to increase sales in the months that had the lowest number of sales, it could be difficult to tell which months fall into that category. If the chart was modified to only display the months that are in the bottom 20% of sales based on the total order amount by month, the chart would be easier for the marketing department to use. You have already created a report that displayed the top five orders for a month. Creating a report for the bottom 20% is very similar.

1. Save the E16.8 report as `E16.9 Bottom 20 percent chart.`
2. On the Chart Expert, click on the Data tab. Click on the Order Date field on the top list on the right, then click the **TOP N** button.
3. Open the Group sort drop-down list and select **BOTTOM PERCENTAGE**. Change the Percentage field to `20`, then check the **INCLUDE TIES** option. The options shown in Figure 16-45 will display the months that are in the bottom 20%, based on the number of orders placed that month.

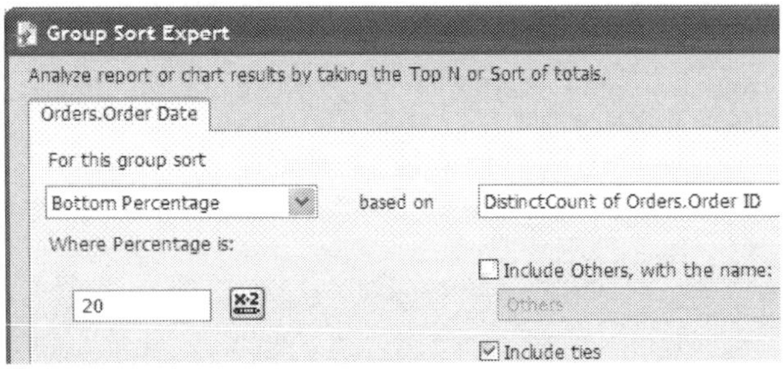

Figure 16-45 Group Sort Expert options

4. Change the Title to `Bottom 20% Of Orders.`

   Delete the Subtitle.

   Change the Group title to `Number of orders.`

   Change the Data title to `Total monthly order amount.`

   The chart should look like the one shown in Figure 16-46.

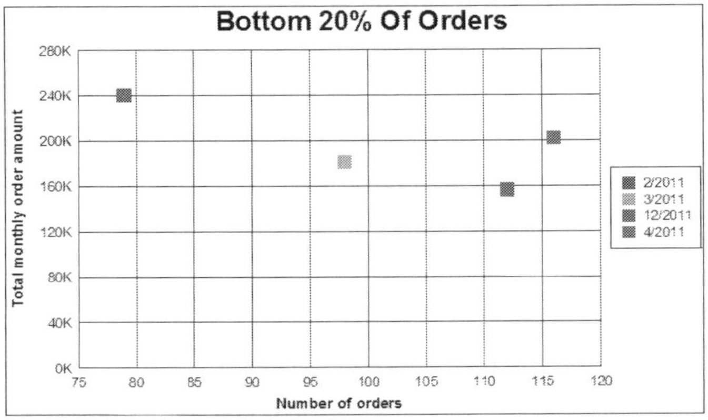

Figure 16-46 Bottom 20% chart

If you create a Top N report and do not add the records on the report that do not meet the Top N criteria to the "Others" group option, any grand total fields that are placed in the Report Footer will include totals for all records that meet the report criteria, whether or not they appear on the report. This means that if the records that do not meet the Top N criteria are not added to the "Others" option, the report grand totals will not be accurate because they will include amounts for detail records that are not on the report. This may not be what you want. If you only want the grand totals to include records that print on the report, in this case the Top N records, you have to create running total fields and place them in the Report Footer instead of summary fields.

Exercise 16.10: Create A Stock Chart

The stock report that you will create will show the average order amount for five regions and the largest order in each region. Stock charts plot minimum and maximum values. The average value will be used as the minimum value and the largest order amount will be used as the maximum value.

The reason that I am using the average value for the minimum is because the lowest value would touch the bottom of the chart which defeats the purpose of the exercise of showing you how a stock chart really does look different then a bar chart.

Create The Selection Criteria

1. Create a new report and save it as `E16.10 Stock chart.`

2. Add the Customer and Orders tables, then click Next.

3. On the Links tab, the tables should be joined on the Customer ID field. If they aren't, create the link by clicking on the Customer ID field in the Orders table and dragging it to the Customer ID field in the Customer table.

   To make sure that link is correct, right-click on the link between the tables and select **LINK OPTIONS**.

   You will see the dialog box shown in Figure 16-47.

   Make sure that the link is exactly like the one illustrated.

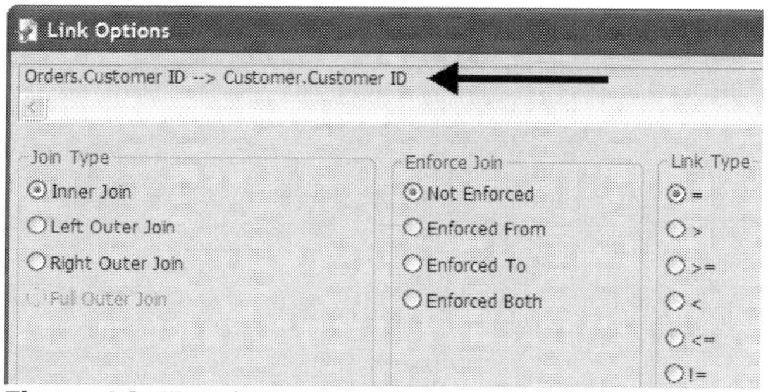

Figure 16-47 Link Options dialog box

4. Create selection criteria to only include customers in the following regions: MA, PA, AL, ID, WI.

Create The Chart

1. Open the Chart Expert and select the Stock High-Low stock chart.
2. On the Data tab, add the Region field to the first list.
3. Add the Order Amount field to the Show value(s) list. Click on the field, then click the Set Summary Operation button. Change the summary type to Maximum.
4. Add the Order Amount field to the Show value(s) list again. Click on the field, then click the Set Summary Operation button. Change the summary type to Average.
5. On the Options tab, check the Show value option. Do not display a legend.
6. Change the Title to `Stock Chart.`

   Add the Subtitle `Avg & Max order amounts for 5 states.`

   The chart should look like the one shown in Figure 16-48.

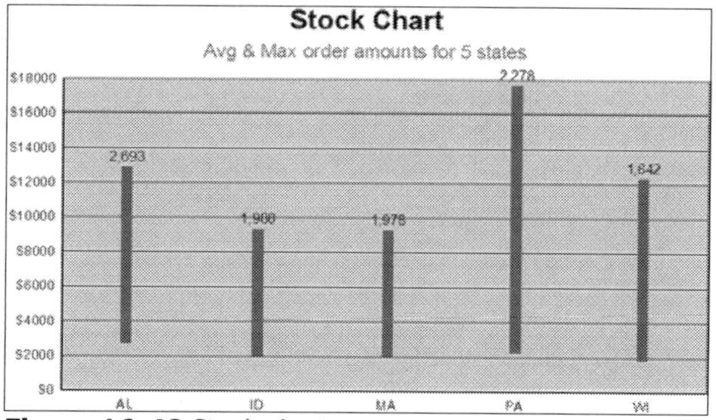

Figure 16-48 Stock chart

Exercise 16.11: Create A Numeric Axis Chart

In this exercise you will create a chart that displays the sum of orders for one company during a specific date range. You will use the options on the Chart Sort Order dialog box to set the frequency of the On Change Of option.

Create The Report

1. Create a new report and save it as `E16.11 Numeric Axis chart`. Add the Customer and Orders tables to the report. Make sure the tables are linked liked they were in Exercise 16.10.

2. Create selection criteria for the Order Date field. The dates should be between 11/1/2011 and 11/30/2011. Create selection criteria that limits the report to only display information for the customer, To The Limit Biking Co.

3. Delete the date field from the Page Header section, if it's there. Add the Order Date and Order Amount fields to the Details section.

4. Change the format of the Order Date field to XX/XX/XXXX, then sort the Order Date field in ascending order.

Create The Chart

1. Open the Chart Expert. Select the Numeric Axis - Date axis bar chart type.

2. On the Data tab, add the Order Date field to the first list. Click on the field, then click the **ORDER** button. Make sure the last option on the Chart Sort Order dialog box is set to **FOR EACH DAY**.

3. Add the Order Amount field to the Show value(s) list.

4. Add a minor gridline to the Data axis option.

5. Check the Show value option, then select the $1 Number format.

6. Change the Title to `Numeric Axis Chart.`

   Add the subtitle `To The Limit Biking Co - Nov 2011.`

   The chart should look like the one shown in Figure 16-49.

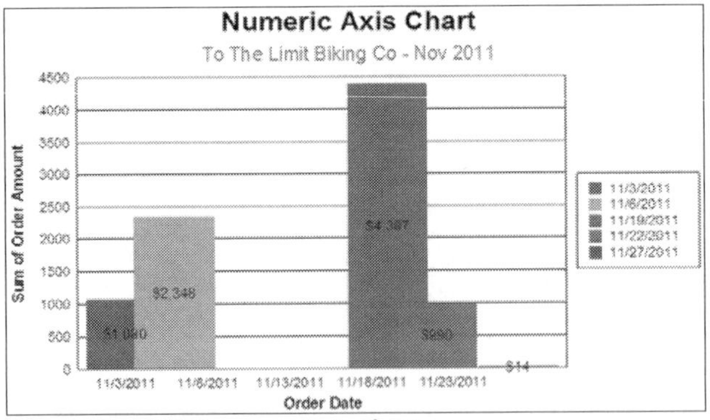

Figure 16-49 Numeric Axis chart

Exercise 16.12: Create A Gauge Chart

In Chapter 14 you read how to create a report that displayed the words True or False in a Boolean field based on the employees salary. This was done to keep the employees actual salary private. In this exercise you will create a chart that will plot how many employees salaries are greater than 50K.

1. Save the Chapter 16 Boolean Suppression Formula report as `E16.12 Gauge chart.`

2. Select the Gauge chart type. On the Data tab, add the **BOOLEAN_STYLE** formula field to the first list, then add the Employee ID field to the Show value(s) list.

3. Click on the Employee ID field, then click the Set Summary Operation button. Change the summary type to Count.

4. Change the Title to `Gauge Chart`.
   Add the Subtitle `Employee salary over 50K`.
   The chart should look like the one shown in Figure 16-50.

   The company has 15 employees.

   If you look at the needles on the chart, you will see that when added together, the values equal 15.

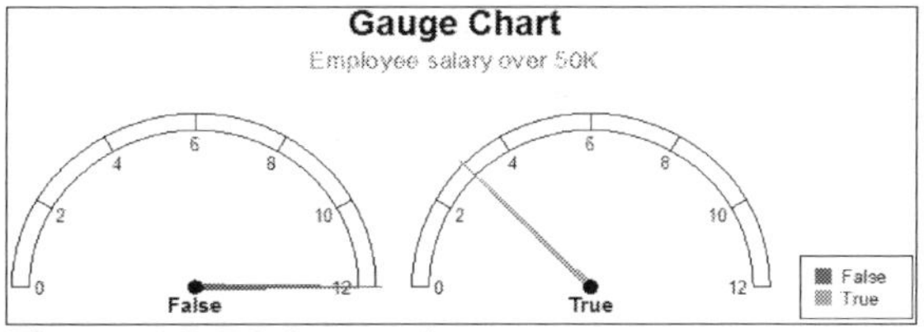

Figure 16-50 Gauge chart

Exercise 16.13: Create A Gantt Chart

In Chapter 13 you created a report that calculated how many days it took to ship the customer orders. Gantt charts require a start and end date. In this exercise you will use the order date as the start date and the ship date as the end date.

The E13.9 Calculate order processing time report currently only has criteria that the order date is greater than or equal to a specific date. The Gantt chart would not be readable if all of the records that are currently on the report were displayed on the chart. To make the chart readable, you will select a few Order ID numbers to display on the chart.

1. Save the E13.9 report as `E16.13 Gantt chart`.

2. Create selection criteria that limits the report to the following Order ID numbers from the Orders Detail table: 1, 1015, 1020, 1069 and 1090.

3. Open the Chart Expert, then select the Gantt chart type and the Use depth effect option.

4. On the Data tab, select the **FOR EACH RECORD** option from the drop-down list, then add the Customer Name field to the first list.

5. Add the Order Date and Ship Date fields to the Show value(s) list.

6. Add the Title `Gantt Chart`.

   Add the Subtitle `Delay in shipping`.

   The chart should look like the one shown in Figure 16-51.

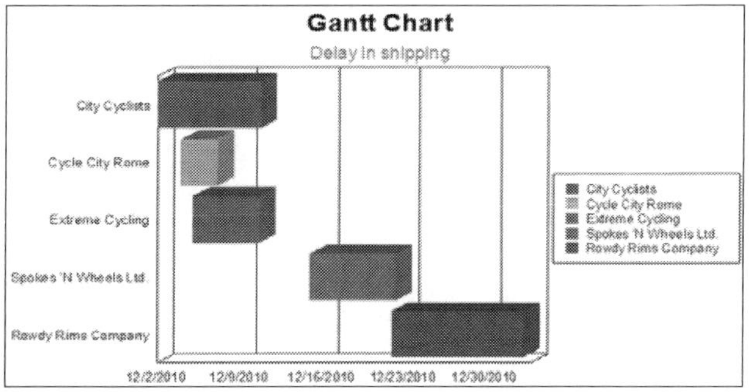

Figure 16-51 Gantt chart

Exercise 16.14: Create A Color Highlighting Chart

In this exercise you will create a chart that will change the color of the bars on the chart to red, if the delay in ship time is greater than or equal to seven days or yellow if the delay in ship time is between four and six days. To reduce the number of order days to something that will make the chart readable, you will add selection criteria to the report.

1. Save the E13.9 report as `E16.14 Highlighted chart`.

2. Add selection criteria to the report so that only orders with an order date between 12/02/2010 and 12/05/2010 will appear on the report. Create selection criteria to only display orders that have a delay in days to ship greater than or equal to two.

3. Select the Side by side bar chart type and the Use depth effect option.

4. On the Data tab, add the Order ID field (in the Orders table) to the first list, then add the Delay In Days To Ship formula field to the Show value(s) list.

5. Change the Title to `Color Highlighting Chart`.
   Add the Subtitle `Yellow = 4-6 day delay, Red = 7+ day delay`.
   Add the Footnote `Orders between 12/2/2010 & 12/5/2010`.
   Change the Group title to `Order Number`.
   Change the Data title to `Delay In Days To Ship`.
   Leave the Chart Expert open to complete the next part of the exercise.

Add The Color Highlighting To The Chart

In this part of the exercise you will create the criteria that will change the colors of the bars on the chart to red or yellow depending on the value in the Delay in Days To Ship field.

1. On the Color Highlight tab, click the New button.

2. Open the first drop-down list and select the Delay in Days To Ship field. Open the second drop-down list and select Is greater than or equal to. Type a `7` in the last field.

3. Select Red as the Format color, then click the New button.

4. Open the first drop-down list and select the Delay in Days To Ship field. Open the second drop-down list and select Is between. Type a `4` in the first field and a `6` in the last field.

5. Select Yellow as the Format color.

   The chart should look like the one shown in Figure 16-52.

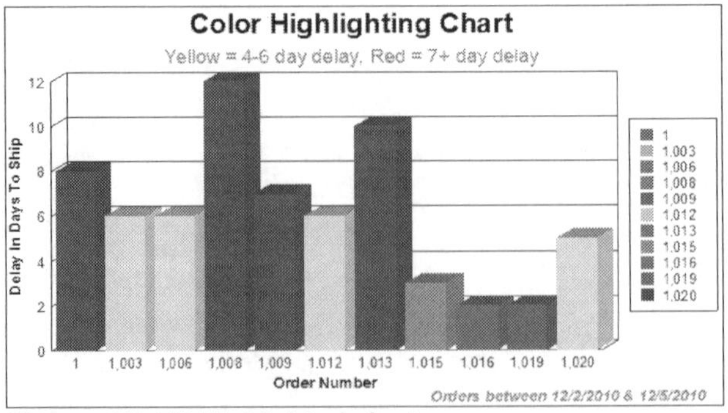

Figure 16-52 Highlighted chart

PARAMETER FIELD BASICS

Parameter fields add interaction between the person running the report and the report. Parameter fields are used to customize reports to better meet the users needs. In this chapter you will learn how to do the following:

- ☑ Use the Create Parameter Field dialog box
- ☑ Create a list of static values for a parameter field
- ☑ Use parameter fields with the Select Expert

CHAPTER 17

Parameter Fields Overview

The reports that you have learned to create so far in this book did not require any input from the people that would run them. You also learned that different users may need slightly different versions of the same report. Based on the report creation techniques that you have learned so far, especially the Select Expert, if one group of people needed to see a customer report for a specific date range and another group of people need to see the same report for specific customers, you would have to create two reports. This is the largest downside to only using the Select Expert to create selection criteria. Using parameter fields to pass data to the Select Expert is a much better solution.

Think about this. If a user requested a report to only show data for one year, the date range would be entered as the criteria on the Select Expert. Now, the same user or a different user needs the same report, but for a different date range and specific customers. The easiest thing to do based on the report techniques that you have learned so far is to open the existing report and save it with a new file name and change the selection criteria to the new date range and add customer criteria. As you can see, this could get out of hand quickly. If the original report used parameter fields to get the criteria from the person running the report, the report could be used for any date range and any customer. Another thing to think about is maintaining all of these reports. If a field needs to be added, you would have to add the field to more than one report.

If you created two parameter fields for the report, one for a date range and another one to select customers, both groups of people could use the same report. A popular type of parameter field is one that passes data to the Select Expert. In addition to being able to pass data to the Select Expert, a parameter field can also pass data to conditional and other types of formulas. This allows the person running the report to have control over the records that will appear on the report without having to know how to use the Select Expert or how to create formulas. The reports that you create that have criteria on the Select Expert can be enhanced by using parameter fields in place of specific (hard coded) values from a table or the value that you type in the second drop-down list on the Select Expert. This would give reports a lot more flexibility.

To help the person that will run a report that has parameter fields, you can include features like default values and drop-down lists. For example, if you were creating a parameter field that needed to allow the user to select a country, you could set a default country if the report is often run using a specific country. You could also create a drop-down list field that contains all of the countries and let the user select the country that they wanted to run the report for.

How Do Parameter Fields Work?

When a report is run that has a parameter field, it prompts the user to select options, which creates all or part of the criteria that is needed to run the report. The information that is gathered from parameter fields is passed to various components of the report, like the Select Expert or a formula, to run the report. Like the Select Expert, parameter fields ask questions that will determine what data will be retrieved for the report. Using parameter fields, the following questions can be answered: Which three months do you want to see the sales reps totals for? Which country do you want to see sales for? Which customers ordered hats in December?

In addition to using parameter fields to gather the report selection criteria, parameter fields can be used to customize and format the report. For example, parameter fields can be used to select the sorting or grouping options or highlight records that meet a certain condition. If a report has confidential information, one of the parameter fields can require the person running the report to enter their User ID. Based on the User ID, parts of the report would be hidden.

While parameter fields are a good way to get input from the person running the report, they may not be the best solution because they can lack functionality that you may need. If you are a programmer, you can create a form in Visual Basic or Visual C++ for example, to get user input. This also allows you to create more input validation rules then are available parameter fields.

Create New Parameter Dialog Box

Now that you know what parameter fields are, how useful they are and how they work, it is time to learn about the dialog box shown in Figure 17-1, which is used to create parameter fields.

Table 17-1 explains the options on the Create New Parameter dialog box.

Reports can and often do have more than one parameter field.

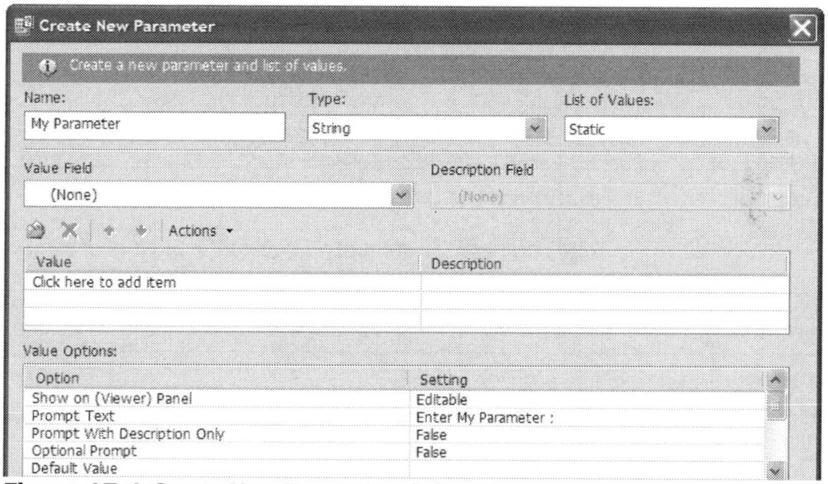

Figure 17-1 Create New Parameter dialog box

There are several ways to open the Create New Parameter dialog box as discussed below.

① Click on the Parameter Fields category in the Field Explorer, then click the **NEW** button on the Field Explorer toolbar.

② Right-click on the Parameter Fields category in the Field Explorer and select New.

③ Click the Field Explorer button on the Standard toolbar to open the Field Explorer, then follow one of the options above in this list.

④ View ⇒ Field Explorer, then follow option one or two above.

Option	Description
Name	This option is used to name the parameter field. The name is how you reference the parameter field. Try to use as descriptive a name as possible, while keeping the name as short as possible. You can use the name of the field in the table that the parameter field will query. You can also use the name of an existing formula. (1)
Type	Select the data type for the parameter field. You should select the same data type as the field or data that the parameter field will be compared to. (1)
List of values	If you want to provide values for the parameter field, there are two types of values: Static values that do not change and dynamic values, which can change each time the report is run.

Table 17-1 Create New Parameter dialog box options explained

Option	Description
Value Field	The options in this field are the fields from the tables that are connected to the report. This field has two purposes: To select the field for the comparison for the parameter field or select the field that will be used to import values for a static or dynamic list.
Description Field	Is used to specify text or another field that will be displayed next to the Value Field in the list. This is helpful when the value field option is an ID field. Often, the person running the report will not understand the values in an ID field. For example, you may need to use the Customer ID field, but display either the Customer ID field and the Customer Name field or display the Customer Name field by itself. The Customer Name field contains data that the person running the report understands.
Insert	Clicking this button retrieves the data that is in the field selected in the Value Field, discussed above.
Actions	The options in this drop-down list, as shown in Figure 17-2, are used to create a list of values or export values.
Value/Description	These two columns function like a table and are used to select specific data from the field that the parameter field is based on. You can also type values in this list. Filling in the Description column is optional.
Option/Setting	The options in this section are used to customize the parameter field. The options will change depending on the data type that is selected.

Table 17-1 Create New Parameter dialog box options explained (Continued)

(1) This is a required option to create a parameter field.

The **APPEND ALL DATABASE VALUES** option adds (imports) all unique values from the table.

The **CLEAR** option removes all values from the list.

The **IMPORT** option imports the values for the parameter field.

The **EXPORT** option copies the values for the parameter field to a file.

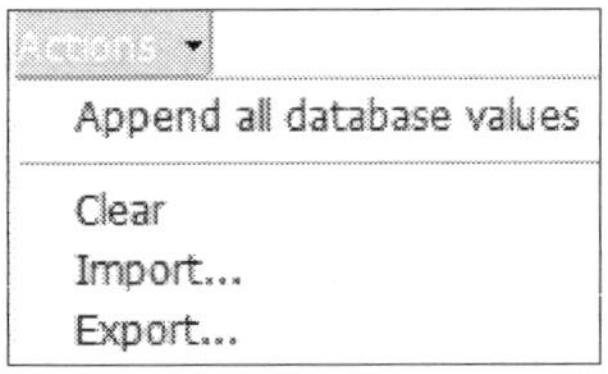

Figure 17-2 Actions drop-down list options

Value Options

Option	Description
Show On (Viewer) Panel	Is used to select whether or not the parameter field will be displayed on the Parameters Panel. It has the following three settings: ① The **DO NOT SHOW** setting hides the parameter field on the Parameters Panel. This is the default option. ② The **EDITABLE** setting allows the parameter field values to be changed when the report is run without refreshing the data. (2) ③ The **READ ONLY** setting allows the parameter field values to be viewed, but not changed. To change the values, press the F5 key or click the Refresh button. (2)
Prompt Text	Is used to enter text that will let the person running the report know what to enter or select for the parameter field.

Table 17-2 Value options explained

Option	Description
Prompt with description only	Is used to select whether the parameter field is displayed with just the prompt text or the prompt text and description.
Optional Prompt	Is used to select whether or not the parameter field is required to have a value. If required, the report will not run until the parameter field has a value. Select True to make the parameter field optional.
Sort Order	Is used to select the order that the values in the parameter field are sorted in. This option is only available for dynamic parameter fields.
Default Value	Is used to select a default value for the parameter field.
Allow custom Values	Is used to select whether or not the person running the report can enter any value or if a value has to be selected from the values available for the field.
Allow multiple values	If this option is set to true, the person running the report can select or enter more than one value in the field.
Allow discrete values	Limits the parameter field to only accepting one value.
Allow range values	Requires the person running the report to enter start and end values.
Min Length	Is used to select the minimum length for the value in the parameter field.
Max Length	Is used to select the maximum length for the value in the parameter field.
Edit mask	Is used to enter an edit mask instead of a range of values for the string field. [See Edit Masks, later in this chapter]

Table 17-2 Value options explained (Continued)

(2) This option allows the parameter field to be displayed on the Parameters Panel.

Data Types

The data type that you select determines how the parameter field will be used in the report. For example, you cannot select a string data type to use in a comparison with a date/time field. Number, currency and string data types do not have the limitations that date, date/time and Boolean data types have.

Number and **Currency** data types can only use the numbers zero to nine and the minus sign. Any other values will generate an error message.

String data types can use all of the number data type options, plus letters and special characters.

Date and **Time** fields may be the most used data type to limit the data that appears on a report. When you use the Select Expert to create criteria for a date field, you have several options including "Is greater than", "Is greater than or equal to" and "Is between". The Create New Parameter dialog box does not have the same options in terms of their names.

Figure 17-3 shows the options available for date/time parameter fields when the report is run.

The following three options are used to specify how to use dates on a parameter field.

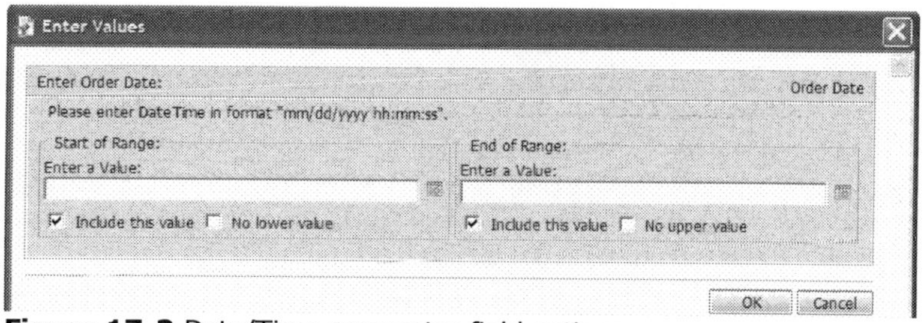

Figure 17-3 Date/Time parameter field options

① **INCLUDE THIS VALUE** If checked, this option will include the date that is entered in the parameter field as part of the selection process. Checking this option on the Start of Range field is the equivalent of the "Is greater than or equal to" Select Expert operator. Checking this option on the Start and End of Range fields is the equivalent of the "Is between" Select Expert operator.

② **NO LOWER VALUE** If checked, the value in the Start of Range field will not be used. (3)

③ **NO UPPER VALUE** If checked, the value in the End of Range field will not be used. (3)

(3) You cannot select both of these options at the same time. If you type 1/1/10 in the Start of Range field and 6/1/10 in the End of Range field and clear the No lower value option, all records that have a value that is less than the value in the End of Range field will be included on the report, even though a date was entered in the Start of Range field. If the No upper value option is checked, all records that have a date greater than 1/1/10 will be included in the report, even though a date was entered in the End of Range field.

If you need to create a date range, you have to set the **ALLOW RANGE VALUES** option to True on the Create New Parameter dialog box. By default, this option is set to False because the **ALLOW DISCRETE VALUES** option is set to True. These two options are mutually exclusive, meaning that only one of them can be set to True for the parameter field.

Boolean Parameter Fields

Boolean parameter fields are very similar to the Boolean formulas. Like Boolean formulas, Boolean parameter fields are used with a Boolean field in a table, which has one of two values: True or False.

Figure 17-4 shows the Value options that are available for Boolean parameter fields. In addition to being able to select a default value of true or false for the Boolean parameter field, you can enter a description for the true and false options.

Option	Setting
Show on (Viewer) Panel	Editable
Prompt Text	Enter My Parameter:
Prompt With Description Only	False
Optional Prompt	False
Default Value	
Boolean group #	
Exclusive group	False

Figure 17-4 Boolean parameter field options

The description should help the person running the report decide which option is appropriate for the records that they want to appear on the report.

The **BOOLEAN GROUP #** option is used to add the Boolean parameter field to a group of other Boolean parameter fields. Creating a Boolean group will remind you of a group of radio buttons that you have probably seen on dialog boxes in other applications, like the print range options on the dialog box shown in Figure 17-5.

Figure 17-5 Radio button group example

The number that you enter in the field is the Boolean group that the parameter field that you are creating or editing should be associated with. If the report has five Boolean fields and two are needed to create one Boolean group, you would enter the same number in this field for these two parameter fields. You would enter a different number for the other three Boolean parameter fields so that they would be grouped together. The three print options in Figure 17-5 would have the same Boolean group number.

This is similar to how summary fields appear on the Data tab of the Chart Expert, as shown in Figure 17-6.

Notice how there are three fields that are in the Group 1 section and three fields in the Group 2 section. That would be the equivalent of two Boolean groups.

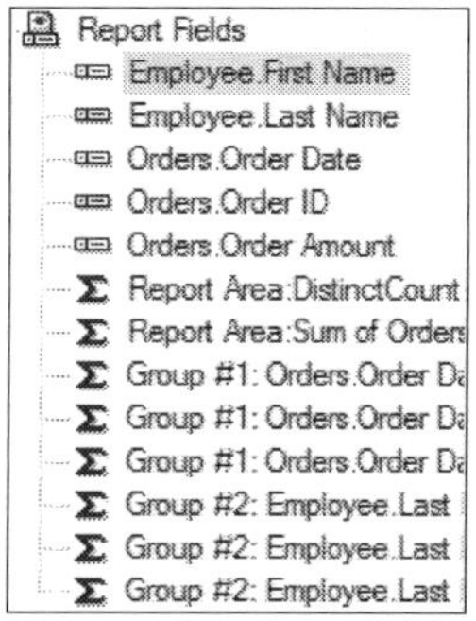

Figure 17-6 Available group fields in a chart

The **EXCLUSIVE GROUP** option shown earlier in Figure 17-4 works with the Boolean groups on the report. This option is used to select whether or not only one option in the Boolean group can be selected. Selecting **TRUE** for this option will only allow one option in the group to be selected. The selected option in the group would will be set to true and the other options will return a value of false.

Figure 17-5 shown earlier, is an example of this because you can only select one of the print options. Selecting **FALSE** for the Exclusive Group option will allow more than one option in the group to be selected. Each option selected will be set to true and the others will be set to false.

Using Parameter Fields With The Select Expert

This combination may be the most used parameter field option. Many of the reports that you have created in this book used the Select Expert to specify which records appear on the report. In programming terminology, these reports are known as "hard coded" because all of the options needed to run the report are coded into the report. At one time this was the only programming option that was available. Today, there are other options and parameter fields are one of these options.

After you create the parameter fields, open the Select Expert and select the parameter field instead of the actual values in the table. For example, in Exercise 8.2 you created the criteria shown in Figure 17-7.

Instead of selecting the specific states (regions) FL and OH, which is the hard coding that I was referring to earlier, you would select the parameter field from the drop-down list on the right. That is how the value in the parameter field is passed to the Select Expert.

Figure 17-7 Select Expert criteria

> What you will find is that you cannot always use the same operator (Is greater than, Is between, etc) with parameter fields that you would when selecting actual values from a field. The majority of the time you will use the "Is equal to" operator with parameter fields on the Select Expert even when the parameter field will be used for a range of values like "Is between 1/1/2011 and 1/31/2011" or when the parameter field is used to select multiple values like "Is one of FL or OH".

When you open the drop-down list on the Select Expert shown in Figure 17-8, you will see all of the parameter fields that have the same data type as the field from the table. Parameter fields are always at the top of the list.

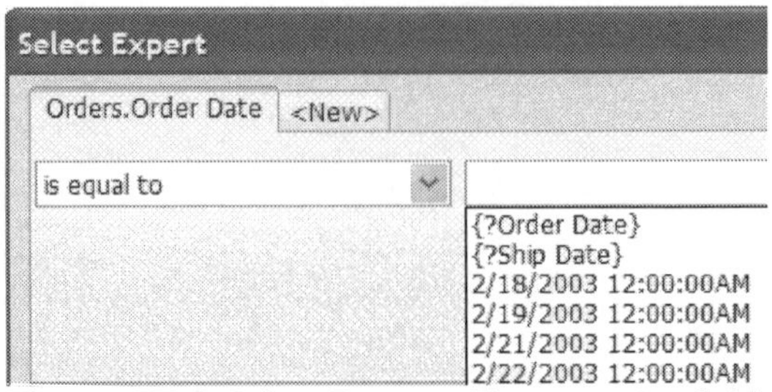

Figure 17-8 Select Expert with parameter field options

If you do not see the parameter field that you are looking for when you open the drop-down list on the right of the Select Expert, it usually means one of two things:
1) That you selected the wrong data type when you created the parameter field or
2) You associated the parameter field with the wrong field. Open the Edit Parameter dialog box, change the data type or field that the parameter field is associated to, then re-open the Select Expert.

You will see the terms "pick list", "list of values" and "prompt". Depending on who wrote the article or documentation, these words when used in conjunction with parameter fields can be used interchangeably. To me, the first two mean the same thing, but prompt, refers to the questions asked on the Enter Values dialog box that you saw earlier in Figure 17-3.

An example of a pick list and how to combine existing reports (which means less reports for you to create or maintain) would be the reports that you created in Exercises 8.1 and 8.2. The report in Exercise 8.1 used the Select Expert to only display customers in one region. The report that you created in Exercise 8.2 displayed customers in two regions. These reports could easily be combined with the use of a parameter field. What would you do if the user needed to run the reports that you created in Exercise 8.1 or 8.2 for different regions next week? Someone, probably you, would have to save the current report with a new name and change the selection criteria for the new regions.

When a report with parameter fields is refreshed, you will see the dialog box shown in Figure 17-9. These options are used to select whether you want to use the parameter values that were selected the last time the report was run or if you want to select new values.

If the option **USE CURRENT PARAMETER VALUES** is selected, the report will run with the existing parameter values and you will not see the Enter Values dialog box.

If the option **PROMPT FOR NEW PARAMETER VALUES** is selected, the Enter Values dialog box that you saw earlier in Figure 17-3 will appear so that you can select new parameter values.

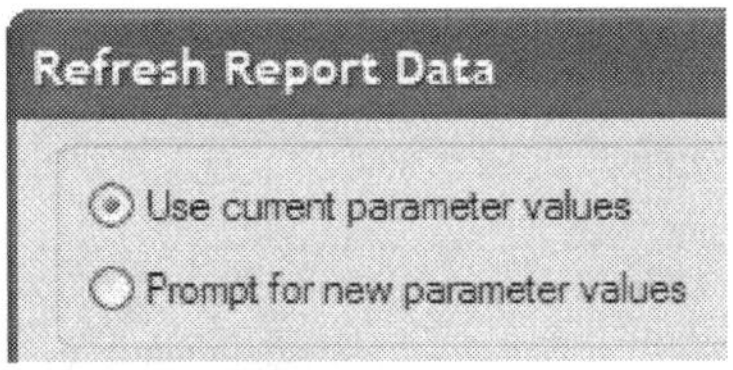

Figure 17-9 Refresh Report Data dialog box

When the Enter Values dialog box opens, it will display the values that were selected the last time that the report was run. You only have to select values that you want to change. I tend to always select this option because it is a good way to double check to make sure that you have the options that you want to use when the report is run.

Enter Values Dialog Box

This dialog box contains all of the parameter fields for the report, as you saw earlier in Figure 17-3. If there is more than one parameter field on the dialog box, you may only be able to select options for the first prompt. Once you select an option for the first prompt, you will be able to select an option for the next prompt. The reason this happens is because sometimes the values in the next prompt are dependant on what was selected in the first prompt. This is known as **CASCADING PROMPTS**. For example, if the first prompt is used to select a country and the second prompt is used to select a state, the only values that will appear in the state drop-down list are states that are in the country that is selected in the first prompt.

Parameter fields appear on the Enter Values dialog box in the order that they are created. The Enter Values dialog box can be customized. You can change the color, fonts and more.

Edit Masks

Edit masks are placeholders that determine how data will be displayed on a report. The Edit mask feature for parameter fields is similar. Edit masks are used to set the rules for how data has to be entered into a field. If an edit mask has 10 placeholders, that means that no more than 10 characters can be entered into the field. Each of the edit mask characters has its own rule. The characters can be combined in the same field as needed. For example, if you were going to use an edit mask for a country field, you may want to force the first character to be an upper case letter and the other characters could be a combination of upper and lower case letters.

Table 17-3 lists the mask characters that you can use. Edit masks provide a lot of flexibility for managing the data that is entered in parameter fields. An edit mask is a series of characters (placeholders) that control the type of data that can be entered in **STRING** parameter fields. The Edit Mask field is at the bottom of the Value Options list on the Create New Parameter dialog box.

The edit mask **>AA** could be used for a state field. AA forces two alphanumeric characters to be entered in the field. **>** forces the characters to be uppercase.

If the values entered are not correct, you will see an error message. Often, the error messages are cryptic and can confuse the person that is trying to run the report. If I use an edit mask on a parameter field, I put as much information in the Prompt Text field as possible to help the person enter the correct data.

Character	Rule
A	Requires that an alphanumeric character be entered.
a	Allows an alphanumeric character, but it is not required.
0 (zero)	Requires a numeric character to be entered.
9	Allows a numeric character, but it is not required.
#	Allows a digit, space, plus sign or minus sign, but it is not required.
L	Requires a letter to be entered.
?	Allows a letter, but it is not required.
&	Allows any character or space, but it is required.
C	Allows any character or space, but it is not required.
. , : ; - /	Allows separator characters, but it is not required.
<	Converts the characters in the field to lower case.

Table 17-3 Edit mask characters explained

Character	Rule
>	Converts the characters in the field to upper case.
\	Causes the character that follows the \ (back slash) to be taken as a literal.
Password	Does not display the actual characters that are entered. Instead, circles appear when text is entered into this field.

Table 17-3 Edit mask characters explained (Continued)

Tips For Parameter Field Exercises

① After saving the existing report with a new report name in step 1 of the parameter field exercises, open the Create New Parameter dialog box, unless instructed otherwise.

② When you see the instruction "Refresh the data", after doing so, you should select the second option, **PROMPT FOR NEW PARAMETER VALUES** on the Refresh Report Data dialog box shown above in Figure 17-9, then click OK or press Enter.

Exercise 17.1: Create An Is Equal To Parameter Field

In this exercise you will enhance the E8.1 Region = CA report by creating a parameter field that will prompt for the state that will be used to run the report.

1. Save the E8.1 report as `E17.1 Is Equal To parameter field`.

2. Type `Region` in the Name field, then change the Type to String. Notice that the **PROMPT TEXT** option at the bottom of the dialog box has the name that you just entered.

3. Open the Select Expert. Open the second drop-down list. At the top of the list you will see the parameter field that you just created, as illustrated in Figure 17-10. Select the Region parameter field, then click OK. You will see the dialog box shown in Figure 17-11 when you preview the report. This dialog box is automatically created and displays the parameter field(s) that the report has.

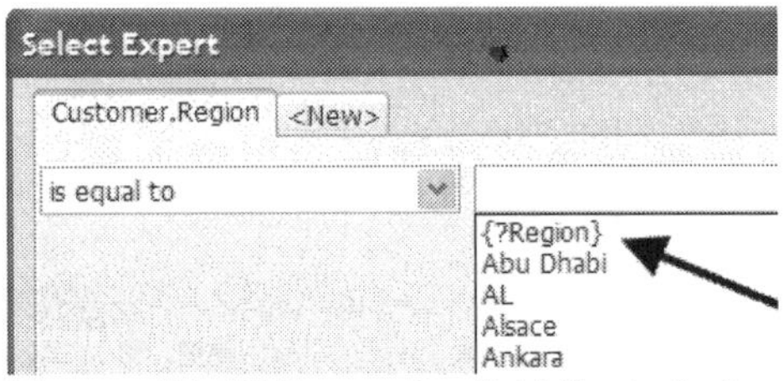

Figure 17-10 Parameter field illustrated on the Select Expert

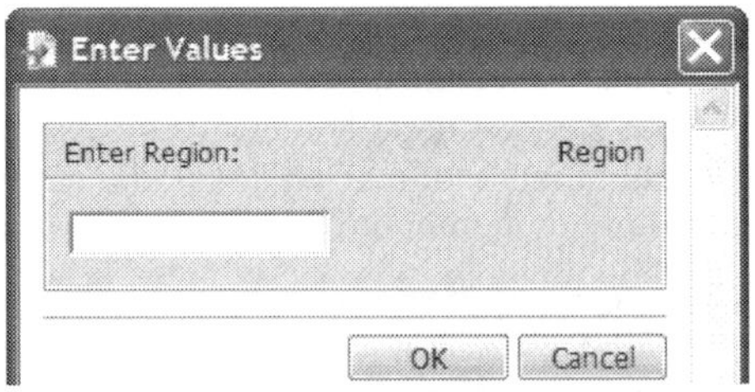

Figure 17-11 Enter Values dialog box

4. Type `CA` in the Region field on the Enter Values dialog box, then press Enter or click OK. You should see six records on the report.

Unless the parameter field has an edit mask, string fields are not case sensitive, which means that you can type "CA" or "ca" and get the same results. When prompted to refresh the data, at this point it does not matter if you refresh the data because you refreshed it a minute or so ago. However, if you were running this report against live data, I would refresh the report every time it is run to make sure that I had the most current data.

> Reports that have a parameter field will not automatically refresh when you switch from the design window to the preview window. Click the **REFRESH** button on the Report Navigation toolbar.

5. Click the Refresh button on the toolbar. You will see the Refresh Report Data dialog box shown earlier in Figure 17-9. Select the second option, then click OK. As you can see, the value that you entered last is still there.

6. Type your first name in the Region field, then press Enter.

Unless your first name is a region in the table, you will not see any data on the report. This isn't what you want to happen. Reports are created to retrieve data, not produce empty reports. If this report used a list of values for the region field, you would have been able to select a region from a list instead of typing it in. That is a better solution.

Exercise 17.2: Create An Is Greater Than Parameter Field

In this exercise you will enhance a report by creating a parameter field that will prompt for the Order Date that will be used to run the report.

1. Save the Chapter 8 Order Date report as `E17.2 Is Greater Than parameter field`.

2. Type `Order Date` in the Name field, then change the Type to Date and click OK.

3. Open the Select Expert, then open the second drop-down list.

Notice that you do not see the parameter field that you just created. That is because the Order Date field is a date/time field. I did this to demonstrate that Crystal Reports does try to help you as much as possible.

4. Close the Select Expert and reopen the parameter dialog box by right-clicking on the Order Date parameter field in the Field Explorer and selecting Edit. Change the Type to Date Time, then click OK.

5. Open the Select Expert. Select the Order Date parameter field in the second drop-down list.

6. Add the Record Number special field to the Report Footer section. Preview the report. You will see the Enter Values dialog box.

Calendar Control

There are two options for entering a date. The date can be typed in or it can be selected from the calendar control. If you entered data in a parameter field that isn't valid, the report would run, but not return any records, which would cause the report to be empty. This is why it is a good idea that parameter fields have a list of values or a way to select data as often as possible. All fields on the Enter Values dialog box are not required. I have noticed that if you leave some types of fields empty and click OK, you will see an error message that says "The value is not valid".

> Notice the icon at the end of the Order Date field shown in Figure 17-12. If you click on this icon you will see the calendar shown in Figure 17-13. Instead of typing in the date, you can use the calendar to select the date.

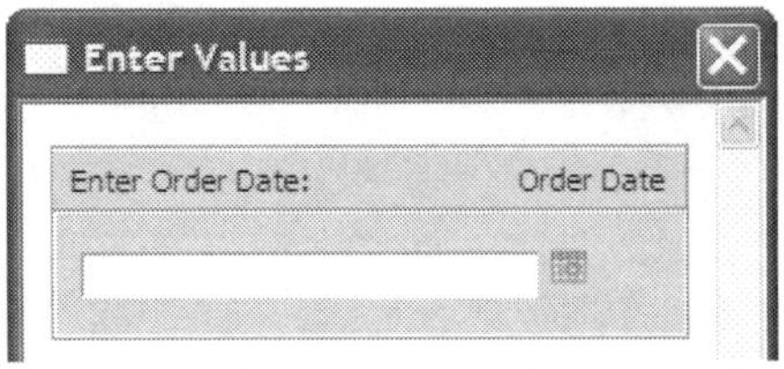

Figure 17-12 Date Time data entry format illustrated

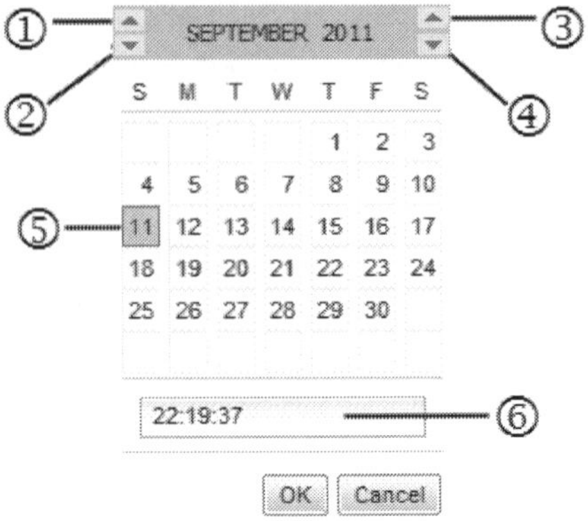

Figure 17-13 Calendar control

> **Date Parameter Fields**
> Crystal Reports 2008 and earlier, automatically added a line of text to the Enter Values dialog box for date fields that had the date/time format that dates and times had to be entered in. This has been removed.

Calendar Control Options

Navigating in this calendar is similar to other electronic calendars that you may have used. If you need a date in the month and year that is displayed on the calendar, click on the date in the calendar. The options are explained below.

① Displays the next month.

② Displays the previous month.

③ Displays the next year.

④ Displays the previous year.

⑤ This is the current day. The current day is highlighted in the calendar.

⑥ Is used to type in a time in HH:MM:SS format. This option is only displayed for Date/Time fields.

7. Select June 24, 2010 in the calendar.

   You should see the date and time on the dialog box, as shown in Figure 17-14, when you run the report. The report should have 3,602 records.

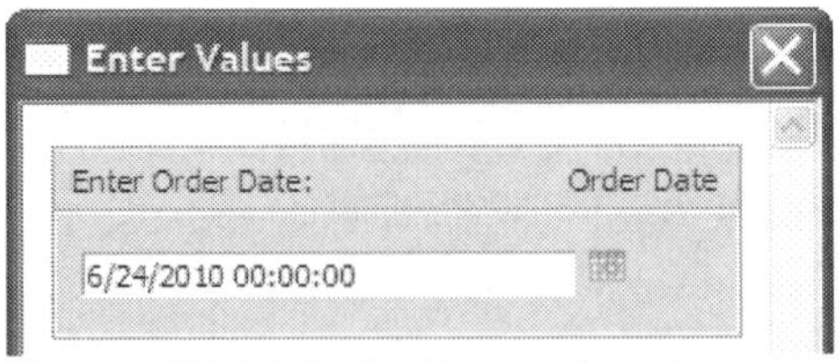

Figure 17-14 Order Date entered

> If you do not type 00:00:00 in the minutes field, you will not get all of the records for the date or date range that you select.

Exercise 17.3: Set A Default Date For A Parameter Field

If you know that the majority of times that a report is run that a certain value will be selected, you can set that value as the default. Setting a default value will still let another value be selected when the report is run. Default values are usually created to save time. In this exercise you will set a default date for the parameter field in the E17.2 report.

1. Save the E17.2 report as `E17.3 Parameter field with a default value.`

2. Open the parameter dialog box for the Order Date field. In the Value Options section, click in the Setting column for the **DEFAULT VALUE** option and type `6/24/2010`, as shown in Figure 17-15.

Option	Setting
Show on (Viewer) Panel	Editable
Prompt Text	Enter Order Date:
Prompt With Description Only	False
Optional Prompt	False
Default Value	6/24/2010 12:00:00 AM

Figure 17-15 Default Value option illustrated

3. Preview the report, then refresh the data. Select the second option on the Refresh Report Data dialog box. You will see the default date that you just added to the parameter field.

4. Select the date 7/15/2011 in the calendar. The report should have 1,977 records. If you see a different number of records, run the report again and type 00:00:00 as the time.

There isn't much use in saving the data with a report that has a parameter value, unless the report will be exported. Reports with parameter fields usually refresh the data.

The remaining exercises in this chapter should not save the data with the report. After completing step 1 in the exercises, open the Report Options dialog box and clear the **SAVE DATA WITH REPORT** option.

List Of Values

If you used a previous version of Crystal Reports, you will notice changes in the list of values option. As you learned in Exercise 17.1, if a parameter field does not have a default value or a drop-down list with values, it is possible that the person running the report will type in the values incorrectly. As much as possible, you should avoid creating parameter fields that allow this to happen. Instead, you should provide a list of values for the parameter field. There are three list of values types that you can create for parameter fields, as discussed below.

① **STATIC PROMPT** The values are stored in the report.
② **DYNAMIC PROMPT** The values are not stored in the report, they are stored in a database.
③ **CASCADING PROMPT** The values are not stored in the report, they are stored in a database.

A list of values is the data that the person running the report will select from. You can use the same list of values for different prompts in the same report. For example, if the report prompted for a customer "Bill to" state and a "Ship to" state, you could use the same list of states for both parameter fields.

List Of Value Categories

There are two list of value categories as discussed below.

① **UNMANAGED LISTS** are stored in the report file. This type of list of values can use report fields or commands as the data source. If you are not going to publish the reports to the Business Objects Enterprise, you can use an unmanaged list of values.
② **MANAGED LISTS** are stored in the Business Objects Enterprise. Managed lists of values are based on a Business View, even if the report is not based on a Business View.

> The dynamic and cascading list of values exercises that you will complete in the next chapter are not for reports that are published on a Crystal Reports or Business Objects Enterprise Server.

Static And Dynamic List Of Values

As you learned in the exercises that you have completed earlier in this chapter, you can create parameter fields that require the person running the report to type in the data when prompted. You also saw that this type of parameter field can cause errors to be generated or produce empty reports. This is not the best solution. You can create a static or dynamic list of values to use with the parameter field. Depending on the data, one type of list of values may be better suited then another. It is easy to get carried away and create all dynamic lists, but if a static list is better suited for the parameter field, you should use it. In addition to static and dynamic list of values, you can also create a cascading list of values, which is a type of dynamic list.

Static List Of Values

Out of the three types of list of values, static lists are the easiest to create. They are best suited for values that do not change or for data that is not stored in a field. An example of a static list of values would be a list of states. Keep in mind that static lists do not change unless you change them. That is the biggest drawback of a static list of values. I personally only use a static list of values if the list is small, because the values are stored in the report which makes the report file size larger. The benefit of static lists is that they are retrieved faster. There are three ways to create a static list of values, as discussed below. You can use any combination of these options to create the list that you need.

① Import the values from a field in a table.
② Type the list of values in manually.
③ Import the list of values from a text file.

Adding Values Manually

There are two ways to add values manually on the Create (or Edit) Parameter dialog box, as discussed below.

① Click on the **CLICK HERE TO ADD ITEM** option in the Value column.
② Click the **INSERT** button.

Exercise 17.4: Create A Static List Of Values Manually

In this exercise you will create a static list of values manually. In Exercise 8.2, the report was limited to two regions: OH and FL. In this exercise you will limit the regions to five, but the person running the report will be able to select which of the five regions will to appear on the report from a drop-down list.

1. Save the E8.2 report as `E17.4 Manual static list of values.`
2. Type `Region` in the Name field.
3. Select one of the ways discussed above to add a value and type `OH` in the first row in the Value/Description section of the dialog box, then type `Ohio` in the Description column.

If the data in the Value column contains an ID number, abbreviation or other data that the person running the report may not be familiar with, you should enter a brief explanation in the Description column. The information that you enter in the Description column will appear in the drop-down list next to the content in the Value column. The description is only used for display purposes.

> You do not have to enter a value in the Description column for every option in the list, only those that you think the person running the report may not understand.

If you have entered a description for every value in the list, you can change the **PROMPT WITH DESCRIPTION ONLY** option at the bottom of the dialog box to True. If you do this, the only values that will appear in the drop-down list on the Enter Values dialog box will be the values in the Description column.

If there is data in a report that you do not want everyone to see, you can create a list of values that will prevent everyone from seeing all of the data. For example, you may not want all sales reps to see sales outside of their region. In this example, you would create a parameter field that lists the regions that you want the sales reps to be able to view. You can create this type of list of values with static or dynamic lists.

4. Add the following regions to the Value column: CA, PA, WI and FL.

5. Change the **ALLOW CUSTOM VALUES** option at the bottom of the dialog box to False.

   In this report, you are only going to allow the report to be run for one of the regions that you added to the static list of values.

   You should have the options shown in Figure 17-16.

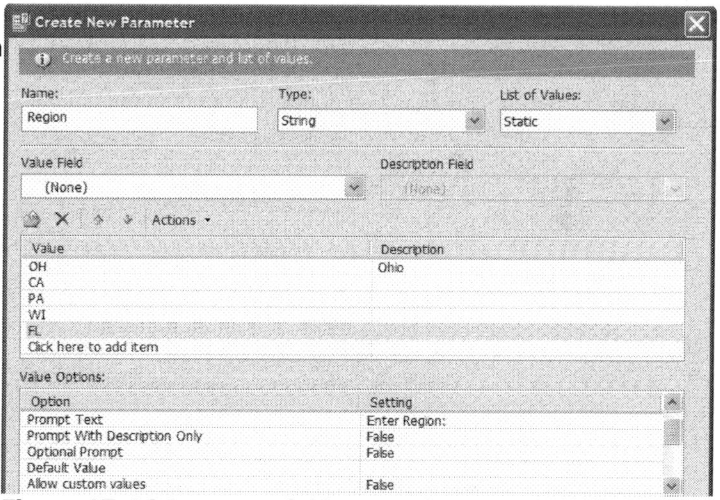

Figure 17-16 Parameter field options for a static list of values

6. Open the Select Expert and select the Region parameter field. Remove the other values from the list. Preview the report.

You will see the Enter Values dialog box. If you open the drop-down list, you will see the values that you added to the static list of values, as shown in Figure 17-17. As you can see, the first option also displays the description that you entered. If you try to type in this field you will see that you can't. That is because the **ALLOW CUSTOM VALUES** option is set to False, as shown above in Figure 17-16.

Also notice that the values are not in alphabetical order. They are in the order that they were added to the Value/Description table. In the next part of the exercise you will learn how to change the order of values in a static list of values.

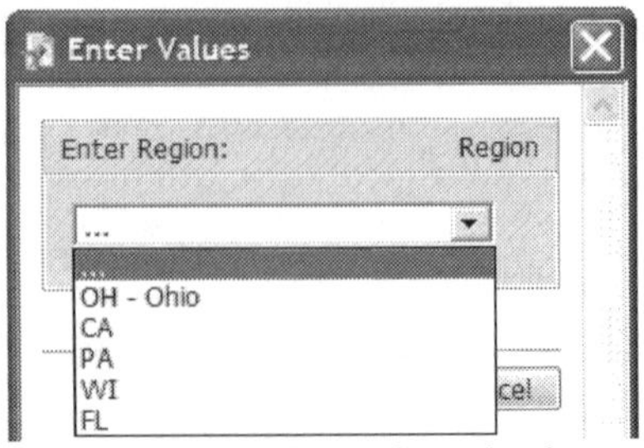

Figure 17-17 Static list of values

If the **ALLOW CUSTOM VALUES** option was set to True on the parameter dialog box, you would see a field at the bottom of the Enter Values dialog box that would let you type in additional values, as shown in Figure 17-18.

The person running the report could select an option from the drop-down list or type in the value that they want.

This would be useful if the static list contained the 10 most used options, which would keep the list small, while providing additional flexibility by allowing data to be entered manually.

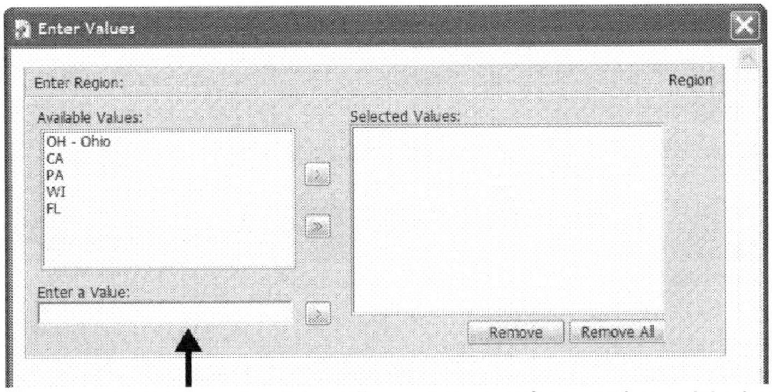

Figure 17-18 Result of the Allow custom values option set to true

7. Select PA from the list and run the report. You should have five records on the report. Leave the report open to complete the next part of the exercise.

Change The Sort Order Of The Static List Of Values

As you saw in the previous part of this exercise, the states are not in alphabetical order. Most lists are in alphabetical order because it is easier to find the value that you need. In this part of the exercise you will learn how to change the order of the items in the list.

> There are two ways to change the sort order of a list of values. The instructions in this exercise are best suited for a list that does not need a lot of changes or for a list that you do not necessarily want in alphabetical order, but just in a different order then the list is currently in.
>
> An example of this would be if you wanted to put a specific value at the top of the list because it is the most used option and then put the rest of the list in alphabetical order. You may have seen this on a web-based form for a country field. You would see "USA" at the top of the drop-down list because the company knows that most of their subscribers or customers are in the USA. Below that option, the rest of the countries are in alphabetical order.

1. Open the Edit Parameter dialog box for the Region field.

2. Click on the CA value, then click the Up button illustrated in Figure 17-19.

   Rearrange the other values in the column so that the entire list is in alphabetical order.

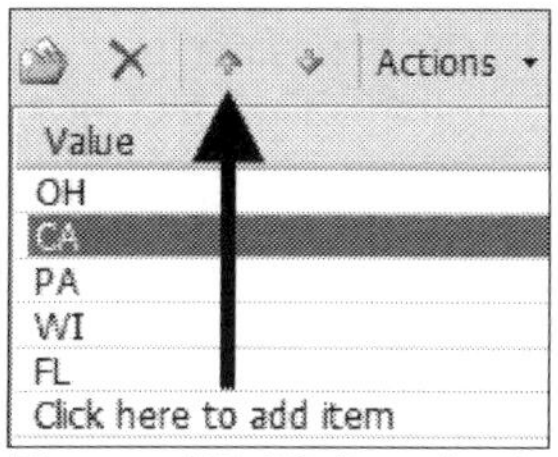

Figure 17-19 Reorder buttons illustrated

3. Preview the report, then refresh the data. Select the second option. When you open the drop-down list, you will see that the values are in alphabetical order.

How To Sort The Entire List At One Time

To sort the entire list at one time, click on the column heading (Value or Description) that you want to sort the list by. You will see the arrow illustrated in Figure 17-20. If the arrow is pointing up, the values will be sorted in ascending order.

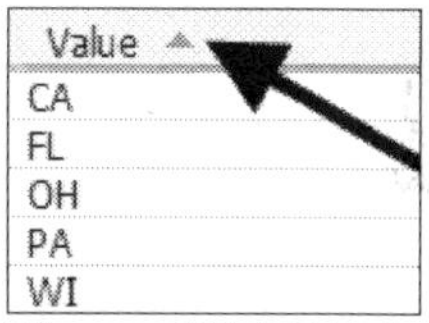

Figure 17-20 Column sorting options illustrated

If the arrow is pointing up and you click on the arrow, it will point down and the values will be sorted in descending order.

Importing A Static List Of Values

The list of values that you created manually in Exercise 17.4 was small, so it did not take a lot of time to set up. Often, that is not the case and you could have 50 or more values for a static list. If the data for the static list exists in a table or text document, it is easier to import the list. If you know that you do not need all of the values in the list that you will import, you have the two options discussed below for removing the values that you do not need. You will have to evaluate which option is best, on a list by list basis.

① Import the list as is, then manually delete or change the options as needed on the parameter dialog box.

② Delete the values or make the changes to the list before importing it as a list of values. If the data that will be imported is in a table, it may not be possible or feasible to change the live data.

If the list of values (static or dynamic) has a description, it will also be imported, if all of the values are imported. If the values are added individually from a database, the Description column will not be imported.

Exercise 17.5: Create An Imported Static List Of Values

In this exercise you will import values from a field in a table to create a static list of values.

1. Save the E8.2 report as `E17.5 Imported static list of values`.

2. Type `Region` in the Name field.

3. Open the Value Field drop-down list and select the Region field.

4. Click the Actions button and select the **APPEND ALL DATABASE VALUES** option.

You will now see all of the values from the Region field from the Customer table. If there were values in the list that you did not want or need, you can delete them by clicking on the value that you do not want and then click the Delete button (the X button after the Insert button).

5. Change the Allow custom values option to False, then click OK.

6. Open the Select Expert and select the parameter field in the second drop-down list, then remove the other values from the list and click OK. When you run the report and open this parameter drop-down list you will see all of the values from the field in the table. If you changed any values on the Create New Parameter dialog box, you will see the changes in the drop-down list. The data in the table was not changed.

> **Parameters Panel**
> This functionality is not available on the Design or Preview tab. It is available on the free Crystal Reports viewer. http://www.businessobjects.com/forms/crystalreports/viewer/

Parameters Panel

The options shown in Figure 17-21 make it easier for people running reports with parameter fields. The options are on the left side of the Preview tab and are activated by default when a report is run or refreshed that has a parameter field. The Parameters Panel toolbar options are explained in Table 17-4.

You can change one of the parameter options by double-clicking in the space below the parameter that you want to change. For example, if you wanted to change the date range, double-click on the 2/18/2010 date. The Enter Values dialog box will open with the prompt to change the date range. After the report is run once, you can select a different date from the Parameters section shown in Figure 17-22, by double-clicking on the date. Once you select the date, click the Apply Changes button on the Parameters toolbar.

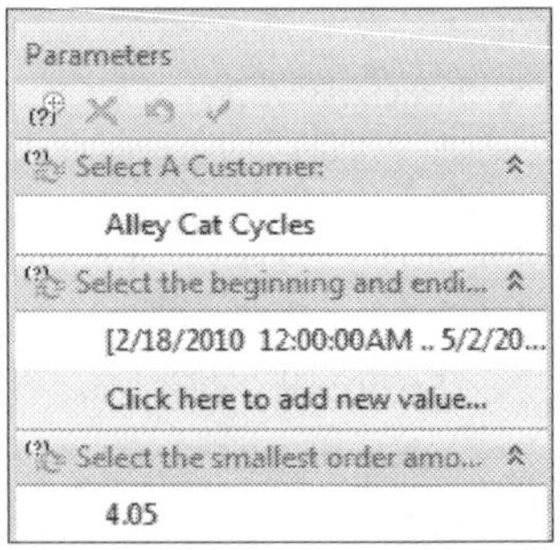

Figure 17-21 Parameters Panel options

Figure 17-22 Calendar in the Parameters Panel

Button	Description
Prompt for parameters	Opens the Enter Values dialog box.
Remove Value	Deletes the last value that was added to the parameter panel.
Revert all changes	Deletes all of the parameter changes since the report was last run.
Apply changes	Runs the report with the current parameter options.
Enter {Value}	Toggles displaying the last value entered on the Enter Values dialog box.

Table 17-4 Parameters toolbar buttons explained

CREATING DYNAMIC & CASCADING PARAMETER FIELDS

Dynamic and cascading parameter fields add more functionality to the parameter fields that you learned how to create in the previous chapter. They filter the data in fields on the Enter Values dialog box. In this chapter you will learn how to do the following:

- ☑ Create a dynamic list of values
- ☑ Create cascading prompts
- ☑ Use the Allow Range value option
- ☑ Use the long list of values options
- ☑ Combine range and multiple values
- ☑ Use formula fields in parameter fields
- ☑ Use parameter fields to sort and group data on the report

CHAPTER 18

Dynamic List Of Values

Dynamic and cascading prompts are probably one of the most talked about requested features. These prompts allow for greater flexibility when creating reports.

In Chapter 3, you learned some basic report design techniques. You also learned that different groups of people may need similar reports. One of the ways that you can create one report that works for slightly different needs is by incorporating dynamic and cascading prompts.

Unlike a static list of values that are not refreshed each time the report is run, dynamic and cascading list of values are refreshed each time the report is run. This means that if new values are added to the field in the table that the parameter field is getting the data from, the new values are also available in the parameter field.

For example, if the dynamic parameter field is based on the product name field and 12 new products are added, those 12 products would also be available in the parameter field list. The opposite is also true. If values are deleted from the field in the underlying table, they would no longer be available in the parameter field list. Dynamic list of values are best suited for data that changes in a table, like new customers or a growing list of products.

> While you will not notice this completing the exercises in this book because the database is stored on your hard drive, dynamic and cascading lists take longer to be retrieved then static lists. Depending on the number of records in the table that the dynamic or cascading list is being retrieved from, you may notice a delay between the time that you open the drop-down list and the time that you actually see the values appear in the list.

Exercise 18.1: Create A Dynamic Region List Of Values

In Exercise 17.5 you imported regions from a table associated with the report. When a customer is added that is in a region that does not currently exist in the values for the parameter field, the E17.5 report would not include the new region on the report, meaning that the report will not contain up to date information because static lists are not automatically updated. In this exercise you will create a dynamic list of values for the Region field, which means that the values in the drop-down list will always be up to date.

1. Save the E8.2 report as `E18.1 Dynamic region list of values.`

2. Type `Region` in the Name field, then open the List of Values drop-down list and select **DYNAMIC.**

3. Click the Insert button (It's the yellow button with the folder icon). You will see a list of fields that are available for the dynamic list. Select the Region field. You should have the options shown in Figure 18-1.

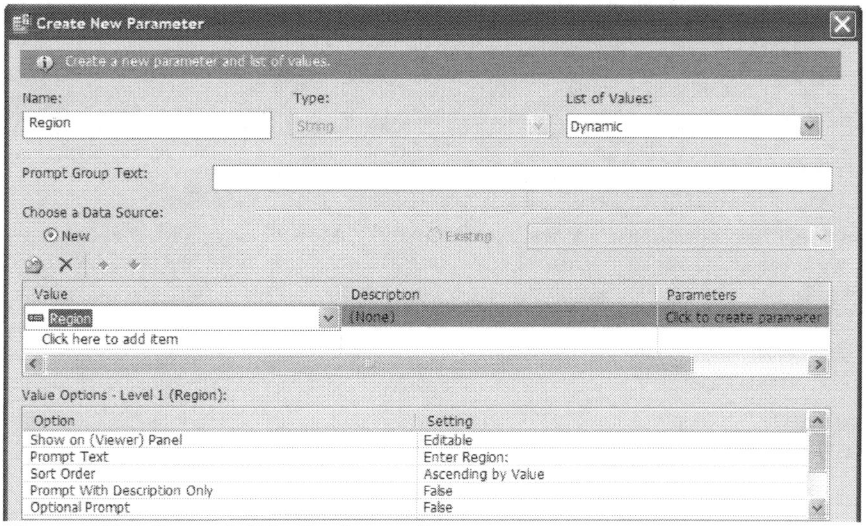

Figure 18-1 Dynamic list of values options

The **EXISTING** option in the Data Source section is only available when the report already has a dynamic list.

The **DESCRIPTION** column works the same for dynamic lists as it does for static lists.

The **PARAMETERS** column is used when creating a dynamic cascading prompt. This is how you create the hierarchy between the fields that will be part of the cascading prompt.

4. Open the Select Expert and select the parameter field, then delete the other values from the Region field.

5. Preview the report. You will see that you can only select one value from the Region drop-down list. Save the changes and close the report.

> If this report was going to be put into production, it would probably be a good idea to change the operator to "Is equal to" so that when you read the formula, it will match the objectives of the report. Otherwise, it may be confusing later if you have to edit the report. If you leave it as it is, when the report is run, only one region can be selected from the drop-down list because the Allow multiple values parameter option is set to False.

Cascading Prompts And List Of Values

Cascading prompts are created like dynamic prompts. Unlike the dynamic list of values, cascading prompts contain related data and you must have at least two parameter fields to create cascading prompts. A cascading list of values will reduce the number of items to select from in at least one of the fields on the Enter Values dialog box.

The difference between dynamic and cascading prompts is that the option selected in the first prompt on the Enter Values dialog box is used to filter the values that will be displayed in the second prompt. An example of cascading prompts would be a list of suppliers and a list of products. The first prompt would contain the suppliers. Once a supplier is selected, the values in the second drop-down list would only contain products for the supplier that was selected in the first prompt.

> When you create cascading prompts, Crystal Reports will automatically change the name of the parameter field. It will be renamed to a combination of the name that you gave the field and the name of the field that it is connected to in the prompt group. You can rename the parameter field in the Field Explorer back to what you had originally named it.

Exercise 18.2: Create Cascading Prompts For Countries And Regions

In this exercise you will create two prompts. The first one is for the country, the second one is for the region. The region drop-down list will only show states (regions) that are in the country that is selected in the first prompt. The Chapter 18 Parameter Fields report currently displays all countries and regions. The cascading prompts that you will create for this report will allow a specific country and specific region to be selected when the report is run.

1. Save the Chapter 18 Parameter Fields report as `E18.2 Cascading prompts for countries and regions`.

2. Type `Countries and Regions` in the Name field, then select the Dynamic List of values option.

3. In the **PROMPT GROUP TEXT** field type `Select a country, then select a region:`.

4. Click the Insert button, then select the Country field. Click in the second row and select the Region field.

5. Open the Select Expert, then click on the Region field on the Choose Field dialog box. In this step, you have to select the last field that was added on the Create New Parameter dialog box.

6. Select the "Is equal to" operator.

   Select the Countries and Regions - Region parameter field.

   Your dialog box should look like the one shown in Figure 18-2. Notice that the Region field is not enabled. When you select a country, the region field will be enabled.

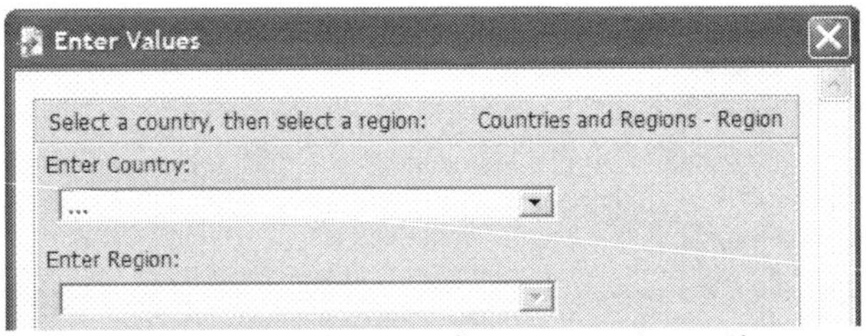

Figure 18-2 Dynamic cascading parameter options

7. Select USA, then select CA. There should be six records on the report.

Did you notice that the only states (regions) in the second drop-down list are for the USA? If you select a different country, you will only see regions in that country. This is the dynamic cascading (filtering) effect.

Exercise 18.3: Create Cascading Prompts For Customers And Their Orders

Many people in a company may have the need to view a particular customers orders. This is the type of report that dynamic cascading parameters were designed to handle.

1. Save the Chapter 18 Customer Orders report as `E18.3 Cascading prompts for customer orders`.

2. In the Name field type `Customer Orders`, then select the Dynamic List of values option.

3. In the Prompt Group Text field type `Select a customer, then select the Order # that you want to view:`.

4. Select the Customer Name field in the Value column.

5. Change the **PROMPT TEXT** option to `Select A Customer:`, as illustrated in Figure 18-3.

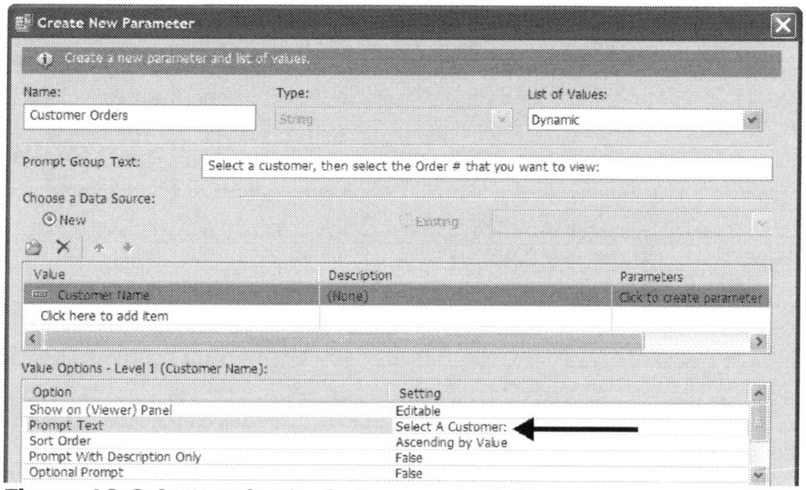

Figure 18-3 Options for the first parameter field

6. Click in the second Value row and select the Order ID field, then change the Prompt Text option to `Select the Order Number that you want to view:`.

7. Open the Select Expert, select the Order ID, then click OK.

8. Select the "Is equal to" operator, then select the Customer Orders - Order ID parameter field in the next drop-down list.

9. Preview the report. Select the customer, Alley Cat Cycles, then select the order number 2300. The order numbers in the drop-down list are for the customer that is selected in the first drop-down list.

   Your dialog box should look like the one shown in Figure 18-4.

   You should see the data for order number 2300.

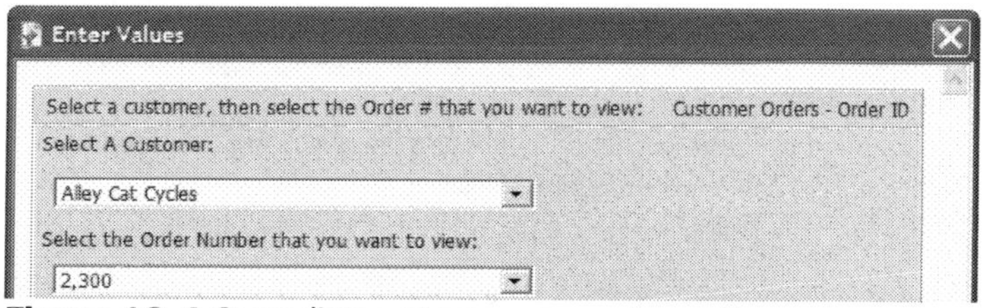

Figure 18-4 Cascading customer parameter options

> What may not be obvious is that once you click OK on the Create New Parameter dialog box, you can't go back and edit cascading parameter field options. For that reason, I create each of the fields for the group separately and then put them in a group parameter field, which you will learn how to do. Doing this allows you to edit each of the fields in the parameter group if necessary.

Allow Range Values And Allow Multiple Values Options

The reports that you have created parameter fields for in this chapter have added a lot of interactivity between the user and the report. This allows the person running the report to have more control over the records that will appear on the report. What you have probably noticed is that each parameter field that you have created only allows one option to be selected. In some instances this can limit the data that displays on reports in a way that is not best suited for the user.

The Create New Parameter dialog box has two options that will allow more flexibility. The **ALLOW RANGE VALUES** option allows the parameter field to accept high and low values, like the "Is between" Select Expert operator. A good use of this option would be for a date range. The **ALLOW MULTIPLE VALUES** option allows more than one value to be selected from the parameter field. A good use of this option would be if you need to select more than one value from the same field. An example is if you needed to select several products to see which ones are not selling.

Allow Range Values Option

When this option is set to **TRUE**, you will be able to use one parameter field to accept two values, a start of range value and an end of range value. More than likely, you will use this to allow date ranges to be entered. When a parameter field has this option set to True, on the Select Expert you have to select the "Is equal to" operator, because the parameter field contains the start and end values in one field. A parameter field with the range value is the equivalent of the "Is between" operator.

By default, the Start and End of Range fields have the **INCLUDE THIS VALUE** option checked. This means that the values entered in both fields will be included in the record selection process. If you clear this option for either field, the value will not be included in the record selection process. This is the equivalent of the "Is greater than" and "Is less than" Select Expert operators.

Earlier in this chapter you read about the **NO LOWER VALUE** and **NO UPPER VALUE** options. When the Allow range values option is set to True, these options are not checked. This means that only records that have a value between the start and end range values will be included in the record selection process. These options were also discussed earlier in conjunction with date fields. These options also work with non date field ranges. If either of these options are checked, the input field is disabled and you can't enter anything in the field. These options can also be used like the "Is greater than" and "Is less than" Select Expert operators.

Only entering a value in the Start of Range input field and checking the No lower value option will retrieve all records that have a value greater than (or equal to, if the Include this value option is also checked for the field) the value in the Start of Range field.

Only entering a value in the End of Range input field and checking the No lower value option will retrieve all records that have a value less than (or equal to, if the Include this value option is also checked for the field) the value in the End of Range field.

Exercise 18.4: Use The Allow Range Values Option With Dates

In Exercise 17.2 you created a parameter field that only allowed one date to be entered. In this exercise you will modify that parameter field to allow a date range to be entered.

1. Save the E17.2 report as `E18.4 Date range parameter field.`

2. Open the Order Date parameter dialog box. At the bottom of the dialog box, change the Allow range values option to True.

3. Open the Select Expert. Change the Order Date operator to "Is equal to", then select the parameter field.

4. Refresh the data. Select the start date 3/1/2011 and the end date 3/31/2011. You should have the options selected that are shown in Figure 18-5.

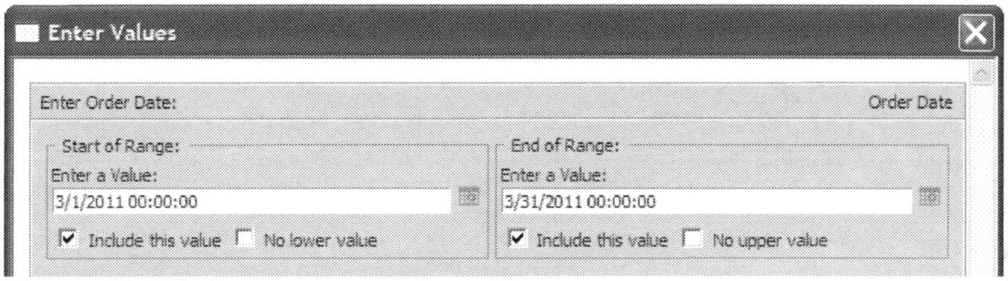

Figure 18-5 Date range parameter options

You can also use the "Is not equal to" operator with range value parameter fields.

If you ran the report again and cleared the **INCLUDE THIS VALUE** option on the Start of Range field, there would be fewer records on the report. That means that some orders were placed on 3/1/2011. To verify that, check the Include this value option, then change the End of Range value to 3/2/2011. Clear the Include this value option on the End of Range field. The reason that I entered 3/2/2011 is to be able to account for the time portion of the date/time field. I find this easier then typing in the equivalent of 11:59:59 PM as the end time.

If you wanted to run the report for one day, you would enter the same date in the start and end of range fields. For Date/Time fields, you would have to include the equivalent of 11:59:59 PM on the End of Range field or you could enter the next day and use a time of 00:00:00.

If you are running a monthly report and do not know if there are 30 or 31 days in the month, enter the first day of the next month that you are running the report for in the End of range field and clear the Include this value option. Doing this will include all records for the prior month.

Using Range Values For Non Date Data

A lot of the time, the range value parameter field is used for dates. You can use range parameter fields for other types of data. Two other uses that come to mind are: 1) To only print records in a zip code range. 2) If you wanted to print a list of customers whose last name started with a specific letter or was in a range of letters, like customers whose last name starts with A through D.

Long List Of Values Options

Parameter field drop-down lists that have a lot of values are now separated into groups of 200 records. If the value that you are looking for is not in the first group of values, open the drop-down list shown in Figure 18-6 and select another level or click on the navigation buttons on either side of the drop-down list.

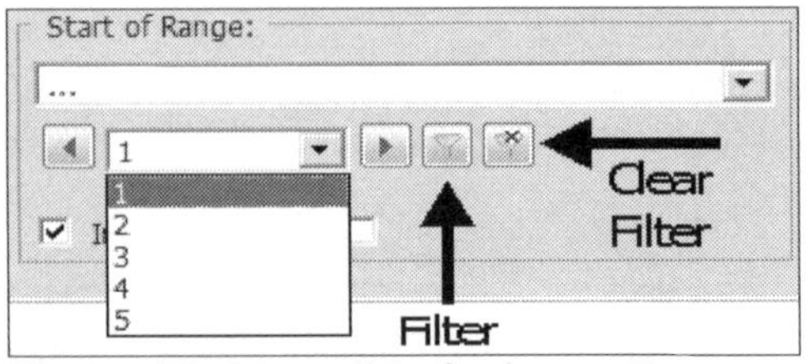

Figure 18-6 Long list of values options

The **FILTER** button is used to create a filter for the values in the entire list.

The **CLEAR FILTER** button removes the filter for the values in the drop-down list.

How To Change The Default Long List Of Values Quantity For Parameter Fields
The information below explains how to change the number of items displayed in a parameter field drop-down list. The path to the registry key that you can change is: HKEY_CURRENT_USER\Software\SAP Business Objects\Suite XI 4.0\Crystal Reports \Report View. If the DWord value **PROMPTINGLOVBATCHSIZE** does not exist, as illustrated in Figure 18-7, create it, then enter the default value that you want to use, as shown in Figure 18-8. Select Decimal as the base value.

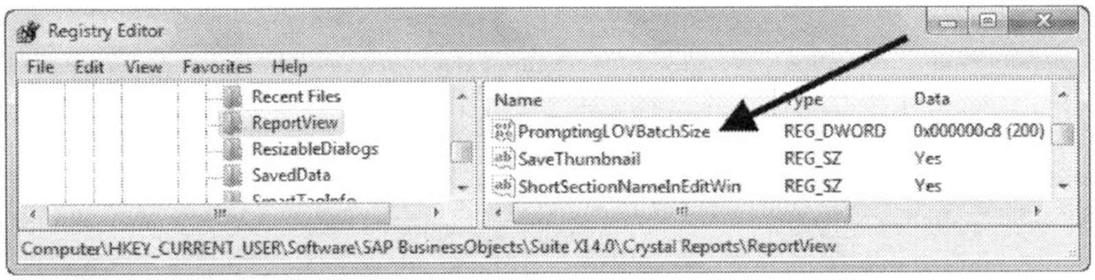

Figure 18-7 Registry key illustrated

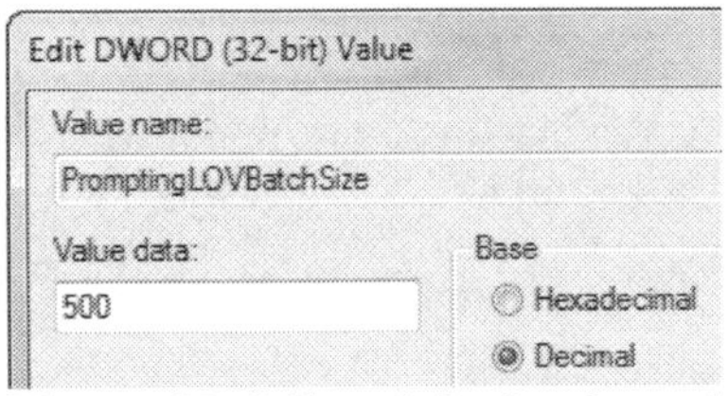

Figure 18-8 New default value entered for the Long list of values

Exercise 18.5: Use The Allow Range Values Option With Currency Values

In the previous exercise you used the Allow range values option with a date field. You can also use this option with numeric and currency fields. In this exercise you will use the option to find all orders that are within a certain dollar amount range.

1. Save the E16.1 report as `E18.5 Currency range parameter field`.

2. Type `Order Amount Range` in the Name field, then change the Type to Currency. Select the Dynamic List of Values option.

3. In the Prompt Group Text field. Type `Enter the order amount range for the report:`, then add the Order Amount field to the Value column.

4. Change the following options, then click OK.
   Prompt Text `Select the order amount:`
   Change the Allow range values option to True.

5. Open the Select Expert and click on the **NEW** tab. Select the Order Amount field, then click OK. Select the "Is equal to" operator, then select the Order Amount Range parameter field.

6. Preview the report. Select the first order amount over $1,000 for the Start of Range value. Select the first order amount over $2,000 for the End of Range value.

7. Clear the Include this value option for the End of Range field. Doing this will only display orders that have an order amount between $1,000 and $2,000.

   You should have the options shown in Figure 18-9.

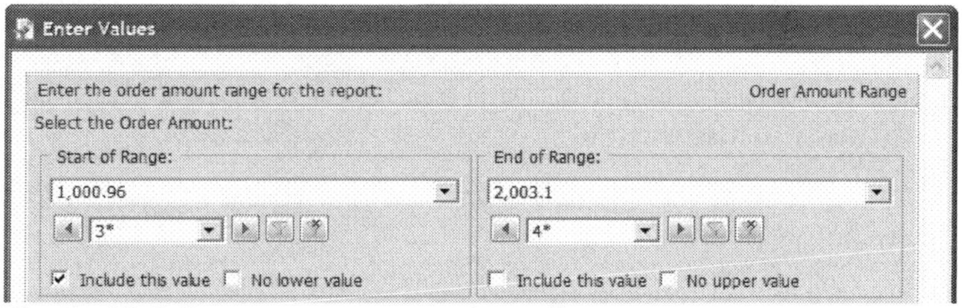

Figure 18-9 Currency range parameter options

Allow Multiple Values Option

When you set this option to **TRUE**, more than one value can be selected in the parameter field. This is the equivalent of the "Is one of" Select Expert operator. In Exercise 18.1 you created a dynamic list of values for the region field. When the report was run, only one region could be selected. You may often have a report request that requires that more than one value be included in the selection process. When the Allow multiple values option is set to True, you are creating what is called an **ARRAY**. This means that the field can contain more than one value.

> If the **ALLOW CUSTOM VALUES** and **ALLOW MULTIPLE VALUES** options are set to True, values can be added from the **AVAILABLE VALUES** list box and typed in manually if the values in the Available Values list box are from a static list. This cannot be done with dynamic and cascading list of values.

Exercise 18.6: Use The Allow Multiple Values Option With A Static List Of Values

In Exercise 17.4 you created a static list of values by manually entering them. As you just learned, in addition to setting the Allow multiple values option to True, setting the Allow custom values option to True also, will allow the person running the report to select values from the static list and type in other values. In this exercise you will modify the parameter field to allow multiple values to be selected from the static list and allow other values to be entered.

1. Save the E17.4 report as `E18.6 Customer multi value parameter field`.

2. Open the Parameter dialog box for the Region field. Change the following options, then click OK.

   Prompt Text `Select the region(s) or type them in below:`
   Change the Allow custom values and Allow multiple values options to True.

3. Open the Select Expert. If you see a warning message that says the array must be subscripted, click OK. Select the "Is equal to" operator on the Region parameter field, then select the Region parameter field.

4. Preview the report. Select the FL and PA regions from the Available Values list and add them to the Selected Values list.

> If you hold down the **CTRL** key, you can click on multiple options in the Available Values list and then click the **ADD** button to add them to the Selected Values list box at one time.

5. Manually add the TX and NY regions to the Selected Values list by typing one value in the Enter a Value field and then click the arrow button at the end of the field.

   Your dialog box should have the options shown in Figure 18-10. There should be nine records on the report.

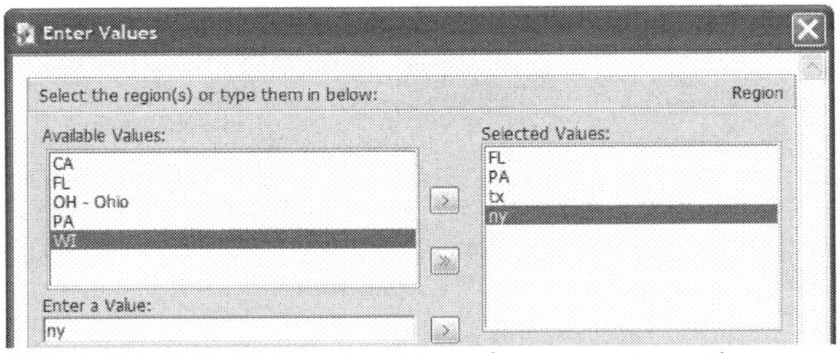

Figure 18-10 Multiple and custom value parameter options

Exercise 18.7: Use The Allow Multiple Values Option With A Dynamic List Of Values

With a dynamic list, there is usually no need to allow custom values. In this exercise, you will modify a report to be able to select the shipping carriers that will appear on the report.

1. Save the Chapter 9 Shipping Info report as `E18.7 Dynamic multi value list`.

2. Type `Ship Via` in the Name field, then select the Dynamic List of Values option.

3. In the Prompt Group Text field type `Select the Ship Via option(s) for the report:`.

4. Add the Ship Via field to the Value column, then change the Allow multiple values option to True.

5. Open the Select Expert and change the Ship Via operator to "Is equal to", then select the Ship Via parameter field.

6. Preview the report.

   Add the last three shipping options to the Selected Values list, as shown in Figure 18-11.

   The report may be easier to read if it was sorted on the Ship Via field.

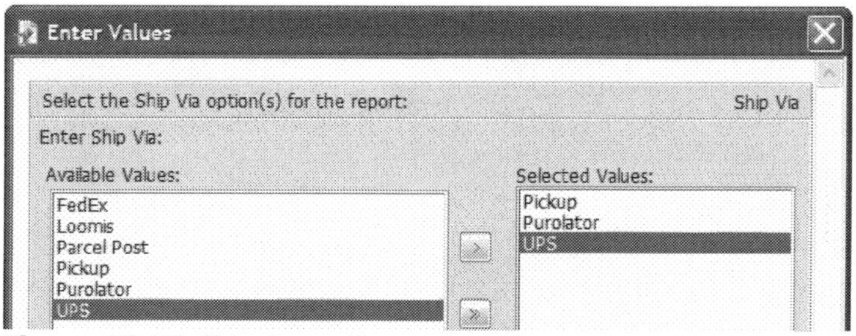

Figure 18-11 Shipping options selected

7. Sort the report on the Ship Via field in ascending order. The first shipping method on the report should be Pickup.

Combining Range And Multiple Values

What may not initially be apparent is that these two options can be combined on the same parameter field. Doing this allows for maximum flexibility and options when the report is run. On a report that uses a date parameter field, you can allow multiple date ranges to be entered.

For example, if you wanted to be able to compare the orders for the first five days of three months, you could enter 1/1/2011 to 1/5/2011, 3/1/2011 to 3/5/2011 and 5/1/2011 to 5/5/2011 on the same parameter field. Another example would be if you wanted to see orders 1001 to 1050 and 1100 to 1124 on the same report. Setting the Allow range values and Allow multiple values options to true would allow you to create parameter fields for both of the examples just discussed.

Exercise 18.8: Combine Range And Multiple Values For A Date Field

In Exercise 18.4 the parameter field that you created only allowed one date range to be entered. In this exercise you will modify that parameter field to allow multiple date ranges to be entered.

1. Save the E18.4 report as `E18.8 Multiple date range parameter field`.

2. Open the Order Date parameter field dialog box. Change the following options, then click OK.
   Prompt Text `Enter the Order Date range(s):`
   Change the Allow multiple values option to True.

3. Preview the report. Refresh the data. After you add the End of Range date, click the **ADD RANGE** button, then add the next date range. Add the following date ranges to the Selected Values list. 1/1/2011 to 1/5/2011, 3/1/2011 to 3/5/2011 and 5/1/2011 to 5/5/2011. Don't forget to set the time to 00:00:00. Your dialog box should have the options shown in Figure 18-12. There should be 95 records on the report.

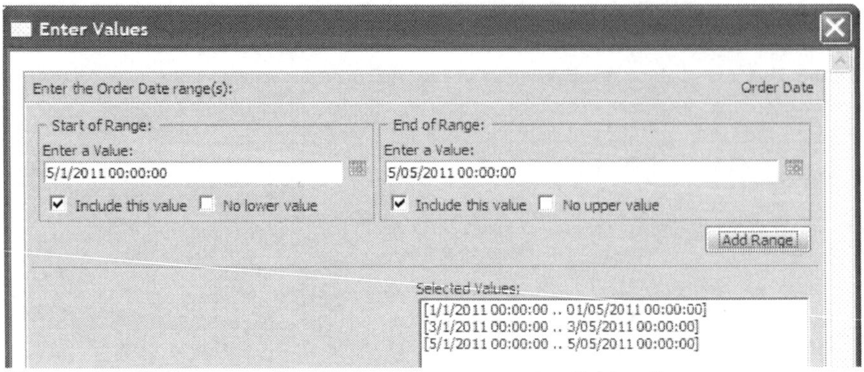

Figure 18-12 Range and multiple values parameter field options

Cascading Parameter Groups And Multi Value Parameter Options

Now that you have learned how to create cascading parameter groups and multi value parameter fields, the options that reports can have are almost endless. If you find that you cannot create the cascading parameter groups that you need, you can create individual parameter fields and add each one to the Select Expert and they will all appear on the Enter Values dialog box.

I prefer this method of one parameter field for each field that I need to query, because I do not have to rename the parameter fields after I create them. This is also very helpful if you need to rearrange the order that the fields appear in on the Enter Values dialog box or if you need to add a new parameter field and place it between two existing parameter fields. This is what you will learn how to do in the next exercise.

Exercise 18.9: Create Dynamic Cascading Prompts For Customers And Their Orders

In this exercise you will create cascading prompts for three fields: Customers, Order Date and Order Amount. The E9.2 report displays the orders by customer. Creating cascading prompts will let the person running the report select a customer and only display orders that meet the date range and order amount that they select. For example, the prompts that you will create in this exercise will let you see all orders placed on or after 1/1/2011 for a specific customer that has order amounts greater than $1,000.

Create The Customer Name Parameter Field

1. Save the E9.2 report as `E18.9 Cascading prompts for customer orders`.
2. Type `Customer Name` in the Name field, then select the Dynamic List of Values option.
3. In the Prompt Group Text field type `Select the customer, date range(s) and minimum order amount:`.
4. Add the Customer Name field to the Value column, then click in the Parameters column. This is what tells Crystal Reports that you want to use this field on the Enter Values dialog box as a cascading prompt field. It should have the same name as the one you typed in the Name field.
5. Change the Prompt Text option to `Select A Customer:`. Click OK.

Create The Order Amount Parameter Field

1. Type `Order Amount` in the Name field. Change the Type to Currency, then select the Dynamic List of Values option.

2. Add the Order Amount field to the Value column, then click in the Parameters column.

3. Change the Prompt Text option to `Select the smallest order amount that you want to see:`. Click OK.

Create The Date Range Parameter Field

1. Type `Date Range` in the Name field. Change the Type to Date Time, then select the Dynamic List of Values option.

2. In the Prompt Group Text field type `You have to select at least one date range. Once selected, click the Add Range button:`.

3. Add the Order Date field to the Value column, then click in the Parameters column.

4. Change the following options, then click OK.
   Prompt Text `Select the beginning and ending order dates from the drop-down lists:`
   Change the Allow multiple values and Allow range values options to True.

Modify The Select Expert Options

1. Open the Select Expert and change the Order Amount operator to "Is greater than or equal to", then select the Order Amount parameter field.

2. Change the Order Date operator to "Is equal to", then select the Date Range parameter field.

3. Click on the New tab, then select the Customer Name field. Select the "Is equal to" operator, then select the Customer Name parameter field.

   The formula on the Select Expert should look like the one shown in Figure 18-13.

```
{Orders.Order Amount} >= {?Order Amount} and
{Orders.Order Date} = {?Date Range} and
{Customer.Customer Name} = {?Customer Name}
```

Figure 18-13 Select Expert formula

Test The Parameter Fields

1. Select the Alley Cat Cycles company, then select the Order Amount 100.4.

2. Select the first and last dates in 2011. This will return all of this customers orders in 2011 that have an order total of $100.40 or more.

   You should have the options selected that are shown in Figure 18-14.

   There should be 29 records on the report.

   Leave the report open to complete the next exercise.

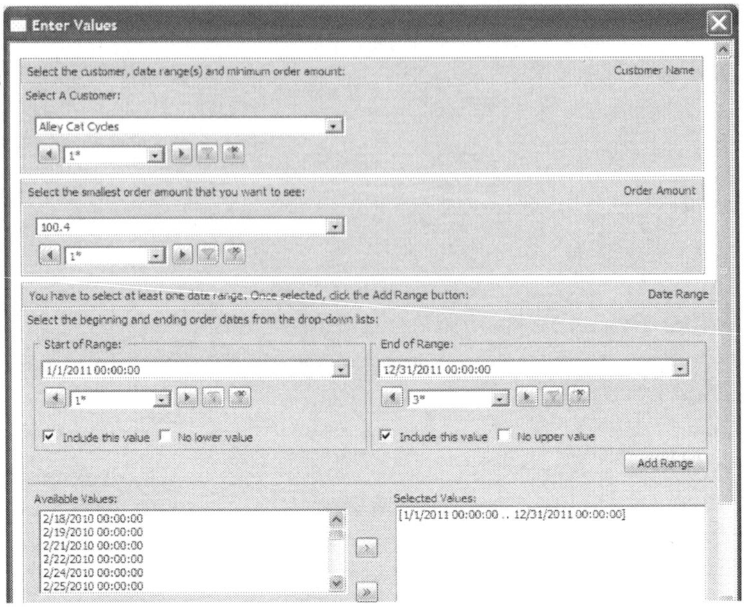

Figure 18-14 Report parameter options

> I don't know why, but you can only rename a parameter field from the Field Explorer. You cannot rename it from the Edit Parameter dialog box. The good thing is that if you rename a parameter field, it is renamed throughout the report.

Using Formula Fields In Parameter Fields

All of the formulas that you have created in this book have been static or hard coded, meaning that they do not change each time the report is run. There will be times when hard coded formulas will not produce the results that are needed. One way to tell if is you get requests for several reports that are very similar. This is often the case for reports that are used in what is known as "What-If" analysis.

For example, someone wants to see the potential revenue gain if they raise the price of the products by 5, 7 or 8%. Hard coded formulas would require you to create three reports, one for each of the potential percent increases. Creating a parameter field that prompted for the percent of increase, allows the report to be flexible and not have to be changed.

A parameter field that is based off of a formula field will allow the user to be able to sort or group the report the way that best meets their needs. Instead of selecting a field name on the Record Sort Expert or Insert Group dialog box, you would select the formula field.

In addition to using formula fields for What-If analysis, you can also base parameter fields off of formula fields that are used to conditionally format data. An example of this is the suppression of data in the E14.5 Suppress Salary GT 50000 report. Another example would be the conditional formatting that you created using the Highlighting Expert.

Top N Reports With Parameter Fields

In Exercise 11.6 you created a Top N report. Like other reports that have formulas, the options that you selected to create a Top N report are hard coded. You can create a conditional formula and use it with the parameter field to be able to run the Top N report with different **N** values.

Exercise 18.10: Create A Parameter Field For A Top N Report

In this exercise you will create a formula that will be used as the basis for a parameter field that will let the person running the report select the **N** value. You will also remove the hard coded date range and add a parameter field to allow a date range to be selected each time the report is run.

Create The Parameter Field

1. Save the E11.7 report as `E18.10 Top N parameter field`.

2. Type `Top N` in the Name field, then change the Type to Number.

3. Change the following options, then click OK.
   Prompt Text `Enter a number between 1 & 100 for the Top N value:`
   Change the Default Value option to 5.
   Change the Min Value option to 1.
   Change the Max Value option to 100.
   You should have the options selected that are shown in Figure 18-15.

Value Options:

Option	Setting
Show on (Viewer) Panel	Editable
Prompt Text	Enter a number between 1 & 100 for the Top N value:
Prompt With Description Only	False
Optional Prompt	False
Default Value	5
Allow custom values	True
Allow multiple values	False
Allow discrete values	True
Allow range values	False
Min Value	1
Max Value	100

Figure 18-15 Top N parameter field options

When you create a Top, Bottom or Percent N parameter field, you can select the Default, Min and Max Values that you want. If you know that the majority of times the users will run the report and select a specific N number, set that number as the default. It is not a requirement to have Min and Max Values.

Create The Top N Formula

1. Open the Group Sort Expert, then click the Formula button.

2. Type `{?Top N}`, as shown on the right side of Figure 18-16. (After I typed the first bracket, the rest automatically filled in)

   Click the Save and close button.

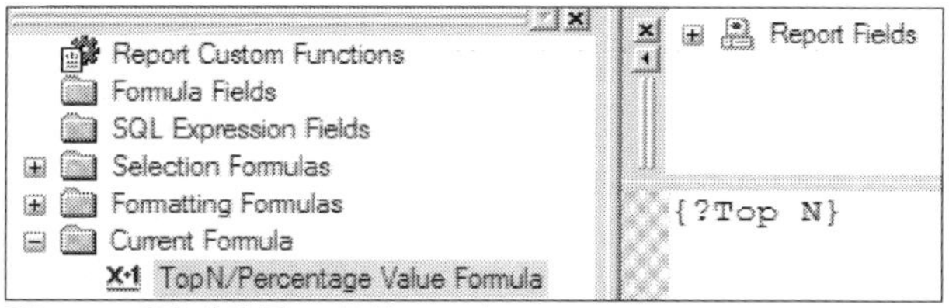

Figure 18-16 Top N Formula

3. Check the Include ties option, then click OK to close the Group Sort Expert.

> If the **INCLUDE TIES** option is not checked and there are ties, only one of the tied groups will be displayed on the report. I could not find a way to specify which of the tied groups will appear on the report or a way to indicate that there is another group with the same number. Therefore, I think the best solution is to always check this option.

The report needs more changes. The current report title will not be accurate because the person running the report has the option of selecting the Top N number and the order date range. Later in this chapter you will learn how to add a parameter field to the report so that it can be printed.

Create The Order Date Range Parameter Field

In this part of the exercise you will remove the hard coded date range and replace it with a parameter field.

1. Open a new parameter field dialog box and type `Order Date` in the Name field, then change the Type to Date Time and select the Dynamic List of Values option.

2. Add the Order Date field to the Value column, then click in the Parameters column.

3. Change the following options, then click OK.
   Prompt Text `Select the date range that you want to see orders for:`
   Change the Allow range values option to True.

4. Open the Select Expert. Select the "Is equal to" operator, then select the Order Date parameter field.

Test The Parameter Fields

1. Preview the report.

   Your dialog box should look similar to the one shown in Figure 18-17.

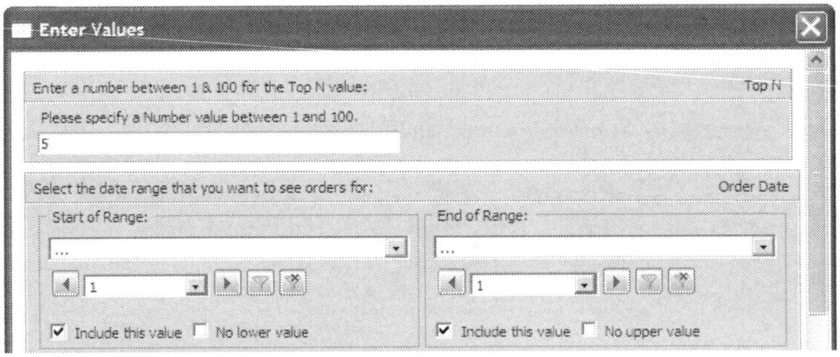

Figure 18-17 Top N parameter options

2. Run the report. If you select a high N number, the chart will be difficult to read. More than likely, you would delete the chart from this report.

Using Parameter Fields To Highlight Data

In Exercise 14.1 you used the Highlighting Expert to conditionally format data when a certain condition was met. The report created in that exercise may be more helpful if an option existed to select the value, in this case, the threshold to use for applying the conditional formatting. The report currently highlights records if the value in the Delay in days to ship field is greater than or equal to three.

Exercise 18.11: Create A Parameter Field To Highlight Rows Of Data

In this exercise you will modify a report to prompt the user to select the delay in days to ship. You will also add a date range parameter. The background color of the row will change to yellow if the record meets the condition.

Create The Order Date Range Parameter Field

1. Save the E13.9 report as `E18.11 Highlight rows of data parameter field`.

2. Type `Date Range` in the Name field. Change the Type to Date Time and select the Dynamic List of Values option.

3. Add the Order Date field to the Value column, then click in the Parameters column.

4. Change the following options, then click OK.
   Prompt Text `Select the date range that you want to see orders for:`
   Change the Allow range values option to True.

Create The Highlight Rows Of Data Parameter Field

1. Open a new parameter field dialog box. Type `Delay in days` in the Name field, then change the Type to Number.

2. Change the following options, then click OK.
   Prompt Text `Enter the minimum number of delay in days to ship that you want to see:`
   Change the Default Value option to 3.
   Change the Min Value option to 1.
   You should have the options shown in Figure 18-18.

Option	Setting
Show on (Viewer) Panel	Editable
Prompt Text	Enter the minimum number of delay in days to ship that you ...
Prompt With Description Only	False
Optional Prompt	False
Default Value	3
Allow custom values	True
Allow multiple values	False
Allow discrete values	True
Allow range values	False
Min Value	1

Figure 18-18 Delay in days parameter field options

Create The Row Color Formula

In this part of the exercise you will create the formula that will change the background to yellow for the rows that have a days to ship number greater than or equal to the number that is entered on the parameter field that you just created.

1. Open the Section Expert and click on the Details section, then click on the Color tab.

2. Click the Formula button and open the Report Fields tree.

Notice on the left side of the Formula Workshop that the conditional formatting formula that you are creating is being applied to the background color option in the Details section.

3. Type `If` in the formula section and press the space bar, then double-click on the Delay in days to ship formula field in the Report Fields section.

4. Press the space bar and type >=, then press the space bar.

5. Double-click on the Delay in days parameter field in the Report Fields section, then press Enter and type `Then crYellow Else crNoColor`.

   Your formula should look like the one shown at the bottom of Figure 18-19.

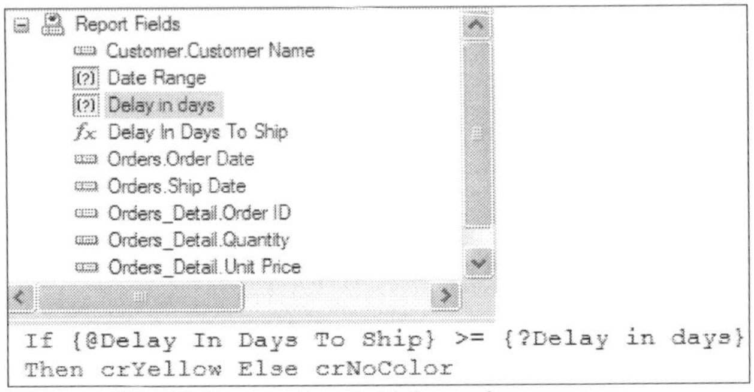

Figure 18-19 Parameter field formula

> If you did not add the crNoColor option, rows that did not meet the criteria would have a black background and you would not be able to see the text.

Add The Date Range Parameter Field To The Select Expert

If you look at the Parameter Fields section of the Field Explorer you will see that the Date Range field does not have a green check mark next to it. That is because the field is currently not being used on the report.

1. Open the Select Expert and select the "Is equal to" operator for the Order Date field.

2. Open the next drop-down list and select the Date Range parameter field.

3. Preview the report. Select the first date in 2011, for the Start of Range value, then select the last date in 2011 for the End of Range value. Notice that the default value that you set is in the Delay in days to ship field. You should have the options selected that are shown in Figure 18-20. The top of the first page of the report should look like the one shown in Figure 18-21. Every row that has a value of three or greater in the Delay in days to ship field has a yellow background.

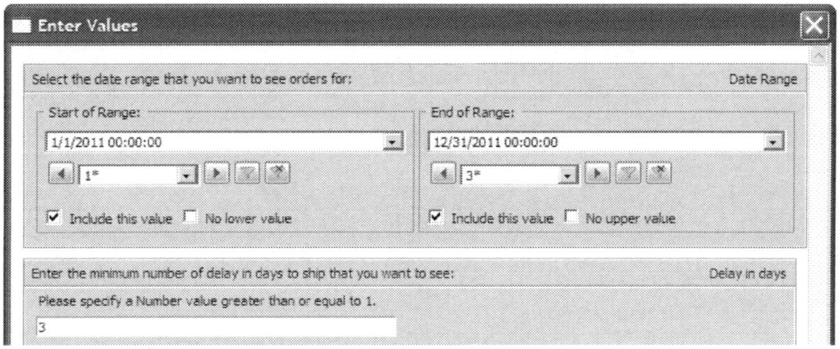

Figure 18-20 Delay in days parameter field options

Customer Name	Order Date	Ship Date	Order ID	Unit Price	Quantity	Delay In Days To Ship
Rough Terrain	01/01/2011	01/01/2011	1,121	$41.90	1	0
Rough Terrain	01/01/2011	01/01/2011	1,121	$809.87	1	0
Hooked on Helmets	01/01/2011	01/08/2011	1,122	$21.90	3	7
Hooked on Helmets	01/01/2011	01/08/2011	1,122	$479.85	2	7
Clean Air Transportation Co.	01/02/2011	01/02/2011	1,123	$1,739.85	3	0
Off the Mountain Biking	01/02/2011	01/09/2011	1,124	$19.90	3	7

Figure 18-21 E18.11 Highlight rows of data parameter field report

Using Parameter Fields To Select The Sorting And Grouping Options

You have learned how to sort and group data by selecting options on the Record Sort Expert and Insert Group dialog boxes. There will be times when a report needs to be sorted or grouped in several different ways. Rather then hard code this information and have to create several reports, one for each field the report needs to be sorted or grouped on, you can create a parameter field that will be used to find out what field the report will be sorted or grouped on. The value collected from the parameter field will be passed to the Record Sort Expert or Insert Group dialog box.

Parameter fields cannot retrieve a formula or table name. Therefore you have to create a formula that uses the value in the parameter field as the field to sort or group on. The formula field is what you will select on the sorting or grouping dialog box.

Exercise 18.12: Create A Parameter Field To Sort The Records

In Exercise 5.1 you created a customer information report. As it is, the report is not sorted or grouped. In this exercise you will create a formula and parameter field that will allow the report to be sorted on one of the following three fields: Customer Name, Region or Country.

Create The Sort By Parameter Field

1. Save the E5.1 report as `E18.12 Sort records parameter field`.

2. Type `Sort By Field` in the Name field.

3. Type the values `Customer Name`, `Region` and `Country` in the Value column.
   Type `State` in the Description column of the Region value.

4. Change the following options, then click OK.
   Prompt Text `Select the field that you want to sort by:`
   Change the Allow custom values option to False.

Create The Sort Formula And Add It To The Parameter Field

1. Create a formula field named `SortBy`. Type the formula shown below.

```
If {?Sort By Field} = "Customer Name" Then
{Customer.Customer Name}
Else
If {?Sort By Field} = "Region" Then {Customer.Region}
Else
{Customer.Country}
```

2. Open the Record Sort Expert, then add the SortBy formula field to the Sort Fields list box.

   Preview the report. The Enter Values dialog box shown in Figure 18-22 will open.

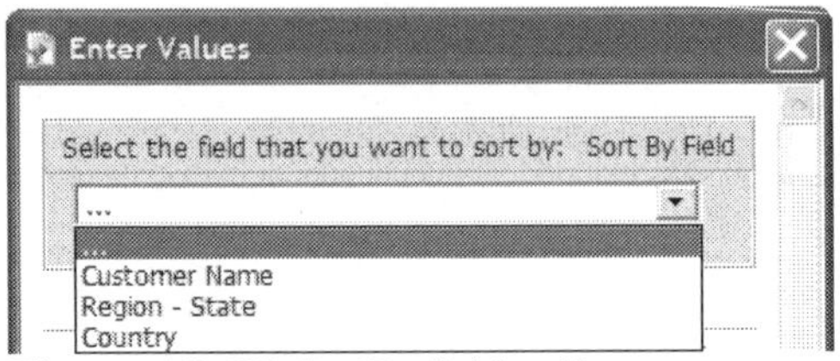

Figure 18-22 SortBy field options

Test The Sort Parameter

1. Select the Customer Name option from the drop-down list. The report should be sorted in Customer Name order.

2. Run the report again and sort the report by Region. Leave the report open to complete the next exercise.

Exercise 18.13: Create A Parameter Field To Group Data

In the previous exercise you learned how to sort the detail records using a parameter field. Selecting the field to group on via a parameter field basically works the same way. The difference is that you attach the formula field to the Insert Group dialog box instead of the Record Sort Expert.

In this exercise you will create a group in the customer information report from the previous exercise. One parameter field that you will create in this exercise is used to select which of the three fields; Customer Name, Region or Country to group on. You will create another parameter field that will be used to select the group sort order, ascending or descending.

Create The Group Sort Parameter Field

1. Save the E18.12 report as `E18.13 Group data parameter field`.

2. Type `Group By Field` in the Name field.

3. Type the values `Customer Name`, `Region` and `Country` in the Value column.

4. Change the following options, then click OK.
   Prompt Text `Select the field that you want to group by:`
   Change the Default Value option to Region. You can select it from the drop-down list.
   Change the Allow custom values option to False.

Create The Group Formula And Add It To The Parameter Field

1. Create a formula field named `GroupBy`.

2. Click on the SortBy formula field under the Formula Fields node on the left of the Formula Workshop. Copy and paste the SortBy formula into the GroupBy formula.

3. Change the word "Sort" to `Group` in two places in the formula.

Create The Group Sort Order Parameter Field

The parameter field that you will create in this part of the exercise will let the person running the report select the sort order of the group, either ascending or descending. Parameter fields are displayed on the Enter Values dialog box in the order that they were created in. The more logical order in this exercise would be to have the Sort By Field last.

1. Open a new parameter field dialog box and type `Group Sort Order` in the Name field.

2. Type the options `Ascending` and `Descending` in the Value column.

3. Change the following options, then click OK.
   Prompt Text `Select the order that you want to sort the groups in:`
   Change the Default Value option to Ascending.
   Change the Allow custom values option to False.

Create The Group And Add The Group Formula To The Insert Group Dialog Box

As you have noticed, the report that you are working on does not have any groups. In this part of the exercise you will create the group based on a formula field and sort the group based on a different formula field.

1. Open the Insert Group dialog box, then open the first drop-down list and select the GroupBy formula field.

2. Check the option, **USE A FORMULA AS GROUP SORT ORDER**, then click the Formula button and type the formula shown below.

```
If {?Group Sort Order} = "Ascending" Then crAscendingOrder
Else
crDescendingOrder
```

3. Refresh the report.

   You should see the dialog box shown in Figure 18-23.

   Run the report a few times, selecting different options.

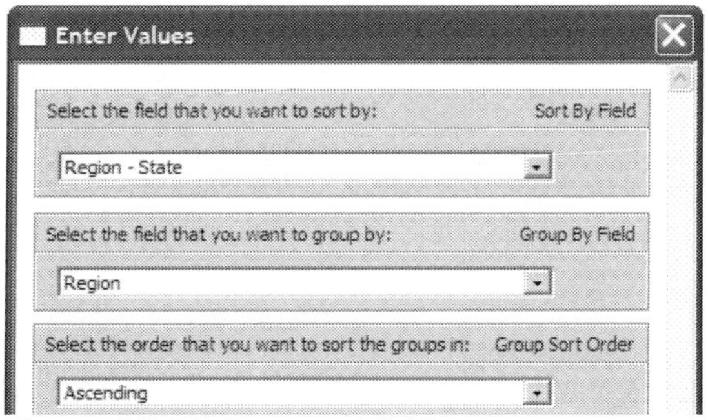

Figure 18-23 Group and field sort parameter options

Boolean Parameter Fields

Boolean parameter fields like Boolean formulas can only have two values: True and False. Like Boolean formulas, you do not have to display the options as true and false. If the Boolean parameter field is not a group, you can use the Description column to enter the text that you want to display in the drop-down list instead of the values, true and false.

Interestingly enough, you cannot use the Description column to change what is displayed in the drop-down list on Boolean group parameter fields. Instead, the name of the Parameter field is used. Therefore, make good use of the Name field.

Using A Parameter Field To Suppress Data

You have learned how to conditionally suppress data on a report. Suppression is often done with a Boolean field. Suppressing data is popular on reports that have a lot of detail records. Being able to select whether or not to suppress detail records allows one to run the report and only see the summary information. Doing this means that one report can be a detail report or a summary report. The Suppress (No Drill-Down) option on the Section Expert requires a Boolean formula when it will be used conditionally.

Exercise 18.14: Conditional Section Suppression Using A Parameter Field

In this exercise you will modify a report so that it can be run as a detailed report or a summary only report.

Create The Suppression Parameter Field

1. Save the E9.2 report as `E18.14 Suppress section parameter field`.

2. Type `Summary Report` in the Name field.

3. Type `Yes` in the first Value row, then type No in the second Value row.

4. Change the following options, then click OK.
   Prompt Text `Do you want to run a Summary Only report?`
   Change the Allow custom values option to False.

Modify The Section Expert Options

1. Open the Section Expert and add another Page Header section.

You need the additional Page Header section because the field headings also have to be suppressed if the report will be run as a summary report.

2. Click on the Formula button for the Suppress (No Drill-Down) option for the Page Header b section, then type the formula shown below. This formula checks to see if the Summary Report parameter field has the value Yes. If it does, the Page Header b and Details sections will be suppressed.

   ```
   If {?Summary Report} = "Yes" Then True
   ```

3. Highlight the formula and press **CTRL+C**, then click the Save and close button. This will let you copy the formula.

4. Click on the Details section in the Section Expert, then click the Formula button for the Suppress (No Drill-Down) option. Paste (Press **CTRL+V**) the formula into the Formula section.

Modify The Report

As mentioned earlier, when the report is run in the summary only mode, the field headings should not print. This is why you created another Page Header section and added the suppression formula to the second Page Header section.

1. Move the field headings to the Page Header b section.

   Refresh the report. You should see the dialog box shown in Figure 18-24.

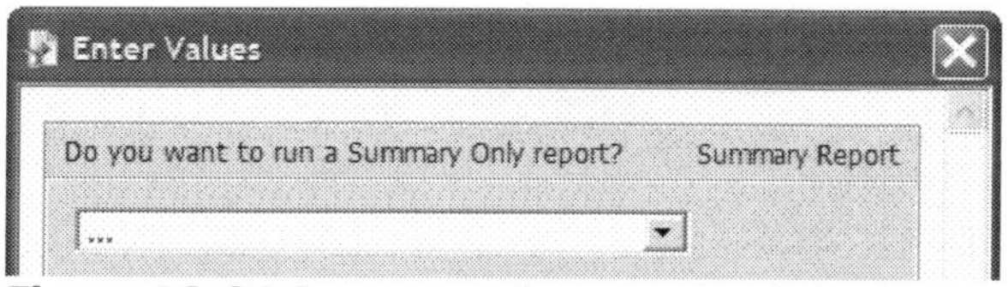

Figure 18-24 Summary only parameter dialog box

2. Select Yes to run a summary report. You should only see summary information on the report. Run the report again and select No.

Managing Data Entry In Parameter Fields

You have created several parameter fields in this chapter. While you took care and entered the data in the parameter fields correctly, it is unrealistic to think that people that run the reports will always enter the correct information in the parameter fields. If the reports are going to be part of an application, there are more options available for helping and guiding users to enter the data in parameter fields correctly then Crystal Reports provides. Crystal Reports does provide three types of options that you can use to help users enter data in the parameter fields correctly. These options are Min and Max field lengths, which use a range of values to limit the data. You have already used these options. The other options are Min/Max value and Edit Masks.

On string parameter fields the **MIN LENGTH** and **MAX LENGTH** options are used. The length refers to how many characters can be entered in the field. The number that you enter in the Max Length field should not be larger than the actual length of the corresponding field in the table. Any items in the Value column have to meet the min and max requirements.

The range limits **MIN VALUE** and **MAX VALUE** are primarily used for number and date fields. These options require that the data entered in the field be in a specific range. For example, if the min value is one and the max value is five, any number less than one or greater than five would not be accepted.

> If a number parameter field is populated with a static list of values and you do not want all of the values to be available, enter the min and max values for the range of data that you want to import, before importing the values for the static list of values.

Adding Parameter Field Criteria To A Report

You have learned how to create parameter fields that add a lot of interaction. The one thing that is missing is adding the parameter field criteria to a report. With all of the parameter field selection combinations that a report can have, including the selection criteria on the report would be helpful. Single value parameter fields can be dragged from the Field Explorer on to the report like other fields.

> Range value and multiple value parameter fields cannot be dragged onto the report and printed like single value parameter fields. If these fields are added to the report, only the first value in the field will print. Printing solutions for these types of parameter fields are discussed below.

Printing Parameter Range Fields

There are two functions, **MINIMUM()** and **MAXIMUM()** in Crystal Reports that can be used to print the range in a parameter field. These functions return the beginning and ending values. The formula below will print the date range on the report as long as the **NO LOWER VALUE** and **NO UPPER VALUE** options are not checked on the Enter Values dialog box. Replace the {?Date_Parameter} field shown below with the name of the parameter field that you want to print.

"Starting Date " & Minimum ({?Date_Parameter}) & " and Ending Date " & Maximum ({?Date_Parameter})

> You can use the Minimum and Maximum functions for any type of range parameter field data. It is not just for date ranges.

Exercise 18.15: Print Parameter Range Fields

1. Save the E18.11 report as `E18.15 Print parameter range fields.`

2. Create a formula field named `Print Date Range`. Type the formula below, all on one line.

```
"Starting Date " & Minimum ({?Date Range}) & " and Ending Date "
& Maximum ({?Date Range})
```

3. Add the Print Date Range formula field to the top of the Page Header section. Make the field at least five inches wide. Preview the report. You should see the date range at the top of the report, similar to the one shown in Figure 18-25. You may have different data on the report.

Starting Date 6/24/2011 12:00:00AM and Ending Date 9/19/2011 12:00:00AM

Customer Name	Order Date	Ship Date	Order ID	Unit Price
Alley Cat Cycles	06/24/2011	07/02/2011	1,761	$21.90
Alley Cat Cycles	06/24/2011	07/02/2011	1,761	$539.85

Figure 18-25 Parameter field range printed on the report

Printing Multi Value Parameter Fields Using The Join Function

If you drag a multi value parameter field to a report, the only value that will print will be the first one. All of the values that are selected in a multi value parameter field are stored in one field and are separated by a comma in the array. The **JOIN** function will print all of the values in the array. The formula below is used to print all of the values in a multiple value parameter field. Replace the {?ShipVia} field with the name of the multi value parameter field that you want to print.

"Shipping Methods Selected: " + Join ({?ShipVia}, ", ")

Exercise 18.16: Print Multi Value Parameter Fields

1. Save the E18.6 report as `E18.16 Print multi value parameter fields.`

2. Create a formula field named `Print Regions`. Type the formula below.

```
"Regions Selected: " + Join ({?Region}, " , ")
```

3. Add the Print Regions formula field to the top of the Page Header section. Make the field longer.

4. Preview the report. Select two regions from the list, then type in other regions. Your report should look similar to the one shown in Figure 18-26. You will have different data on the report.

Regions Selected: CA , FL , WI , TX

Customer Name	Address1	Region	Country	Postal Code
Sporting Wheels Inc.	480 Grant Way	CA	USA	92150
Rockshocks for Jocks	1984 Sydney Street	TX	USA	78770
Trail Blazer's Place	6938 Beach Street	WI	USA	53795

Figure 18-26 Multi value parameter field printed on the report

Deleting Parameter Fields From A Report

You may need to delete a parameter field from a report. If you do, follow the steps below.

1. Right-click on the parameter field in the Field Explorer that you want to delete and select **DELETE**. You will see the message shown in Figure 18-27. This message is letting you know that once you delete the field it cannot be undone.

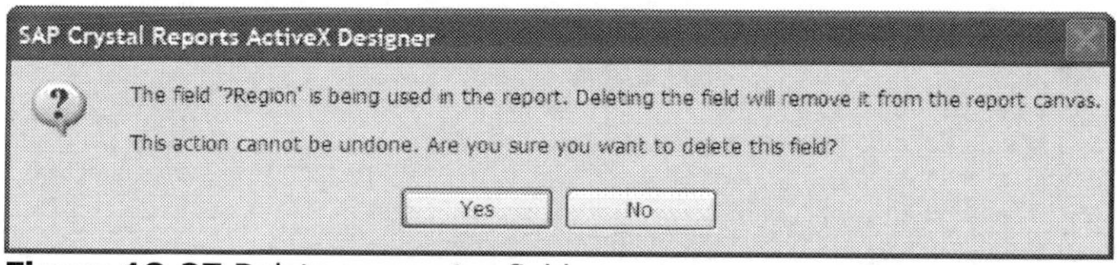

Figure 18-27 Delete parameter field message

2. Click Yes.

You may see the message shown in Figure 18-28.

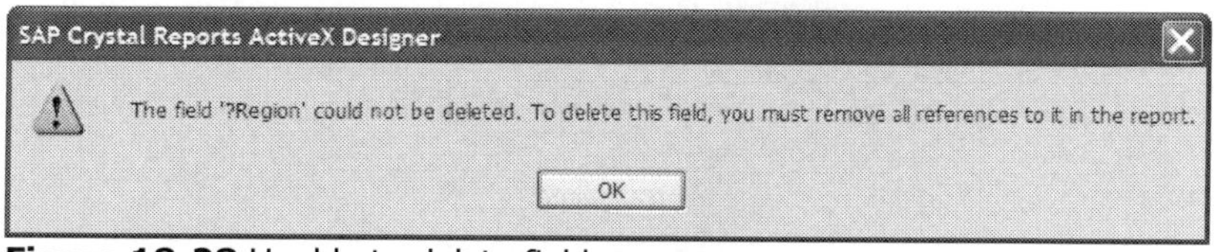

Figure 18-28 Unable to delete field message

This message is letting you know that the parameter field can't be deleted because it is being used in the report. Before you can delete a parameter field, you have to delete it from the place(s) that it is being used in the report. In this example, it is being used on the Select Expert. If it was being used on the report to display the criteria that was used to run the report, you would have to delete it from there. The parameter field could also be used in a formula.

3. Click OK, then delete the parameter field from all of the places that it is being used in the report. Once you do that, repeat step 1 above and the parameter field will be deleted, then save the changes.

Customizing The Enter Values Dialog Box

Attributes of the Enter Values dialog box can be modified. You need to have some web design experience to modify the Enter Values dialog box, in particular, HTML (Hypertext Markup Language) and CSS (Cascading Style Sheets). This is beyond the scope of this book, but I wanted to let you know that the dialog box can be modified.

The file that you would modify is promptengine_default.css. This file is in the folder listed below if you selected the default installation path when you installed Crystal Reports.

C:\Program Files\SAP BusinessObjects\Crystal Reports for .NET Framework 4.0\Common\crystalreportviewers\prompting\css\

If you plan to modify this dialog box, keep in mind that any changes that you make will be applied to all Enter Values dialog boxes that point to the CSS file that you modify, not just one report. You should make a copy of this file before making any changes to it. Some of the features that you can change are listed in Table 18-1.

Enter Values Dialog Box Changes	
Font	Background color
Font size	Prompt text box
Font color	Prompt button
Border	Size of text in a drop-down list

Table 18-1 Some of the Enter Values dialog box options that can be changed

INDEX

D

E

F

M

N

O

P

Q

R

S

T

U

V

W

X

Y

Z

No Stress Tech Guides

ISBN: 978-1-935208-23-5

ISBN: 978-1-935208-22-8

ISBN: 978-1-935208-15-0

ISBN: 978-1-935208-18-1

ISBN: 978-1-935208-24-2

ISBN: 978-1-935208-11-2

ISBN: 978-1-935208-19-8

ISBN: 978-1-935208-00-6

ISBN: 978-1-935208-26-6

ISBN: 978-1-935208-14-3

ISBN: 1-935208-01-2

ISBN: 978-1-935208-05-1

ISBN: 978-1-935208-25-9

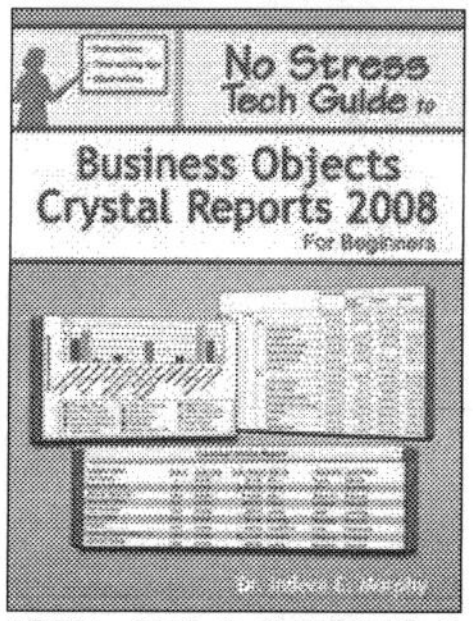

ISBN: 978-0-9773912-9-5

ISBN: 978-1-935208-16-7

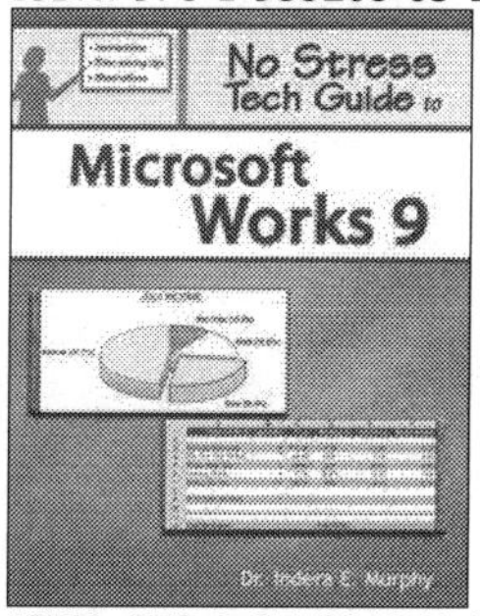

ISBN: 978-0-9773912-7-1

Visit us online to see the entire series www.tolanapublishing.com

Made in United States
Orlando, FL
04 November 2026

90219748R00197